SPORTSELECTION

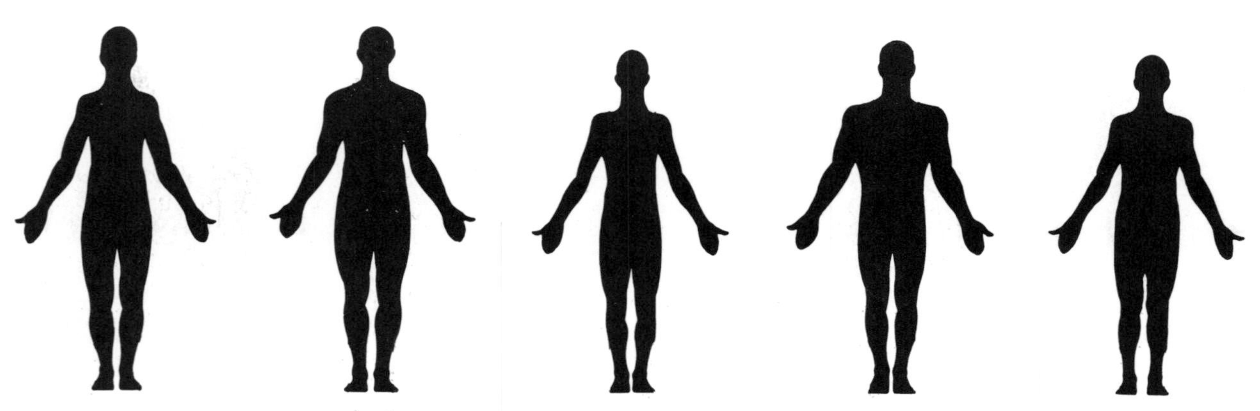

SPORTSELECTION

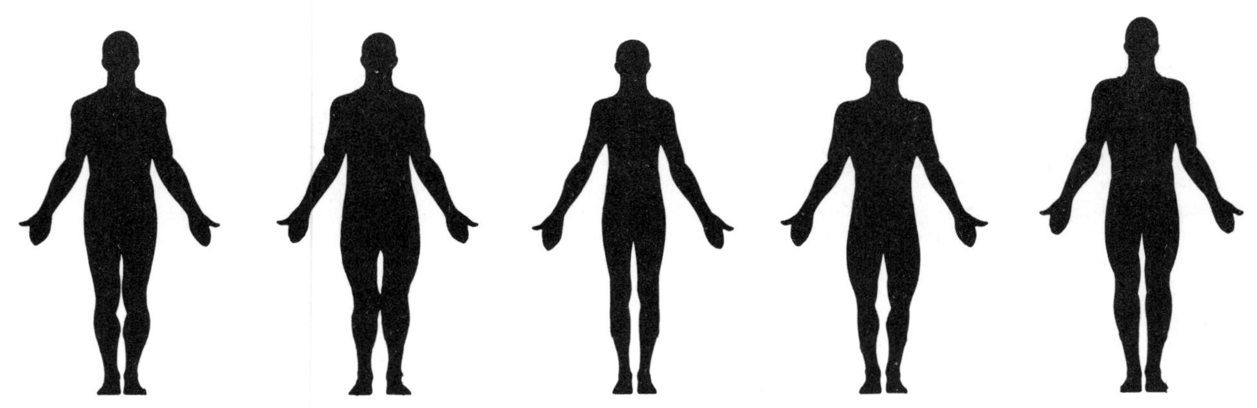

ROBERT BURNS ARNOT, M.D.
AND CHARLES LATHAM GAINES

PELHAM BOOKS

First published in Great Britain by
Pelham Books Ltd
44 Bedford Square, London WC1B 3DU
1984

A portion of this book appeared originally in *Outside Magazine*.

ISBN 0 7207 1562 8

Printed in the United States of America
Set in ITC Bookman
Designed by Beth Tondreau
with the assistance of Mary A. Wirth

Grateful acknowledgment is made to the following for permission to adapt copyrighted material:

Edward R. Burke, U.S.O.C.: U.S. National Team Bicycle Sprint Test.

J. E. L. Carter (ed.): "Measurement of Bodily Proportions," from *Physical Structure of Olympic Athletes*, Part I: The Montreal Olympic Games Anthropological Project. Basel: Karger, 1982.

Charles J. Dillman, U.S. Ski Team: "Hexagonal Obstacle Test."

Laux Company, Inc., Harvard, Mass.: Two tables from the article "Measurement of Cardio-Respiratory Fitness and Body Composition in a Clinical Setting," by Michael L. Pollock, Ph.D.; Donald H. Schmidt, M.D., and Andrew S. Jackson, Ph.D., from *Comprehensive Therapy*, Vol. 6, No. 9, 1980.

McGraw-Hill Book Company: "Bicycle Ergometer Test" from Table 10-4, *Textbook of Work Physiology*, by Per-Olof Astrand.

Jim Page, U.S. Nordic Ski Team: "Agility Run Test."

Warren Witherell, Burke Mountain Ski Academy, Vermont: "Concrete Block Jump Test."

John Wiley & Sons, Inc., Dr. Kenneth Cooper, and Dr. L. H. Getchell: "Cooper Twelve-Minute Run Test," as it appears in *Being Fit: A Personal Guide*, by Bud Getchell and Wayne Anderson.

WE DEDICATE THIS BOOK
TO OUR RESPECTIVE FAMILIES,
WITH A PARTICULAR THANKS TO PATRICIA GAINES—
WHO SUFFERED US.

ACKNOWLEDGMENTS

A great many people assisted in the preparation and completion of this book. The authors would like particularly to thank: Patricia Gaines; Lauren Stager; Jan Bagley; Bill Strachan and Connie Sayre at Viking; the staff and student body of Stratton Mountain School, and especially Hermann Goelner; Chuck Dillman; Bill Drake; Jack Groppel; James Counsilman; Bill Rodgers; Peter Cavanaugh; Ed Burke; the staff at *Velo News*; Francesco Moser; Per-Olof Astrand; Bengt Saltin; Dieter Hanneman; Ulf Bergh; Bill Evans; Ellie Henneman; Bruce Ogilvie; Skip Sheldon; Carleton Chapman; Dave Kanereck; Andy Glass; Brian Whipp; and Hans Howard.

For advice and information, we would also like to thank: Jeff Tesch, Phil Wilson, Marty Hall, Doug Peterson, Bill Koch, John Caldwell, Bill Marolt, Steve Lathrop, Tom Corcoran, Hermann Muckenschabl, Howard Chivers, Vic Braden, Bob Nirschl, Carl Hedrick, Jane Katz, Dave Costill, Tom Beneson, Fred Hayward, Arleone Dibbin, Ben Harvey, Reed Lockhart, Mike Bissner, Bill Dillinger, Nancy Arnot, John Howard, Peter Mooney, Grace Jones, Bob Gregor, Jim McGuire, Bob Mann, Ralph Paffenbarger, Allen Ryan, Lars Hermanson, Richard Edwards, Bill Morgan, Jack Wilmore, John Ivy, Captain Jim Wright, Bob Singer, E. A. Fleishman, Richard Schmidt, J. A. Adams, Stan Grillner, Marsh Tenney, Stan Plagenhof, Bert Zarins, Lyle Micaeli, Art Boland, Roy Shephard, Hansel Stedman, Dave Lamb, Gideon Aeriel, E. Asmussen, Eric Jaeger, E. Buskirk, Reggie Edgerton, John Sutton, Eric Hultman, J. Keul, Elmar Kornexl, Skip Knuttgen, and Paavo Komi.

CONTENTS

PART II: THE PERFORMANCE REQUIREMENTS OF ALPINE SKIING, TENNIS, WINDSURFING, RUNNING, SWIMMING, CYCLING, AND CROSS-COUNTRY SKIING

PART III: TESTING YOURSELF FOR SPORTSTALENT

PART IV: INTERPRETING YOUR TEST RESULTS AND MAXIMIZING YOUR SPORTSTALENTS

PART V: IDENTIFYING AND DEVELOPING SPORTSTALENT IN CHILDREN AND ADOLESCENTS

APPENDIX

KEY TO LOGOS

The logos below represent the key components in human performance. The page heads of *Sportselection* are indexed with these logos to allow you quick access to these parts of the human machine in each chapter of the book and to serve as visual reminders of the components.

CONTROL SYSTEM

MOTOR ABILITY

MOTOR PROGRAMMING CONTROL SYSTEM

TRAITS

EYE

CONVERGENT VISION

BINOCULAR VISION

HEART AND LUNG

HEART

LUNG

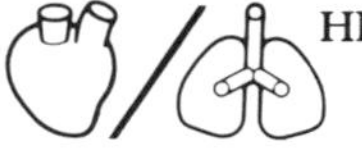
HEART/LUNG

BODY COMPOSITION

PHYSICAL DIMENSION

BODY PARTS

MUSCLE

ENDURANCE

SPRINT

EXPLOSIVENESS

ELASTICITY

FAT

INTRODUCTION

This book could not have been written before now. Though sportstalent testing has been carried on for years in other parts of the world, notably in Russia and in Eastern Europe, it is only recently that sports scientists in this country have become aware of the methods and procedures of that testing to the point where principles from various branches of sports science could be extracted, mingled, and synthesized.

Even more recent is the perception, here and abroad, that screening for sportstalent by testing might be systematized. Since the early 1960s, sportselection for individual sports has been practiced in Russia and certain Eastern European countries. East Germany has successfully screened and tested for swimming and crew, Rumania for gymnastics, and Czechoslovakia for tennis, to name a few examples. But in none of these countries has a comprehensive multisport *system* of testing and screening for sportstalent been developed and applied. Lacking the resources and population necessary to excel at a wide variety of sports, these countries and others in Eastern Europe have chosen to employ sportselection discriminately to achieve success in a small number of sports.

Discriminate sportselection was developed in Europe because it was the only method by which these small countries could effectively compete with larger countries in athletic contests. Sportselection satisfied a unique, twofold need: to identify accurately in a small population the very best talent that existed for one or more carefully chosen sports, and to ensure that the expensive coaching, training, and sports-science resources that would have to be put to the identification and development of that talent would not be wasted. For those purposes it was necessary for a country such as East Germany, for example, to mount an all-out, well-organized national effort at sportstalent identification and development. Once launched, that effort was devastatingly effective. In the 1968 Olympics, in which East Germany competed for the first time as an independent country, East German athletes won a total of nine gold medals, as compared with forty-five won by American athletes. In the 1976

Montreal Olympics, East Germany (with a total population smaller than that of New York State) won forty-seven gold medals to thirty-seven for the United States.

Frank Shorter, the American hero who set off a national running boom, was beaten in the marathon at Montreal by the virtually unknown Waldemer Chierpinski, an East German—and Chierpinski was racing against a world-class field in the marathon for the first time in his life. When a dejected Shorter told television reporters that he would not—and the United States should not—compete in the Olympic Games again without benefit of the sophisticated sports science being employed by the East Germans, he was voicing for perhaps the first time ever this startling truth: Americans simply did not know how to train, and too often they were playing the wrong sports in the wrong ways. At Sarajevo the low USA medal count showed the situation had changed little.

Until the 1976 Olympics there was no perceived need for scientific sportselection in America. We were a large country with a proud athletic history; and a country, moreover, that believed in the democracy of sports—we believed that all athletes are created equal. However, our experience with the East Germans at Montreal in 1976 demonstrated graphically that many of our national training methods were sadly out of date, and that we were not effectively using our vast resources to identify and develop Olympic sportstalent. Traditionally, we have tended to channel our better athletes into the nationally popular and remunerative team sports of football, baseball, and basketball, thus robbing our Olympic development programs of considerable talent. When that became embarrassingly apparent in Montreal, for the first time in the country's athletic history Americans began to feel the need for a scientific sportselection process.

There had been a selection process for sports in this country before—but it was anything but scientific and anything but democratic. Although the organized, analytical sportselection of Eastern Europe still seems unattractively authoritarian to many Americans, the fact is that what had passed for sportselection in this country is far less egalitarian and less fair than the scientific Eastern European version. Stubbornly unscientific and "democratic," American sportselection has tended to use the wrong values to determine sports ability and the wrong method for actualizing that ability in both children and adults.

We are brought up in this country to believe in a sports myth—the myth of the "natural athlete." From childhood, we are conditioned to believe that an individual either is genetically athletic or is not, and that athletic talent comprises a single unchanging set of abilities. As children, all of us knew a "natural athlete"—a boy or girl who seemed to perform at sports more easily and with more skill than the rest of us—and most of us assumed that this person's athletic ability was a God-given talent that could be employed successfully in any sport. More often than not, however, such early sports ability is the product of nothing more mysterious than early physical maturity and/or effective encouragement by parents or coaches, and while that ability can be, and often is, employed successfully in the performance of a number of sports during childhood, it is no more likely to result in adult sports achievement than ability that is unmasked later in an individual's life.

Motor skills and explosive speed are athletic abilities that can become apparent very early in a child, and often those two abilities, particularly in combination with early signs of physical maturity, are perceived to represent overall athletic talent. But there are many athletic abilities, and a great number of them (such as the abilities central to distance running or cross-country skiing) do not become evident until adolescence or later. Because we are so accustomed to thinking of athletic talent as an all-or-nothing thing and a single package of skills, very often an individual who does not show early athletic promise is given up on as an athlete, and made to give up on himself or herself, *before* that individual has been given a fair chance to determine what he or she is capable of. Lack of encouragement by coaches and parents, regardless of a child's demonstrated physical ability, can also *stunt* athletic growth, and quite often does. An enormous percentage of adult Americans have been put off sports participation, sometimes permanently, in their youth, either from lack of encouragement or because their athletic abilities went unrecognized.

The fact is that sportselection in this country has too often meant sports rejection. Since a systematic methodology for matching particular athletic abilities to particular sports has never existed here, children and adults usually wind up being "naturally selected" into sports that, more often than not, are wrong for them. This natural selection of sports in America is really not natural at all, since a number of sociological factors heavily influence it. A child in this country commonly finds himself or herself playing a sport because a parent played it; because a parent wants the child to play it; because the sport is popular in the child's particular region of the country or has some tradition in the child's racial or ethnic background; or because of hero worship or the associations of fame and riches with the sport. Similarly, an adult in this country typically enters participation in a sport for social reasons, for health or beauty reasons, or because of some momentary national or regional craze for the sport. While there is nothing necessarily wrong with any of these methods of selecting a sport, none of them allows for anything more than an accidental matching between a particular individual's physical, mental, and psychological capacities and the demands of the particular sport. And because that matching is so rarely achieved in American sportselection, much if not most such selection results in failure and rejection. According to a recent Louis Harris study, fully 50 percent of America's kids experience some sort of sports failure as their first major failure in life. Some of these kids will never participate in sports again. Others will grow into maturity participating poorly at sports that, at worst, can be so wrong for them as to cause physical injury and, at best, can never provide them with the joy of athletic self-actualization.

Sports participation by region.

We believe that athletic talent is an important resource, one to be nurtured and prized in the same way we encourage and value academic and artistic talent. We believe that the traditional laissez-faire, "natural" process of sportselection does not result in either accurate recognition or proper utilization of sportstalent. And we believe that the time has come for a more scientific, systematic approach toward sportselection, one that allows for the free, full development of each individual's athletic ability. Moreover, we believe that there is a palpable *need* now for such an approach.

The fitness boom in America, which sometimes seems to have been with us forever, really began during the Kennedy years as a relatively confined and largely upper-middle-class concern with "vigor"—with bracing physical activity for its own sake—and as a significant part of the "Camelot" image of those years. That concern was enlarged by literally millions of Americans over the course of the 1960s and early 1970s as exercise was more and more understood to be good preventive medicine, particularly in regard to coronary artery disease. If the first phase of the

American fitness boom was recreational and culturally image-serving, and the second medically motivated, the third phase, beginning sometime in the mid-1970s, could be called ornamental—Americans, in staggering numbers, began to exercise not only to feel better but to look better. Now there is very strong evidence to suggest that the country has entered a fourth phase of the boom—increasingly, Americans want to be fit for athletics: they want bodies that are not only healthy and good-looking but capable of athletic performance. This relatively new, widespread desire to utilize fitness has led in recent years to record numbers of Americans participating in sports, many of them for the first time in their lives, and that unprecedented mass entry into sports has created a pressing need for a new, easily available understanding of how sports work and of how we can most productively participate in them.

In effect, millions of Americans are now serious sports consumers, and yet there is very little good consumer advice. Though there is a surfeit of "fitness writing" available in bookstores and on magazine stands, and quite a few good books and periodicals on individual sports, none of this literature details the exact physical requirements of a sport; nor does it make the reader consider how his or her physical capacities meet those requirements and/or can be improved by them. What is really needed is a literature of scientific and systematic sportselection—a literature that will allow and encourage Americans to choose the right sport to participate in. We see this book as a beginning of that literature—the first comprehensive and analytical attempt to provide a scientific context for the understanding and selection of participation sports, and the first real consumer guide to athletics and fitness ever published, one, we hope, that will steer its readers clear of the boredom, frustration, poor performance, and injury that can and do result from uninformed and misinformed sportselection and fitness programming.

It has been tacitly assumed by sports scientists and coaches for years that the only workable sportselection analysis was a purely deductive one that would track all possibly significant factors in an athlete's performance over the course of an important period in his or her development, with the hope that certain of those factors would announce themselves as being critical to that development. This method—necessarily an expensive and time-consuming one—has been employed occasionally in this country and in other places by individual coaches and scientists with some success in identifying elements of sports-talent within particular sports. But too often, in an attempt to keep the method purely deductive and objective, coaches and scientists have purposely kept themselves at arm's length from what they knew (or could learn) about the nature of a particular sport, and have tracked performance factors indiscriminately. Such an approach, by consciously ignoring the world's accumulated knowledge on the athletic performance of the specific systems of the human body, can, and often does, identify performance factors that are essentially irrelevant to the performance of a sport. One such deductive sportselection analysis, done in Austria on young Alpine skiers, managed to determine that the most significant single contributor to Alpine skiing success was parental income.

We believe that no effective and *comprehensive* sportselection method is possible without a thorough understanding of each individual task involved in a given sport, and an equally thorough understanding of how the various human systems (the brain, the heart, the muscles, and so on) go about performing those tasks. Our aim in this book, therefore, has been to offer both a complete task analysis of each sport treated in the book and an integrated systems analysis of each of the human physical and mental systems that are active athletically. There is now enough scientific information available in the fields of biomechanics, neurophysiology, and exercise physiology to make such a systems analysis of the body athletic possible—and to our knowledge this book represents the first time it has ever been attempted. New technological methods such as computerized motion analysis have allowed three-dimensional, high-speed examinations of sports on a task-by-task basis, and in our analysis of the human mental and physical systems that are operative in sports we have attempted to demonstrate not only how each system functions athletically but how all of them work together to complete sports tasks. One of the major barriers to devising an effective sport-selection methodology has been the traditional feeling that any given sports performance comprises so many different physical and mental capabilities—some of them unidentifiable—that it is virtually impossible to weight those capabilities as to their relative significance. However, through our own laboratory research and that of colleagues, we have found that it *is* possible to assign relative importance to different capabilities within a sport, once the physical and mental systems inherent in that sport are well enough understood and the different tasks involved in the sport clearly enough identified, and we unashamedly make such assignments here.

The aims of this book, then, are to let you know through a carefully integrated systems analysis precisely how your body and mind function, both separately and together, in the performance of seven different sports; to let you know precisely what each of those sports demands of you and which of your capabilities are most significant to performing well at any one of them; to enable you to identify your inherent aptitude or talent for each of the sports, and to tell you how that aptitude can be maximized.

This information has never before been integrated and presented as a whole, and we believe that it could not have been done until now. In integrated form, as an overall *system* of sport-selection, we further believe that the materials herein have wide practical application for a wide variety of people:

- If you are entering or about to enter athletic participation for the first time, this book will help you to identify your athletic abilities and to choose a sport for which you have some natural talent. By helping you to identify precisely your sportstalent, and by stripping away the mystiques and hype from the seven sports it treats, it may also give you the confidence to take up some sport other than the broad-entry sports of running and swimming—a sport that you might otherwise never have tried; and that same confidence might keep you from being intimidated by what you hear about the sport's difficulties from some "local expert."
- If you already participate occasionally in one or more of the sports treated here, the book can enlarge your athletic enjoyment by expanding your knowledge of that sport or sports and of yourself as an athlete. It will indicate your strengths and weaknesses at whatever sport you presently practice and therefore can help you improve your performance; and it may very well point you toward a new sport for which you have talent but may never have tried.
- If you are anything from a serious weekend practitioner to a world-class competitor at one of the sports here, we are convinced that this book will have plenty to teach you about your sport and about yourself as an athlete. It can be very helpful in enlarging your performance understanding of your sport, and by providing you with an exact profile of your strengths and weaknesses, it can make you a better strategist. It will also give you access to a common "sports language" through which you will be better able to appreciate and understand what a wide variety of athletic activities have in common. And if you don't have all of the time you'd like to train, this book will help you maximize the time you have.
- If you are a parent, this book will help you to supervise your child's physical education intelli-

gently and to direct that child safely and productively into sports at the right times during his or her development.

- Finally, this book will make you, no matter who you are, a better sports spectator by allowing you to understand more of what you see.

Though there is much scientific information contained here, this is really a layman's book. It is directed to anyone who wants a comprehensive understanding of the mental and physical requirements of the sports treated, and of the intricate, interlocking athletic capabilities of the human mind and body. It is for anyone who wants to know what he or she is capable of athletically, and/or who wants improved sports performance. It is our belief that people naturally enjoy things they do well more than things they do poorly, and the real object of this book is to encourage enjoyment of sports. It is not our interest here to direct anyone away from sports participation he or she presently enjoys, but rather, by presenting in layman's terms information that heretofore has been the exclusive domain of science, and by codifying and systematizing that information into a true sportselection method, to make sports participation more informed and thus more rewarding for everyone.

HOW TO USE THIS BOOK

Parts I–IV should be viewed by the reader as containing interdependent material and should be used accordingly. Our first thought on how to write this book was simply to prepare an introduction to a book of sportselection tests. That format quickly proved inadequate, as we realized that the tests would not stand alone—that they would appear superficial and arbitrary unless seated in a context consisting of: (1) a detailed analysis of how the various human mental and physical systems operate athletically; (2) a task analysis of each of the sports we deal with that would identify exactly what those sports require of the human athletic systems; and (3) a comprehensive interpretation of the test results, and suggestions as to how sportstalent, once determined, might be maximized. Those three contextual concerns became, respectively, Parts I, II, and IV of this book. The tests themselves are contained in Part III. Each part of the book has an introduction that outlines an approach to it, but it is important that the reader realize that the order of the parts is not arbitrary: they are designed to be read in the sequence in which they are presented.

It is, of course, possible to wander around in this book or to read only one or two of its parts, and to do so productively. We believe that Part I, for example, taken by itself and notwithstanding its necessarily scientific nature, is an interesting, unified, first-of-a-kind dissertation on how the human mind and body perform at sports, and that it can be read as such. And we believe that Part II can be read and enjoyed separately as a unique, synthesized task analysis of seven sports, one that reduces each of those sports to the essential demands it makes on the human body and mind. But just as Parts I, II, and IV provide a necessary informational context for the tests, the tests render the information contained in those parts usable and personally applicable. The tests provide, in effect, a workshop in which the reader can put to personal use the rest of the book's materials.

The central aim of the testing section of this book is to identify raw, undeveloped talent for the seven sports we deal with. To achieve that end, we have tried to devise tests that delineate as clearly as possible individual abilities and capacities for measurement, and that assess pure, genetic talent rather than acquired skills. In the tennis section, for example, we do not test for how well someone hits a forehand (an acquired skill), but rather for the endowed structural abilities that underlie a good tennis game—abilities such as explosiveness, agility, and good anticipation, which someone who has never played tennis is as capable of having as someone who plays it regularly.

These are field tests that you can administer to yourself in your own home or neighborhood, and necessarily they do not have the precise measurement capability of laboratory tests. But for the purposes of this book the tests do not need that capability, since they are intended to identify raw, gross talents for a number of sports in a large and heterogeneous group. These tests are *not* designed to make fine distinctions of ability among already accomplished athletes within any homogeneous group (such as Olympic swimmers, professional tennis players, Category I cyclists, and so on), since such distinctions can be made only by sophisticated laboratory testing.

Any test results may raise more questions than they answer. By way of addressing what we have found to be common questions that may and do arise from these tests, and in order to try to provide a substitute for the sort of personal interpretation and clarification of test results one would normally receive in a laboratory environment, we have posed some of those questions here and answered them.

1. I have been running middle distances recreationally for a couple of months. I enjoy it and would like someday to compete at it, but my results on your tests for running indicate that I have little or no talent for the sport. Does that mean I should stop running, even though I enjoy it?

First of all, you might enjoy another sport, one you have more talent for, even more than you presently enjoy running, and we suggest that you take the tests for a number of the other sports in this book to find out whether you have some talent for one or more of them that you might not yet have discovered. If you don't want to take up another sport but would like to improve your running, Part IV of this book will let you know which aspects of your running can be improved and which cannot. The chances are that you can make significant improvements in your running through proper training, and that training may also unmask some talent you have for the sport that did not show up in your test results.

2. I have never before been "athletic" but I'd like now to take up a sport. I took the tests for most or all of the sports in your book and find that I have little or no talent for any of them. Does this mean I have no chance of participating successfully in one of those sports?

No, it doesn't necessarily mean that. Your poor test results may be due to your being overweight and out of shape. If you are serious about wanting to take up a sport and are overweight and out of shape, we suggest that you lose weight and use one of the aerobic sports here to get in good enough shape to determine accurately what your true aptitude for that, or another, sport is. If you are not in poor shape or overweight, examine your individual test results again for any high score on a particular test. Such a score will, in and of itself, indicate some talent for that sport. You should then refer to Part IV for ways to maximize that talent and to enlarge your other capabilities for the sport.

3. I have been a good (or competent, or expert, or world-beater) tennis player for years and yet I had low scores on your tennis tests. What the hell is *wrong* with you guys?

This scenario is perfectly possible, particularly for a participant in one of the skill sports treated here (tennis, Alpine skiing, and windsurfing). Chances are that the person who asks this question has been playing tennis for years, and has developed a game that allows him or her to substitute experience and strategy for talent.

This person probably also has effective ground strokes—a tennis talent that cannot be tested for outside a laboratory and that, again, is at least partially a function of experience. Furthermore, we suspect that though this questioner may in fact be *a world-beater at his local club, John McEnroe probably doesn't have to worry much about him.*

4. I had wonderful scores on your tests for Alpine skiing and yet I can hardly get down the bunny slope without falling. What *is* wrong with you guys?

The person who asks this question has all the underlying structural abilities to be an excellent competitive or recreational skier. (Anyone who has high scores on the tests for a particular sport has the requisite talent to excel at that sport, regardless of how well he or she now performs at it.) This questioner can't ski well at present because he or she doesn't know how to ski well. With good instruction, leading to the formation of an accurate "image of correctness"—a mental image of how to ski well—this person's natural talent for the sport will certainly emerge, and he or she might really become the world-beater that Questioner 3 claims to be. The confidence engendered by knowing you have a real talent for a sport can and should encourage you to go out and aggressively learn that sport.

5. I presently play a little golf and racquetball. I like those sports, all right, but I'm not particularly good at them, and I want to find a sport for which I have some real aptitude. My results on your cross-country skiing tests indicate that I have exceptional talent for that sport, but I don't like cross-country skiing (or I live in Miami and have no opportunity to do it). What do you suggest?

Much of this person's talent for cross-country skiing, a highly aerobic sport, is transferable to other aerobic sports (just as certain elements of talent at one skill sport, such as windsurfing, are transferable to another, such as Alpine skiing). The large heart-lung capacities, for example, that are necessary for good performance at cross-country skiing would serve this person well in cycling, running, or crew; and his or her considerable heart-lung endurance capacity would be valuable in a number of "stop-go" sports such as soccer and basketball. The primary purpose of these tests is to help you identify your athletic assets, not to lock you into any particular sport. Once you know what those assets are, you can be as creative as you want in finding a sport you enjoy that utilizes as many of your greatest individual sportstalents as possible.

6. Why these seven sports? Why didn't you deal with golf, say; or football, baseball, and basketball?

The sportselection methods of this book could be (and, we believe, will be) applied to any sport. We chose to deal with Alpine skiing, tennis, windsurfing, running, swimming, cycling, and cross-country skiing for a number of reasons.

First, because all those sports are "life sports"—that is, they can be taken up at any age and practiced either recreationally or competitively well into middle age and beyond. It is rare that anyone begins participation in a team sport much beyond college age, or continues regular participation in one into middle age. All the sports listed above are sports that can be taken up at any period of life, practiced regularly, and competed at (often with continuing improvement), by men and women, for a lifetime. Each of them, moreover, is demanding and varied enough in training, practice, and opportunity for improvement to continue, almost indefinitely, to interest anyone who participates in it. Perhaps for that reason all these sports are enormously popular throughout the world, and that fact, along with the authors' personal involvement and familiarity with them, was a second reason for our choosing them.

Third, good performance at any one of these seven sports is a result of specific mental and physical abilities and/or capacities working together. Good performance at each of them requires a number of different underlying physical and mental talents and traits that are critical to that performance, and thus each of these sports is particularly well served by the sportselection process of assigning relative values to different talents and traits and then fitting those weighted talents and traits to the specific performance requirements of the sport. In other words, we wanted to deal with sports that could really utilize a systematic selection process, as opposed to sports like golf and riflery, in which only a single system of talents and traits is critical, or the major team sports in which each position (for example, quarterback, defensive tackle, and wide receiver in football) is likely to be characterized by a different set of talents and traits.

Part V, "Identifying and Developing Sportstalent in Children and Adolescents," applies some of the book's overall premises and methods to a discussion of children and adolescents in sports. It does not include sportselection testing for children because such testing, when done systematically to allow for all the different developmental stages of childhood and adolescence, could fill a separate volume. Part V is really an addendum to the rest of the book, one designed for parents, physical educators, and anyone else concerned with the healthy, happy, and productive introduction of children into sports and with their athletic development. It can also be understood and used by adolescents themselves, and we hope that it will be.

"How-to" sports books and sports-medicine books have traditionally taken an empirical approach to their materials, deriving qualitative principles from observation and trial and error as opposed to scientific analysis. We see this book as being in the vanguard of a second generation of sports books that will proceed from objective, measurable analysis toward the formulation of quantitative principles—principles that might help free participation in sports from the subjectivism, cant, and witchdoctory that have burdened it for years. Each of us has the right to participate in sports to our full capacity for enjoyment and good performance, and this second generation of sports books will help us to do that by substituting real and systematic knowledge of sports and the human athletic machine for subjective observations on those subjects, thus making the sports consumer in this country—the athlete or would-be athlete—informed for the first time.

There is no need to fear the coming of scientific sportselection in America. The purpose of a systematic sportselection method such as the one presented in this book is not to channel people into sports they don't want to participate in, but to make available to everyone who wants it sufficient self-knowledge as an athlete or potential athlete to make *informed* sports-participation choices on an individual level. The sportselection process advanced here is nothing more than a scientific method for recognizing athletic talents and for finding a pattern to those talents that matches the pattern of demands posed by a particular sport. The primary aim of this method is to make people aware of what they are capable of athletically, of who they really are as athletes or potential athletes.

As individual sportselection becomes more and more refined and precise, we believe, its applications will broaden. Very soon we will see a truly scientific, nationwide approach to coaching and training for adults and children—one based on sportselection—that will begin to replace the old subjective approach and make available to people other than world-class athletes the best and latest information from sports science.

Sportselection, we believe, will soon begin to allow athletes to match precisely their equipment to their specific abilities and anatomical characteristics. For example, runners will be able to select shoes that are custom designed for their weight, speed, stride length, the position of the foot at impact, and the degree of foot pronation; tennis players will be able to buy tennis racquets built to the specifications of their anatomical dimensions, forearm strength, stroke mechanics, and the nature of their game.

And we believe that sports instruction in this country will soon begin to benefit enormously from sportselection. Sportselection will allow instruction to become personal rather than general, to deal directly and effectively with an individual's particular strengths and weaknesses. New microelectronic devices will make custom-tailored instruction of this sort capable of radically improving athletic performance, especially among athletes without much natural coordination.

Over the next decade, these and other applications of sportstalent recognition—applications that derive directly from sportselection—will allow more Americans to enter sports earlier and to develop higher athletic skills faster than ever before. They will also allow many Americans who have been discouraged from sports participation by a system that prejudicially selected them out to select themselves back into sports, on the basis, this time, of what they know their true capabilities to be.

All of this will not happen overnight, of course —but it will happen. In this country, when a better way of doing something comes along, it is adopted. The old "natural" sportselection process has always been wasteful and inefficient, and often, particularly when it applied to children, psychologically and physically damaging, but it has survived until now for lack of a workable alternative. With this book, and with others that will follow it, that alternative has finally arrived.

PART I

HOW THE BODY PERFORMS AT SPORTS

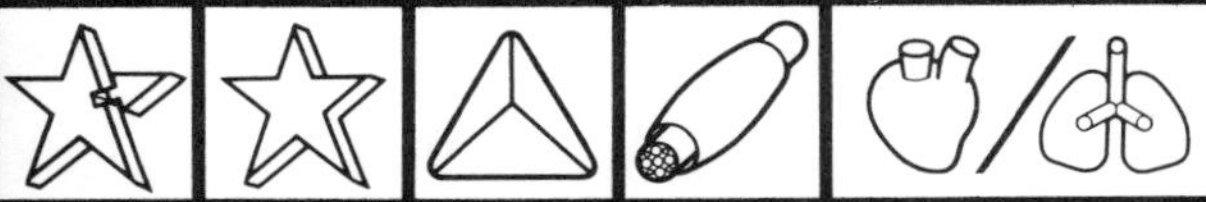

INTRODUCTION

Part I should be thought of by the reader as an owner's manual—a systematic, part-by-part guide to how the body operates athletically. The human body has a number of specific components (the heart, lungs, muscles, and so on) that have very specific athletic functions. These components vary widely from person to person—in size, in shape, in type, in capacity—and each of us possesses a unique combination of them that provides us with distinct sports-related talents. In order to understand yourself as an athlete, you need to understand *how* these components operate, both individually and in concert with each other; Part I is designed to allow you to do that.

The guide is divided into three sections: the Control System, the Heart-Lung Package, and Body Composition. The first section deals with the essential aspects of how the mind controls the body mechanically and psychologically during the performance of sports—with such aspects as the learning of new skills and their storage in permanent memory, the relationship between an individual's genetically determined abilities and aptitude for a particular sport, and the regulation of such psychological functions of the brain as anxiety and arousal. The second section of the guide deals with how the heart and lungs function in sports, both separately and together, to remove the waste products of exercise and to supply oxygen to the body at the speeds and volumes that it requires. The final section describes the athletic operation of the body's frame and its various skeletal and muscular parts.

This is the first comprehensive layman's guide to how the human body performs at sports. We have gathered the salient facts and principles of the subject from individual scientists and laboratories throughout the world, and from much of the available literature on biomechanics, exercise physiology, motor behavior, sportsvision, and sports psychology, synthesizing those facts into a primer on the human body athletic. We have tried to make Part I of this book as practical and usable as any good owner's manual, and in doing so we have avoided highly scientific terminology. The terms defined in the glossary section of the

IDEAL BODY TYPES

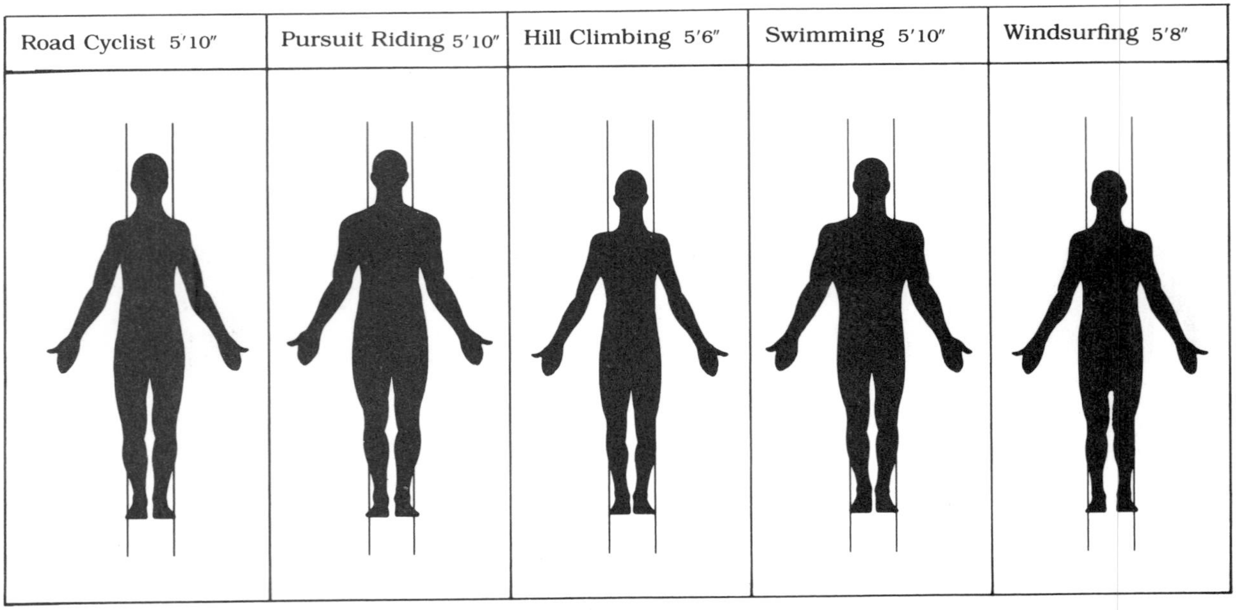

Road Cyclist 5′10″	Pursuit Riding 5′10″	Hill Climbing 5′6″	Swimming 5′10″	Windsurfing 5′8″

Appendix, terms that are used throughout this book, are derived from science, but through aptness and increasing use they have become basic to a new sports language spoken and understood by more and more athletes, coaches, and students of sport. If you are a serious athlete, and/or if you read the technical sports magazines, such as *Velo News* for cycling, *The Runner* for running, or *Ski Racing* for Alpine skiing, you are undoubtedly familiar with many of these terms. If not, any interest you now have in sports will be made more informed and articulate by knowing what these terms mean and by understanding how they relate to each other within the context offered here.

There are a number of ways to use Part I, as there are for any owner's manual. If you are the kind of person who, when you buy a new car, reads the entire manual to get an overall sense of what you have and how it should operate, then by all means use this part of the book in that way. That, in fact, is probably the best method. But you can also make good use of this part by referring back to it, as you need or want to, from later parts of the book. If you are a tennis player, for example, and begin by turning to the section on tennis, you will probably find it helpful in the Control System section of that chapter to come back to the Control System section in Part I for useful background information, in much the

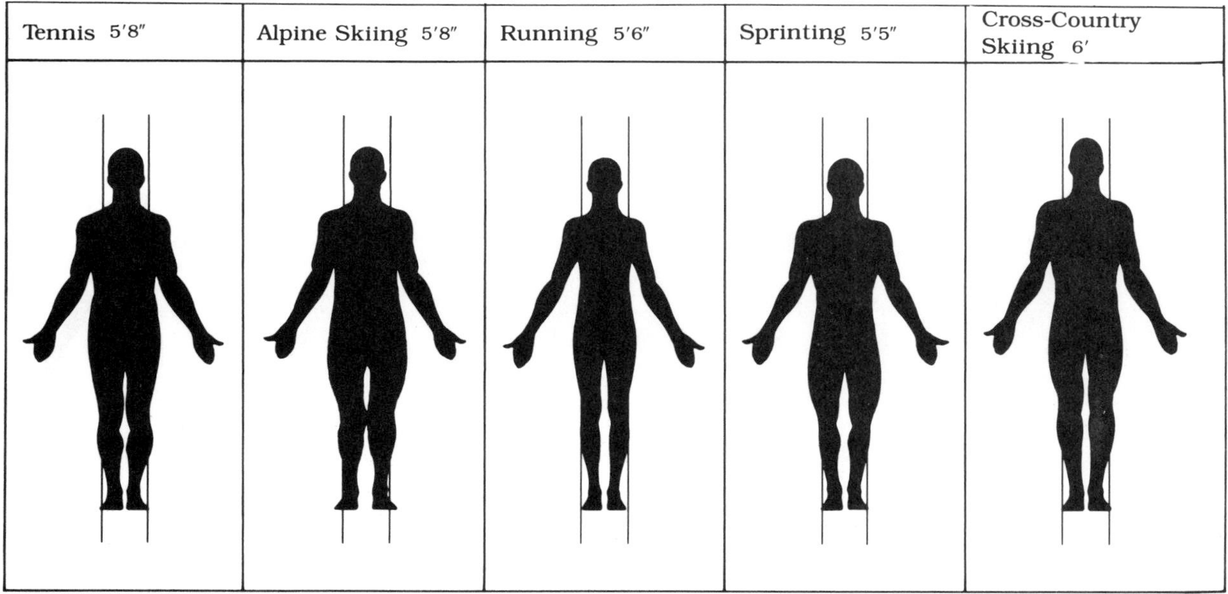

same way that you might find it helpful when confronted with a flat tire on a new car to refer to the paragraph in the owner's manual on changing tires. If you are a runner and begin reading the Heart-Lung Package section here but skip the rest of Part I, you might find it helpful in understanding your results on some of the important tests for running to come back to the Body Composition section here. However you choose to use Part I, if you are interested in learning, or improving your performance at, Alpine skiing, windsurfing, or tennis, we advise that you read the Motor Learning segment of the Control System section for what we believe to be the best information anywhere on the learning process for skill sports.

Finally, we have designed Part I to function as a book within a book, a small reference work on the body athletic. In addition to contributing to an overall picture, each subject treated here is self-contained and may be understood on its own, which will allow you to refer to Part I over and over again for accurate information on a wide variety of sports- and fitness-related subjects.

IDEAL BODY COMPONENTS	Alpine Skiing	Tennis	Windsurfing
Heart	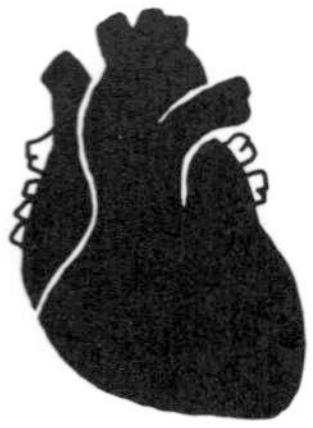	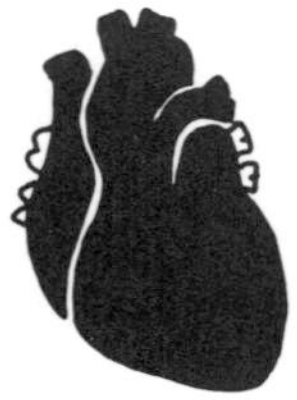	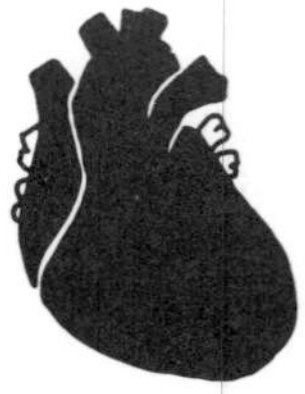
Lungs	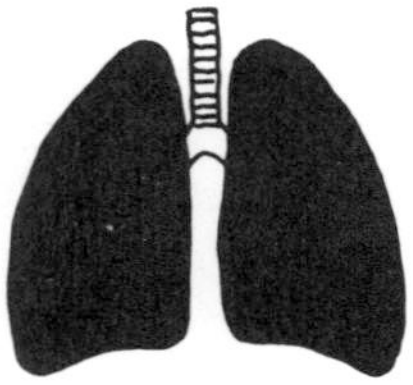	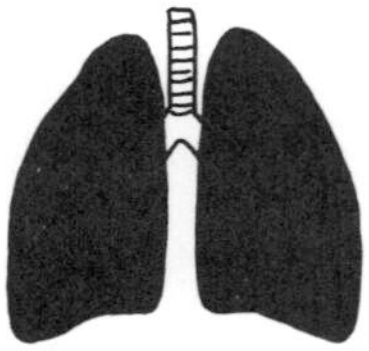	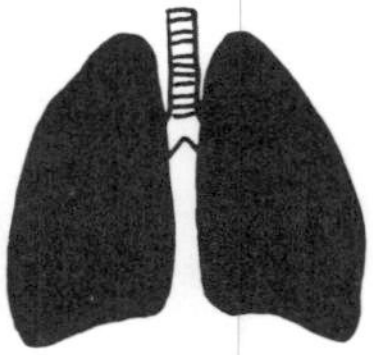
Muscle fiber type: ● *Endurance* ○ *Sprint*	60/40 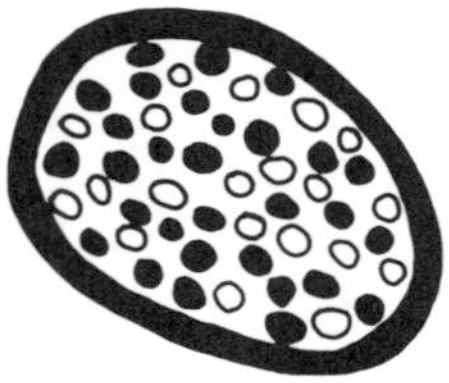	60/40 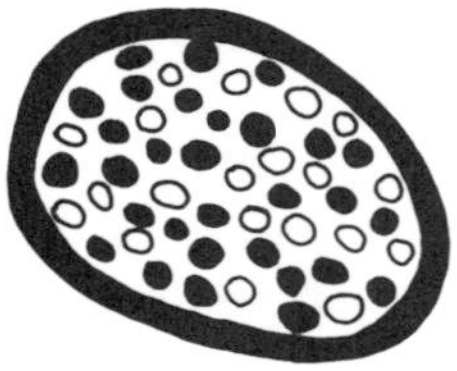	40/60 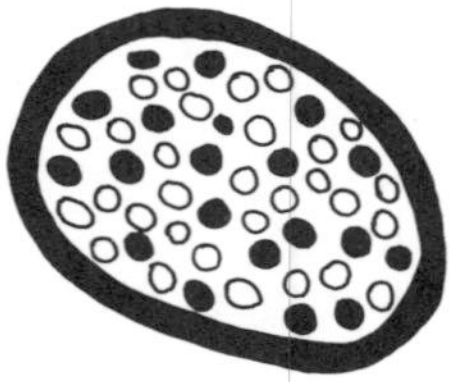
Frame	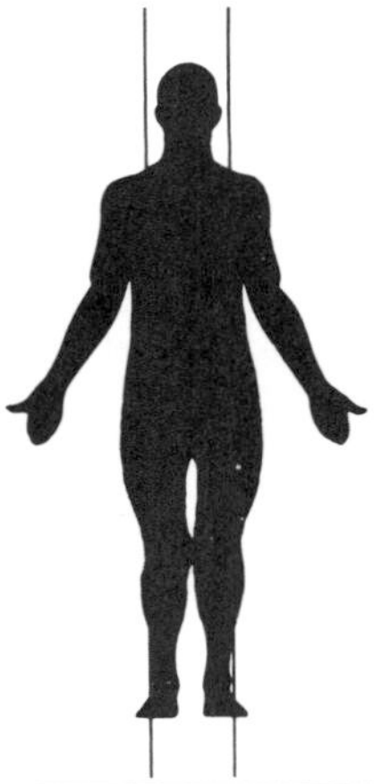		

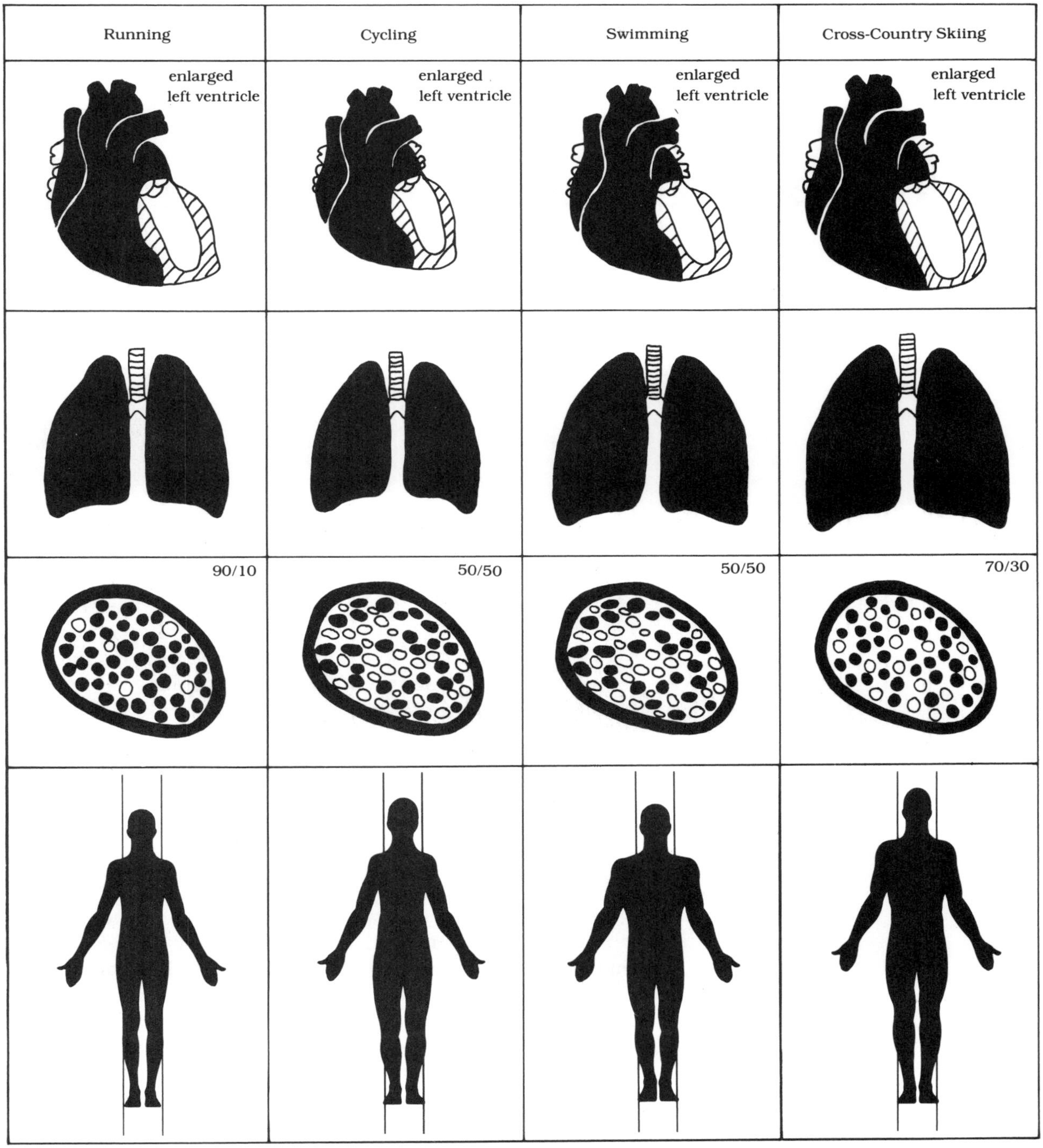

Running	Cycling	Swimming	Cross-Country Skiing
enlarged left ventricle	enlarged left ventricle	enlarged left ventricle	enlarged left ventricle
90/10	50/50	50/50	70/30

THE CONTROL SYSTEM

The human nervous system is an immensely complex organ whose anatomical parts include the brain, the peripheral nerves, the cranial nerves, and the spinal cord. The Control System is that part of this organ which, through a network of receptors and effectors, controls everything we do physically by evaluating the need for action and then executing it. The Control System operates on three different levels: receiving and evaluating sensory input; planning and beginning a response to that input; and effecting, controlling, and adjusting the response. Within those three broad categories of activity the Control System has seven specific functions and components that are critical to the performance of sports.

Reception

In order to perform physically the body needs to have information about its own movements and where it is in space. No single sense can provide the body with that information; it must be supplied to the Control System as an integration of sensory inputs from a number of sources. In addition to telling us what we are doing and where we are while doing it, the Control System can also tell us whether or not we are doing something correctly, by comparing the action to a centrally stored standard reference for that action.

THE CONTROL SYSTEM

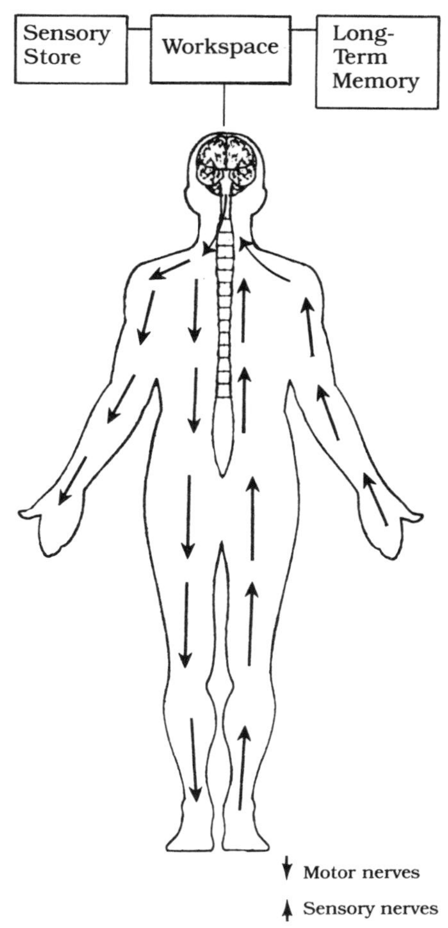

Sensory input for the performance of sports comes from the eyes, ears, and limbs. The eyes tell us both where things are in space (*exteroceptive information*) and where and how the body is moving in relation to those things (*proprioceptive information*). The primary receptive function of the ears is to locate objects and determine their movement in relation to the hearer (for example, the rate of a race car closing from behind, the speed of a tennis ball coming off a racquet, the velocity of a sweet-spot drive in golf). But a little-known fact in sports is that the ears not only pinpoint critical action around us, they also help to complete a three-dimensional picture for the athlete at any given moment, a picture that cannot be provided by the eyes alone. Good quarterbacks, for instance, have an uncanny ability, sometimes described as having "eyes in the back of their heads," to complete a three-hundred-and-sixty-degree picture of what is going on around them—linebackers rushing from behind, running backs coming around for handoffs, receivers running pass patterns—only part of which can be visualized. The ears also have a proprioceptive function, which tells us about our own movements: the sound of skis over snow can tell us how fast we are skiing and how well we are turning; the sound of a golf downswing can tell us how fast we are moving the club head.

While vision and hearing both serve some proprioceptive functions, the bulk of the work of locating where each part of the body is in space is left to the inner ear and to nerve receptors in the limbs. The inner ear serves as the body's gyroscope—discharging messages to the Control System whenever the head turns, the discharge speeding up as the rate of turning does—and any athlete with a good sense of balance will have especially sensitive inner-ear receptors.

To complete any given kinesthetic picture begun by the inner ears, hearing, and vision, the Control System must know where each limb is and what it is doing. It is given this information by position and pressure receptors in the limbs. Though there are pressure receptors throughout the body, they are most densely packed on the palms and fingers of the hands—where they are so sensitive they can actually read, as they do in recognizing Braille—and on the soles of the feet, where the minutest changes in pressure register subtle shifts in balance.

The position receptors are located in joints, tendons, and muscles. Joint receptors are triggered, or fire, only when a joint reaches the end of its range of motion; tendon receptors increase their firing as muscle tension increases; and muscle

THE CONTROL SYSTEM AT WORK

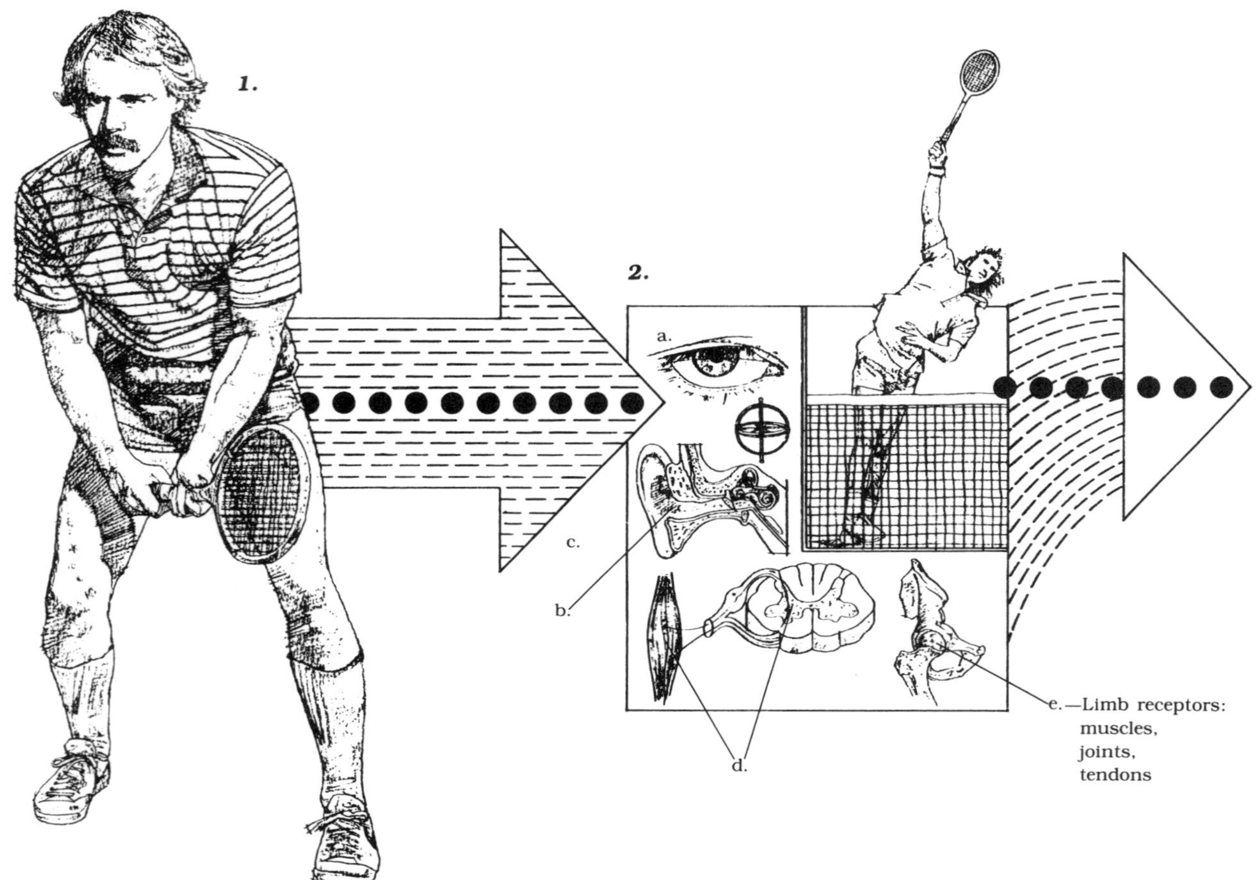

1. *Tennis player anticipating a serve.*
2. *Receptor organs sensing information critical to return of serve.* ***a.*** *The eyes follow the opponent's service and the ball's flight path.* ***b.*** *The ear listens for ball strike, timing, or character (twist, spin, hit on wood).*
c. *The inner ear registers balance.* ***d. e.*** *Muscle position and tension and joint position let control system know readiness and position of limbs prior to moving them.*
3. *Information sensed by receptor organs is stored here momentarily and then replaced by new data.*
4. *The workspace of the control system looks at highly selective data in the SSTS, then chooses and slots into play an action (motor response) which is the return of serve.* ***a.*** *Computational power of control system.* ***b.*** *Brain's battery (the RAS), which at full tilt powers the brain at a high state of arousal.* ***c.*** *Motor program represented as a sequence on videotape from Long-Term Memory.* ***d.*** *Assembled components of new motor program returned to Long-Term Memory after practice.*
5. *Long-Term Memory.* ***a.*** *Library of completed motor programs.* ***b.*** *Underlying motor abilities.* ***c.*** *Past memory of opponent's service pattern.* ***d.*** *Motor programs readied for action.*
6. *Execution of motor program from brain's motor cortex through spinal cord to muscles.*

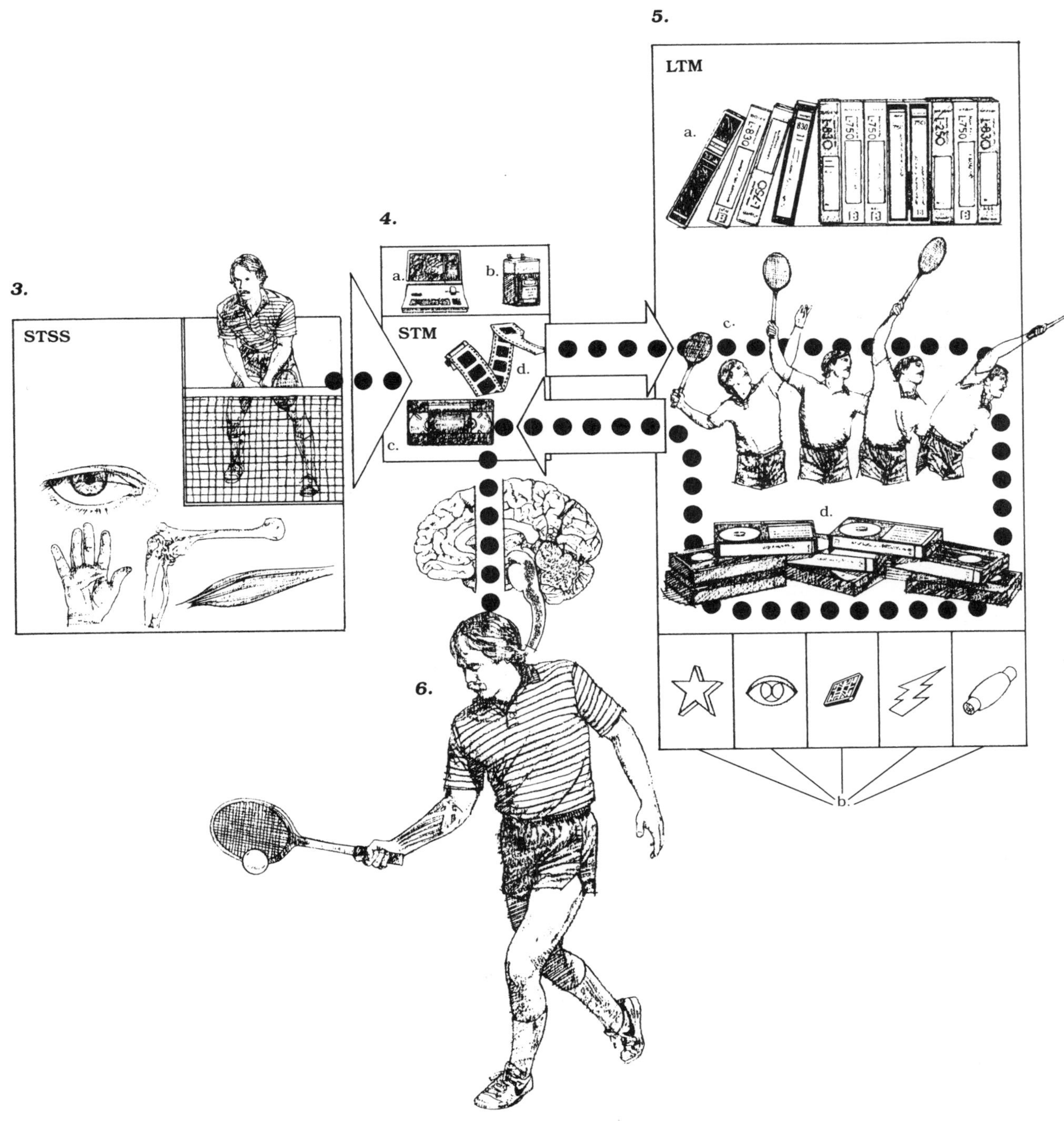

5.
LTM
a.
c.
d.
b.
4.
a.
b.
STM
d.
c.
3.
STSS
6.

As motor control first emerged from neurophysiology and psychology as a separate area of research, Jack Adams became one of the great early pioneers in this major field. His work has formed much of the basis of our understanding and portrayal of human memory. Since virtually all we know about memory and learning in sport is inferential, Adams's elegant work is necessarily highly inferential.

receptors assess the length of a particular muscle and how quickly it contracts, thereby signaling when a braking action on the limb is required.

In any athletic performance the Control System samples a huge number of sensory inputs from all these receptors, assembling from them as complete a picture as possible of the athlete's surroundings, and integrating the body's precise spatial orientation within those surroundings. An ultimate refinement of this process can be seen in the triple-axel jump of a figure skater, where at any given second the athlete knows his or her precise three-dimensional spatial orientation, how it varies from a standard of correctness, and if it does, how to correct it.

Memory

During any athletic event, literally millions of bits of sensory information are made available to the Control System by the receptors. The storage of this information in various ways, the selection of relevant details from it, and the initiation of proper responses to it are all functions of memory.

There are three separate, sports-related memory banks, the design and uses of which are so similar to those in the electronic computer that original computer architecture may well have been intuitively patterned after them. These three banks are the Short-Term Sensory Store, the Short-Term Memory, and the Long-Term Memory.

The Short-Term Sensory Store (STSS) receives all sensory information provided by the eyes, the ears, the inner ears, and the limb receptors. The STSS holds massive amounts of sensory input, much of which is extraneous to whatever activity the body is engaged in at a particular time, and while the STSS has a virtually limitless capacity, the information in it fades quickly unless rapidly reinforced. For example, visual events usually remain in the STSS for only a few milliseconds, and the *maximum* length of time they can be stored there is only one second.

The STSS stores only raw information; through a process called *selective attention*, the Control System selects from this bulk of details what information to pass along to the Short-Term Memory. Policemen are often perplexed by the fact that there can be a different version of an automobile accident for every observer of it. This is so because unless an observer has directed his or her selective attention to the exact instant of the accident's occurrence, all the raw visual information the eyes

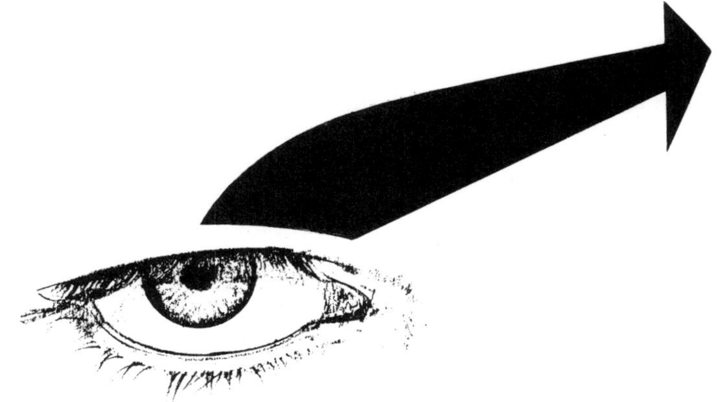

Selective attention not directed at ball; STSS will not retain information.

pick up will simply fade from the STSS and be lost by the time the witness focuses on the accident.

There is a very small channel between the STSS and the Short-Term Memory that, unlike the STSS, can easily be overloaded, even with relevant sensory information. Therefore, relative to the enormous capacity of the STSS, only a very small amount of information can be passed along at any given time from it to the Short-Term Memory. However, the superb athlete (for example, a quarterback in the middle of a play, focusing both on receivers and on rushing defensive linemen) can, by rapid shifts of attention, make a large variety of information available to his Short-Term Memory despite this limited channel capacity.

The Short-Term Memory (STM) is the Control System's work space, in which information from both the STSS and the Long-Term Memory is processed. Compared with either of the other two storage banks, the Short-Term Memory has an extremely limited capacity of only six to eight items at a time; and those items are short-lived, remaining in the STM for a maximum of

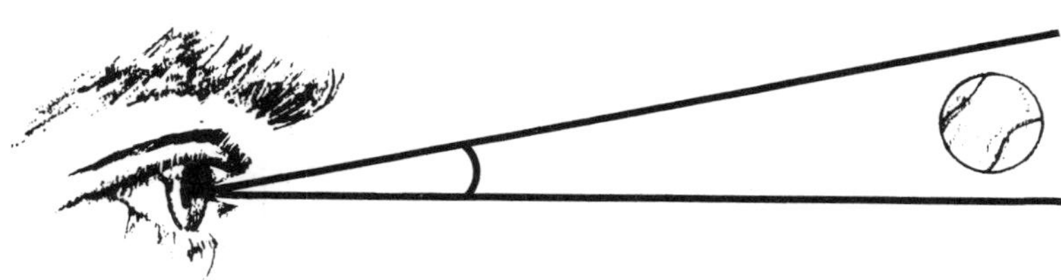

Selective attention focused on ball.

Motor programs readied for return of serve after recognition of service pattern. Stored motor programs above; raw motor abilities below.

Completed motor programs in LTM.

only sixty seconds, which is why, for example, we can forget phone numbers between the time we get them from Directory Assistance and the time we find a pencil. The developed ability to hold more than six or eight items at a time in the Short-Term Memory is due to a process known as "chunking"—or connecting various pieces of information by one or another form of association.

The information in the Short-Term Memory is what we are actually aware of at any given moment, and what we are aware of is essentially consciousness: who we are at a given time. Awareness has constantly available to it two seemingly limitless stores of information: the STSS, from which current sensory information is extracted; and the Long-Term Memory, in which relevant past experiences and a library of motor skills and programs may be stored and later retrieved. After specific sensory information has been selected from the STSS and compared with relevant past experience, available motor skills are unshelved from the Long-Term Memory and combined within the work space of the Short-Term Memory in order to initiate movement.

The Long-Term Memory (LTM) stores not only past experiences but also the entire library of motor skills that we have mastered to that point. In contrast to the Short-Term Memory and the Short-Term Sensory Store, the Long-Term Memory has a virtually limitless duration and a capacity so large that no maximum value for it has ever been found. Once learned and stored in the LTM, motor skills are protected from loss—which is why, for example, an individual is still able to ride a bicycle after fifty years of not having done so. If a learned skill does fade from the LTM, it is because of some active form of interference or because the skill was never well enough practiced to reinforce the original memory trace. Practice does constantly reinforce learned skills by increasing associations and by retrieving currently practiced information from the Short-Term Memory.

As an example of how the Short-Term Sensory Store, the Short-Term Memory, and the Long-Term Memory work together in the performance of an athletic act, picture a tennis player about to return a serve. The player's work space, or STM, recognizes a pattern, stored in the LTM, in the serving motion of the other player that may tell something about the direction and force of the coming serve; the player's STSS tells him the position of his extremities, a critical precondition for initiating action, and based on this information he readies those extremities for the anticipated serve; the mechanism of selective atten-

tion sweeps his STSS for information about the position of his opponent, his own movements, and the position of his racquet and the oncoming ball; long before he actually returns the serve, a motor program is selected from his LTM and slotted into the STM, where it must be initiated by his body well in advance of the ball's arrival; and finally his STM compares the action of his swing, while he is making it, with a trace in his LTM that, based on his past observation and practice, the player perceives to be a standard of correctness. Finally, the necessary work of the memory done, the player returns the serve.

The overall amount of memory available through the Short-Term Sensory Store, the Short-Term Memory, and the Long-Term Memory does not appear to vary much in normal adults. However, the Control System's use of memory can vary radically from individual to individual depending on how effectively selective attention can scan the STSS, the judgment used in choosing the appropriate program, the number and refinement of motor programs available to the STM, and the degree of arousal and anticipation called up in an individual about to perform a particular act.

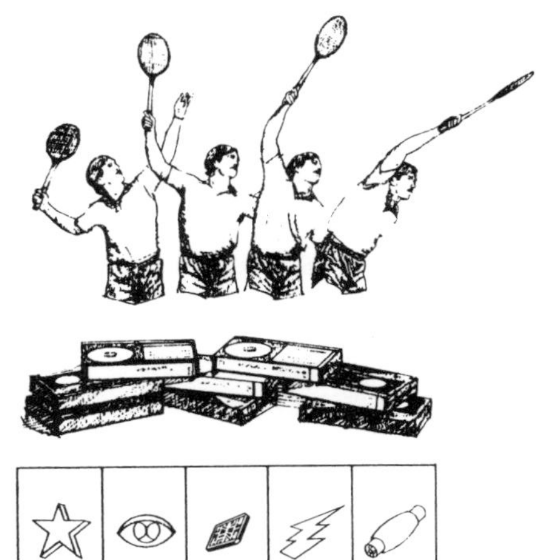

Selecting appropriate readied motor program and slotting it into STM.

Abilities

We have all known someone whom we considered to be a "natural athlete," but in fact there is virtually no such thing as a single, general athletic ability. For each physical skill there are several underlying structural motor abilities whose excellence is genetically determined and that are changed little by practice. Multilimb coordination, reaction time, speed of limb movement, manual and finger dexterity, arm/hand steadiness, aiming, agility, and balance are examples of motor abilities. There are more than a hundred of them and practically no one is born with a package of superior abilities large enough to make for overall athletic skill. Even among world-class athletes there is little connection between seemingly similar skills, because those skills have in common few underlying abilities. Even different types of ball throwing have different underlying abilities; as a result, professional football players generally do not throw baseballs as well as they do footballs. In skills that are even closer, such as downhill and slalom skiing, there is rarely any significant crossover in ability among world-class skiers.

At the schoolyard level, certain children may appear to be natural athletes, but this is usually because those youngsters are

The pioneering work in Sportselection was done by Edwin Fleishman. He was the first to define the underlying structure of human performance, especially as applied to motor abilities, in a wide range of activities, from early pilot selection through much of industry and sport.

In addition to the enormous amount of research he has done, Richard Schmidt has written* Motor Control and Learning, *which is the first work to integrate the complex and revolutionary studies in this field in a single volume. Schmidt's teaching, writing, and research have been invaluable to us in understanding the Control System.

larger and stronger than the others. Because of early success in one sport, these children tend to venture quickly into others, while those without early athletic success, even children with great underlying abilities, will likely avoid continued participation in sports. Although they are not genetically poor athletes, such children develop a skill deficit that is more a function of their personality and social environment than it is of their inherited potential for sports.

Though the existence of the natural athlete is largely a myth, there *are* a very few people who are simply born with a large library of superior motor abilities and a capacity to learn skills quickly—such people might be called motor geniuses. True motor genius lies in the right-brain from birth. While the left-brain is traditionally the seat of the intellect, the right-brain contains the three-dimensional spatial and motor-learning capacities that allow for the development of athletic intelligence. Right-brain, or motor, genius is much rarer than intellectual genius: in skiing, for instance, it might be present in one skier, worldwide, in an era.

Motor Learning

We have described motor abilities as underlying structural genetic traits, a large number of which in combination may form a motor skill. For instance, the skill required to execute a single well-made slalom turn in Alpine skiing requires dozens of underlying abilities in balance, speed, strength, coordination, and agility.

When the Control System first executes a particular skill, a trace of it is formed in the Long-Term Memory; the inscription of this trace represents motor learning. This trace is strengthened by each successive rehearsal of the skill. Although early on, the competence with which a skill is performed is almost entirely dependent on abilities, any later perfection of it comes through practice.

How does someone learn a skill such as windsurfing? First, the person has to want to do it. Second, the higher the windsurfing goal he sets for himself, the better he'll be at it. Whatever that goal is, the individual next needs to build for himself an image of the physical movements involved in windsurfing. Based on his present inventory of physical skills and past experiences, he begins to construct this image in his memory as he begins to practice. This early phase of motor learning, in which the student has formed only a weak and spotty *standard of correctness*, is known as the cognitive, or thinking, phase. During

this phase, the truer the standard of correctness formed by the student from his instruction, the better he will do. He will also benefit substantially at this stage of his learning from some knowledge of how the windsurfing rig and board work mechanically, and from a sense of the physical context of windsurfing, a feel for the various conditions of the wind and water. During this time when a student is learning *what* he is supposed to do rather than how to do it, any input such as books, films, and discussion, as well as formal instruction, is helpful to the process. This cognitive phase is particularly crucial in the development of a skill for adults without a large library of motor skills and abilities, because such adults are simply not prepared to learn from demonstration alone. First-rate athletes are often characterized by the capacity to learn a new motor skill by critical observation and imitation of that skill, and this capacity can considerably speed up the cognitive motor-learning process, as well as ensure the correctness of that process.

In the second, or associative, phase of motor learning, a student begins to think less about what to do than about how to do it, and the trace of the skill in his motor memory becomes strengthened by practice and refinement. At this stage our windsurfer is no longer falling into the water while an instructor shouts at him from the bank, but actually sailing the board and finding out what works for him and what doesn't in improving his new skill. Now he can also improve by watching other windsurfers more skillful than himself, strengthening the trace of the skill by absorbing what he sees other people do—by modeling his own performance after more correct demonstrations of it. Learning requires less effort, both mental and physical, than it did at the cognitive phase; the student does things faster and more easily, and he retains more of what he learns.

During the third phase of motor learning, the student practices the various movements comprising a skill until they become automatic—until, at the point of ultimate mastery of the skill, he no longer has to think at all about what he is doing or how he is doing it, and his movements just seem to happen on their own. At this point, our windsurfer is off the windward side of Maui, where, driven by a thirty-knot wind, giant open ocean rollers with twenty-five-foot faces crash onto a shallow offshore reef. He makes his way out through the surf by riding up each successive face, and at the crest of each wave he flies off the top, up to forty feet in the air, and delicately uses his sail to parachute the board down onto the next roller. Beyond the reef he executes a duck-jibe on the crest of a breaking wave to surf

We are indebted to Professor Richard Schmidt for his keen insights into building a proper image of correctness and the practical implications this has for coaches, trainers, and athletes.

down its face and back across the reef. Each turn, or jibe, down the face of the waves is made in milliseconds, and even fractional errors in timing can send the windsurfer "over the falls," to be crushed by tons of water. Everything he does in this context has to be automatic, and to an observer on the beach trying to work cognitively through what the windsurfer is doing, the performance of the skill on this level will seem unimaginable.

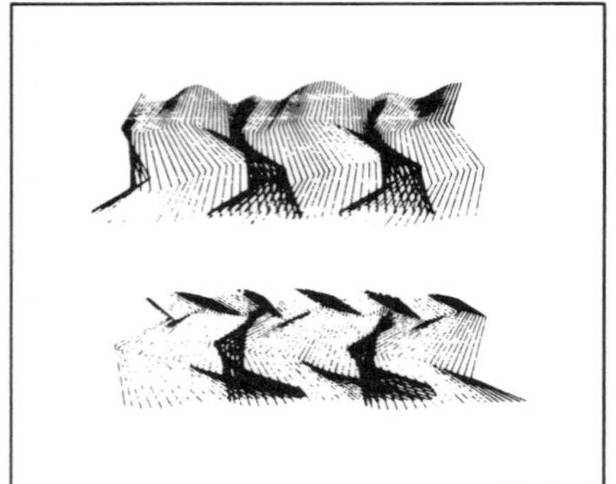

Computerized Motion Analysis provides an accurate reproduction of movement patterns.

Motor learning on any plane will not occur without both *practice* and the error detection provided by a *knowledge of results* (KR). A knowledge of results is simply an awareness of the outcome of a particular physical movement or sequence of movements. A simple form of knowledge of results in basketball, for example, is knowing that the ball did or did not go through the hoop. An accurate knowledge of results is not only the single most important factor in learning new skills—motor learning may not happen at all without it—it is also a terrific motivational device, giving the learner both an ongoing interest and a will to succeed. As long as an individual continues to practice a sport he will improve at it if accurate and constructive feedback is provided. This feedback takes two forms: a knowledge of results and a *knowledge of performance* (KP) that produced those results.

While KR has been traditionally fairly easy to measure by some objective standard of outcome (in tennis a stroked ball will either go in or go out), until recently it has been virtually impossible for an athlete to be provided with a knowledge of the complex movement patterns, or performance, that produced the results. The greatest modern technological breakthrough in sports has been the development of *Computerized Motion Analysis* (CMA) as a method of providing an accurate visualization of errors committed in movement patterns, making radical improvement in sports performance possible not only for the Olympic athlete but for the weekend athlete as well, to whom CMA and its offshoots offer accurate, scientific feedback rather than the often faulty, nonspecific, and inconsistent comments offered by friends or coaches.

Dr. Charles Dillman pioneered in the use of computerized motion analysis in his work with the U.S. Ski Team and with track and field athletes. He is currently Director of Biomechanics for the U.S. Olympic Committee at their training center in Colorado Springs. His excellent judgment and insight allowed for the reduction of extremely complex data into simple coaching points.

Here are some particular things you should know about knowledge of results:

1. The more precise the KR, the more learning occurs and the better the performance is. An athlete who wants to improve should not accept from a coach a comment like "Nice going," but rather should ask precisely what it was he did correctly. In a

tennis lesson a direction such as "Get your racquet back earlier" should ideally be combined with information as to how *far* back in actual inches, and *how early* in actual seconds.

2. KR can serve an important motivational function by keeping the learner stimulated to practice longer and harder.

3. As an athlete becomes more competent at a skill, his own internal error-detection mechanisms increasingly substitute for KR in his improvement.

4. For athletes without a highly developed error-detection mechanism (typically the less skilled athletes), KR is critical and therefore should be sought in its most accurate form. Though any repetitive form of correct KR is valuable, some forms are much more valuable than others. Verbal instruction is often frustrating for both coach and athlete because of the constantly repeated, usually large number of verbal attempts necessary to close the distance between the coach's standard of correctness (which may or may not be correct) and the athlete's. Although the use of videotaping in assessing an athlete's performance has been widespread in the past twenty years, there is little evidence that it is effective. If the skill being performed is complex, videotaping tends to provide too much information to the athlete at one time and thus is confusing. Computerized Motion Analysis provides by far the best form of KR when the physics of the sport have been worked out and the CMA is presented in a meaningful form.

5. For the KR to take hold, there must be an interval between a given KR and the next trial of the skill.

6. The ultimate perfection of a given skill is proportionate to the overall number of KRs given in the development of that skill. Practice, in other words, does make perfect . . . with enough KR.

The final output of motion analysis describes the speed at which limbs move. This is most effectively done by saying how quickly limbs move around a joint, i.e., the upper and lower leg around a knee, as measured by degrees per second.

The more you practice a given motor skill, the better you get at it, and world-class performances in all sports occur only as a result of extensive practice. Here are some conditions for the productive practice of skills:

1. Continuous events (such as running, swimming, and cycling) must be practiced as a whole, but sports involving discrete skills may be effectively practiced part by part. The improvement in performance that occurs as the result of component training is known as *positive transfer*. For example, the improvement in a person's tennis game that might result from hitting dozens of backhands off a ball machine, without having to employ the skills of moving to the ball, is an instance of positive transfer.

2. The good tennis player is often concerned that the wrist flick in his squash or racquetball stroke will interfere with his tennis stroke; and in fact in any situation in which two skills are strikingly similar but employ different phases of speed within the same sequence of movement (for example, the tennis and the squash strokes), there may be some loss of skills through the mechanism of *negative transfer*. Such loss is actually rare; more often, loss of skill results from mental confusion over two seemingly similar skills.

3. Practice of one skill very similar to another results in practically no positive transfer to the second skill. Practicing a ski-jumping motion indoors, for example, will produce very little, if any, improvement on a ninety-meter ski jump.

4. The above fact has led to the invention in aviation of simulators that are so precise that they provide a very high positive transfer of skills. For dangerous, or expensive, or inaccessible sports such as race-car driving or acrobatics, this sort of realistic simulation makes very good sense as a method of improving skills.

5. Varied practice leads to greater depth of learning. A skill will be more fully and deeply learned if it is practiced in all the diverse conditions in which it is performed. Skiing, for instance, is improved if it is practiced on varied kinds of terrain and snow conditions.

6. "Mass-practice"—the practice of several skills at the same time—can actually impair learning. But the advantages of mass-practice are that it allows more learning to take place over a shorter period of time and that it contributes to a greater depth of learning.

As is true in any type of learning, certain people will learn a particular motor skill more quickly than others. The speed with which an individual learns a motor skill can be demonstrated on a graph known as a *learning curve*. Though learning curves are useful devices to separate fast and slow learners, they show learning only as a gradual process, when in fact it can occur in sudden, intuitive leaps.

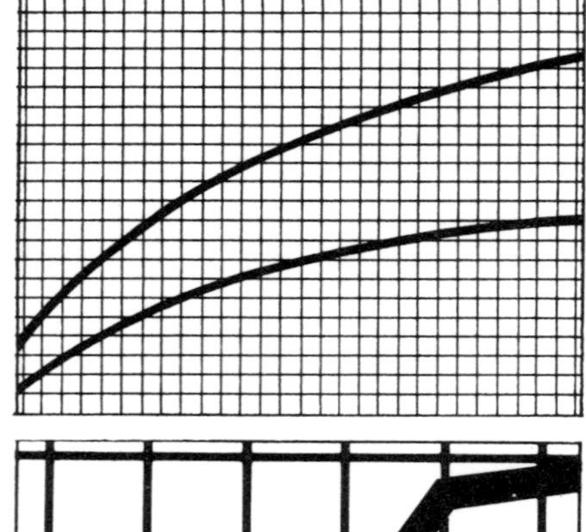

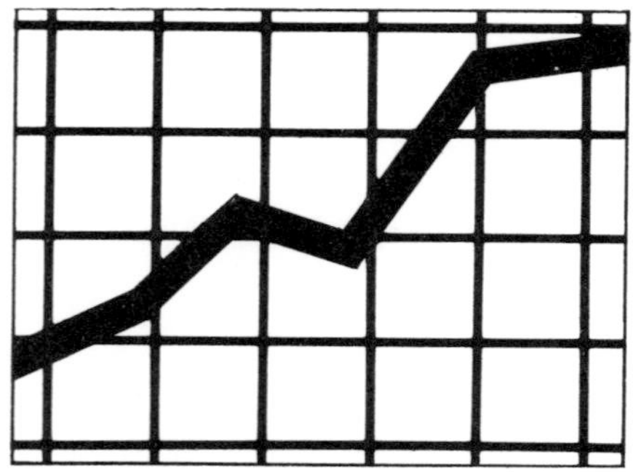

Above: Examples of fast and slow learning curves. Below: Magnified portion of learning curve reveals learning occurs in sudden jumps.

Motor Programming

During the motor-learning process, memory traces are etched and reinforced in the Long-Term Memory. These traces are stored and recalled for future use as *motor programs*. Any given motor program comprises a number of separate skills linked together. In forming a program for a new sport, already existing

skills (such as grasping, throwing, kicking, or jumping) are linked together into new combinations.

Each motor program is a general set of specifications, rather than a detailed blueprint, for the performance of a particular action. In sports it is impractical to have a bewildering variety of movements available in the performance of a single action. A tennis player, for instance, standing at the net, is better served by a limited number of programs for the backhand volley than by a vast array of them. Motor programs in sports, therefore, deal only with three broad specifications for movement: sequence, phasing, and force.

Sequence is the order in which movement progresses, and it is invariable in any given motor program (for example, the hip-flexion, knee-flexion, leg-extension, and foot-strike sequence of running is always the same). *Phasing* refers to the relative amount of time during which a particular muscle group is active within a sequence of movement. The same motor program, and therefore the same phasing, is active in a marathoner running at speeds between six and a half and five minutes a mile; but if the runner drops the speed to seven and a half minutes per mile, the phasing is distinctly different and its pattern is commonly recognized as jogging. One step in running at five minutes a mile might take a quarter of a second. A number of muscles are involved in taking that step, and each of them is engaged for its own fixed percentage of the time required to take it. When the runner slows to a jog, those fixed percentages change, causing a visible difference in the phasing pattern of the movement.

Just as each segment of a movement occupies a fixed percentage of the time required to complete the movement, regardless of speed, the *force* produced by each of the movement's segments is also fixed in relation to the other segments. If two movements are in the same motor program and you double the force of one of those movements, you automatically double the force of the other. In a push-up, for example, even though the pectoral muscles of the chest and the triceps muscles in the backs of the arms don't bear an equal burden, if you double the force provided to a push-up by the pectorals, you will double the triceps force as well.

While observing marathoner Bill Rodgers, Boston track coach Bill Squires remarked, "Running is like dancing except that there is only one step, and you had better learn it well." Coach Squires was commenting on the fact that any runner, through a range of speeds, has an observably distinctive style that is repre-

sentative of a single motor program. A given motor program is composed of specific and set relationships among sequence, phasing, and force: the motor program is defined by those relationships, which cannot be changed.

Imagine taking a leisurely walk at, say, an eighteen-minute-per-mile pace. As you take a step, your hip muscles contract, pulling your knee forward, after which your foot swings forward and strikes the ground. The sequence, phasing, and force ratios with which all this is accomplished will remain the same even as you pick up the pace of your walk to twelve minutes a mile. If your hip muscles at this pace contract twice as quickly and three times as powerfully, then your leg will swing through twice as quickly and three times as powerfully. But if at twelve minutes a mile you break into a slow jog, keeping exactly the same speed at which you were walking, you are now executing a different motor program and you will notice that although the same objective of travel at twelve minutes per mile is being accomplished, the phasing and force of the jogging movement are completely different from those which characterized and defined your walk. Although the sequence of the two movements is similar, certain muscle groups are now contracting more powerfully and for longer periods of time, changing both phasing and force.

Perhaps nowhere is the structure of a motor program more important than in tennis, where basic ground strokes *are* your game. Most tennis players believe that they have a whole range of shots available to them. In fact, what they have is a few basic shots that vary only in the racquet speed and height employed to execute them. In a slow game, a tennis player without good basic ground strokes can take advantage of the time he has to correct mistakes and of the fact that spatial errors increase dramatically with speed. In a Wimbledon match the very high speed of play means that there is no chance for correction during a given movement and therefore the motor program for each stroke must be perfect.

The Mind

Americans have always believed that there is a nonphysical dimension to the performance of sports, a psychological dimension where will, determination, and the old Pete Rose "try" have a place. It used to be thought that the "psychological" aspect of sports was a sort of spirit aspect, unidentifiable and observable

only in its effects; but now we understand that aspect to be largely biological, and increasingly it can be evaluated, measured, and modified by hard science. To the argument that this new understanding robs sports of their "human" elements, we would answer that, in fact, it makes sports *more* human by providing the athlete with some knowledge of, and some control over, the part played by the mind in athletic performance.

There are three specific biological functions of sports psychology that together put a driver with personality, motivation, anxiety, and goals into the driver's seat of the Control System, which in each individual is already biologically defined by its own peculiar potentials and limitations. These three functions are attention, anticipation, and arousal.

Attention. As we have seen, during the performance of a sport huge amounts of input data supplied by the eyes, the ears, the inner ear, and the limb receptors enter the Short-Term Sensory Store along parallel tracks, forming there a vast repository of sensory information. In order for any programmed movement to occur, the Short-Term Memory must focus on this information and select individual items from it via the mechanism of selective attention. Also necessary for the occurrence of movement is the retrieval of a motor program from the Long-Term Memory, the slotting of it into the work space of the Short-Term Memory, and the initiation of it as movement. Since the channel between the Short-Term Memory and the Short-Term Sensory Store is very narrow, as is the channel to motor program selection and initiation, attention is a limited capacity. It is impossible, for example, to run fast and figure out a complex mathematical problem at the same time, since both acts require attention (but the math problem might be solved at a jog, which requires little or no attention). If, in fact, you can execute *any two* motor tasks at the same time, one of them is making little demand on your attention. Some sports, such as downhill skiing and whitewater canoeing, are so totally demanding of attention that the expression "they take your mind off everything" is literally true.

For the performance of any activity requiring a high level of skill, many sensory inputs are necessary and many motor programs must be chosen; the mechanism of selective attention makes it possible to shift from one input to another and to choose and initiate a motor program. The good athlete has a continual sweep of attention through the entire sensory store and is able to focus intently on particular sensory data, to maximize the information derived from those data, and to switch focus quickly. Such a high level of athletic attention demands

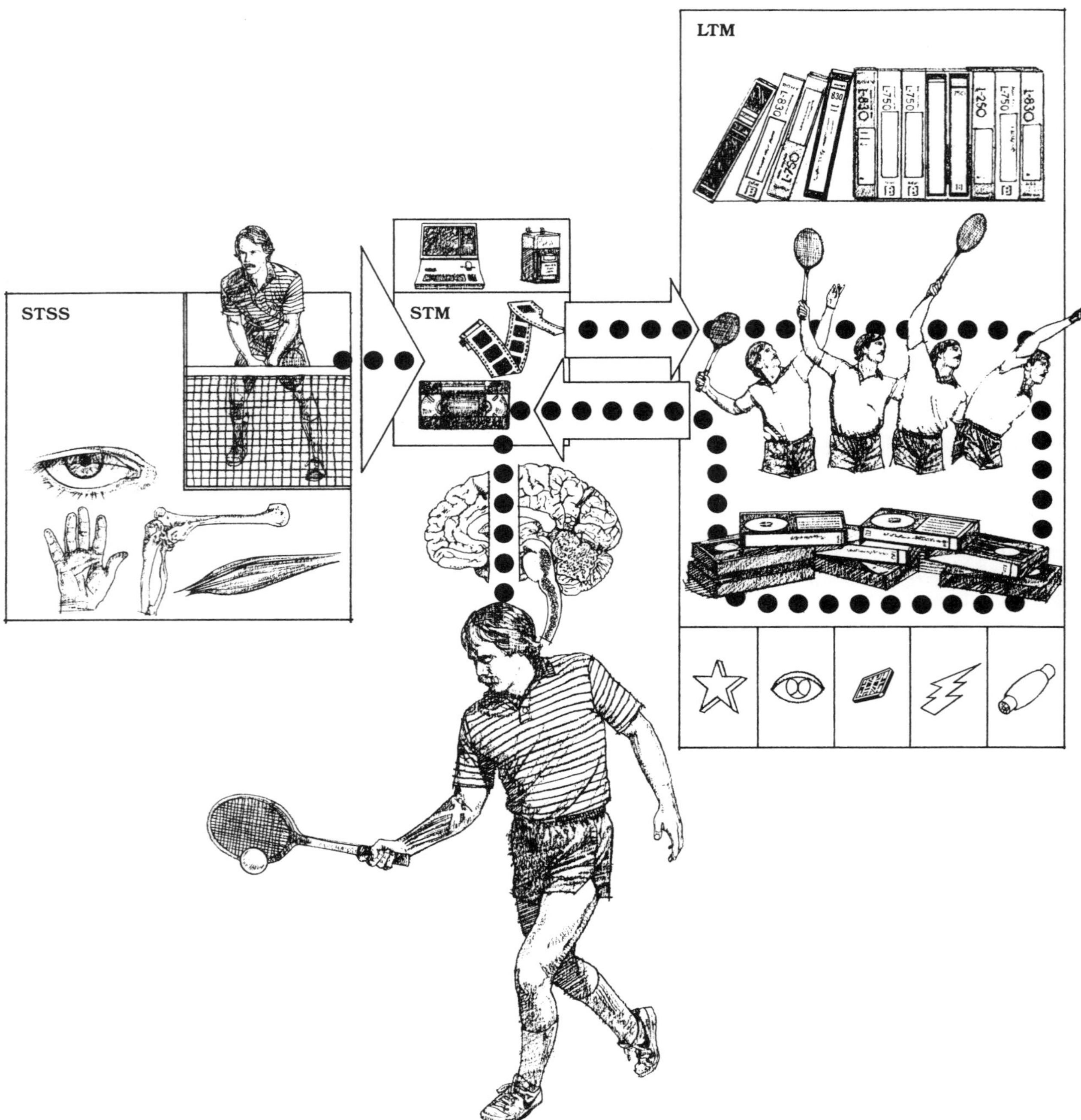

Return of serve: executing selected motor program with updated sensory data.

an enormous amount of effort, and results in real and measurable physiological fatigue.

Attention is required at the initiation of a response but can diminish quickly thereafter—which accounts for the fact, for instance, that a tennis player can run to the net while, at the same time, following through on a stroke. The attention required to execute a motor program also diminishes rapidly with practice of that program. Another characteristic of attention with important applications in sports is that too much attention directed at sensory stimuli slows the response. An FBI marksman, for example, will have no problem firing quickly at a single pop-up target representing a criminal; the same marksman, presented suddenly with six pop-up targets, only one of which is the criminal, will be dramatically slowed in his response by the extra demands made on his attention of having to select the proper target.

In sports, attention is the focused desire to perform well; to sustain attention for any length of time—either in the perfection of skills during practice or in the actual performance of the sport—one must expend tremendous and fatiguing mental effort, and few athletes are willing or able to do this. Of two athletes possessing similar skills and the requisite body components for a sport, the one better able to maintain attention through practice and into competition will invariably perform better—giving credence to the general feeling that fierce determination and concentrated effort will win in the end. It is equally true, however, that all the attention and determination to win in the world can't make up for a lack of the biological components necessary to compete at a given sport.

As skills in a sport become increasingly automatic, a good athlete is able to direct less attention to selecting and executing motor programs, and more to the overall strategy of the sport. A beginning tennis player, for example, is usually too concerned with actually returning a shot to pay much attention to the overall strategy of the game, while the expert tennis player is often thinking two or three shots ahead. On the highest levels of strategic play at any sport, an athlete is able to cut reaction time significantly by bypassing the time required for response selection through the mechanism of anticipation.

Anticipation. Selective attention means scanning for the appearance of a particular stimulus, then searching for an appropriate response. Anticipation, on the other hand, involves guessing when a stimulus will appear and pre-slotting an appropriate response into the Short-Term Memory, thereby sub-

In sports science the most commonly used measurement is the millisecond, 1/1000 of a second. Since winning times in skiing, track, bobsled, and other short events are measured in 1/100 of a second, it is increasingly necessary to break parts of movement into even finer parts in order to understand them. Here are some examples:

EVENT	*MILLISECONDS*
Reception of a visual signal	*100*
Reaction time, minimum	*180*
Movement time, minimum	*200*

stantially reducing reaction time. In the average person, the amount of time required to react to something seen or heard is 180 milliseconds; if an athlete can accurately anticipate the sight or sound, he can decrease reaction time by up to 150 milliseconds. For anticipation to work at all, the proper response must be pre-selected. If an athlete pre-selects the wrong response to his anticipation, his reaction time will lengthen because he has to reselect the proper response; and should he actually have begun to execute the wrong response, he will be forced both to take corrective action *and* to select the proper response—in effect, at least doubling his normal reaction time. An offensive lineman in football, who is trained to get off the snap of the ball on hearing a particular series of signals called, may have a zero reaction time between the actual snap and the initiation of his movement. Knowing the sequence of numbers leading to the snap signal, he is able to anticipate that signal and to expend no time in executing an already slotted-in and correct motor program. On the other hand, a defensive lineman who guesses that a running back is going off-tackle will have a slower reaction time to the back's actually going off-center than he would have had if he had not guessed at all; and if he were both to guess and to *move* off-tackle, the time it would take him to react to the actual play would double or more.

In addition to temporal and spatial anticipation, there are two more sports-important types of anticipation: receptor and effector anticipation. Their operation is usually thought of as "good timing," and is distinctly different from the operation of the sort of "start-gun" anticipation involved in the football snap, the face-off in hockey, or the start in sprinting. In tennis, for instance, *receptor anticipation* is the anticipation by the Control System of the point at which the ball will arrive in front of a player. The Control System does this by a sort of automatic triangulation (similar to a navigator's system of measurement) that gauges (through information given it by the eyes) the location of the ball at multiple points along its path. By an extremely complex integration, or judgment, of those locations, the Control System is able to calculate the ball's trajectory, velocity, and acceleration. Based on these calculations, the Control System determines when the ball is going to arrive at a point where the pre-slotted motor program for hitting it must be initiated. The tennis ball becomes the stimulus, like the signal called in football, and at an exact location and speed, it triggers the player's motor program for hitting it. At this point, receptor anticipation has told the player when to initiate the program. It is able

to do this because the Control System knows through *effector anticipation* that the time required for the player to swing through and meet the ball at a particular point is exactly the same as the time required for the ball to reach that point. When there is a mismatch between the anticipated time of the ball's arrival (supplied by receptor anticipation) and the time required for the swing (supplied by effector anticipation), a player will hit the ball too early or too late, or not at all.

In all sports there are disastrous consequences for faulty anticipation, while correct anticipation can provide a player with one of the best of all athletic advantages.

Arousal. The part of the brain stem known as the Reticular Activating System (RAS) functions as the brain's battery. A particular level of arousal represents the degree to which the RAS has stimulated the brain at any given time. A given state of arousal can be either high or low, and either focused or scattered. A paranoid schizophrenic, for example, may be highly aroused, but the individual's arousal will be widely scattered by delusions, hallucinations, and so on. A severely depressed person, on the other hand, may be very narrowly focused on a single morbid concern and in a very low state of arousal. In athletics, in both practice and competition, there is an ideal level of arousal, appropriate to an individual's level of experience, as well as a correct focus for that arousal. This ideal level of arousal in sports is best understood by means of the Inverted-U Hypothesis (see illustration): as arousal increases, performance improves along a curve up to a maximum beyond which performance decreases even as arousal continues to increase.

In a low state of arousal there is an enormous number of visual, auditory, and positional stimuli in the STSS, on any one of which attention is poorly focused. As arousal increases, the selective attention begins to focus on particular stimuli that it believes important to performance. As arousal heightens to the optimal level, the selective attention narrows its focus to only the most relevant stimuli, and as arousal increases beyond that optimal level, the selective attention's focus becomes so narrow that important stimuli are ignored, adversely affecting performance. At too-high levels of arousal, though attention is very tightly focused, it is also very easily distracted to unimportant and even irrelevant stimuli. The state of arousal in a club tennis player suddenly dropped onto Centre Court at Wimbledon across the net from John McEnroe is likely to be so high that he may completely ignore McEnroe's position on the court (and even his own, for that matter) in an effort to concentrate on the

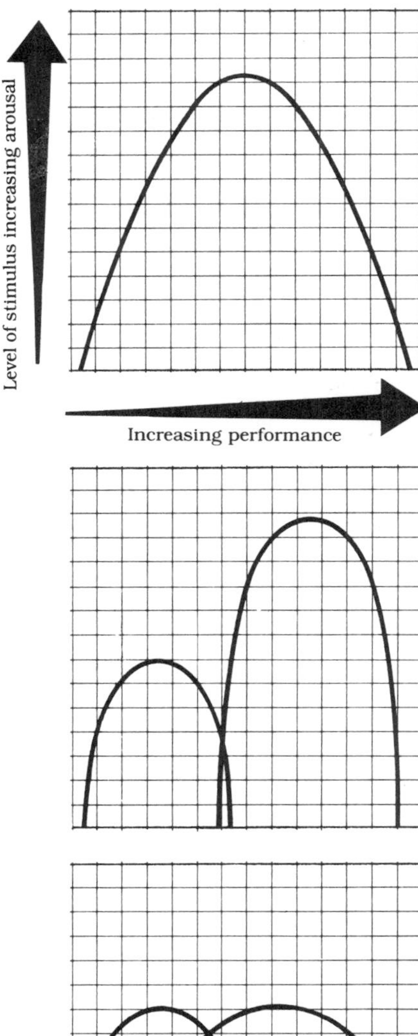

Inverted-U curves illustrate levels of performance for beginner vs. expert (middle) and introvert vs. extrovert (bottom).

ball. Such arousal can border on pure animal fright, and a loud noise from the crowd, the movement of a ball boy, a gust of wind, or any number of other things might distract our club player to a point at which he could barely function.

Different degrees of arousal are required to maximize different skills. Simple repetitive skills requiring little selective attention or anticipation, such as tasks on an assembly line, are improved by arousal, as are some skills that are performed so quickly that there is no time for correction, such as the quick draw of a gunslinger. High levels of arousal not only improve performance but are necessary in sports such as sprinting and weight lifting that involve speed or force but not high levels of precision. High arousal would help a barroom brawler become "fighting mad" and might add to his strength, but it might also make him easy prey to the precision of a cooler, less highly aroused combatant.

For complex skills and tasks that require considerable precision, and for tasks performed slowly enough to allow for ongoing minor corrections, too much arousal is counterproductive. A biathlon athlete, for example, who drops to the ground when going from the skiing phase of his sport to the marksman phase, has to decrease his physical level of arousal consciously in order to shoot accurately. Similarly, a basketball player must avoid a high state of arousal in order to decide between dribbling, passing, and shooting, or to summon up the steadiness and precise gradations of muscular control necessary for a shot from outside the key. The accuracy of a high-pressure shot in basketball is likely to be adversely affected by anything that pushes the player's arousal beyond its optimal level, such as a coach shouting encouragement or a crowd cheering (or jeering). Overarousal of this sort can actually be observed in an electrical muscle test when an athlete stiffens or tightens muscles—thereby giving meaning to the old coaching advice, "Stay loose."

Exactly where the optimal level of performance lies in an individual's state of arousal is the function of two things: practice and the personality trait commonly known as anxiety. The peak of the Inverted U-shaped Curve represents the optimal level of performance for a given skill. A beginner at a sport needs little arousal to reach his performance peak, which is not particularly high; as he progresses within the sport to a high level of skill, he requires a higher level of arousal to reach his peak, which through constant practice is also becoming higher. The level of arousal provided by a match at Wimbledon's Centre Court that might bring John McEnroe to a peak performance might completely cripple a club player by arousing him so far beyond the peak of his Inverted U-shaped Curve that he literally could no longer function. However, if that club player were a true extrovert with a low-anxiety trait in his personality, Centre Court might bring out the greatest game of tennis he had ever played, because his peak performance level, although itself not very high, had coincided with a very high level of arousal. A high-anxiety-trait player, on the other hand, doesn't need Wimbledon to make him fall apart—he can do that during any club match in which the anxiety is too high for him.

Any good coach is aware of a player's level of skill; a great coach can also judge the anxiety trait of the player, as well as his various states of arousal. Before a major competition that coach will know that the highly anxious player may be overly aroused and need calming down rather than further motivation. The coach will know, too, that the extroverted player with a low-anxiety trait may be bored and little aroused by the same competition, and so will require a degree of coaxing that would cripple the first player. A coach has few problems motivating an athlete with a high-anxiety trait, who does not need a lot of arousal to try his best, whereas a low-anxiety-trait, extroverted athlete will need constant motivation to stay sufficiently aroused to play well. Constant high-level motivation is also necessary for *any* athlete who performs at the world-class level, because at that level such enormous effort is required to reach optimal performance, even in practice.

Arousal represents the level of energy supplied by the brain stem for the processes of selective attention and anticipation. In topflight competition these processes are extremely fatiguing, and to be sustained, require very high levels of mental energy in the form of arousal, levels very few athletes can reach. The motivation necessary to achieve this level of arousal is the most important single factor limiting a world-class athlete, and inasmuch as this is true, psychological factors do indeed constitute the ultimate ceiling for the performance of sports. The criteria of physical attributes necessary for world-class performance at sports are very stringent; for most of us, who don't aspire to play sports at the world-class level and don't have to meet those criteria, motivation is even more important than it is for the world-class athlete if we are to play sports at our highest levels of ability.

Sports Psychology

The field of sports psychology deals with (1) identifying individual psychological traits that are specific to a sport, (2) designating the best years for performance at a sport, (3) dealing with psychological problems that may detract from athletic performance, and, most directly, (4) improving sports performance by means of specific learning and training tools that control mental processes.

An athlete's psychological problems can severely limit performance. They are no different from the everyday psychological problems that affect us all, such as depression, anxiety, adjustment difficulties, acute emotional reactions, or lack of motivation. Clinicians deal with these problems on an individual and personal basis, and since their treatment involves the entire breadth of psychiatric diagnosis and treatment, it is inappropriate for them to be discussed in this context. A determination of the best years in which to learn to perform individual sports will be left to the sports chapters of this book. Here we are concerned with the two remaining functions of sports psychology mentioned above.

While sports sciences have long disagreed on the exact physical requirements necessary to athletic performance at particular sports, there *is* general agreement on the psychological traits necessary to such performance. Standard personality profiles have for a long time been used to determine personality traits. Athletic inventory tests have added a sports dimension to the determination of psychological traits by amplifying the personal preferences found in them. Both personality profiles and athletic inventory tests are part of overall psychometric testing, which is also capable of specifying aptitudes, abilities, and skills, and how they differ from sport to sport.

Among the psychological traits important to sports that have been isolated and tested are dominance, aggression, sociability, self-control, single-mindedness, persistence, acceptance of criticism, meanness, and anxiety. Independent of other traits, sociability determines, at a very early age, a person's desire and ability to play team sports. The hockey coach Herb Brooks, in choosing the 1980 American gold medal hockey team, deliberately did not seek the highly skilled extroverts, but rather the "team players" who were characterized by a high degree of sociability and unselfishness. (A solo mountaineer, on the other hand, would likely be found to lack sociability and have little need for approval or an audience.)

On a high competitive level in certain sports the criteria of necessary psychological components are as rigid as the necessary criteria of physical components. In a well-known study of race-car drivers, men and women drivers were virtually indistinguishable on paper—to the extent that a researcher could literally have thrown the completed test sheets into the air and not been able to identify the participants by sex. In the tests, levels of dominance, aggression, single-mindedness, and self-control were found to be almost identical in both men and women. Moreover, it was these *psychological traits* that were crucial to the drivers' success at racing, not the physical ramifications of their being either men or women.

Mental processes must be developed and trained just as physical skills are. Many of the early tools of sports psychology were applied to modulating the state of arousal in athletes by training in motivation and relaxation. Different types of motivation were used to increase arousal, and different relaxation techniques—including yoga, Zen, self-hypnosis, transcendental meditation, instrumented biofeedback, and psychotherapy—were used to diminish it.

The early tools used to raise and lower the curtain of anxiety in athletes were relatively gross ones. Sports psychology now has more precise tools available, and the most important of those is known as *mental imagery*. Fighter pilots are able to practice extremely dangerous skills safely in simulators that recreate as realistically as possible the conditions of air war; mental imagery in sports training is simply mental simulation, the visualization of a skill or a combination of skills, outside the actual context of the sport. Mental imagery has two unique and valuable functions where sports are concerned. First, a motor program may be withdrawn from the Long-Term Memory, slotted into the Short-Term Memory, and test-run there by means of mental imagery, resulting in a substantial positive transfer of skills to the motor program. During this sort of visualization, electrical traces of muscular activity will have the same pattern as in actual execution, though the muscular power settings are so reduced that no real contraction of the muscles takes place. A gymnast who is consistently making a particular mistake in his routine will likely make the same mistake in his mental imagery of it. A figure skater who is unable to execute a triple-axel jump will often find that the visual trace of the jump disappears from her imagination at the same point at which the jump falls apart for her on the ice. Given a proper mental image, the gymnast will be able to visualize his routine toward correctness, and the

figure skater will be able to complete her visual trace of the triple axel and actualize it on the ice.

The second important function of mental imgery is that it allows an athlete to run through a variety of circumstances that might occur during his performance for which he would otherwise be unprepared, to overcome anxiety in advance by mentally controlling the emotions aroused by competition, and to deal with whatever real risks might be involved in the competition. A downhill skier, for example, can lie indoors on a couch and use mental imagery to feel and control the anxiety that might paralyze him in the hours and minutes before his race; he can deal in advance with the known risks the race will present, such as icy corners and compressions; and he can prepare himself for unforeseeable hazards or circumstances, such as a spectator on the course, fog, or a windblown patch of snow.

Any sort of practice at a sport, whether it is done through visualization or on the field, is virtually useless unless it is systematically measured for correctness and progress. The greatest contribution of sports science to sports psychology has been the ongoing development of psychological and biomechanical monitoring systems by which technical correctness and physical progress can be measured, thus providing sports psychology with its first objective feedback. The relatively recent availability of these monitoring systems to ordinary weekend athletes has given them an exciting new opportunity for major improvement in their athletic performance.

Though we have acknowledged in this chapter that the mind in its various functions can and does play a crucial role in the performance of sports, it is also true that any sport makes specific and unyielding demands on genetic abilities and physical components in particular combinations. Given the motivational demands for continued high levels of sports arousal, the tremendous mental energy required to maintain selective attention, and the physical wear and fatigue involved in increasing levels of training and competition, any athlete would clearly do well to choose a sport with which his or her psychological traits, underlying abilities, and physical components are well matched.

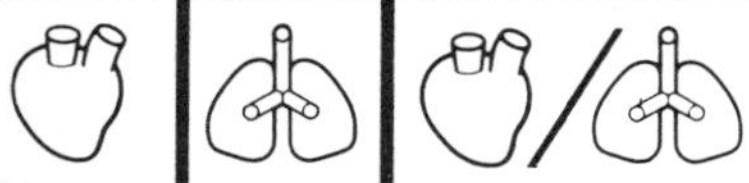

THE HEART-LUNG PACKAGE

THE HEART

Since the time of the ancient Greeks, it has been known that exercise can enlarge the human heart, and that fact has historically promoted misconceptions about the relationship between exercise and health. A failing heart is often enlarged, and until relatively recently, medical science had no way of distinguishing between the apparently enlarged dynamic heart of the athlete and the enlarged sick heart.

The father of cardiology, Giovanni Lancisi, who died in 1720, was the first scientist to observe the condition of the sport-enlarged heart, and Jean Corvisart (1755–1821), a French physician, was the first to consider it diseased. In 1879 Beneke, a German cardiologist, claimed that the athlete's enlarged heart would inevitably lead to a premature death. And in 1927 when a pair of Austrian doctors named Deutsch and Kauf determined in a study of oarsmen and swimmers that the transverse diameters of the hearts of championship swimmers were on average 30 to 40 percent larger than normal hearts, their subsequent reaction to discovering progressive heart enlargement in athletes was to pull them out of training until the enlargement stopped.

We know today that the enlarged sick heart, swollen with backed-up fluid from an inability to pump effectively, is radically different from the athlete's large heart, which can be, and often is, healthier than the normal heart. We also know today what

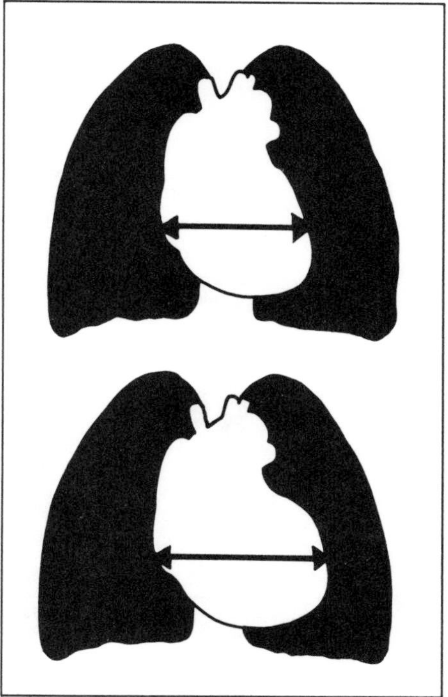

Normal heart (above) and enlarged heart (below).

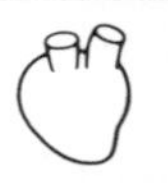

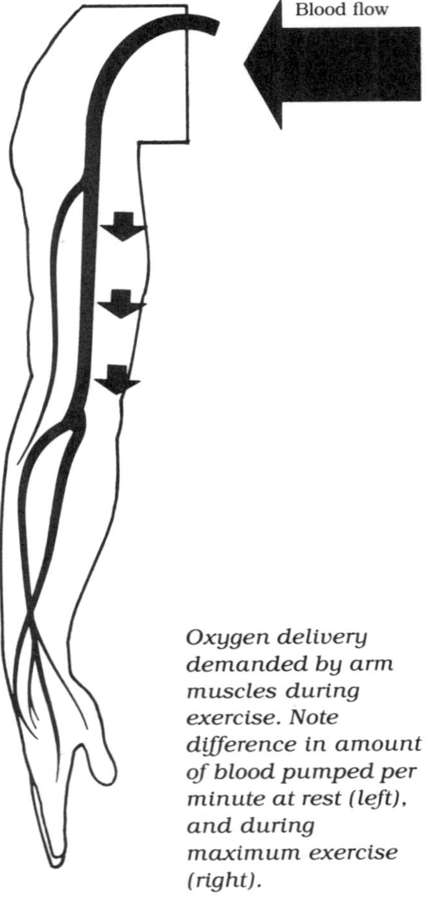

Oxygen delivery demanded by arm muscles during exercise. Note difference in amount of blood pumped per minute at rest (left), and during maximum exercise (right).

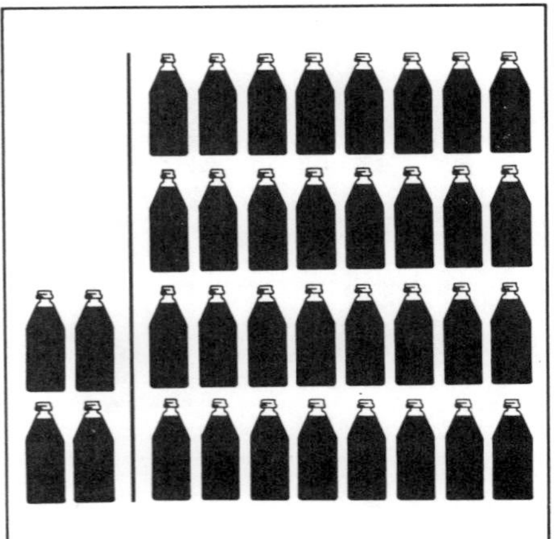

causes the sports-enlarged heart: its size, like that of any other muscle, is partially an adaptation to the amount and type of work it does—when the heart is put to increased work loads often enough in sports or in training, it appears upon examination and in laboratory tests to respond by increasing in size.

Pumping

Athletic training and sports participation impose increased work loads on the heart because in order for exercised muscles to function over a period of time they must have a continuous and increasing supply of oxygen; the job of the heart is to effect that supply by pumping the blood that carries the oxygen to the muscle cells. It is a job the heart takes seriously (in a body exercising heavily, 60-plus percent of the heart's output of blood goes to the muscles, as opposed to the 4 percent sent to the muscles in a body at rest), and at which it works hard (at rest, the normal heart has an output of about four liters of blood per minute; the working heart of a marathoner or cross-country ski racer can have a pumping output of more than *thirty* liters per minute).

The work that the heart does in sports training and performance can be broken into two basic types: *volume work* and *pressure work*.

The heart's volume work, which is of particular importance in all aerobic sports, is to pump out blood in enough volume to the exercising muscles to meet their demands for oxygen. During sports activity the heart can respond to the muscles' increasing need of oxygen in two ways, both of which increase its volume output: by pumping at a faster rate, on orders from electrical impulses which are regulated by the demands of the muscles and the nervous system; or, more effectively, by actually ejecting more blood per heartbeat by increasing its pre-load and/or decreasing its after-load.

Pre-loading works like this: as the heart pumps out blood, the muscles in the exercising limbs pump it back to the heart in sufficient volume to force the heart to stretch to accommodate the blood, with no increase in contractility, thereby enabling more volume output without an increase in heart rate. This capacity of the heart to pre-load before contraction is characteristic of endurance athletes and is a wonderful compensatory and self-saving device in that it imposes a lesser work load on the heart than would an increase in the number of heartbeats to a level sufficient to pump the same amount of blood.

The second way in which the heart ejects more blood per heartbeat is to empty itself more fully. When the main valve of the heart, the aortic valve, is pushed open by the contracting heart muscle in the act of expelling blood, it encounters a certain pressure in the aorta, a certain amount of resistance to its pumping effort. (The condition of consistently high, nonathletic-related resistance to that effort is known as high blood pressure.) If that resistance, or *after-load*, is low, as it will be in a well-trained athlete, the heart is able to empty itself more completely by expelling more blood.

The volume of blood the heart is capable of processing by all of its methods is critical to the performance of endurance sports—so critical that "blood doping" is occasionally used in those sports as a method of increasing overall volume, and therefore pre-load, by transfusing more blood into the system; and so critical that any volume drop of the blood, such as that caused by dehydration, can ruin an athlete's chances of performing well. And the *manner* in which the heart processes its blood volume is as good a gauge as any of overall cardiac fitness. At any given work load and at any given heart rate, an athletically trained heart will have a higher pre-load (it will accommodate more blood before contraction), and a lower after-load (it will empty more completely), and will thereby expel more blood during contraction, than an untrained heart. This trained heart will have a larger pumping chamber than the untrained heart and therefore it will be, as Giovanni Lancisi noted, larger. But, contrary to centuries of speculation, it will probably also be healthier.

That is not necessarily true of an athlete's heart made larger by the pressure function of the heart's work. During certain kinds of exercise (for example, weight lifting, wrestling, and equestrian sports), prolonged strong contractions of muscles compress the arteries running through them and bringing them blood. After a while this compression will diminish the blood supply to the muscles, and at very strong contractions will completely shut it off. The pressure work of the heart is to continue to force the blood into these contracting muscles.

Different muscle groups begin to compress their blood supply at different levels of contraction—the calf, for instance, at 30 percent of maximum contraction; the forearm at 20 percent. As these contraction levels increase, the blood flow to the muscle is more and more limited, forcing the heart to contract more forcefully to attempt to push the blood through the compressed arteries. At around 70 percent of the maximum contraction of any muscle, the heart can no longer drive the blood, and blood

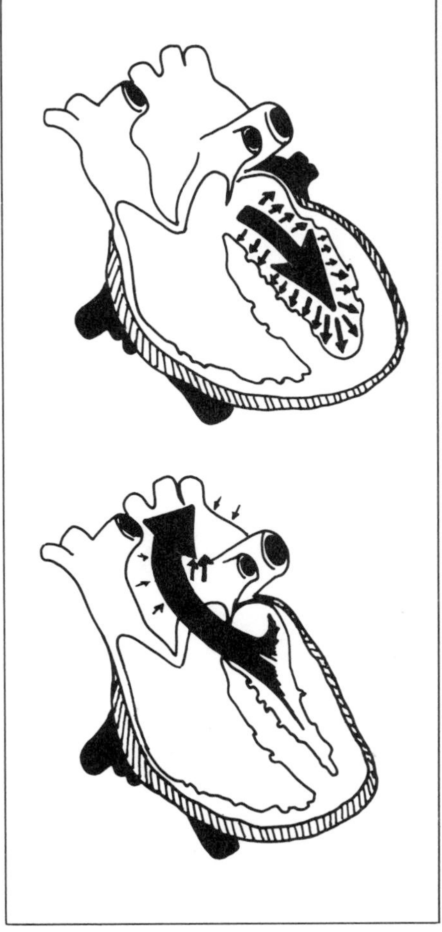

Preload (above): Degree of filling prior to contraction.
Afterload (below): Degree of resistance to blood outflow from heart during contraction.

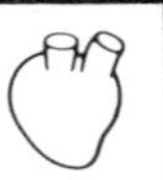

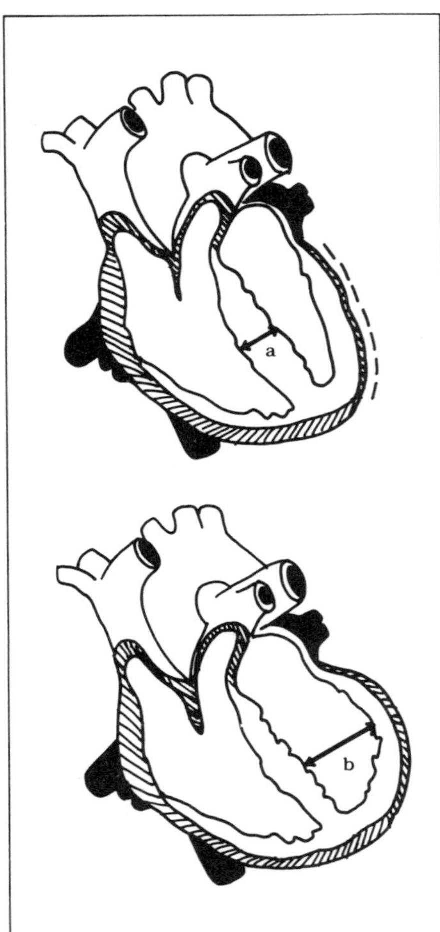

Heart before contraction. Normal-size heart with large septum (a) in response to pressure work (above), and with large ventricle (b) in response to volume work (below).

flow will stop completely until the contraction is relaxed. Long-term training and/or competition in the sports that demand this pressure work of the heart will make the heart larger by increasing the thickness of the septal wall if not the entire left ventricle, building that part of the heart muscle by constantly stressing it. (It will also increase the contractility of the left ventricle and improve its ability to empty itself without the help of a big pre-load.) But it is a more taxing kind of labor for the heart than the endurance athlete's volume work, and may not be as good for it.

Failure

During athletic performance or training the heart can fail in its necessary work in two ways, the second more serious than the first.

Just as skeletal muscle cells have to be constantly supplied with oxygen, so does the heart, with the added condition that the heart cannot allow any lapse at all in oxygen delivery and consumption. When less oxygen is delivered to the heart than it needs, the condition known as *ischemia* (a relative lack of oxygen) occurs. If that condition persists for any length of time, damage to the heart cells can occur, then instability of the heart's electrical system, and finally death of individual heart cells—which can never be replaced.

As the heart starts to do rate, volume, or pressure work during sports or training, it begins to require more oxygen than it does when at rest. That requirement is met both by the fully oxygenated blood inside the heart and, more critically, by the fully oxygenated blood coursing over the surface of the heart and into it through the coronary arteries. When blood cannot reach the heart normally in either of these two ways, ischemia results. Though there are numerous heart disorders, both acquired and congenital, that can produce ischemia, two are significant for athletes.

When the onset of exercise is so sudden (*sudden spontaneous exertion*) that the oxygen demands of the heart muscle can't be met immediately either by direct supply from within the heart or by the blood flowing through the coronary vessels, ischemia can result momentarily, even in the youngest and best-conditioned athletes. It can also occur when the heart's delivery system is inadequate. As exercise load increases, oxygen demand by the heart muscle increases, too; this demand escalates even further if the work of the heart is being performed more by

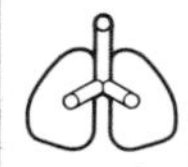

rate than by volume, and it is more likely to become excessive if the work is pressure work. If the caliber or diameter of the coronary arteries is smaller than normal (either because the individual was born with abnormally small blood vessels or because of disease-related blockage within otherwise normal vessels), a level of oxygen demand by the heart can be reached that simply can't be met.

Potentially more dangerous than the cell damage and even cell death caused by ischemia is the *electrical instability* that can be caused in and around the heart muscle when it is oxygen deprived. Normally the heart is made to contract by electrical impulses that course regularly through its conducting system. Under conditions of stress or exercise either a congenitally abnormal conducting system or one affected by ischemia can cause these electrical impulses to become irregular or erratic. Though electrical irregularity in the heart during exercise is harmless more often than not, it can occasionally be fatal, and therefore constitutes a more serious potential exercise-related failure than simple ischemia. It should be mentioned that electrical irregularity can also be caused by something as simple as a viral infection. Similarly, extreme overheating and/or dehydration, both potential consequences in the body of exercise, can also set up rhythm disturbances in the heart's electrical system, sometimes fatal ones.

THE LUNGS

The respiratory system is composed of two parts: the gas-exchanging organs known as the lungs, and the respiratory muscles in the chest wall that act as a pump to ventilate the lungs. In sports the two key functions of this system are the loading of oxygen onto red blood cells and, more important, the dumping of excess carbon dioxide (CO_2) that begins to accumulate in the blood at the onset of breathlessness during exercise.

When we inhale, air is transported through a series of increasingly small passages to millions of air sacs in the lungs, from which oxygen is loaded onto the red blood cells as capillary blood courses through the membrane wall of each air sac. The more red blood cells that go by, the more oxygen that can be transported into the system and thereby be delivered to the

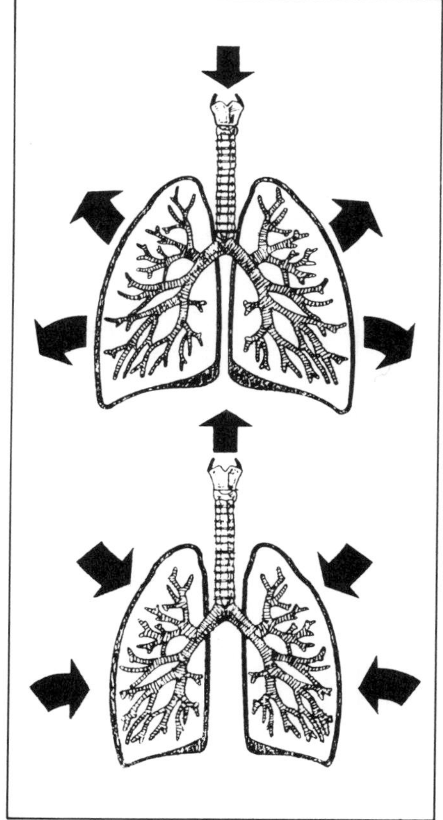

Loading oxygen onto red blood cells (above) and dumping excess carbon dioxide (below).

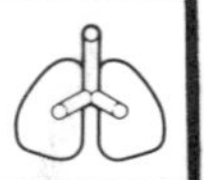

muscles. When exercising muscles begin to demand more oxygen, the heart and lungs act in concert to meet that demand: the heart begins to pump more blood through the lungs, and the lungs begin to pump more air, bringing more oxygen into the air sacs for deposit into the blood.

The lungs respond in two ways to the muscles' demand for more oxygen: by pumping faster (rate) and by sucking in more air (volume). As with the heart, volume increase is more efficient than rate increase—a volume increase moves new air in and out of the lungs, while a rate increase moves some stale air back and forth through the large airways without totally expelling it. At high levels of exercise a threshold is reached at which the removal of excess carbon dioxide that has accumulated in the blood as a result of heavy exercise becomes a more critical function of the lungs than the delivery of oxygen, and the lungs respond by moving a greater amount of air, both by volume and by rate, than would be required simply to meet the oxygen demand. The point at which the lungs begin to perform this second duty, the dumping of excess CO_2, is referred to by the British, appropriately enough, as the "puff point," and is known scientifically as the anaerobic threshold (AT).

The more air an endurance athlete can move in and out of the lungs quickly, to carry off excess CO_2 and to supply the blood with oxygen, the better that athlete will perform. The ability to move air quickly is limited by two factors: the size, or maximum volume capacity, of the lungs; and the amount of endurance work capable of being performed by the respiratory muscles.

Human beings have from birth a certain genetic lung capacity that, like the heart's, can be substantially enlarged only during the years of adolescence. After adolescence, though the respiratory muscles can be strengthened through training, the capacity of the lungs remains fixed. Though it is not the only contributing factor, this volume capacity of the lungs is crucial to the upper limits of aerobic power in endurance sports and of recovery rate in stop-and-go sports. Where an average sedentary 150-pound man might be expected to have a lung capacity of 3.5 liters, a top marathon runner, even at 140 pounds, will likely have a capacity of about 5 liters. For a 180-pound, fifteen-year-old East German crew athlete, 6-liter lungs are essential; and Juha Mieto, the giant Finnish cross-country skiing racer, has a lung capacity of more than 7 liters—*twice* that of the average sedentary 150-pound man.

But lung capacity alone doesn't tell the whole story. The speed with which air can be expelled by the lungs is also critically im-

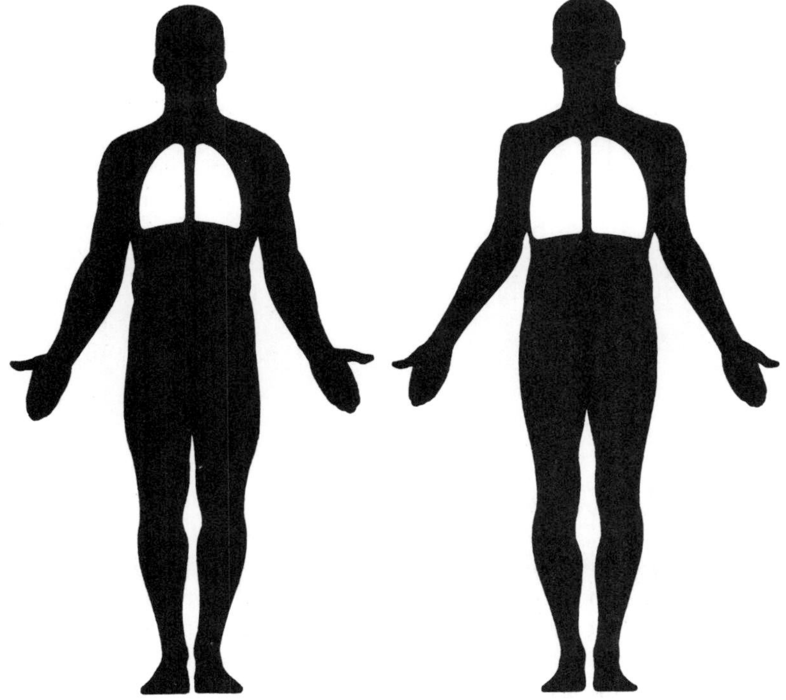

The lung size of an average 150-pound man (left) might be 3.5 liters; of a 140-pound marathoner (right), 5 liters.

portant, in that it determines the respiratory rate and therefore the amount of air the lungs can process. It is almost axiomatic that a top endurance athlete must be able to expel at least 80 percent of the maximum functional lung capacity in one second. The gauge, known as *maximum minute-ventilation*, reflects both the fixed functional capacity of the lungs and the speed of exhalation; this speed is controlled by the respiratory muscles and is influenced by any resistance in the airways such as might be caused by asthma, smoking, or bronchitis. Any normal individual without such resistance and with a relatively high lung capacity could be expected to move more than 100 liters of air in a minute. The sedentary person, in fact, may differ little from the trained endurance athlete in the amount of air the lungs can move over the course of one minute, but the ability to sustain a high minute-ventilation for more than five minutes at a time is characteristic only of top endurance athletes. This trained ability to unload excess CO_2 from the blood at high minute-volumes over a prolonged period is so important that it can be said to be the single most vital determinant for winning in endurance sports among athletes with similar constitutions.

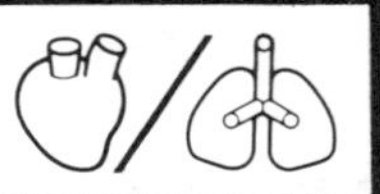

One of the three major chairs of exercise physiology at the Karolinska Institute is held now by the founder of modern exercise physiology, Per-Olof Astrand, who has been not only an outspoken spokesman for fitness but also one of the most prolific researchers of his time. His early work uncovered the secrets of oxygen consumption, making him the true father of the aerobic era.

To give you some idea of the upper limits of minute-volume, Alberto Salazar in his 1981 world-record 2:08:13 marathon probably maintained a minute-ventilation of 140 liters a minute; Bill Koch, the 1982 World Cup cross-country ski-racing champion, regularly maintains minute-ventilations of up to 160 liters a minute over the course of a 1-hour 15-kilometer race; and Rheinhold Messner, the great Austrian mountaineer, climbing in thin air to the top of Mount Everest, alone and without supplemental oxygen, was moving in excess of 200 *liters* of air per minute.

HEART-LUNG POWER

As we have seen, the heart and lungs work together in the performance of sports. They are partners in a transport system whose two critical functions in athletics are oxygen delivery (the measure of which is known as maximum oxygen consumption), and the dumping on of CO_2 (the onset of which is known as the anaerobic threshold).

Since the 1920s, scientists and coaches have sought to place a single value on the transport function of the heart and lungs in exercise—a value so accurate that it could actually be used to rate athletes and even to determine athletic winners in advance. Since the 1930s, maximum oxygen consumption has come the closest to providing that value of aerobic power. Now, in the 1980s, this obscure-sounding standard has so pervaded the world of endurance sports and fitness that it has come to occupy a place in the everyday vocabulary of athletes and coaches all over the world. In Sweden, in fact, it is known simply and accurately as the *Kundy*, or condition number, and is used to relate in a single number an individual's overall fitness.

The term *maximum oxygen consumption* (VO_2 Max) refers both to the maximum oxygen-transport capacity of the heart and lungs and, equally important, to the ability of the skeletal muscles to offload and combust the fuel the oxygen delivered to them. While a large heart and lungs would seem to guarantee a high VO_2 Max, they do so only in sports that use all the major muscle groups, such as crew and cross-country skiing, and then only if those muscle groups are able to offload and con-

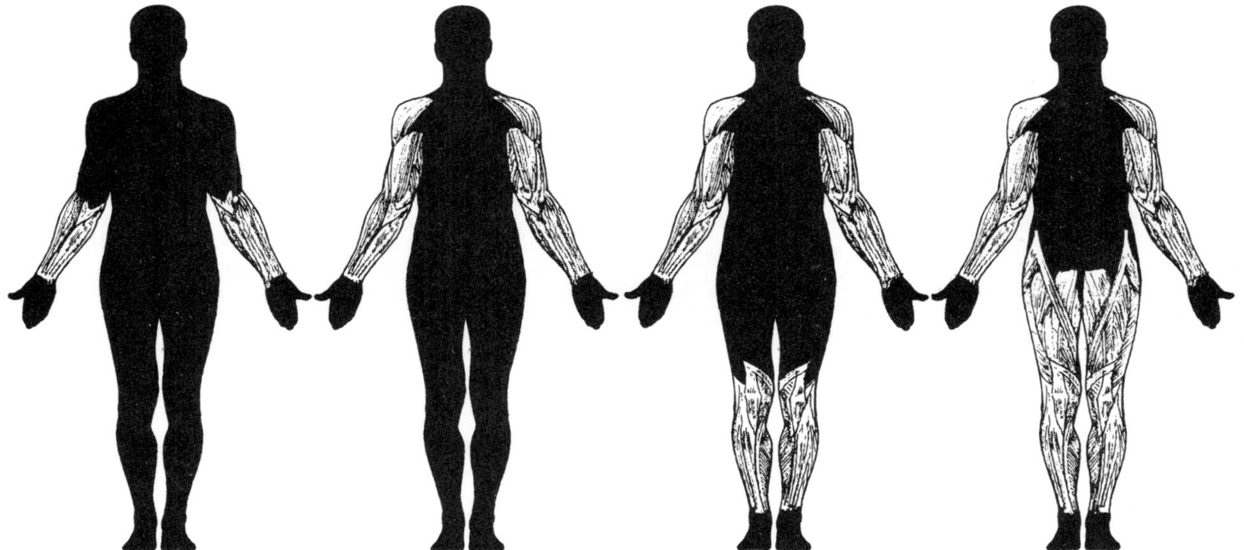

Oxygen demand increases as use of muscle mass increases.

sume oxygen at the highest levels. In sports there are few absolute delimiters, but VO_2 Max is one. It is the body's horsepower rating, defining the upper speed limits of a competitor in endurance sports; and without the capacity to consume oxygen at very high levels no endurance athlete will perform at the world-class level.

Not only is VO_2 Max an absolute delimiter in endurance sports; there is, as well, a structural upper limit to it that is 100 percent genetic: an untrained adolescent or adult beginning aerobic training may expect an improvement of up to 30 percent over his or her untrained VO_2 Max, but no more.

There are very few sports that consistently tax an athlete's VO_2 Max to its limits, and therefore the functional percentage of oxygen consumption usable over a long period of time is at least as important a criterion for continued high levels of performance as is VO_2 Max in all athletic events lasting up to an hour. Furthermore, even the most extraordinary athlete cannot operate at VO_2 Max for more than seven minutes at a stretch, because the excess CO_2 load built up in the blood by severe muscular activity overwhelms the ability of the transport system to dump it and lactic acid builds up in the exercising muscles, making them functionally useless by shutting them down.

In any aerobic sport, as an individual increases the pace over a period of several minutes, a level of intensity of muscular ac-

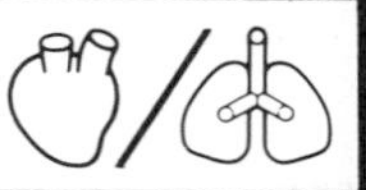

tivity is reached at which excess CO_2 is dumped by the muscles into the blood in exponentially increasing quantities. This level, as we have said, is known as the anaerobic threshold (AT), or "puff point."

In an extraordinarily well trained athlete the lungs are able to increase their minute-ventilation and sustain exercise at the anaerobic threshold by means of vigorous respiratory muscle contractions for up to thirty-five minutes or longer (though, in fact, few athletes are well enough trained to sustain high minute-ventilations at the AT for more than a very few minutes at a time). An untrained athlete, or one who trains at a leisurely pace, can have an AT that occurs at as little as 30 percent of maximum oxygen consumption. Vigorous physical training at the AT can, over the course of years, push the threshold to 90 percent of the athlete's maximum oxygen consumption, but this is very rarely the case. Though there is a genetic ceiling on an athlete's VO_2 Max, few athletes are well enough motivated or have good enough training programs to push their anaerobic thresholds close to that ceiling; and whereas training can bring

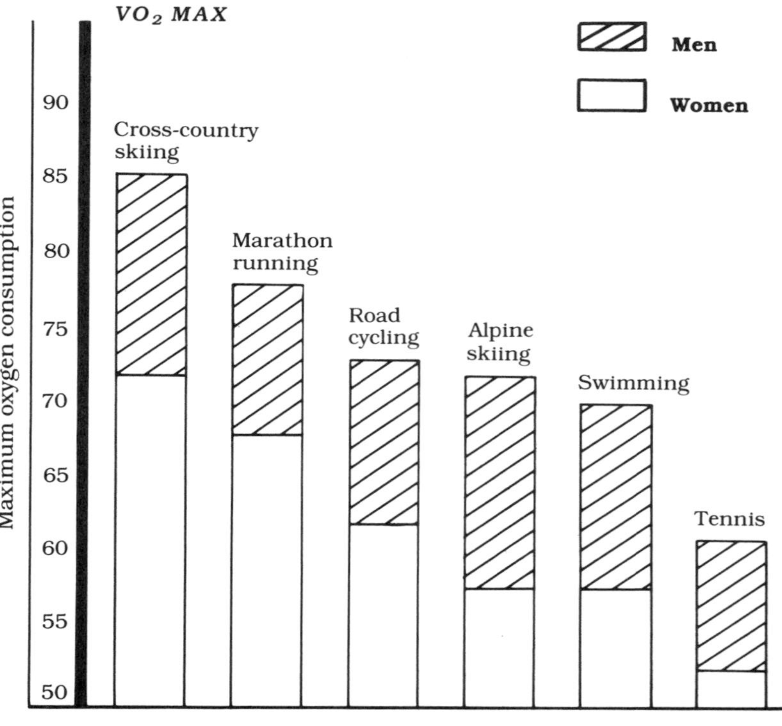

about only a 30 percent increase in VO_2 Max, it can effect as much as a 50 percent increase in the AT, making improvement of the AT the great hope of the weekend aerobic athlete.

While the exercise scientist in the laboratory may postulate sports requiring constant levels of exertion, few endurance sports and no stop-go sports actually do demand such levels. In most athletics, therefore, the most important function of the oxy-transport system is not fixed-rate oxygen delivery but the *speed of oxygen delivery*, along with the system's ability to recover from an excess CO_2 load. Various cross-country ski racers, for example, with similar maximum oxygen consumption levels and anaerobic thresholds, will perform differently in a given race depending on the speed with which their transport systems can meet the increased oxygen demand of climbing a steep hill and the speed at which excess CO_2 can be dumped, or blown off, during recovery downhill. In stop-go sports, such as ice hockey and soccer, the speed of oxygen delivery and the rate of dumping CO_2 in recovery outweigh the importance of either maximum oxygen consumption or the anaerobic threshold.

As a final point, the heart and lungs can be taxed and therefore trained to a high level of oxygen demand and CO_2 dumping either by continuous vigorous effort, such as that found in a 10,000-meter road race or a 1-mile open-ocean swim, or by back-to-back, stop-and-go demands such as those made by soccer.

BODY COMPOSITION

For centuries coaches have attempted to identify athletic ability in different sports by the physical appearance of the athlete, and all of us tend to make visual connections between the way certain people look and certain sports—between a lean, seven-foot man, for example, and basketball. Over the last few decades that tendency to make qualitative visual assessments of athletic ability or potential has been formalized into a set of rigid, quantitative measurements known as anthropometrics. Purely visual assessments of bodies *can* identify certain athletic abilities, even if imperfectly, in much the same way we can identify visually the varying performance potentials between, say, a Ferrari and a Mack truck. The Ferrari *looks* fast, and likely is; the truck is *probably* as powerful as it looks, but not necessarily. No amount of looking at an athlete, not even the most sophisticated visual assessment, can reveal the individual's heart-lung engine or the Control System that drives the machine. Nor can such an assessment tell you, except in the most general way, how the machine is constructed.

The body composition of fat and muscle and the proportions of the skeleton are determined in an individual from before birth and they circumscribe that person's athletic potential for a lifetime. In making an individual evaluation, the anthropometrist measures height; weight; length, width, and circumference of all body segments; and size of fat stores. The goal in

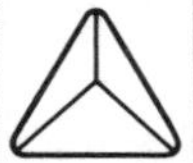

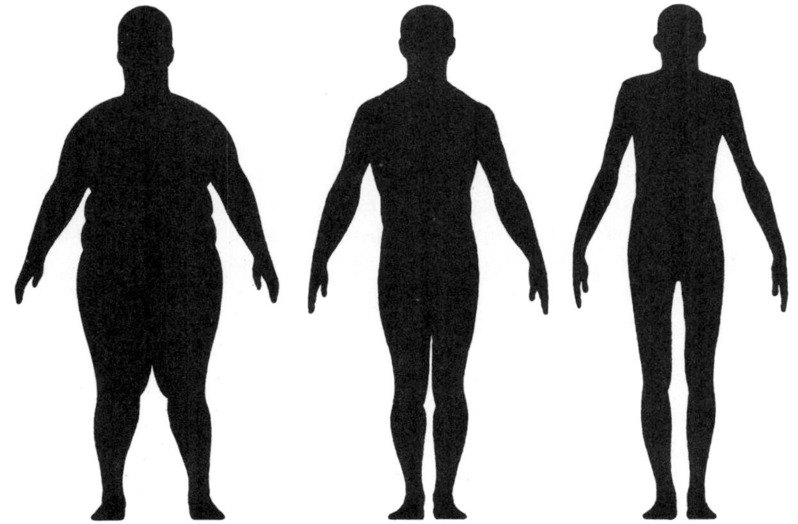

From left to right: endomorphic, mesomorphic, and ectomorphic somatotypes.

taking these measurements is to reduce them to a simple but accurate index that can convey precisely the athletic potential of a given physique. This specific index, comprising an individual's degree of fatness and muscularity and proportions, is known as the person's *somatotype*. There are three somatotypes: ectomorph, endomorph, and mesomorph—which follow our general and traditional sense of how physiques divide into lean people, fat people, and muscular people. Convenient as those categories are, however, the modern anthropometrist knows that no individual fits precisely into any one of them, and that the proper function of somatotyping is not to caricature but to characterize individuals by the degree to which they are, on a scale, measurably endomorphic, ectomorphic, or mesomorphic.

Ectomorphy describes the linearity of the skeleton, and someone at the far end of this scale will appear tall and slender. *Endomorphy* is the scale that describes the degree of an individual's fatness or leanness, and an endomorph is an individual at the fat end of that scale. *Mesomorphy* describes the degree of muscularity in an individual relative to his height, and most athletes are mesomorphs of one kind or another.

In somatotyping a person for the purposes of athletics, two techniques are employed by the anthropometrist: the individual is given a numerical score on a scale of 1 to 6 for the degree to which he or she possesses each of the three somatotypic charac-

Lindsay Carter, an immensely resourceful professor at San Diego State University, has led the cooperative groups researching the body composition of top athletes. His work at the Montreal Olympics is the most complete ever on all aspects of an athlete's frame, dimensions, and body parts.

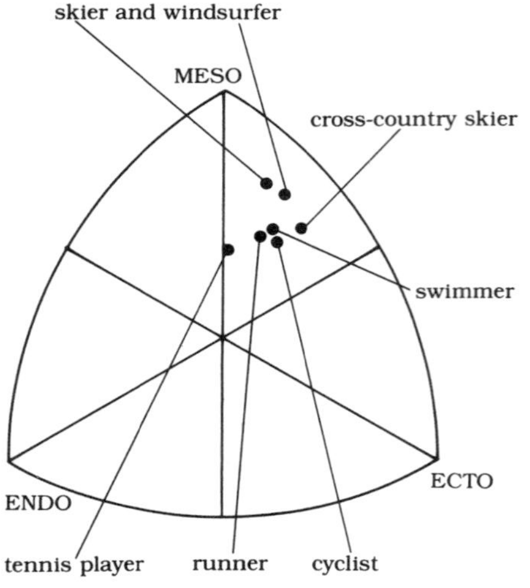

teristics, and these scores are then plotted on a somato chart to determine how the individual's numerical sequence fits into the requirements for a particular sport. Some sports, such as gymnastics, canoeing, and boxing, require a very specific type of physique, while other sports—jogging and cycling, for example—permit a wider range of somatotypes and thus can accommodate a wider scattering of numerical sequences. A somato chart helps a sports scientist visualize how a person's physique relates to the specific requirements of individual sports. Moreover, the athlete can see for himself on a somato chart how his physique matches those of top athletes in his sport by comparing it to the "phantom frames" that are prototypical of that sport.

Though somatotyping serves a useful purpose for sports scientists by grossly describing the structural requirements of various sports, it remains a purely descriptive device and adds little to the understanding of how the body performs athletically. Until recently the task of sports science was mostly descriptive: the compilation and evaluation of data within narrow academic fields and the use of those data to describe physical characteristics of the body. The goal of modern sports scientists is to help athletes to perform better; in order to do this, they have to do more than simply describe the sizes of hearts and lungs and frames in athletes—they must be able to understand how those components work and how their various performances might be improved. The science of kinanthropometry has made it possible to achieve this knowledge through investigation of how the muscles work in relation to particular frames. Having described the Control System of the athletic body, and its heart-lung power plant, we will deal here with the sports aspects of skeletons, muscles, and fat stores with which the kinanthropometrist is concerned.

THE SKELETON

The skeleton is the bony part of the body's frame that supports the fat, muscles, and internal organs. There are three aspects of the skeleton that are important to sports: its overall size, its proportions, and the sizes of its individual parts.

Skeletal size is the grossest, or most general, sports delimiter,

although it can be specifically important. A basketball center, for example, simply *has* to be over a certain height to be effective in his position. At any given height, a skeleton can be either small, medium, or large. At six feet two inches in height, a skeleton must be large and dense in order to support a defensive lineman's 100-plus pounds of muscle, or small and light to allow the marathoner to weigh the two pounds per inch of body height necessary for top performance at the sport.

Once an athlete's skeletal size has been determined to be appropriate for a certain sport, the next evaluation must be of proportion. Different sports have different ideal proportions among skeletal parts. Good runners, for instance, have legs that are long in proportion to their upper bodies. Top Alpine skiers, on the other hand, have trunks that are long in relation to their lower bodies. While proportions like these have been observed and described in sports for years, it is only recently that kinanthropometrists have examined the mechanical advantages they provide to the athletes who possess them.

Finally, the skeleton is important to sports performance in the sizes of certain of its individual parts. A narrow pelvis is a real necessity for a sprinter, because it allows a more direct line for the legs to follow than a wide pelvis would; long arms are necessary to boxers; big hands and feet are an obvious help to swimmers, as are long thighs to runners and big chests to oarsmen and cross-country skiers.

MUSCLE

Muscles contract: their single function is to do so, and it is through their contractions that all human movement, athletic and otherwise, is made possible. The skeletal parts of the body are connected by the muscles, and for movement of these parts to occur, the muscles attached to them must shorten by contracting. Just as there are different kinds of hearts and lungs, psychological traits, and motor abilities, so there are sports-specific aspects of muscular activity that are unique from athlete to athlete. These aspects can best be understood within the context of the entire muscular-effector system of the motor cortex, motor neurons, and muscle fiber.

The Muscular Command Center

Muscles are the effectors of the Control System, the means by which it executes a given motor program. The Control System initiates and executes all physical movement from the area of the brain known as the *motor cortex*, and every part of the body (hand, foot, leg, arm, and so on) is controlled from a specific location within the motor cortex. Each location commands a bank of motor units, which are composed of muscle fibers and a nerve known as a *motor neuron* that, when activated by an electrical impulse from the motor cortex, causes the fibers to contract. These motor units exit from the spinal cord near the parts of the body they are responsible for controlling. When movement and, therefore, muscular contraction is required from one of those body parts, the motor cortex sends a command for the movement in the form of an electrical current, and the appropriate bank of motor units responds with varying gradations and refinements of muscular force.

The Regulation of Muscular Force

A muscle contracts because it is stimulated to do so by an electrical current originating in the motor cortex. This current arrives at particular muscle fibers via a motor neuron attached to those fibers. A single motor neuron attached to a variable number of muscle fibers comprises what is known as a *motor unit*, and any given muscle is made up of a number of these motor units. The refinement of the muscular contraction is dictated by the number of muscle fibers controlled by a particular motor neuron. The very fine, subtle movements of the eye are possible because each motor neuron controlling the muscles of the eye is responsible for only three to six muscle fibers; each motor neuron regulating the muscles of the leg, on the other hand, controls up to two hundred fibers, making the movements of the leg much less refined.

Just as there are gradations in the refinement of different muscular contractions, so are there gradations in the speed and force of those contractions. Increments in the speed and force of muscular contraction are controlled by a surprisingly simple and economic principle known as the *size principle*, which states that motor units are recruited for muscular contraction by the sizes of the motor neurons they contain. Motor neurons conduct electrical current; as is the case with wire, the larger the diameter of the nerve, the more current it can conduct. In

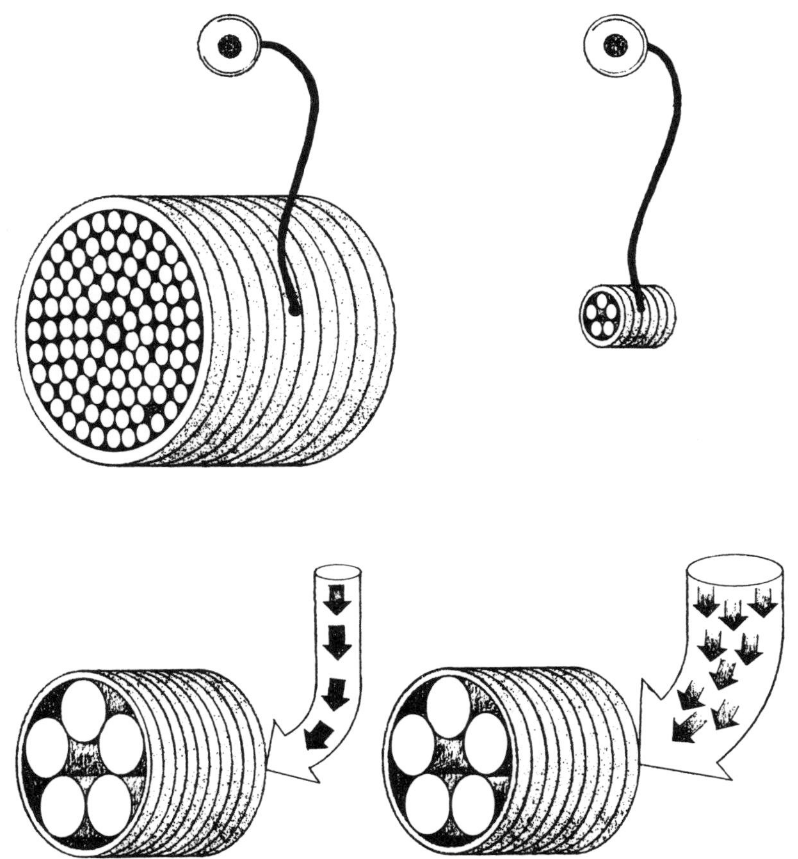

Gross motor control in the leg (1 nerve for 200 muscle fibers) vs. fine motor control in the eye (1 nerve for 5 muscle fibers).

Size Principle: small nerve size—early recruitment; larger nerve size—increasing speed and power.

any physical movement motor neurons are recruited in a fixed sequence from the smallest to the largest to produce increasingly faster or more powerful contractions of the muscles involved in the movement. Because more current is required to produce a faster or stronger contraction than a slower, weaker one, only smaller-diameter motor neurons are recruited for slow, weak movements. In increasingly faster or stronger movements, motor neurons of larger and larger diameter are employed. Slow, weak movements can begin when the rate of electrical current through the smallest motor neuron reaches five impulses per second. During the fastest, most powerful muscular contractions—contractions that recruit all the available motor neurons—this rate in the largest of those nerves can reach a level as high as seventy impulses per second.

A brilliant professor at Harvard Medical School, Ellie Henneman is responsible for the size theory of neurologic recruitment, which first showed the differences between those of us born with endurance or sprint. His continued interest in sports medicine has allowed us to proceed from the most basic scientific theory to practical coaching implications.

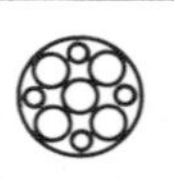

Bengt Saltin, a professor at Copenhagen's August Kroogh Institute, holds one of the three major chairs in exercise physiology. His work on single muscle fibers gave us much of our current understanding of the differences between sprint and endurance muscle fiber type.

Muscle Fibers and Whole Muscle

To meet the demands of movements ranging from weak to strong, slow to fast, and sporadic to continuous, the body provides two types of muscle fiber: slow-twitch, or endurance, fiber; and fast-twitch, or sprint, fiber. Each motor neuron controls a pool of muscle fiber of one of these two types. The size of a given motor neuron determines the type of muscle fiber attached to it: endurance fiber is attached to and controlled by small motor neurons, and sprint fiber by large motor neurons. The proportional composition of sprint and endurance muscle in an individual is a direct and genetic function of the relative percentage of large and small motor neurons possessed by that individual. A sprinter is born and not made, possessing from birth a large percentage of fast motor units (large motor neurons and sprint muscle fiber). Conversely, a successful marathon runner will have, from birth, a high percentage of the endurance fiber and small motor neurons that comprise slow motor units.

The composition of any human muscle is mixed, varying from an even percentage of sprint and endurance fiber to nearly 100 percent of one or the other. The muscles within a given body will sometimes have different mixes of the two fiber types. A cross-country skier, for example, may have nearly 100 percent sprint fiber in the deltoid muscles of the shoulders, which do the fast work of poling, and nearly 100 percent endurance fiber in the quadriceps muscles of the legs, which must perform the slower, continuous work of kicking and gliding.

Both sprint and endurance muscle fiber have certain particular characteristics that define them.

Sprint muscle fiber is characterized particularly by its capacity to reach a peak force of contraction three times faster and ten times more powerful than endurance fiber, and by its corresponding ability to relax more quickly from contraction. Sprint muscle fiber has a larger diameter than endurance fiber and therefore is able to exert a greater absolute muscular tension,

Muscle fiber type:
• Endurance
○ Sprint

100% Endurance

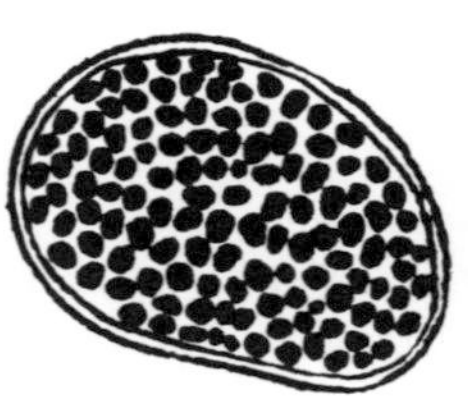

70/30

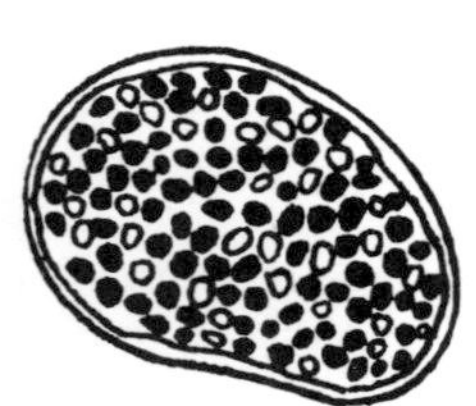

50/50

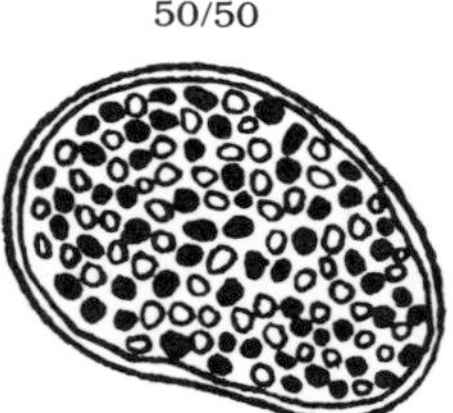

30/70

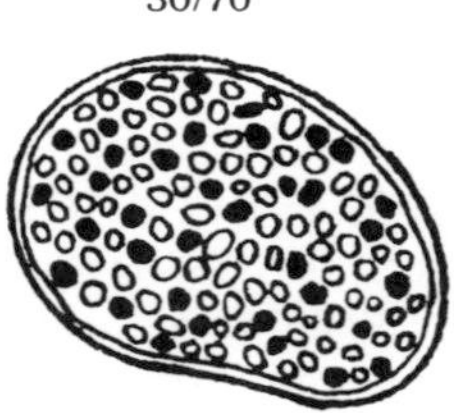

100% Sprint

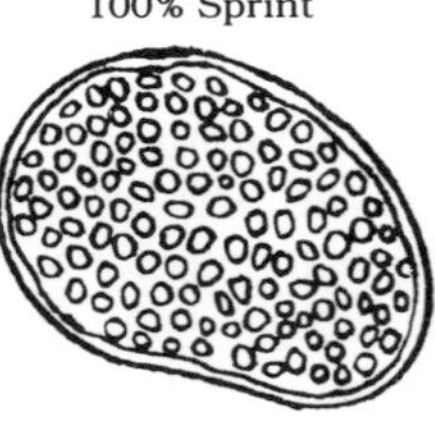

since such exertion of tension is a function of the size of a muscle fiber's cross-sectional area. Sprint fiber is also far more susceptible to having its cross-sectional size, or diameter, increased even further through training than is endurance fiber, which accounts for the fact that endurance athletes often have trouble adding muscular size, even on the same weight-training programs that quickly bulk up athletes with more sprint muscle fiber.

Sprint muscle is able to produce the energy necessary for the exertion of great amounts of power far more quickly than endurance fiber can. The biochemical fuel source for this energy production is predominantly sugar, which is stored in the muscle as glycogen. Though sprint muscle fiber can break down and thus feed on glycogen up to ten times as fast as endurance fiber can in order to meet the energy demands made of it, it pays a price for feeding this quickly. Though sprint fibers combust fuel furiously, they do so incompletely, and the residue of glycogen breakdown is left in the muscle as lactic acid. The inside of a muscle cell has a certain acidity—slightly more acid than neutral—that forms the necessary environment for the muscle's biochemical reactions to occur. As lactic acid accumulates in the muscle it causes a rise in the acidic environment of a muscle, at first slowing and finally shutting down its biochemical production of energy, and therefore its capacity to contract. Since the exertion of high speed and power causes lactic acid to accumulate quickly, sprint muscle fibers can be recruited and used only for brief periods of time. In fact, even the fast motor neurons recruiting sprint fiber are fatigable.

Simple day-to-day functions such as walking and adjustments in posture would not be possible if all muscle fatigued quickly. For this reason, all continuous movements recruit a range of muscle fibers progressing from the practically indefatigable to the quickly fatigued.

Endurance muscle fiber is capable of slower and less powerful work than sprint fiber is, but it can work for a much longer period of time—for the more than two hours, for example, necessary to run a marathon. Endurance fiber is capable of such long-term work because it is able to combust its fuel completely and thus suffers no impairment of function from the buildup of lactic acid. Endurance fiber is structurally different from sprint muscle fiber: the biochemical processes that permit the complete combustion of fuel require oxygen that is transported within the fiber to locations known as *mitochondria*, and endurance fiber contains about twelve times more mitochondria

As the level of lactic acid increases, energy production falls.

	ENDURANCE	SPRINT
Speed	Slow	Sprint
Power	—	Lots
Endurance	Yes	—
Fat—slow-burning fuel	Fat	—
Sugar—fast-burning fuel	—	Sugar
O_2 stores	Large	—
Fatigable	No	Yes
Size potential	Slight	Large
Peak force	Low	High
Relax quality	Slow	Fast
Color	Dark	White

than sprint fiber does. To support continuous work over an extended length of time, endurance fiber also has a greater oxygenating blood supply than sprint fiber does, and three times the capacity to store oxygen within individual muscle cells.

In any movement, endurance fiber is the first to be recruited, and it is the only fiber used in light- to medium-intensity work. It is, therefore, highly resistant to fatigue. Because it almost always operates at relatively low degrees of force and speed, endurance fiber can use fat as a fuel supply, thus sparing the body's limited supply of glycogen, and its cells have a fat-storage capacity three times larger than the cells of sprint fiber do.

It would be ideal if there were a muscle fiber type that combined the long-term work capacity of endurance fiber with the speed and force capacities of sprint fiber, and, in fact, there is such a type. It is known as *intermediate fiber*, though it is really sprint fiber with some endurance characteristics (notably, increased oxygen-storage capacity, more and larger mitochondria, and more fat content) that are attained by prolonged endurance training.

All sports make varying demands on sprint and endurance muscle fiber. It is possible to jog with no significant use of sprint muscle fiber, and a punch thrown in boxing makes no significant demands on endurance fiber. But most sports make demands on both types of fiber, in proportions that vary from sport to sport and from moment to moment within each sport. In soccer, a forward may begin a particular downfield play at a slow jog. As the intensity of play increases he will sequentially recruit more and more endurance muscle fibers, so that he can roam the field comfortably over a period of time. If the ball is passed to him and he makes a drive at the goal, he will break through a recruitment threshold (the anaerobic threshold), and for power and speed he will begin to tap what banks of sprint fibers he has. If he has proportionately few sprint muscle fibers to call on, their recruitment will come late, after virtually all the endurance fibers in the legs are in use, and he will not produce much of a burst in speed or power. If, as is likely, this forward has a high proportion of sprint fibers in his legs, those fibers will kick in early in the recruitment process and result in the true breakaway speed his position requires. Of course, the trade-off for this speed is that it cannot be sustained for long, and the muscle fibers producing it will fatigue rapidly no matter how well trained the athlete.

David Costill started as a coach. Certain that there was a more objective method of coaching than the strictly empirical techniques in use, he returned to school and earned a doctorate in biochemistry. He is now one of the most productive biochemists in exercise physiology, and his work in carbohydrate loading and fluid replacement is widely known to serious athletes throughout the world.

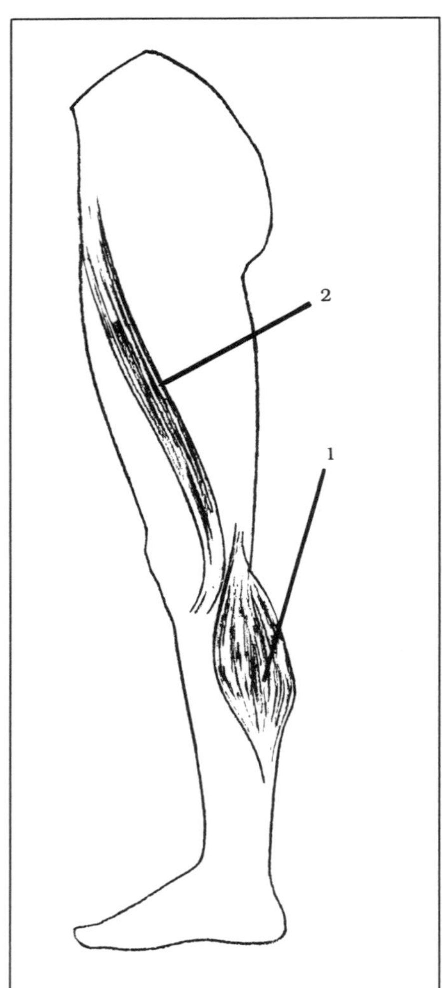

1. Calf muscle—high connective tissue content; very elastic.
2. Thigh muscle—low connective tissue content; inelastic.

Up to this point we have discussed only the fibers composing muscles, but whole muscles, which are made up of tens of thousands of individual fibers, have identifiable qualities of their own.

Muscle is held together by connective tissue that interlaces in and around muscle fibers, running parallel to them, and encases the muscle as a whole. This connective tissue condenses at both ends of a muscle into what we know as tendons, providing the muscle's attachments to the skeleton, and it gives the entire muscular unit an elastic quality, or springiness, that varies widely from muscle to muscle. The gastrocnemius muscle of the calf, for example, has a high connective-tissue content, making it very elastic. When a runner while sprinting forceably elongates the calf muscles and the long, elastic Achilles tendons connecting them to the feet, he stores large amounts of a type of energy known as kinetic energy in the stretched connective tissue of the muscles, adding considerably to the force of the muscles' active contractions and to his overall speed. Any runner whose gastrocnemius muscles and Achilles tendons lack elasticity will not be so fast as he might. The sartorius muscles of the thighs, on the other hand, have a low connective-tissue content and are therefore relatively inelastic and incapable of storing much kinetic energy.

No matter how much elasticity a muscle possesses, when it is maximally stretched it becomes inelastic and stiff, and the tendons then provide structural strength to the entire unit; this strength is four times that of the muscle itself at peak contraction. The measurement of this end range of motion is commonly referred to as flexibility, but is scientifically known as *joint looseness*. While there is no proven connection between joint looseness and overall athletic performance, too much looseness can be a real liability in sports that require rapid changes of direction and acceleration, such as basketball, tennis, and soccer, while too little of it would seriously restrict a gymnast or a figure skater; and so the quality of joint looseness or flexibility is largely sports-specific. While an individual may have an overall flexibility trait, certain joints may be far more flexible than others; and certain joint flexibilities are critical to particular sports, such as shoulder flexibility to swimming and hip flexibility to tennis. As is commonly recognized, an individual's flexibility diminishes with age; but contrary to much popular belief, women, except in four particular joints, are not more flexible than men.

The point at which a given tendon attaches to a bone deter-

mines the amount of leverage the muscle has when it contracts, and this leverage is important to athletic performance in that it increases the efficiency with which the muscle is used. If you were to hold the short end of a seesaw you would be able to move the long end up and down quickly, but would have trouble lifting a person sitting on the long end; conversely, if you were to hold the long end, you could leverage, or lift, a person on the short end with relative ease, but could move that end up and down, even unweighted, only slowly. The triceps muscle in the rear of the arm has a short fulcrum and is designed for the speed of movement necessary to throwing and cross-country ski poling; the powerful gastrocnemius muscle of the calf forms a long fulcrum where it inserts into the foot, increasing that muscle's leverage for a long jump or hurdle.

There are two other sports-important aspects to leverage. The first is that the longer a limb, the more leverage it can exert, which is why distance runners tend to have long thighs and good oarsmen have long arms. The second is that every muscle has a point of optimal leverage, which usually occurs near the middle of its range of motion, where, during contraction, the muscle has its largest diameter. In a pull-up, for example, the biceps muscles have little leverage at the beginning of the movement; their leverage increases up to about the halfway point of the movement, where the biceps become largest, and then decreases again as the chin approaches the bar and the exercise becomes most difficult.

In addition to their elasticity and leverage, a third quality of muscles important to sports is their dimension. The greater the diameter of a muscle, the more speed and power it can generate. The largest-diameter muscles will have a high degree of explosive force, which is why boxers, weight lifters, speed skaters, gymnasts, and track cyclists have large muscles in those parts of their bodies that have to generate force. The ultimate achievable diameter of a given muscle in an individual is genetically limited, and this diameter is a direct function of how long the muscle is. Even if a limb is very long, the muscle on it needn't be, and a short muscle on a long limb cannot become as wide and therefore as strong as a long one.

Whole muscles have identifiable performance characteristics, as well as qualities, that have very specific applications in sports. To understand these characteristics it is essential first to understand the necessary trade-off between force and speed in the contraction of a muscle. That trade-off is best expressed by a chart known as the *Force-Speed Curve* (see page 67).

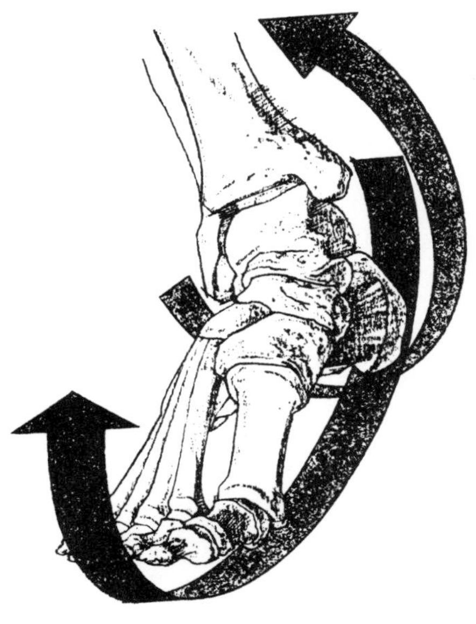

Joint looseness.

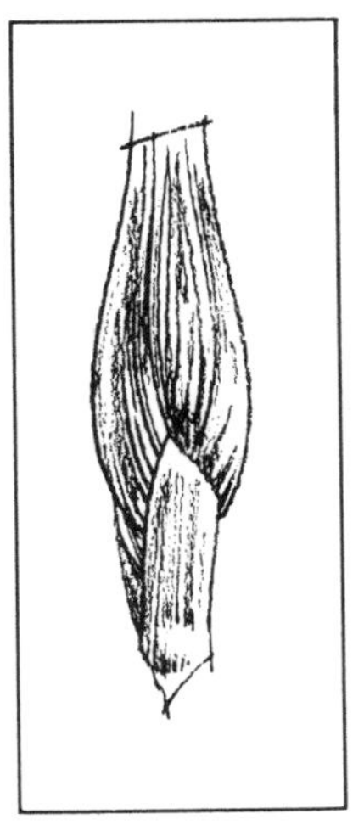

Triceps (left): short fulcrum; high speed; low leverage.
Gastrocnemius (right): long fulcrum; low speed; high leverage.

A very heavy weight can be lifted by the biceps only at a very slow speed, but the biceps can contract very quickly when no weight is being lifted by them. Gradations between no weight and heavy weight are plotted on the Force-Speed Curve to express the maximum force available at specific speeds. A Force-Speed Curve, in effect, describes a muscle's overall performance, and each muscle in a given body will have a different curve that characterizes its performance as being adequate or inadequate to a particular sport. Through training, the curve for any muscle can be improved—meaning that there will be more force generated by it at a specific speed.

Speed, force, and acceleration are the three performance characteristics of a muscle, and they are determined variously by a muscle's fiber type, its Force-Speed Curve, its temperature, and its size and elasticity.

Muscle speed allows a cyclist to pedal continuously at 120 RPMs, a boxer to deliver a punch in 60 milliseconds, or a sprinter to run at 25 miles per hour. Speed differs from muscle to muscle within a body. It is greatest within a given muscle when the weight load on that muscle is the lightest, and when it is maximally stretched prior to the contraction. The higher the percentage of sprint fiber in a muscle, the greater that muscle's speed will be and the faster the muscle's ability to relax in order to maintain its speed.

For a group of muscles to accelerate the human body rapidly, as the leg muscles do in the first 25 meters of a 100-meter dash,

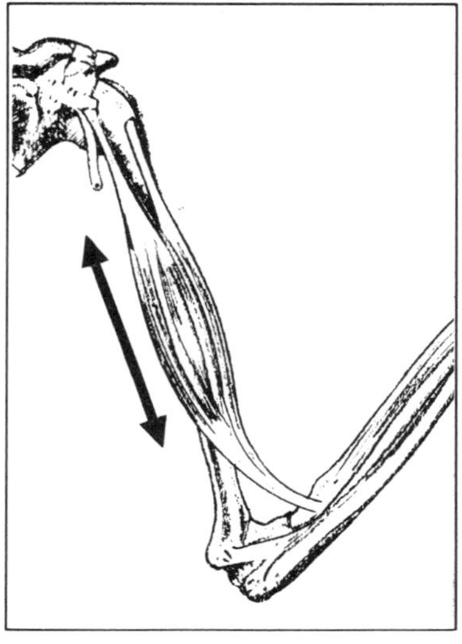

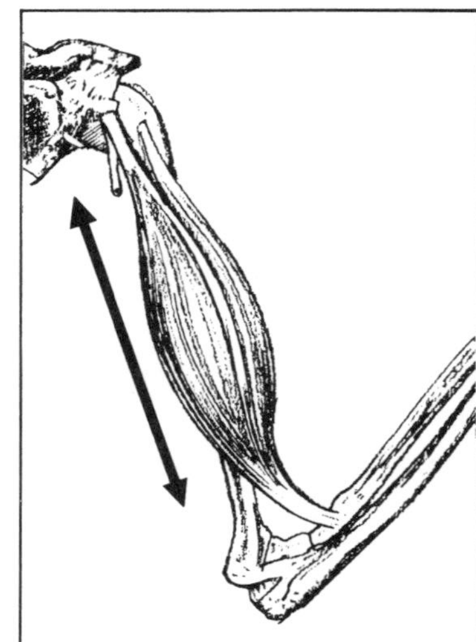

Short muscle (left): less size and, therefore, less power potential. Long muscle (right): greater size and power potential.

The Force-Speed Curve is relatively fixed for any particular muscle. As speed increases, available power decreases.

they must have a high percentage of sprint muscle fiber, high-speed Force-Speed Curves at whatever resistance is being encountered, and the proper temperature. A muscle's temperature at rest is 37°C.; with warm-up that temperature can go as high as 43°, augmenting the power of the muscle by as much as 50 percent. Muscle elasticity also increases with a rise in the temperature, and the muscle becomes more relaxed—as a result, it is less likely to tear and its suppleness of movement is increased. Most muscle groups operate in opposing pairs—when one flexes, the other extends. Another requirement for acceleration is that opposing muscle groups be able to relax as quickly and completely as possible, and this is also a function of their temperature and fiber type.

Big muscles can exert more force than small ones because their maximum diameters are larger, and any muscle exerts its maximum force at its maximum diameter. Two conditions determine the force of any given movement: how short, or flexed, the muscle is when it encounters a load, and how fast it is flexing. A prizefighter's punch can deliver a force of up to 1,000 pounds, much more weight than his arm could lift. This considerable force is made possible by the tremendous speed of muscles shortening in the boxer's shoulder and arm when those muscles encounter their load (in this case, his opponent's head), and by the delivery of that speed to the load at the optimal extension of the fighter's arm.

As the fastest human motion, a boxing punch is delivered at the farthest end of the Force-Speed Curve. At the other end of the curve is high-force, low-speed work. A muscle can best accomplish this kind of work when it has already developed 60 percent of its maximum isometric tension before encountering the load. In a curl with a barbell, for example, the biceps will operate most effectively if they are 60 percent tensed before they begin to move the weight up toward the chest.

FAT

Despite its bad reputation, fat is a body component that is important for sports. Fat is the body's largest energy reserve and is functionally limitless in most people. Healthy human beings range from between 5 percent and 40 percent body fat, and there is an ideal percentage for every sport. A high percentage of

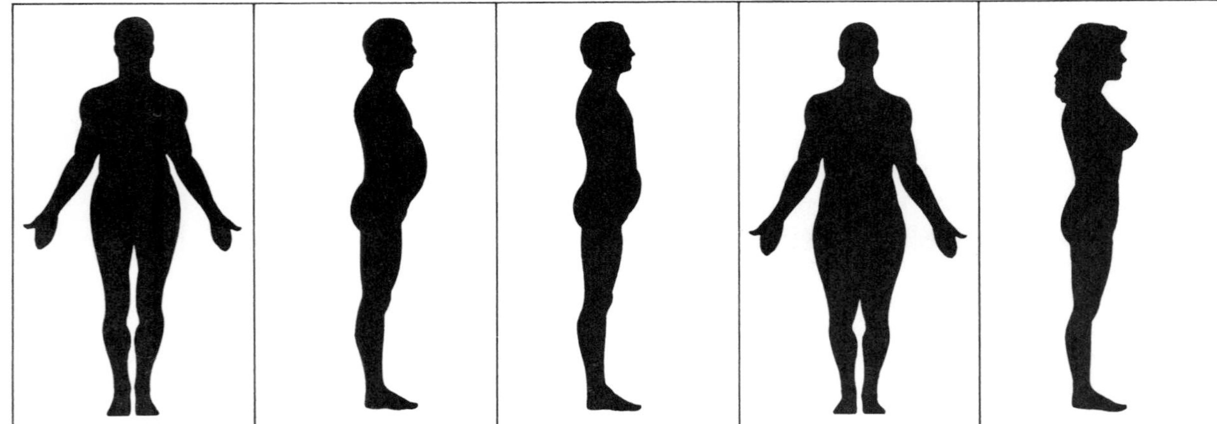

Fat is genetically stored at different sites.

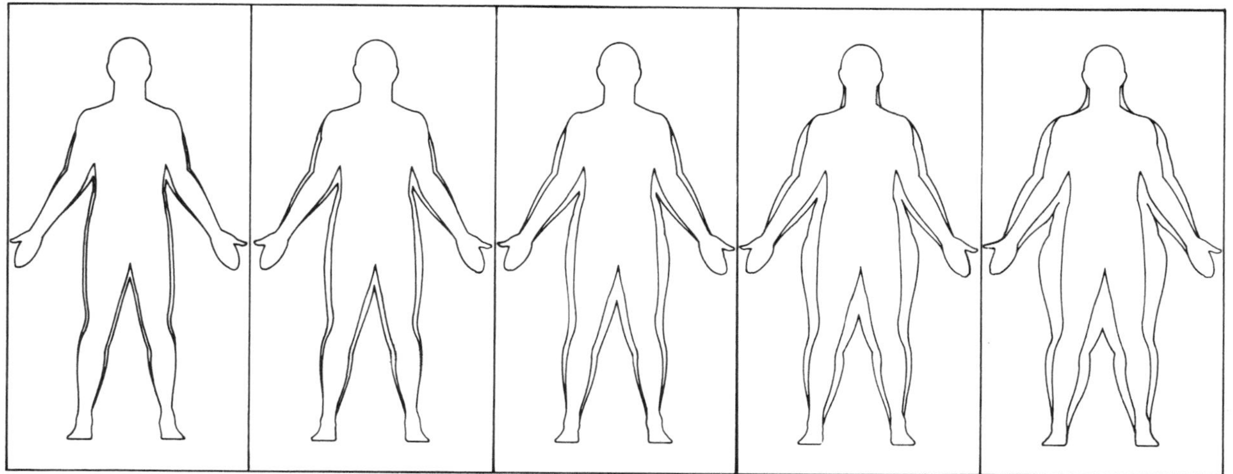

Fat is added in layers throughout the body, but larger increases occur at the genetically determined sites.

body fat provides extra and helpful flotation for long-distance swimmers, and is a source of insulation against convective heat loss in the water. In ultra-long-distance running, too low a body-fat percentage can limit an athlete's performance by shorting the runner on fuel. And in numerous sports, such as golf, baseball, weight lifting, hockey, and field events, a relatively high percentage of body fat is inconsequential.

In other sports, too much fat is a definite liability. In any endurance sport in which the body weight must be lifted, as it is in cycling or skiing up hills, gymnastics, and running, body fat is an obvious hindrance as extra weight for the athlete to carry. The lowest percentages of body fat are found in gymnasts and long-distance runners, to whose performance every extra ounce is critical. The percentage of body fat, though important, is less critical in other endurance sports, such as cross-country skiing and cycling, than it is in running (where the fat must be lifted with every step) because during the gliding and coasting phases of those sports the extra weight is not being lifted.

Individuals vary in the locations and sizes of their depots for storage of fat, which can be depleted through training, although they cannot be preferentially eliminated. Women, who must carry more body fat than men to support lactation and pregnancy, have heavier deposits of fat in the breasts and hips than men do. Other specific body-fat stores that differ in size from person to person are located at the sides of the waist and in the lower abdomen, the buttocks, the backs of the arms, and the thighs.

One final sports-important characteristic of fat is its ability to prevent convective heat loss. This characteristic could be dangerous in the summer for an athlete with a high percentage of body fat, whose body could not dump as much heat as it might need to. And even in the winter, an athlete is better served by keeping warm with an extra layer of clothing than by extra fat.

PART II

THE PERFORMANCE REQUIREMENTS OF ALPINE SKIING TENNIS WINDSURFING RUNNING SWIMMING CYCLING AND CROSS-COUNTRY SKIING

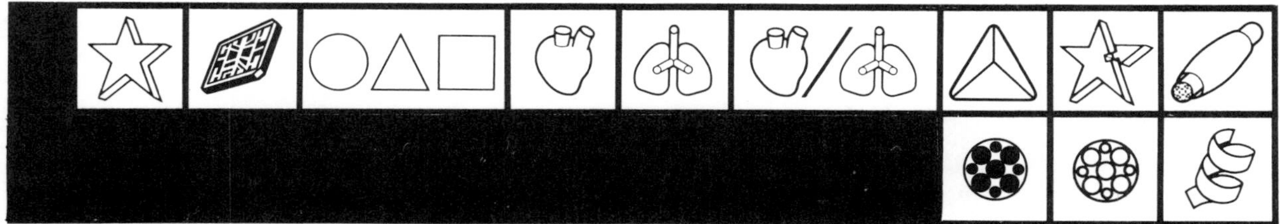

INTRODUCTION

Part II examines seven sports from the point of view of what they demand physically and mentally of their participants. If each of us is a distinct athletic machine endowed with unique talent for sports, each sport is also distinct in the set of performance demands it makes on us. In any great athletic performance, an exactly appropriate and fully adequate group of human mental and physical skills is brought to bear upon the execution of a particular set of mental and physical tasks. To understand clearly the tasks that comprise the performance of a given sport, and to know precisely what capacities and talents you have to bring to the accomplishment of those tasks, is really to know yourself as an athlete.

There is often a considerable gap between the actual performance requirements of a sport and what those requirements are commonly perceived to be. This part of the book is designed to lower the entry barriers to the seven sports it deals with by separating the true performance requirements of those sports from popular misconceptions that too often would cause us to believe that performance at any sport is an all-or-nothing thing—that we either have a single mysterious ability for a particular sport or we don't. In America, commercial hype also often tends to obscure the real performance requirements of a sport. We can be led to believe that a particular tennis racquet is all we need for a good net game, that a hot new pair of sneakers will allow us to run like Bill Rodgers, or a new pair of skis to ski like Phil Mahre. This part of the book is designed to tell you what you *really* need to play good net, to run fast marathons, or to ski well.

It can also increase your enjoyment in watching the sports dealt with here, whether you participate in them or not, by allowing you to understand more of what you see—from the anatomies of the athletes to the strategies they adopt, or are forced to adopt, because of the physical components they bring to the sport.

If you have never participated in one of the sports here and think you might like to, the section on that sport can provide you with a clear idea of what will be required of you by that sport and, therefore, a sense of how well suited to it you are. Learning about its requirements might also help you to decide you are not well equipped for a particular sport, and lead you into another one that you might enjoy more and/or participate in with more success.

If you already play or compete in one of the sports described here, the section on that sport will almost certainly teach you things you don't already know about its performance requirements and give you new insights into yourself as a participant or competitor. You might, for example, be surprised to learn how important your heart and lungs are for good performance in Alpine skiing, even if you have skied for a long time. And we believe you can learn something new, even if you are an out-and-out expert at one of these sports. We have found that even world-class competitors often have an imperfect understanding of the performance requirements of their sport, and therefore train and compete less effectively than they might.

If you *are* an expert at one of these sports and are interested in taking up another one, we believe that this part of the book will allow you an easy transfer to the new one by letting you see clearly, without mystique or technical jargon, how your physical components and talents in one area can be used effectively in the other. We recommend, in fact, that everyone would do well to read a number of these sections, not just the one on the sport he or she is most interested in.

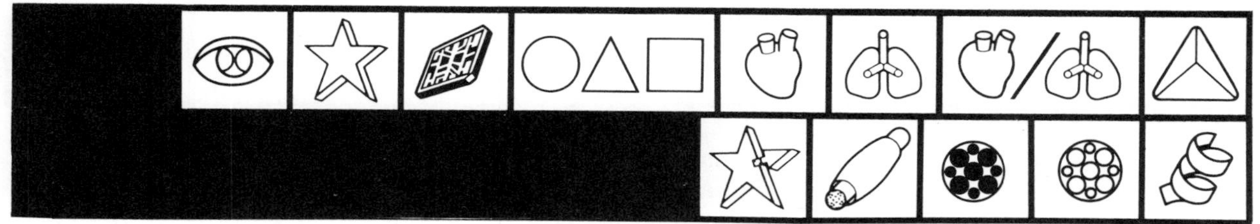

ALPINE SKIING

Formal international Alpine ski racing has been conducted since the 1920s, and from the beginning there have been a number of strong national influences on its development. It was the British who, in the early 1920s, developed Alpine skiing from a method of simply getting downhill on cross-country skis into its earliest recreational and racing forms. From the late 1920s through the 1950s the sport was dominated by the Swiss, and even more strongly by the Austrians—one of whom, the great Tony Sailer, won three gold medals in the 1956 Winter Olympics. The 1960s began with a gold medal win at Squaw Valley by the Frenchman Jean Vuarnet, who along with George Joubert was to become the premier ski theorist of the decade and, with Joubert and Honoré Bonnet, a coach of the most dominant team in Alpine ski-racing history—the French national team of the late 1960s, which included Jean-Noël Augert, Patrick Russel, Alain Penz, Anna and Marielle Goitschel, and the incomparable Jean-Claude Killy.

Vuarnet and Joubert seemed almost to have a formula for the creation of great ski racers, but since their teams of the late 1960s, and since the popularity explosion of Alpine skiing in the early 1970s, no one nation has been able to dominate the sport. Instead, it has been dominated since then by particular individuals, most of them—such as Gustavo Thoeni, Ingemar Stenmark, Steve Podborski, and Phil Mahre—from countries

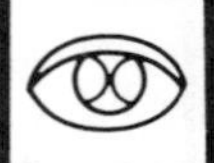

that had not previously been associated with championship Alpine skiing.

It would seem, perhaps, that a nation with the Alpine ski resources of Austria, Switzerland, and France should be able to produce great ski racers one after another through the decades, but modern ski-racing history indicates that periods of national dominance over the sport are in fact very unusual—that great ski racers are born rather than made, and that the true motor genius that makes them great cannot be taught or otherwise transferred to other skiers, though its form and style may be imitated.

THE CONTROL SYSTEM IN ALPINE SKIING

Reception

In no sport is dynamic visual acuity more important than in Alpine ski racing, and one of the crucial distinguishing differences between ordinary ski racers and very good ones is that the latter are able to focus farther ahead of themselves on a given racecourse. While a beginning racer will likely be visually conscious only of the gate he is passing through, and the intermediate racer might be aware of the following gate as well, the expert will use his dynamic visual acuity to assess everything on the course from wherever he happens to be to two, three, or even four gates ahead; thus he can plan the line he will follow through the poles and pre-select the motor programs necessary for following that line.

Dynamic visual acuity is also extremely important to the serious recreational skier, who uses it to pick a line through moguls, to avoid other skiers, and to adjust in advance to changing snow conditions on a given run. The components of good visual acuity in both competitive and recreational skiing are an accurate perception of depth (especially in flat light), the ability to localize and discriminate key objects (such as gates, moguls, and other skiers) in advance, and the ability to track these objects and to saccade quickly between them.

As a person skis, the Short-Term Memory, the Control System's work space, scans the Short-Term Sensory Store for information that will make up an overall performance estimate on

where the skier is, where he is going, how fast he is skiing, and how well balanced and in control he is. The eyes provide much of this information, but that information is augmented by data provided by the ears, the inner ears, and the limb receptors. The ears serve primarily to assess the overall speed of the skier, evaluating the sounds of things passing by, the sound of the air he is parting, and the sounds of his skis traveling over the snow. The inner ears serve as the skier's balance alarm system, alerting him whenever his balance is thrown off. The limb receptors tell the skier where his limbs are, allowing him to position them properly to initiate and finish turns, or to reposition them after a skid or near-fall or an uphill skate. They also provide feedback on the nature of individual turns—how much edge was required, how much the skis chattered, how far forward the knees were or should have been—so that the skier can make necessary corrections in his next turns. And, finally, the receptors on the bottoms of the feet relay positional information to the skier on how pressure is being applied to the skis from front to back during a turn, and from side to side when he is trying to ride a flat ski for more speed on flats or in soft snow.

Abilities

Motor abilities are so overwhelmingly important in Alpine skiing that ski-racing development programs in Austria and the United States are more concerned with identifying these abilities in potential young ski racers than with any other form of talent recognition. When in the late 1960s the Austrians undertook to catch up to the French national racing program, they discovered that many of their skiers had been able to make their way to the national team level without possessing extraordinary motor abilities and that, once there, these skiers were able to compete but not to win on the World Cup circuit. To remedy this situation the Austrians established a series of thirty-two motor-skills tests at the University of Innsbruck and began to administer these tests to ten-year-old boys and girls in an attempt to locate wherever they could find it the phenomenal motor abilities that characterize the world's top skiers. Since then, and since the Austrians' subsequent successes with this sort of testing, the United States has also undertaken such a program, and it is already starting to bear fruit.

The motor abilities most important to skiing—skills that come under the general headings of balance, agility, coordination, and rate control (timing)—are genetically determined—

Honoré Bonnet is widely known as the coach who led the French Ski Team to the top of the World Cup circuit and coached Jean-Claude Killy to three gold medals at the 1968 Winter Olympics in Grenoble. He combined a great knowledge of the scientific training principles contained in the French ski technique with the phenomenal personality and character of a great coach.

that is, an individual is born with them. The Mahre twins, Steve and Phil, are an excellent example of how genetic these abilities are, in that their results on all kinds of physiological and anthropometric tests are so close as to be almost indistinguishable.

Motor Learning

Ski schools have proliferated all over the world in the past twenty years, while schools for other sports, such as running, swimming, and cycling, have not—a fact that demonstrates not only that skiing is popular but also that it is not easy to learn. Many ski schools, both in the United States and abroad, have been accused of teaching form rather than substance—of getting quickly and incompletely past the difficult break points in learning by teaching students on short, soft, easy-to-turn skis, which makes it necessary for them to relearn skiing whenever they are confronted with difficult terrain, or longer, stiffer skis, or icy conditions. All motor learning can be described by a learning curve along which an individual improves, and many people mistakenly believe that they can learn to ski in one smooth progression along this curve. In fact, more often than not, learning takes place in sudden, insightful jumps at certain points along the curve, known as "break points," where difficult new pieces of technique must be acquired. Some people learn skiing more easily and faster than others. These people, whose learning curves for skiing are steep, may pass in a single day a particular break point (say, the transition between a stem christie and a parallel turn) that would take someone with a shallow curve in skiing a year or longer to pass. The very fastest learners are apt to be young, bold, and highly motivated, and they almost always possess a large number of the appropriate motor skills. But no matter how quickly someone learns to ski, or how proficient the student becomes in one set of skiing circumstances (for example, packed powder snow and gentle terrain), without a varied depth of experience at the sport, the skier's technique will quickly fall apart in unfamiliar circumstances.

Depth of experience is necessary not only to the amateur skier but to the competitive racer as well. While Jean Vuarnet was coaching the Italian ski team in the early 1970s, he set out to teach the perfect slalom turn on an evenly graded hill with uniform snow conditions. While one of his racers, Gustavo Thoeni, because of his great depth of previous racing experience and his superior motor skills, was able to implement that turn anywhere and under any conditions, another, Piero Gros (later a great racer himself), who had less experience, would blow out of a course if a gate was placed dramatically higher and shorter than the gates on Vuarnet's practice course.

Most people never learn to ski very well, no matter how many lessons they take or skiing manuals they read. This is because it is very difficult to form an accurate image of correctness for skiing from verbal directions, written materials, videotapes, or even from watching experts. An accurate image of correctness is an understood three-dimensional mental picture of how something is done, and no present method of teaching skiing is capable of constructing that picture very well. Of course there are always exceptional learners—people with good spatial abilities who can quickly create for themselves an accurate image of correctness from almost any instructions—but for most of us, a vivid, correct, three-dimensional picture of what we are supposed to do is all but impossible to glean from any of the traditional methods of learning to ski. These methods are also inadequate, for the most part, for correcting errors—making it very difficult for learning skiers to improve—which is why at any major ski area one sees so many poor skiers. Some ski instructors and coaches, notably Burke Mountain's Warren Witherell, bypass altogether the traditional emphasis on technical correctness in teaching skiing, and concentrate instead, often with very good success, on getting the student recreational skier or racer to focus on results—on getting the skis to carve and hold a line, for example, no matter what technique he or she uses to achieve the required angulation.

Motor Programs

Any motor program for skiing is created by a skier calling upon underlying abilities and whatever skiing motor skills he or she already has to imitate an image of correctness for a particular movement or turn; the trace of the program in the Short-Term Memory is then continually strengthened by practice and filed away in the library of the Long-Term Memory. The repetition of a program modeled on an accurate image of correctness is the

basis for sound learning in skiing, as it is for any sport. Because expert skiing involves so many separate skills, skiing is necessarily learned—and motor programs formed—by linking together just a few skills at a time, such as the pole plant, knee bend, and unweighting that initiate any turn. As a skier gets better and better, older skills become increasingly automatic, enabling the student to concentrate on the development of new ones and, overall, on a larger and larger package of skills—which are linked into more and more complex motor programs. The beginner with very few skills linked together into only a few simple motor programs, the execution of which absorbs all the attention, cannot fathom the seeming ease with which the world-class racer dominates a steep, fast, icy course. This expert's ease is a result of how automatic a great number of skills have become.

Though it is super motor ability that allows some people to become great skiers, it is possible for an individual who is not a motor genius (Billy Kidd, for example) to become a national and even a world-class ski racer—if he has the crucial ability to critically analyze and emulate skillful performance—by developing the requisite number of complex motor programs and acquiring the needed depth and variety of experience.

Attention, Anticipation, and Arousal

Ski racing requires all the attention a skier can bring to it, and then some. Even though a racer's movements, once initiated, are almost entirely automatic, a very high level of attention is necessary to plan and perform one exactly correct turn after another, and to adjust constantly to very fine gradations of speed. On any advanced level of skiing the key focus of attention is anticipation.

Even though motor programs can be readied for initiation in fractions of seconds, the high speeds of advanced skiing make it possible to travel many feet in less than a second, and therefore the skier has to be able to use anticipation to pre-select and preslot the appropriate programs prior to initiating them. A ski racer must pick a line down through a course, which means determining in advance exactly where to turn at each gate. Following that line during a race requires the racer to anticipate and set up for each turn before reaching it, and how consis-

tently this is done may well mean the difference between winning and losing. Similarly, a fast recreational skier will need good anticipation in variable snow conditions, on unfamiliar terrain, and in moguls.

In any sport, performance improves with increasing arousal up to a peak beyond which performance begins to fall off as arousal continues to increase. Because of the high speed, physical danger, and sheer excitement involved in competitive skiing, the control of arousal is usually more critical to good performance than the excitation of it. As an accurate measure of a racer's state of arousal, the number of heartbeats per minute may be at its maximum in the starting gate, before any exercise is done. Where 50 beats per minute might be a skier's resting rate, his heartbeat might well reach 170 per minute in the gate, an escalation that would almost certainly indicate too much arousal for good performance. (So damaging to performance are very high levels of anticipatory arousal that NASA will disqualify astronauts from training programs because of them.) Therefore, the job of the successful ski racer becomes, first, to know the level of arousal at which he or she performs best and, second, to achieve that peak level at precisely the appropriate time, without suffering the debilitating physiological and psychological drain of too much arousal too early.

THE HEART-LUNG PACKAGE IN ALPINE SKIING

Ingemar Stenmark amazed Scandinavian physiologists when he not only gained the highest scores ever recorded on a standard battery of overall physical tests but also managed to outperform many marathon runners on the test for maximum oxygen consumption. With a score of seventy milliliters per kilogram he proved that Alpine skiing is a strenuously aerobic sport.

The Heart

Although the heart of an Alpine skier typically will not be so large as that of a cross-country skier, and will not pump as

much blood per beat, the number of heartbeats per minute during intense skiing will be very near the skier's maximum heart rate. For the experienced skier this high heart rate correlates directly with aerobic power, and the individual is often capable during high-speed skiing of operating at maximum oxygen consumption. This is not true of the less experienced skier, whose high heart rate is more likely to be a reflection of anxiety or of the anaerobic demands of the more static work of less advanced skiing.

The Lungs and Heart-Lung Power

Because skiing is so much more aerobic than is generally recognized, big lungs and strong respiratory muscles are crucial both to the racer and to the expert mogul skier, allowing them to service the demands of the body for oxygen and also to blow off the heavy loads of CO_2 that accumulate in the blood while racing and skiing moguls. Ordinary recreational skiers who stop every few hundred feet down a trail because they are out of breath or because their legs are burning are suffering from an overaccumulation of lactic acid in the muscles, an overaccumulation that would not occur if the heart-lung system were better conditioned, allowing them to ski more aerobically. Occasionally, racers and recreational skiers alike will actually forget to breathe (or will take only very shallow breaths) while skiing, and this practice severely damages performance by limiting the supply of oxygen to working muscles and by limiting the blow-off of accumulating CO_2.

All skiers would like to produce as little lactic acid as possible, since when it builds up in the muscles, specifically in the thighs, the result is not only pain but also an eventual shutdown of the muscles. The higher a skier's anaerobic threshold and the faster the speed of oxygen delivery the less lactic acid the individual will produce at a given work load. A skier's anaerobic threshold can be elevated and the speed of delivery improved by training, and good overall aerobic training makes Alpine skiing a safer, more healthful, and more enjoyable sport for everyone.

BODY COMPOSITION IN ALPINE SKIING

Somatotype and Skeleton

The typical Alpine ski racer is a true mesomorph, with the advanced muscularity necessary to perform well at the sport. Though most ski racers, particularly slalom racers, have traditionally been relatively small, this pattern is changing. Because the new gate poles release at snow level, larger skiers are now able to come as close to the poles as smaller skiers can, thus running steeper, straighter lines between gates than they were able to do with the old poles, and dispelling the myth that smaller skiers are necessarily faster because of their lower centers of gravity. In America in 1983 several skiers more than six feet tall competed successfully on the FIS circuit—something that wouldn't have been thought possible five years ago—and some experts believe that larger skiers may soon come to dominate world ski racing.

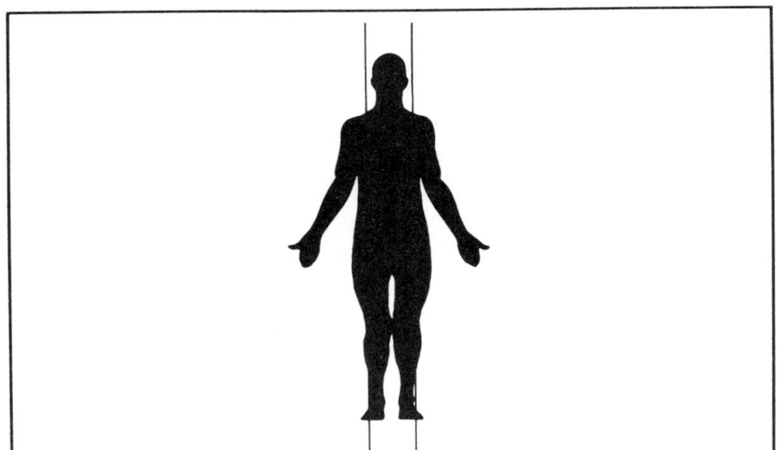

Alpine skier: true mesomorph with a low center of gravity.

However, as a determining factor in Alpine ski racing overall physical size is less important than either the proportions or the characteristics of individual body parts. Maintaining bal-

ance is the single most important physical requirement of Alpine skiing, and a low center of gravity increases the body's stability: relatively short lower legs and thighs, therefore, are real assets to the skier. The bowleggedness often found in football running backs would seem to be another asset in lowering the center of gravity, but in fact most top ski racers are knock-kneed, a condition that automatically centers the knees over the inside, or carving, edge of the skis. Though an Alpine skier will tend to have a relatively tall sitting height, a heavily muscled upper body is a disadvantage, since large upper-body muscles are unnecessary in skiing and serve only to raise the body's center of gravity. Good Alpine ski racers will also tend to have broad shoulders and pelvises, both of which add to a side-to-side sense of balance; a wider pelvis also allows the independent leg action and the wide-tracked stance that are central to modern racing technique. Finally, the frames of Alpine ski racers tend to be big-boned, as measured at the wrists, elbows, and ankles.

Muscle

Top Alpine ski racers are very powerful athletes, as is reflected in their overall muscularity on somato charts. They are especially strong in the quadriceps muscles of the thighs, where they have the highest isometric (static holding) strength among all athletes in proportion to their size. They also have considerable dynamic strength in their upper legs but, surprisingly in such a fast sport, that strength is highest at slow muscle-contraction speeds, since most skiing, even the fastest, is done at a high-power low-speed point on the Force-Speed Curve.

Though ski racers typically have a high percentage of sprint muscle fibers in their legs, they also need more than a little endurance fiber as well, in order to do as much of the work of skiing aerobically as possible; the percentages, therefore, of sprint to endurance fiber in a racer's thighs will ideally be closer to 60-40 than to 90-10—a proportion that allows for the "power endurance" necessary to ski racing. The best slalom racers are the ones who are able to maintain 50 percent of peak muscular power in their thigh muscles for the greatest number of contractions, and their ability to do that is a function of their having at least 40 percent endurance fibers in those muscles. A muscle's power is a result not only of the number of sprint fibers comprising it but of the muscle's overall size as well, and Alpine ski racers will almost always have large thigh muscles, regardless of their percentage of sprint fiber.

George Joubert and Jean Vuarnet described skiing as a sport of flexibility and balance. In fact, except in the case of the hip, where flexion and extension correlate very closely with success in ski racing, joint flexibility is largely unimportant to successful skiing. What Joubert and Vuarnet undoubtedly meant by flexibility is properly called muscle elasticity, and good muscle elasticity is critical to Alpine skiing in that it allows a skier to move fluidly. Any muscle has an inherent elasticity, but this can be increased if a skier is properly warmed up and relaxed. An inelastic muscle not warmed up and tense that is suddenly put to vigorous exercise is in danger of being torn and incapable of the supple, fluid movement that characterizes good skiing.

At least 20 percent of the work of Alpine skiing is anaerobic, and therefore lactic acid is produced in the muscles—at levels as much as two and a half times greater in the expert or racer than in the beginner. The ability to perform the anaerobic work of skiing is so critical that—assuming equal ability among racers—those racers with the highest lactic-acid buildup in their thighs at the end of a race will more than likely be those with the fastest times. Of the three ski-racing events—slalom, giant slalom, and downhill—giant slalom causes the highest lactic-acid buildup in a racer and therefore makes the greatest anaerobic demands.

The levels of muscular contraction characteristic of most forms of Alpine skiing demand, for fuel, sugar stored as glycogen rather than as fat, and when this sugar is depleted any skier's energy disappears, performance plummets, and injury becomes more likely. A skier's sugar levels can drop by as much as half in a given day, and by as much as 80 percent over the course of a ski week.

Fat

While the percentage of body fat is important primarily to athletes who have to carry their weight uphill, it is not unimportant in skiing down hills, where even a little too much fat can interfere with agility. Though some extra body weight in the

form of fat is not a disadvantage to a downhill specialist, among slalom racers there is a high correlation between success and leanness, and the ideal percentage of body fat for all ski racers is around 10 percent for men and 20 percent for women.

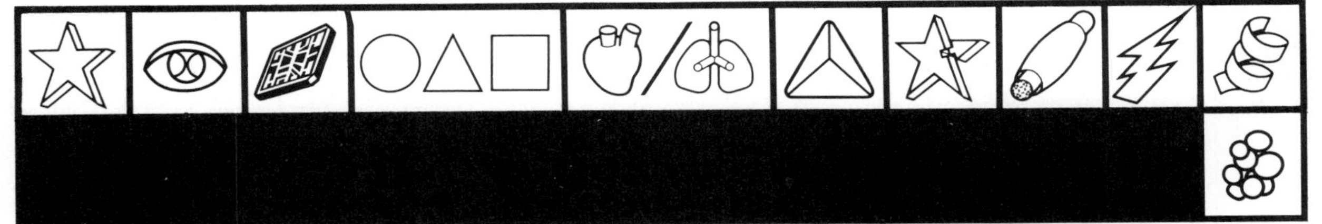

TENNIS

In his fine book *Tennis for the Future*, Vic Braden writes: "Tennis seems innocently simple to those who are outside the fence looking in. There are no sand traps to worry about, or moguls, or blitzing linebackers, or 7–10 splits. The court looks so huge and the net seems so low that people tend to think, 'Heck. This game's a piece of cake.' " As Mr. Braden goes on to point out, however, people don't tend to think that for very long after picking up a racquet. While it is as true of tennis as of other sports in this book that it can be played for fun and exercise by almost anyone, it is also true that *good* tennis makes many and various demands on the Control System and the body, and very few of the millions of people who play tennis do it very well.

Though certain physical talents, characteristics, and abilities can contribute greatly to playing good tennis, the combination of a normal person's physical assets does not so much limit the individual's overall potential at the sport as define the *type* of tennis game he or she can play with the most success. Good tennis is almost purely a function of good strokes, and the ability of the Control System to develop such strokes is much more important to the game a person will finally have than are size, speed, strength, and flexibility. Because of this, and because of the crucial role sportsvision plays in tennis, it can be said of tennis more accurately than of any of the other sports treated here that it is truly a Control System sport.

THE CONTROL SYSTEM IN TENNIS

Reception and Anticipation

At high levels of play the visual demands of tennis are so great that they literally cannot be met by the human eye. The eye can track the arc that a tennis ball follows at a maximum speed of only thirty degrees per second. At ball speeds faster than this—speeds at which virtually all competitive tennis is played—the eyes cannot actually "follow the ball," but continually lag behind it and catch up to it in a series of jerks that fix the ball at a number of different points, or slices, along its arc. Each slice is perceived by the brain a hundred milliseconds after the ball has actually reached that point in space, which means that the tennis coach's advice to "follow the ball all the way into the racquet" is, in fact, impossible. At any given point in a ball's flight we are seeing where the ball was a tenth of a second ago, not where it is at that moment. Thus, in order to initiate a response to an approaching ball (a return of serve, for example), the Control System must *anticipate* the exact instant of a ball's arrival at a particular point in space, since it cannot know it. Though actually watching the ball *into* the racquet is impossible, the farther in *toward* the racquet a player is able to track an approaching ball, the more accurately he or she can anticipate its arrival at the proper point of contact with the racquet, and therefore the better he or she can time the stroke.

Fixing ball at different points along its arc.

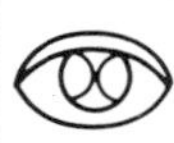

Good stroke-timing is also a function of the number of visual fixes, or slices, a player is able to take along a ball's arc: the more slices a player sees, the better the individual is able to characterize the trace of the overall arc and to determine the speed—and spin, if any—of the approaching ball. In order to locate a number of positions for the ball along its approaching arc, the eyes must continually refocus and converge on the ball. The closer the ball gets to a player, the more strenuous this visual work is and the more important it is to continue it. Binocularity—the ability of both eyes to converge and focus on an approaching object and to fix by triangulation that object's exact position in space—may be the single most important ability in tennis, and very few players have it to any degree. Even though possessing genetic visual-convergence ability, a player may not have the concentration necessary to apply it throughout the ball's entire flight, particularly as it nears the racquet, where the most important positional readings are taken and the most visual work is required.

Vision in baseball and the racquet sports is widely misunderstood and misrepresented. It is impossible, for example, to read the print on a hard-hit tennis ball or to see the stitches on a pitched baseball, just as it is impossible to watch a ball into contact with a racquet or a bat. Both visual tracking and binocularity are improvable by training, but no matter how sophisticated these abilities become, their real function in tennis, as in baseball, is to allow a player, through effective visual cuing, to accurately *anticipate* where a ball will be in space when hitting it.

The inner ears, feeding balance information into the cerebellum, provide the same sense of balance in tennis as in other sports, and hearing can supply a player with some information, supplemental to that provided by the eyes, on the force and spin with which a ball is hit.

Just as the cues taken from visual tracking can tell a player when a ball will arrive at a precise point in space, effector anticipation (provided by a stream of positional readings flowing into the Control System from the limb receptors in the legs and racquet arm) allows the player to know exactly how long it will take, in the course of a given stroke, for the racquet head to reach a particular point in space. The proper matching up of these two systems is known as good timing: for a stroke to be perfectly timed, the racquet head has to meet the ball at an exact location; the player's eyes allow him to anticipate when the ball will arrive at that location, and his limb receptors allow him to an-

ticipate when the racquet head will arrive there. He will hit the ball early, late, or perfectly, depending on where the two anticipated vectors meet.

Abilities, Motor Learning, and Motor Programs

The large participant crossover between recreational tennis and skiing is undoubtedly due in part to the fact that the same abilities of agility, balance, and gross body coordination so important to good skiing are also important to tennis. All the agility, balance, and coordination in the world, however, will not result in a first-class tennis game unless they are combined with good strokes, which are the heart of tennis and have as their only identifiable underlying physical ability a coordinated, uninhibited throwing motion (underhand for ground strokes and overhand for serving) that is free of unnecessary muscular activity. Beyond this physical ability, good stroke production is primarily the result of effective motor learning, an ability of the Control System.

A tennis stroke does not come naturally; it has to be learned, and it is very easy to learn it incorrectly. Any tennis player really has only one basic stroke for the forehand and one for the backhand, though these strokes can be employed in various ways for various effects. And once a player has learned the backhand and forehand strokes it is very difficult to change them—so difficult that many players will go to almost any lengths (buying new racquets, trying new spins and slices, developing a lob) to avoid starting over on basic ground strokes. The reason it is so hard to change a poor stroke into a good one is that, once learned, the mechanics of any stroke, no matter how poor, very quickly become automatic, and any attempted improvement to those mechanics will feel unnatural, awkward, and strained—if not impossible. Anyone who wants to play better tennis, however, will find that the single most effective way to do that is by improving ground strokes, no matter how difficult that may be.

Stroke improvement is accomplished at the conceptual level of motor learning by the formation of a proper image of correctness—an image constructed from studying diagrams in books, watching good players play, taking tennis lessons, and so on. As in Alpine skiing, however, an accurate image of correctness in tennis is difficult to form because of the problems involved in trying to extract usable three-dimensional information from two-dimensional or verbal sources or from watching the fast,

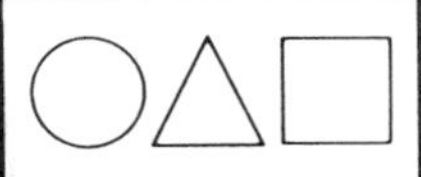

complex play of experts, during which the human eye cannot really keep up with the ball. Even when an accurate image of correctness has been formed, it is difficult to match the actual body positions to it, as is demonstrated by the fact that a great majority of learning tennis players believe they are obeying their coaches' instructions to bend their knees and rotate their hips, even when videotapes show that they are not.

An additional barrier to the formation and proper imitation of an accurate image of correctness is often the tennis coach or pro, who too frequently is unable to communicate instructions effectively, either because of the difficulties of rendering three-dimensional movements into verbalized form, or because of the inability of the student to understand such instructions. Despite all these difficulties, a good image of correctness for a tennis stroke *can* be formed, imitated, and traced into the Short-Term Memory. The trace is then deepened and the stroke made more and more automatic by practice; and enough practice of good strokes will result in the machinelike accuracy and regularity of production that characterize the very best players.

Though strokes form the central motor programs in tennis, no matter how good a player's strokes are, he will be unable to hit them if he is not in the right place at the right time. Agility, balance, and coordination are the abilities underlying the programs for footwork and body positioning that allow a player to be where he has to be on the court to use his strokes.

Attention, Anticipation, and Arousal

At the higher levels of competitive play, tennis demands more attention than any player can possibly bring to it. Though other sports, such as Alpine skiing, may demand longer sustained periods of concentration, no sport requires more intense and focused attention over short bursts of time (during which individual points are played). Concentration in tennis must be not only focused but constantly and rapidly shifting as well—be-

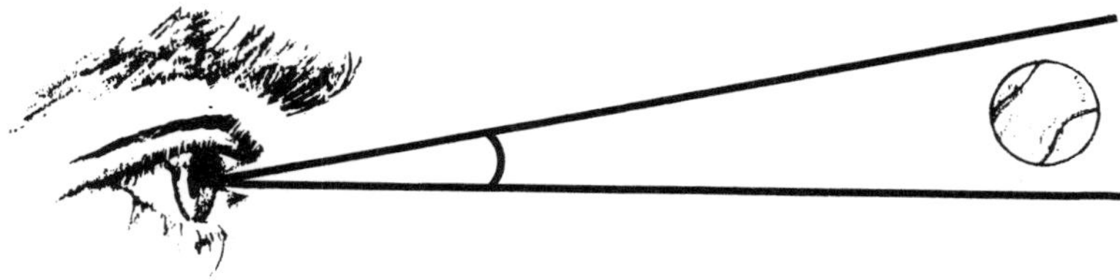

Selective attention—concentrating on the ball.

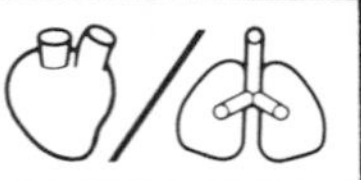

tween the player's own position, the position of the opponent, and the position of the ball. Unfortunately, there is a high potential for distractibility in the sport. The periods of rest between points tend to invite everything from neurotic thoughts about one's game to cloud-watching and listening to spectators—forms of inattention that are often carried back into play. The best players not only give all the concentration they have to individual points but find ways to keep themselves focused between points as well.

As we have said, good anticipation is crucial to good tennis. Tennis is the only so-called hand/eye sport treated in this book; by definition such a sport is one in which anticipation by the eye must coordinate with anticipation by the hand, and in no sport is such coordination, and the timing it requires, more important to successful performance than it is in tennis.

Tennis produces large amounts of mental stress, and the ability to handle pressure and at the same time play well is a function of having enough confidence in your game to keep yourself from becoming aroused beyond the point at which your best play is possible. Overarousal is more often a hindrance to good play than underarousal, as tennis tends to create its own stresses; but playing substantially under your arousal peak on the Inverted U-Shaped Curve will also hurt your game. One way to make the mental tensions of tennis work for you is to sustain throughout a given set or match a positive mental image of yourself at your best, playing as well as you possibly can, and thus forcing the stress to push your actual stroke-by-stroke performance toward that image, rather than away from it.

THE HEART-LUNG PACKAGE IN TENNIS

Since the average tennis point lasts only three seconds (a serve, a return of serve, and a second shot by the server is actually a longer-than-average tennis point), and since even at the world-class level a point very rarely lasts any longer than thirty seconds, tennis makes no major demands on the heart and lungs. World-class tennis players do have relatively high maximum oxygen consumptions, but this aerobic capacity is more impor-

tant in maintaining stamina, tolerating heat, and recovering quickly between points than it is in actual play. Moreover, although it has been recently established that racquet sports will build some aerobic capacity, the high capacities found among world-class players almost certainly have some genetic component and, to the degree that they are developed, are done so largely by such adjunctive training as interval running.

Though a large heart is not particularly important in this sport, large lungs will allow a tennis player to blow off more efficiently whatever CO_2 buildup is caused by the anaerobic work of a given point. And though a large, well-trained heart-lung package is not absolutely crucial to playing good tennis, an aerobically well trained player will have a definite physiological advantage, particularly in a long match, over an untrained player of equal skill.

BODY COMPOSITION IN TENNIS

Somatotype and Skeleton

World-class tennis players are typically ectomesomorphs—lean, muscular athletes—although they don't have to be. Overall body composition does not so much limit an individual's potential at the sport as define the type of tennis game he or she is likely to play with the most success. The more athletic, mesomorphic player is likely to develop an aggressive serve-and-volley game, while the less athletic one will probably have more success playing defensively from the baseline. Since a big serve-and-volley game requires power, height, and speed to be effective, it tends to attract not only the more athletic, mesomorphic players but the taller ones as well; shorter players—with lower centers of gravity and therefore more mobility—are more often drawn into playing court-covering, retrieval tennis.

As in skiing, a relatively low center of gravity is thought to be helpful in tennis regardless of a player's height, which means that, ideally, the legs will be somewhat short in proportion to the upper body. Long arms are also a slight advantage for the extra reach they provide, and for the extra height they allow a player's serve.

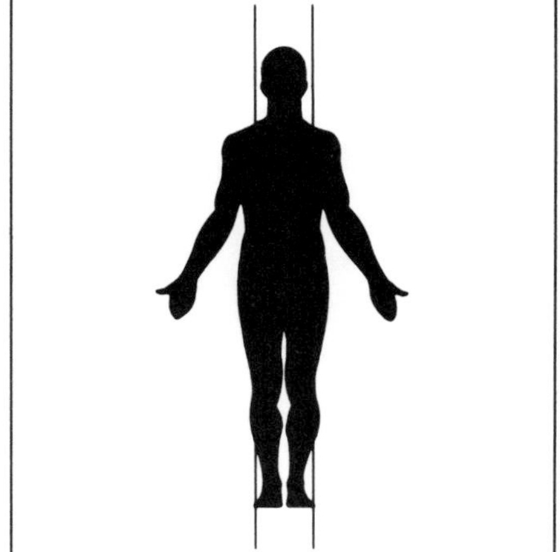

A typical tennis player is an ectomesomorph; it is advantageous to have a low center of gravity and long arms.

Muscle

The first two steps taken toward a tennis ball usually determine whether or not the ball will be reached, and therefore instantaneous speed, or explosiveness, is much more important in tennis than either aerobic or anaerobic power. Even in baseline play, a player rarely needs to take more than three steps to reach a ball. Therefore, the quickness with which the body's inertia can be broken and the amount of speed that can be generated within the first second are the crucial determiners of how fast a player can cover the court. Short-burst, explosive speed is a result of a high percentage of sprint fibers in the leg muscles; and the larger the cross-sectional size of those muscles, the more explosive speed they can deliver. Since tennis makes so few endurance requirements of the muscles, and since sprint fiber can be trained to become fatigue-resistant, the higher the percentage of sprint muscle fiber in a tennis player's legs, the better.

Anaerobic strength in the thighs allows a tennis player the important ability to get down to a shot over and over again during the course of a match. But the muscles most crucial to stroke production are those of the forearm; if they are strong they not only can produce solid strokes but will serve as a protective barrier to injury, specifically tennis elbow.

The basic ingredient of a good tennis stroke is a smooth, continuous movement throughout the entire sweep of the racquet. Such a movement is produced by a full, unrestricted range of motion in the shoulder joint; ideally, the range should extend to 270 degrees for the serve and 250 degrees for ground strokes. The length of both backhand and forehand strokes in tennis, and therefore their potential power, is influenced by the degree to which the hips can rotate, and therefore a full range of motion in the hip joints is another key prerequisite to success in the sport. Since lateral speed in tennis is almost as important as forward speed, and since a loose knee joint is counterproductive for side-to-side quickness, any tennis player is well served by knee joints that have little lateral flexibility. Though it has long been believed and written that floppiness in the wrist is detrimental to good strokes, good *flexibility* in the wrist joint, in combination with firm muscular control, actually makes for better stroke production than does little or no wrist flexibility.

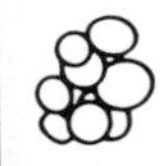

Fat

Though a relatively high percentage of body fat may occasionally be observed even in expert players—as witnessed by the Martina Navratilova of a number of years ago—more than about 12 percent for men and 18 percent for women cannot possibly help your game, and can hurt it by making you tire more quickly, particularly when it's hot; by slowing you down; and by limiting your range of motion on the court.

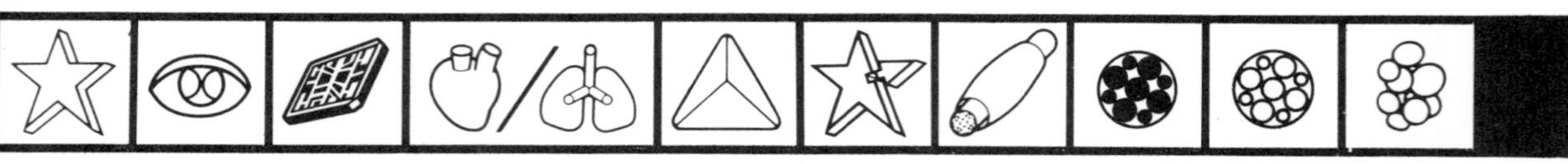

WINDSURFING

Windsurfing is the fastest growing water sport in the world. Though there are a number of competitive variations—from standard triangular-course racing to judged freestyle competition—the most dynamic, thrilling, and demanding form takes place, either competitively or for sheer fun, in high winds and big surf. It is that form with which we will deal primarily.

Since the sport is so new, and since so many people are coming into it fairly well along in their athletic careers, windsurfing has become a sportstalent testing ground, allowing people to assess for themselves, without previously established criteria, how steep their athletic learning curves really are (that is, how quickly they learn new motor skills), and how appropriate their abilities and body components are to the sport. In that sense it is unique among the sports treated in this book.

THE CONTROL SYSTEM IN WINDSURFING

Reception

During the performance of all sports the Control System scans the STSS for raw sensory information supplied by the eyes, the ears, and the limbs, and selects what it believes to be the appro-

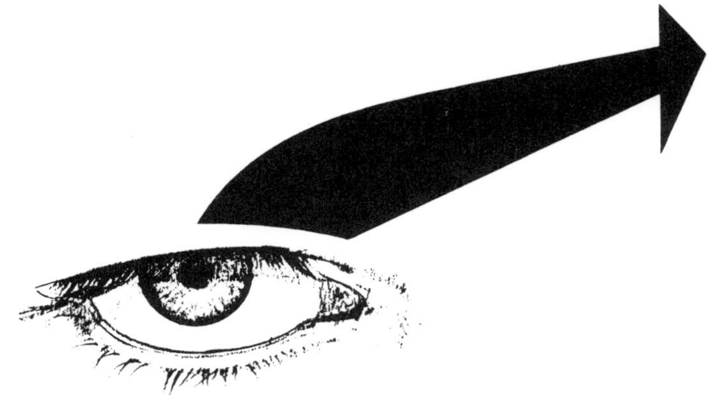

A windsurfer must constantly employ visual dynamic acuity.

priate data. In most sports we are conscious of this process—conscious, for example, of the Control System scanning for the sound of the start gun in sprinting, or for the sight of a rider breaking away in cycling. Pure reaction-time response to raw pieces of information supplied by the eyes, ears, and limbs is common to many sports, but a more complex type of response by the Control System is demanded by windsurfing.

While a ball in tennis or baseball is of a predictable size and shape and approaches a player at a predictable speed, the size and speed of waves are constantly changing and a windsurfer in heavy surf can predict when a wave will arrive under him and what shape that wave will have when it does arrive (building, breaking, or broken) only by a very sophisticated form of Control System integration. The windsurfer attains this integration by using his dynamic visual acuity to scan the sail, the board, and the waves, locating and tracking them relative to his position. The effectiveness of the integration depends, first of all, on how well the windsurfer's dynamic visual acuity works—on the number and accuracy of the readings it can take on wave speed, shape, and height—and, second, on how much information on waves he already has stored in his memory, with which he can compare those readings.

A windsurfer's ears become very important when he is riding down the face of a wave, enabling him to determine where the wave is breaking behind him and how fast the crest is closing. Like the gymnast and high diver, a windsurfer in heavy surf is often in body positions other than vertical, and occasionally will find himself upside down. In these circumstances the balance information provided by the inner ear to the cerebellum is highly integrated to provide an orienting frame of reference for

the head. Three-dimensional spatial orientation for the body is provided by positional information coming from the limbs and, again, integrated by the Control System, and this information allows the brain to know where each part of the body is, even though the body might be upside down.

Abilities, Motor Learning, and Motor Programs

A given motor program consists of as many as hundreds of separate skills linked together. Most basic skills are learned early in childhood, and most motor programs employ different combinations of those skills. Thus it can come as a real shock to a reasonably athletic adult to stumble onto a sport for which he doesn't possess even the most basic building-block skills—as is often the case with windsurfing. Although underlying abilities important to the sport may be present in an individual (such as agility, balance, multilimb coordination, and postural discrimination), even an experienced Alpine skier will likely find it difficult to remain standing upright on a tippy six-foot-long jump board the first time out. Like all such programs, the motor program for windsurfing is finally put together by linking increasing numbers of skills, starting with the most basic, such as standing on the board, uphauling a sail, and sheeting in, and progressing to skills as specialized and difficult to master as the duck-jibe, water start, and wave jumping.

Since very few of these skills are familiar to most people, a considerable amount of attention is demanded to build effective motor programs for windsurfing. For a beginner it is difficult, and sometimes impossible, to link more than two or three of the new skills together; and yet windsurfing in high surf demands long strings of many skills, so thoroughly practiced that they are completely automatic and the Control System's attentive function can therefore shift to overall planning and survival.

Motor programs.

Windsurfing is perhaps the best testing ground there is for adult motor-learning abilities. Because it is generally recognized that motor learning in the sport proceeds in steep jumps rather than smoothly along a curve, a beginner is often apt to ask "Can I do it?" rather than "How well can I do it?" These steep jumps are likely to include: successfully uphauling the sail and sheeting in on flat water; coming about; jibing; high-speed jibes; linked turns; and wave jumping. Although these skills are unfamiliar to most people, one *can* learn them and string them together, and no jump between any two of them is any more difficult or demanding than the jump between, say, the stem christie and the parallel turns in Alpine skiing.

THE HEART-LUNG PACKAGE IN WINDSURFING

Though the beginner might be winded occasionally from pulling and hauling the equipment or from swimming to catch the board, windsurfing itself makes very few strenuous demands on the heart or the lungs, and none that could be considered limiting to a healthy individual at any level of the sport. On the highest levels it is possible to sustain some aerobic activity by surfing, or turning and jumping continuously through a shore break, but that activity is very mild compared with what is required in cycling or cross-country skiing. The demands made on the heart and lungs in windsurfing are mostly anaerobic ones, created by oxygen debt in strenuously and quickly exercised muscles.

BODY COMPOSITION IN WINDSURFING

Somatotype and Skeleton

The windsurfer is typically mesomorphic, with varying degrees of ectomorphy, or leanness. Like slalom ski racers, windsurfers are well served by being short and light. In fact, for the 1984 Olympic triangle races, a body-weight limit of 140 pounds has been set because a standard-size board is being used in those races and its hydrodynamics would be badly affected by any greater weight. However, because boards and sails can be customized for any height or weight, body size and proportion do not rule anyone out of the sport.

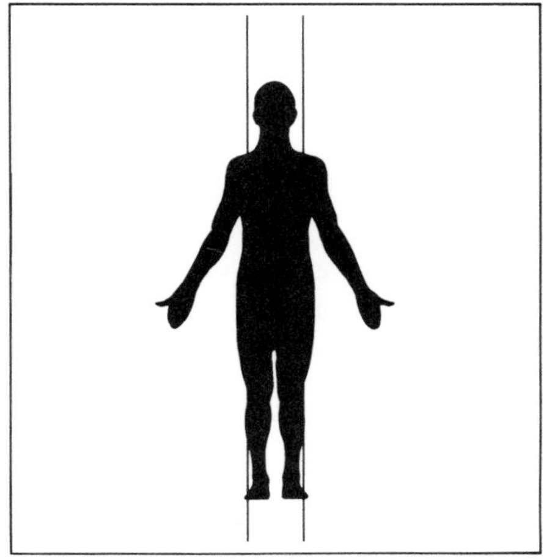

Windsurfer: a knock-kneed mesomorph with a low center of gravity.

Certain body proportions are important in windsurfing, however, particularly those that lower the body's center of gravity.

Legs that are short in relation to trunk length—and small stature overall—are real advantages. Long arms are a help because of the leverage they provide on the boom, and because of the reach required for fast jibes, water starts, and uphauling the sail. A windsurfer is also helped, as is an Alpine skier, by being slightly knock-kneed, so that foot pressure can be applied to the board more quickly in order to carve turns.

Muscle

A more or less even mixture of sprint and endurance muscle fiber types is ideal for overall enjoyment of windsurfing, allowing both for quick, powerful turns and for the long, static holds of straight-line sailing. The big-surf windsurfer is best served by a higher percentage of sprint fiber—up to 80 percent in the thighs—for the split-second turns and jumping required by this variation of the sport.

Many non-windsurfers think the sport requires a lot of upper-body muscular strength, but once a basic finesse has been achieved, it really doesn't. Though in moderate to heavy winds the older boards and rigs could overpower an individual, the newer, lighter boards and wind-specific customized sails require far more finesse and technique than strength to handle them well; and the new techniques of both water and beach starts have obviated any need to haul large, heavy rigs out of the water. While the sport does not demand any unusual muscular force, the wrists, biceps, and lower back of a windsurfer should be well conditioned to prevent soreness from overuse.

Fat

A recreational windsurfer's percentage of body fat is not particularly important, so long as whatever fat there is doesn't restrict agility and range of motion. However, since lightness is a real advantage in this sport, windsurfers on the competitive level tend to have very low percentages of body fat.

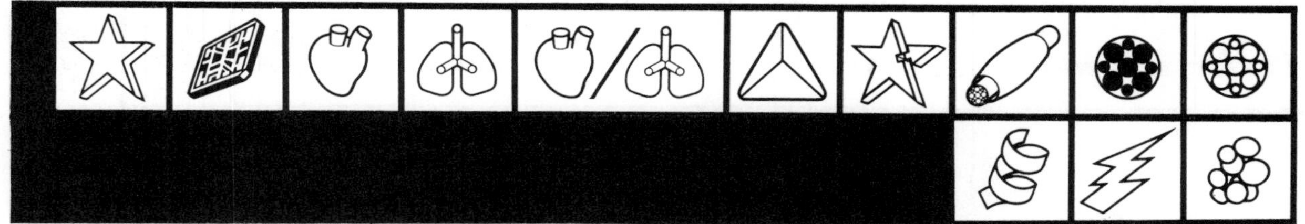

RUNNING

Running is the most regularly practiced of the aerobic sports. This is true despite the fact that many of the hundreds of thousands of people who practice it are not physically well suited to do so; and it is true *because* running has the lowest barrier to entry of all the aerobic sports. Almost anyone can run—anyone with a pair of sneakers who can put one foot in front of another—but the sport actually encompasses a spectrum of physical activities, from jogging very short distances at very low speeds to running under-five-minute miles over the course of a marathon or farther. Most people who run recreationally jog at slow-to-medium speeds over intermediate distances. For many this type of running is not the one best suited to them, and for some it is actually a counterproductive form of exercise. Whether they are engaging in the sport recreationally for general health and fitness, or are racing competitively, or are in training for another sport, runners should be aware of the specific physical capacities they have and then choose the particular type of running that will make the best use of those capacities.

THE CONTROL SYSTEM IN RUNNING

Reception and Motor Programs

In running, the Control System performs primarily a monitoring function, as opposed to the readying and initiating of different motor programs required of it by most other sports. When a person is jogging, the Control System has little to do but casually monitor the external environment: the eyes watch out for dogs and potholes, and notice flowers; the ears listen for traffic or bird song. As the jogger picks up speed, the Control System begins to focus on internal monitoring—directing attention to a tightening hamstring, a cramp in the calf, a burning thigh muscle, shortness of breath, or falling blood sugar—in order to solve small problems in the body before they become big ones, and to sustain a steady pace. In well-trained competitive runners this internal monitoring is so sophisticated that they can actually compute how fast they are going (to within less than a second per quarter mile) from the information provided by the Control System on the length and rate of their stride.

There is really only one motor program for running at speeds from six and a half to four and a half minutes per mile (the speeds that define running, as opposed to jogging or sprinting), and it is even more difficult for runners to modify this program—by changing their stride rate and length at a given speed—than it is for tennis players to modify their basic ground strokes, which means that an individual is pretty much stuck with his or her running style. That style, whatever it is, is a function of an individual's physical components and how well trained those components are.

Running speed is a function of stride rate and stride length.

THE HEART-LUNG PACKAGE IN RUNNING

The Heart

Clarence DeMar ("Mr. Marathon"), seven-time winner of the Boston Marathon, had the largest healthy heart ever examined at autopsy, with coronary arteries nearly three times larger than average. This enormous heart was the result of years of volume overload produced by running. More than any sport except cross-country skiing and crew, distance running distends, or pre-loads, the heart by stretching its main pumping chamber prior to contraction. This pre-loading is effected by the accessory pumping action of leg and respiratory muscles, which return to the heart a blood volume that is, in a trained runner, 30 percent larger than normal. When a pre-loaded heart contracts, it expels as much as two and a half times more blood than a normal heart, both because it was pre-stretched before contraction and because the expulsion of blood into the arteries and muscles after contraction meets less resistance in the trained runner than it does in a normal person. This chronic volume-overloading of the heart, which is common to runners, leads to enlargement of the heart's main pumping chamber and therefore to the overall size of the organ, but not to an increase in its muscle thickness. And this volume-enlarged heart, with large pre-load and lowered after-load, is a more efficient, healthier heart, capable of more work for fewer contractions, or beats, than a smaller heart. It should be said again that heart size, and thus ultimate endurance capacity, is not totally a function of training: some people are born with larger hearts than others and, everything else being equal, those people will make the great distance runners.

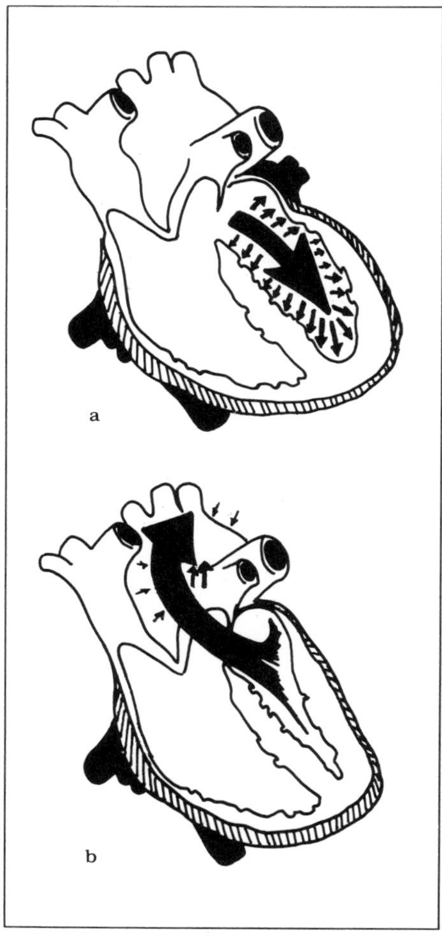

Running: a. high preload; b. low afterload.

The Lungs

Lung volumes for particular body sizes are larger among competitive distance runners than among any other group of athletes. Top distance runners develop reduced resistance to expiration and great endurance in their respiratory muscles, allowing them to exchange large volumes of air, as much as 207 liters per minute acutely, or 120 liters per minute over a long period of time (for example a 10,000-meter race). Such runners

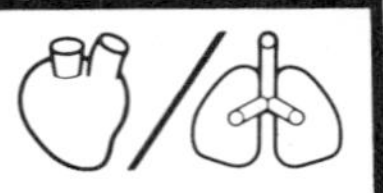

are also able to diffuse gases more quickly within their lungs, thus increasing the effectiveness of oxygen transport in the blood and CO_2 unloading.

Heart-Lung Power

The unusually large heart-lung machine for a given body size found in many runners is a result of both genetic endowment and good training. One would expect such a machine to be capable of consuming large amounts of oxygen, and in fact top runners all have a very high VO_2 Max. Steve Prefontaine, an American 5,000-meter record holder, had a maximum oxygen consumption rate of 84.4 milliliters per kilogram, rivaling that of the best cross-country ski racers and oarsmen. VO_2 Max alone, however, cannot be used to predict winners in middle- or long-distance races; what is functionally more important to a distance runner is the percentage of VO_2 Max available to him without his having to cross his anaerobic threshold and begin producing intolerable amounts of lactic acid. As an example, Steve Prefontaine, with a VO_2 Max of 84.4, and Frank Shorter, with 72.4, each ran a three-mile racecourse in twelve minutes and fifty-two seconds. Their time was the same despite Prefontaine's greater VO_2 Max because Shorter was able to tap a higher *percentage* of his VO_2 Max before reaching his anaerobic threshold.

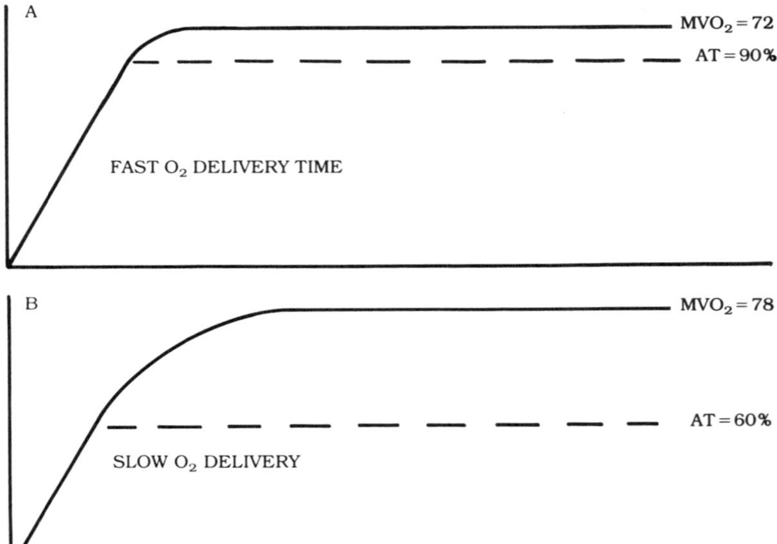

Runner A has a VO_2 Max of only 72 ml/kg but can use 90% of it for middle- and long-distance races and both quickly delivers oxygen and recovers from O_2 debt.

Runner B has a higher VO_2 Max at 78 ml/kg than Runner A but can only use 60% of it in middle- and long-distance events; Runner B builds more oxygen debt due to slow delivery time and recovers more slowly from this debt. With better training Runner B could beat Runner A; the potential is there but undeveloped.

The speed of oxygen delivery is important to a runner mostly at the start of a race, and the faster the oxygen is delivered to him there, the smaller the oxygen debt he will incur. Speed of oxygen delivery can be trained in an individual, but regardless of how fast it is, it is increased by a quick, hard start—which is why so many middle-distance racers begin at a fast pace. The speed of recovery in a runner is also affected by training, and by the intensity of the exercise he is performing. Bill Rodgers, who is famous for his hill running, is able to pick up his pace *before* reaching the crest of a hill because his recovery on the backside is so rapid. Rodgers was one of the first runners to realize that lactic acid is best burned off by running at speeds at or just below the anaerobic threshold, rather than far below it, and thus he maintains a fast pace down the backsides of hills, pulling ahead of many runners who believe that slowing down is the only way to get rid of their lactic acid.

BODY COMPOSITION IN RUNNING

Somatotype and Skeleton

Runners in New York's Central Park on a spring Sunday appear to come in all imaginable sizes and shapes, but as running becomes increasingly specialized into competitive disciplines, such as sprinting and marathoning, the necessary criteria of body shapes and sizes for good performance narrow considerably.

Pure sprinters are mesomorphic, with heavily muscled upper bodies that drive them forward for the first twenty-five meters of a race until they are upright. Also characteristic of this type of runner are a narrow, forward-tilted pelvis for optimum leverage and tracking; a long, springy Achilles tendon; a small calf and foot for a low swing-weight below the knee; a large quadriceps for driving the knee forward; and a very high percentage of sprint muscle fiber in the legs.

Compared with sprinters, distance runners are considerably less muscular, and are leaner, although—contrary to what used to be thought desirable—not necessarily any shorter. While the average height among world-class marathoners is a relatively tall five feet ten inches, they all carry as little weight as possible for their height in order to maximize the power output of their

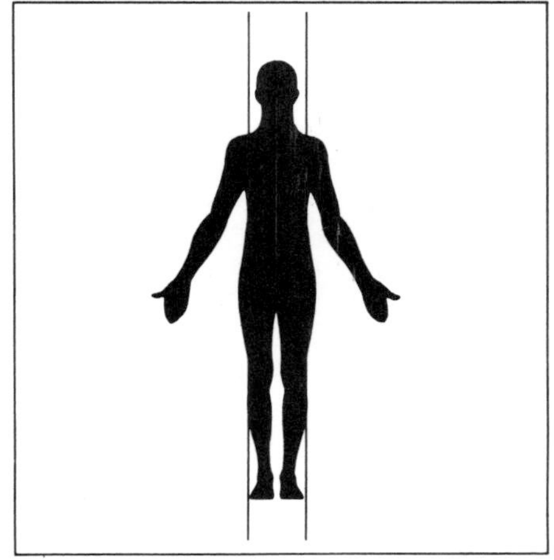

Runner: ectomorph, high center of gravity, low body weight for height.

heart-lung machines. In fact, it is axiomatic that an aspirant world-class marathoner cannot weigh more than two pounds per inch of body height. Unlike the sprinter, the distance runner will likely have an underdeveloped upper body (for lower wind resistance), with undersized upper arms as the most distinguishing anatomical characteristic. (Since the arms are not used for drive but only for balance in distance running, more than the minimum weight there would only give the heart-lung machine extra weight to pull.) Other physical characteristics distinguishing the distance runner from the sprinter are a slightly wider (though still narrow) pelvis, longer legs, and a shorter trunk.

Muscle

More than by overall body size or the proportions of individual parts, a runner's abilities are determined by the fiber composition and elasticity of the muscles.

The more elastic a muscle is, the more kinetic energy it can store, and therefore the more powerfully explosive are its contractions. This principle is particularly important for sprinters, much of whose speed is a result of the ability of the long, springy Achilles tendon to store kinetic energy while being prestretched, and then to add that energy to the contractions of the calf muscles. Elasticity is almost equally important to distance runners in that it allows them to transfer kinetic energy from step to step, keeping their momentum going.

A runner's muscle fiber type determines the distances he can run, his speed over those distances, and the strategies he will do well to employ in different races. The true sprinter has as much as 90 percent sprint muscle fiber in his legs, and this fiber gives him explosiveness out of the blocks, power to accelerate, and sustained short-term speed. Middle-distance runners have a more even mix of endurance and sprint muscle fiber types, giving them some sustained speed over distances, but also a marked ability to accelerate. The pure long-distance runner will have as much as 98 percent endurance muscle fiber, enabling him to run for very prolonged periods of time, if at slower speeds than either the sprinter or the miler.

A distance runner with 98 percent endurance fiber will have very little kick at the end of the race and, like Bill Rodgers, must make his move for the lead miles before the finish. A distance runner with, say, 70 percent endurance fiber and 30 percent sprint fiber will have substantial kick ability at the end of a race,

but may be unable to stay with a runner like Rodgers long enough to use it. Muscle fiber type is so completely a limiting factor at the ends of the combination spectrums that runners with 90 percent sprint fiber may not in fact be able to run marathons at all, while those with 90 percent endurance fiber will have none of the acceleration and speed necessary for even the lowest level of sprinting competition. These limitations to running imposed by muscle fiber type are important for recreational runners to keep in mind: if they have a high percentage of sprint muscle fiber, they shouldn't waste their time jogging, because it's an exercise they will always do poorly at, and one that will require few, if any, of their real athletic abilities.

The amount of fuel stored in the muscles at any one time absolutely restricts the speed at which an individual can run continuously. A highly trained endurance runner can store two and a half times the normal amount of glycogen in the muscles, and since even that is depleted by races and training, the time necessary for repletion is crucial to a runner. This time can vary from a low of about seventy-two hours for a world-class marathoner to a week for the casual runner.

Fat

Though the percentage of body fat is less important to the sprinter than to the endurance runner, neither wants to haul much fat, and while world-class endurance runners perform best when they carry under 6 percent fat, women are advised to carry about 11 percent.

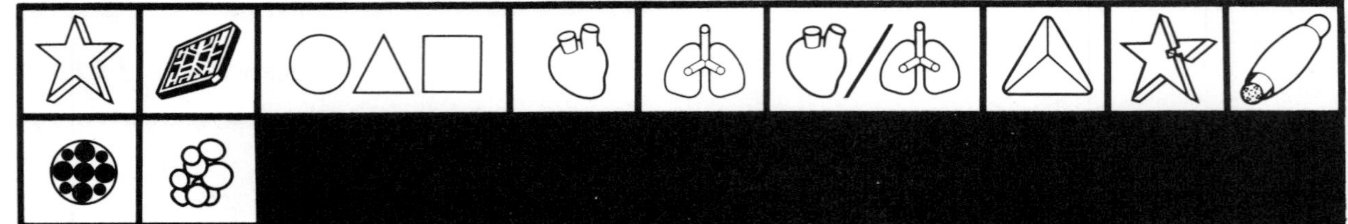

SWIMMING

Swimming for pleasure and exercise is an activity in which virtually everyone can participate. Because in this sport there is no impact between parts of the body and a hard surface, because the work of swimming is distributed among all the major muscle groups, and because of the body's natural buoyancy in the water, the fun and good exercise of swimming can be enjoyed, under a physician's guidance, by many people who cannot participate in other sports: the very old, obese and crippled people, and people with severe orthopedic and arthritic problems. Swimming can also provide continued aerobic training for athletes injured in other sports; even with a broken limb, the runner, skier, or cyclist can continue to get aerobic workouts in a pool.

Unlike such sports as cross-country skiing in which good technique is required to get much exercise, effective workouts can be had in swimming at every level of ability, and in fact a beginner or a swimmer with poor strokes will expend up to five times as much energy as an expert if the two are swimming side by side at the same speed. One of the things that tells us is that swimming improves according to the ability of the swimmer to get the maximum propulsion from, and the minimum resistance to, a given expenditure of work. While the inexperienced swimmer wallows from side to side in the water, losing much if not all momentum by hesitating between strokes and

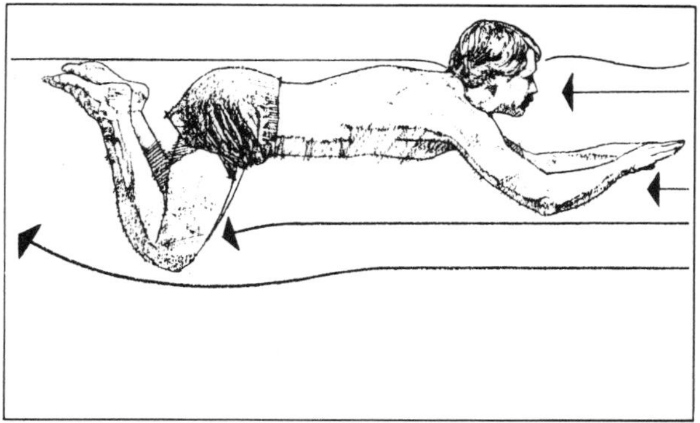

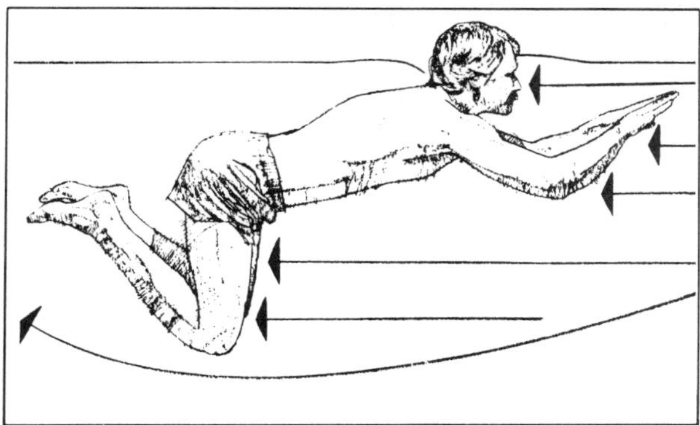

Left: good hydrodynamic position, low drag; right: poor hydrodynamic position, high drag.

generally creating a lot of water resistance, the expert or competitive swimmer will maintain, with less work, a fast, smooth pace through the water with an even hydrodynamic application of power.

Though it is true that practically everyone can swim for pleasure and exercise, very few people swim well—not, usually, because of any physical restrictions, but because of an incomplete understanding of how the body performs at the sport and because of a lack of feel for the water.

THE CONTROL SYSTEM IN SWIMMING

Reception

To move efficiently, a swimmer must have a constant supply of sensory information on his or her stroke-by-stroke performance in the water. This information is supplied by the receptor components of the Control System, feeding data into the Short-Term Sensory Store—data on the swimmer's speed, force, evenness of propulsion through the water, correctness of form, and the amount of water resistance. Their eyes tell swimmers how straight a line they are swimming, the condition of the water, and where they are in relation to landmarks or other swimmers, but cannot tell them anything about their technique. The gyroscopic function of the inner ears, when integrated with other sensory information in the cerebellum, provides swimmers with

James "Doc" Counsilman was the first U.S. coach to bridge the gap between science and sport. His scientific basis for swimming technique not only grounded coaching on a purely objective level but also produced years of world championship U.S. teams and America's top medal winner of all time, Mark Spitz. Counsilman coached the U.S. Olympic and Indiana Swim Teams for almost two decades.

a sense of direction and a reference to how straight a line they are swimming, particularly in the open ocean. The limb receptors supply information on propulsion and speed, and, to a lesser extent, on technique. Expert competitive swimmers can tell from the force of their muscular contractions, the stresses across their body joints created by those contractions, and the amount of water resistance encountered by their hands and feet during propulsion how fast they are swimming to within a tenth of a second in a 100-meter race—a knowledge of results almost as accurate as that provided by a stopwatch.

Though the information on speed and propulsion supplied to the Control System by the limb receptors is phenomenally precise, the information they transmit on technique, particularly on its underwater phases, is often inaccurate. Because the receptors are less at home in water than in air, and because while one is swimming there can be no visual reinforcement of their readings, the receptors cannot make such extremely precise determinations as to where the limbs are that they are able to make in skiing, for example, or in tennis, and therefore are able to pass along to the Control System only general and inexact assessments of technique.

Abilities and Motor Learning

Because there are great natural swimmers who, untaught (or with improper coaching), develop strokes that are both fluid and mechanically correct, we can infer the existence of certain basic motor abilities that underlie the sport. Although swimming is not a high-skill activity in the sense of requiring great precision of movement and lightning-quick reaction times, swimmers are well served in the development of their strokes by such inherent motor abilities as multilimb coordination and gross body coordination. No one ability or combination of abilities, however, can yet be identified as necessarily producing good strokes, which are the most important skills in swimming. Potentially good competitors, therefore, can better be identified by an assessment of their strokes than by an evaluation of their motor abilities.

Motor learning in swimming is defined by James ("Doc") Counsilman, the great Indiana University coach, as "a change in movement patterns due to reinforced practice"—that is, the correct trace for a given stroke, stored in the Long-Term Memory, is reinforced with an improving image of correctness. In swimming, good coaching is the best method of improving this image of correctness and, therefore, of improving stroke mechanics.

For coaching to be effective in any sport, it should take place in nurturing surroundings—in an environment without excessive anxiety and one that engenders enthusiasm and the desire to learn. Within such a situation there are two methods by which a swimming coach can impart to student athletes an image of correctness: by describing the sensations that the coach thinks should be felt by the students during the correct execution of a particular stroke; and by describing the technical details of proper stroke mechanics. In coaching the breaststroke, for example, a former champion breaststroker–turned–coach might have little or no technical knowledge of stroke mechanics and might teach simply by verbalizing what the components of the stroke should feel like when done the way he used to do them. This coach's effectiveness is a direct result of his ability to make his athletes understand him, and it is likely that some, even most, won't—particularly those without much natural ability. A purely technical "blackboard" coach, on the other hand, might teach the breaststroke in terms of its angles of entry, phasings, and muscular-activation sequences; and while this method of coaching potentially provides the clearest picture of what should be done, it, too, may be poorly understood by certain athletes (particularly younger ones and those with non-technical minds), even when it is done very well. Efforts along both of these lines have been successful, since swimmers of different intellectual and physical maturities respond variously to different kinds of coaching. The important thing is not how it is done, but that somehow the image of correctness be effectively transmitted by the coach to the student athletes, establishing a gauge against which the students can measure their developing knowledge of performance.

During the process of motor learning in any sport, control of the muscles progresses from a cognitive level to a subconscious, more automatic level. This progression is of particular importance in swimming, since during the early, cognitive phase of learning swimmers are likely to be extremely ungainly, as the medium is new to them. They will likely exert considerable muscular force, unnecessary to a direct line of propulsion, and fail to relax antagonistic muscle groups, thereby creating excessive tension in those muscles. Doc Counsilman has said, "No one can think out a precise movement in swimming"; but as movements become more automatic, progressing to the subcon-

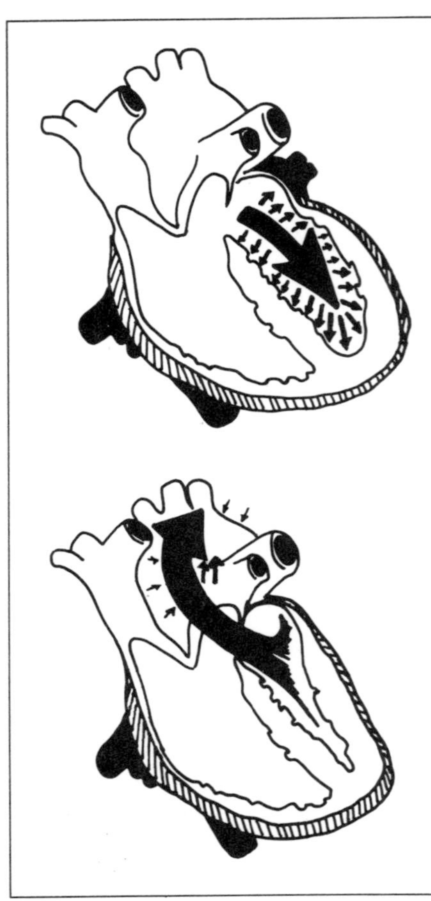

Swimming: high preload, low afterload.

scious level of performance, they become faster, more precise, and less tense.

Motor learning in swimming is unusual in that there is little positive transfer from learning the components of a stroke separately—the backstroke, for example, cannot be effectively learned by working out the sequence, phasing, and force of the arm stroke. After forming some image of correctness (by watching other swimmers, as a result of coaching, mental visualization, reading, and so on), beginning swimmers will learn a stroke better and faster by getting in the water and trying it than by breaking the stroke down and practicing its parts.

Motor Programs

There is a separate motor program for each of the strokes in swimming, and since the sequence, phasing, and force of any stroke is fixed throughout a range of speeds, it is important that beginning swimmers learn each stroke correctly at the outset, thereby forming for it a correct motor program that will continue to be of use as they improve at the stroke. Once formed, a faulty motor program is very hard to correct, and it will plague a swimmer's attempts to improve.

Attention, Anticipation, and Arousal

Selective attention is employed in swimming primarily to navigate and to gauge speed; in competitive swimming it also monitors muscle fatigue and air hunger as well, and returns control to the cognitive level whenever a swimmer needs to make a turn in a race. Anticipation is also important in turns: a racer can shave fractions of seconds off his time by initiating flip-turns at exactly the right moments. It is important as well at the start-gun beginning of a race.

There is much pain involved in competitive swimming, and many hours must be spent in a pool in preparation. Considerable arousal, therefore, is necessary if a swimmer is to train and compete successfully over a period of time, and traditionally, in the United States and elsewhere, adolescents have been best able to meet the severely taxing and asocial demands of competitive swimming and to bring to those demands enough consistent arousal to perform well.

THE HEART-LUNG PACKAGE IN SWIMMING

The Heart

The first noticeable change to occur in an adolescent heart trained by swimming is the permanent dilation of its pumping chamber. The large amounts of blood continuously directed back into the heart by the accessory pumping action of the lungs and the many muscle groups that are active in swimming cause this dilation. After the first year or so of heavy training, an adolescent's heart will increase in overall size as well and—unlike most muscular growth, which disappears when the muscles are no longer being exercised regularly—such heart enlargement has been found to persist in some swimmers for decades after they become sedentary.

A competitive swimmer's heart has to be large in order to deliver the huge volume of blood required by many muscles working at the same time; and in order to deliver this blood efficiently, not only must the heart have a high pre-loading capacity, but its pumping effort must be met with little resistance in the aorta. Because of the amount and type of work done by the heart in swimming—and because of the many, many hours that even the youngest competitors must give to training for the sport—swimmers tend to develop very large hearts, and to develop them early. Some fifteen-year-olds, in fact, have hearts as large as those of top adult marathon runners.

The Lungs

An adolescent beginning competitive swimming who is not genetically endowed with large lungs is very likely to be made quickly uncomfortable by the restriction on breathing rate and time for inhalation imposed by the sport. For this reason, swimmers are naturally selected for their large lung capacity, an absolute requirement in the sport. This is true not only because of the limitations on breathing imposed by submersion in water, and the high oxygen demand and strict necessity to blow off CO_2, but also because the lungs provide important flotation to the swimmer, and the larger they are the more buoyancy they give. Breathing while swimming is more difficult than breathing on land because there is less time to inhale, because an unnatural breathing rhythm is imposed by the stroke rate, and

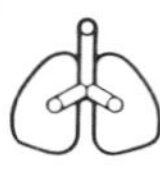

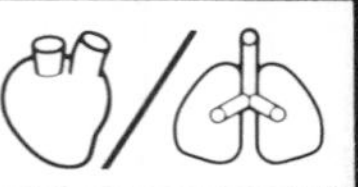

because water compresses the lungs, robbing them of their full expansion capacity. To overcome these difficulties, a well-trained swimmer will breathe more deeply at a slow stroke rate and less deeply as the stroke rate quickens, and will exhale more fully than normal after each breath.

Compression of lung in water (left) compared to normal size (right).

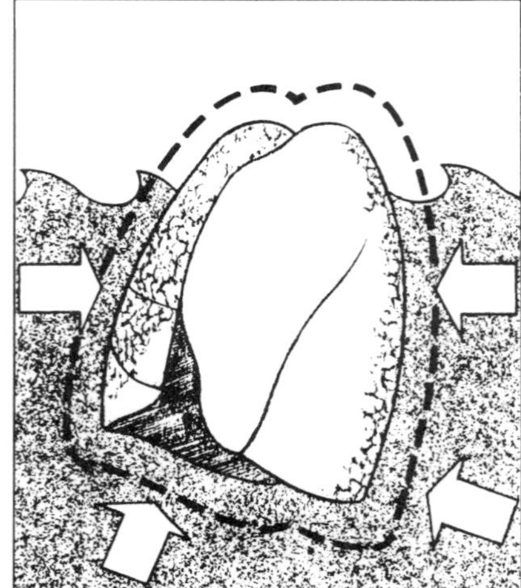

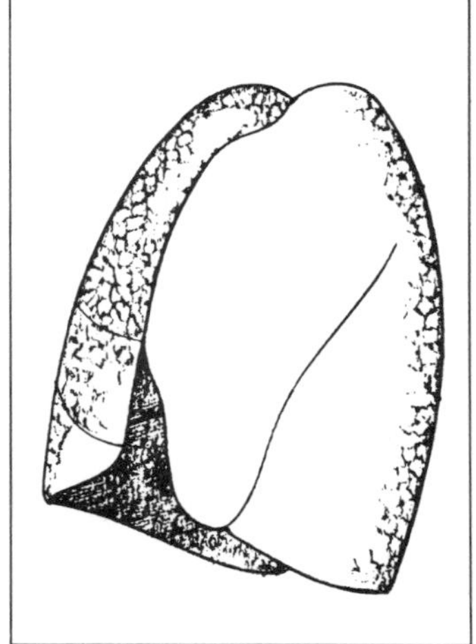

Heart-Lung Power

Given the number of muscle groups used in swimming and the large heart-lung capacity characteristic of top competitors, one would expect a swimmer's oxygen-consumption level to be similar to that of a cross-country skier or oarsman, but it is much lower—even lower than a runner's. This is probably true because in a number of strokes, including the crawl, the large muscles of the upper legs perform relatively little work. Though oxygen-consumption levels in swimming are not as high as they are in a few other sports, they are higher than those found in most, and it is a demonstrated fact that the better the swimmer, the higher the maximum oxygen consumption. Oddly, perhaps, the highest maximum oxygen consumptions found in the sport today are about the same as the highest of twenty years ago, though racing times in all of the strokes and events have dropped dramatically since then. Swimmers have bettered their times not by developing more aerobic power but by swimming with more efficient hydrodynamic technique and with more anaerobic power.

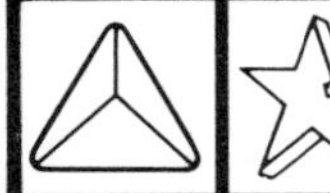

As soon as a swimmer reaches the speed of one meter per second and sustains that speed for a couple of minutes, that individual is swimming at the maximum oxygen consumption level; any further increase of speed will come from anaerobic exertion and will produce substantial lactic acid in the muscles and an oxygen debt potentially larger than the swimmer's oxygen consumption. The faster the rate of oxygen delivery, the less lactic acid is built up in the muscles at a given speed, and swimmers can increase their speed of oxygen delivery through training. They can further minimize the damaging effect of lactic acid on performance by pacing themselves and accelerating throughout a race, so that the level of lactic acid builds with their speed up to the finish. In any race of more than seven minutes' duration a swimmer is forced to swim at a pace that does not build lactic acid, and therefore, by definition, at a pace at or below the anaerobic threshold. Proper pacing is critical to competitive swimming not only to control lactic-acid buildup but because any time speed doubles in water, the resistance to that speed quadruples, and the oxygen cost of producing it is multiplied eight times. Swimmers, therefore, must be very careful as to when and how they accelerate.

BODY COMPOSITION IN SWIMMING

Somatotype and Skeleton

On somato charts, swimmers are typically balanced mesomorphs, meaning that they are taller and leaner than the average athlete but with a high degree of muscularity. Even in adolescence, when most competitive swimming begins, swimmers tend to be taller and more muscular than their friends, not because swimming makes them so but because the sport requires those overall bodily characteristics.

The ideal body composition for a swimmer is one that creates the least amount of water resistance for the greatest amount of propulsion. There are two types of water resistance, viscous and turbulent. The viscosity, or thickness, of any medium creates a particular resistance to passage through it, and that resistance in water rises as a swimmer's speed increases up to 2.1 kilometers per hour, at which point the effort to break viscous resis-

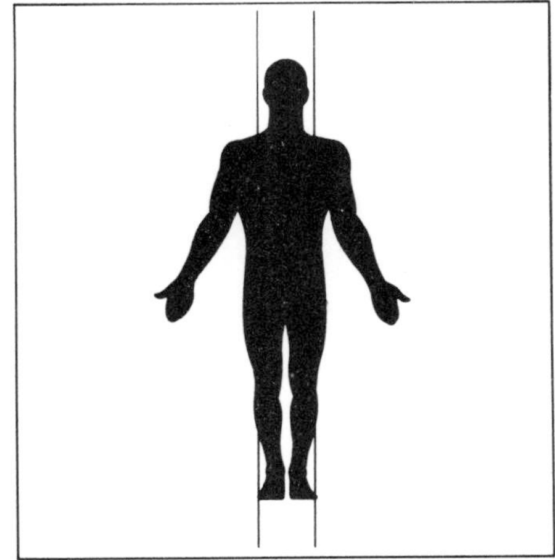

Swimmer: balanced mesomorph.

tance actually brings the swimmer's body partially out of the water in a hydroplane. At 7.2 kilometers per hour, viscous resistance is further broken by the formation of a bow wave at the swimmer's head. Turbulent resistance is created in the water by the suction of small eddies within the turbulent flow that are produced by the act of swimming, particularly by the feet, and this resistance increases with the amount of turbulence a swimmer creates.

One would expect that the more frontal area a swimmer's body presented to the water, the more viscous resistance the individual would encounter, and in fact when two bodies are dragged passively through the water the larger one does meet slightly more resistance. But in actual swimming the amount of viscous resistance encountered by a particular swimmer is less a function of size than it is of how high the person rides in the water. Women have considerably less drag in the water than men do because they ride higher in it due to less upper-body density of muscle and bone and more fat around their thighs—fat that keeps their legs from sinking as much as men's legs do. This higher ride in the water allows women to expend less energy than men in swimming at the same speeds. It does not, however, allow them to swim faster: men have, on average, a 25 percent higher maximum oxygen consumption than women, and the extra propulsion provided by the bigger muscles of men more than makes up for the higher flotation of women.

The upper body creates most of the speed in swimming, and swimmers tend to have long hands, wide shoulders, deep chests, and long, muscular upper and lower arms. Their waists and hips tend to be hydrodynamically narrow—as do their thighs, where no great muscular strength is necessary. They also tend to have narrow leg bones, which makes their legs relatively light. These bodily proportions, in combination with the overall somato type for swimming, are so crucial to success in the sport that any individual who diverges widely from them should not expect to do particularly well at competitive swimming.

Muscle

Because of the enormous aerobic load borne in swimming by the upper-body musculature—greater than in any other sport—all competitive swimmers average more than 60 percent endurance muscle fiber in their upper bodies. So that more oxygen can be made available more quickly to the muscles, the en-

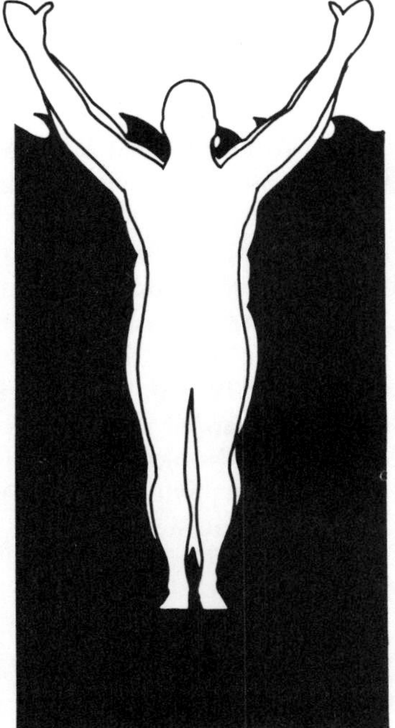

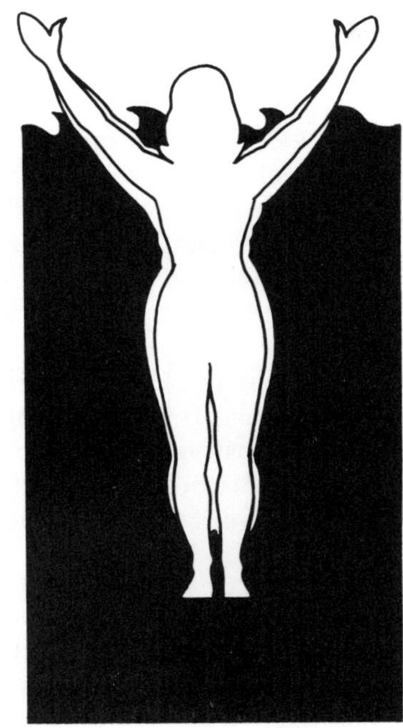

A high percentage of body fat results in increased buoyancy.

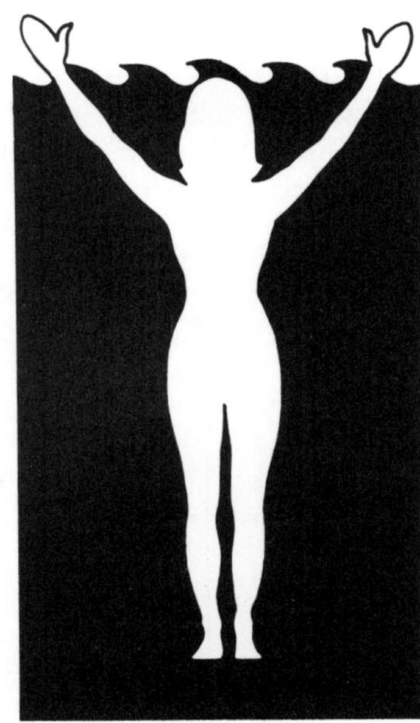

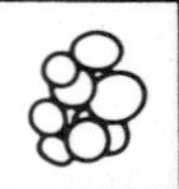

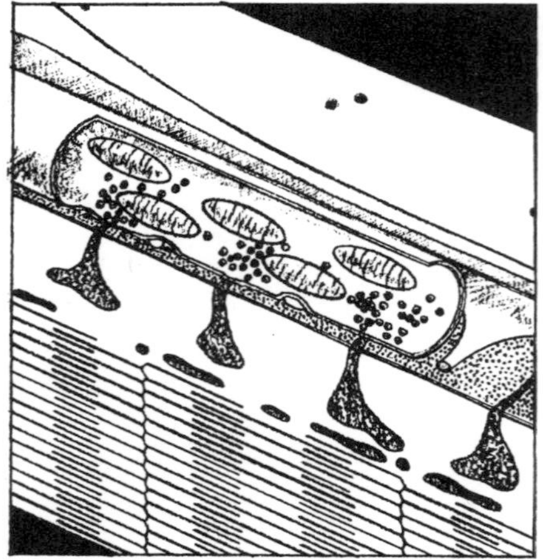

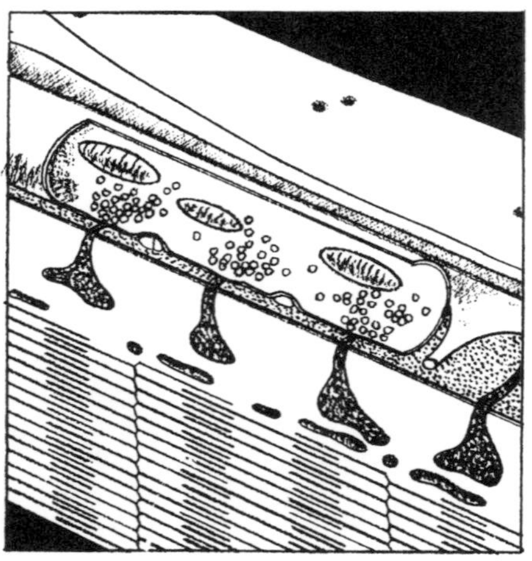

Endurance muscle (top) contains up to 700 mitochondria per cell. Sprint muscle (bottom) has as few as 50 per cell.

durance muscle fibers in swimmers are smaller than normal, are surrounded by a large number of capillaries, and contain very large mitochondria that are densely packed with aerobic enzymes. What sprint fiber there is in a trained swimmer's active body muscles is converted entirely to endurance activity, and is characterized by larger mitochondria and more aerobic enzymes than are found in sprint fibers.

Over the past twenty years, swimmers, particularly women, have become radically stronger, and the increase of anaerobic strength among competitors has made a major contribution to their extraordinary contemporary performances. Anaerobic strength is produced by large-diameter muscles, and swimmers do have larger-than-normal muscles in their upper bodies.

Joint flexibility, or range of motion, in the shoulders and ankles is critical in swimming—so critical that swimmers have more flexibility in those two joints than other athletes.

Fat

It has long been axiomatic that body fat is an advantage to a swimmer in that it increases flotation and thus decreases drag in the water and the amount of effort required for propulsion. In long-distance swimming, such as Channel or ocean swimming, this is unquestionably true: body fat gives more distance for less effort and also provides insulation against the cold. For swimming at the usual 200- to 400-meter competitive distances, however, muscular power compensates for any lack of buoyancy, and any more than a small amount of fat will prove more cumbersome than helpful.

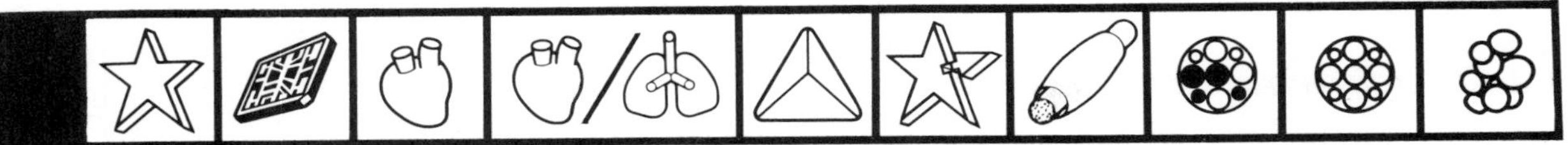

CYCLING

While one out of every three people in the United States owns a bicycle, few Americans have traditionally viewed bicycling as a sport. The Tour de France has for decades been one of the most popular European sporting events, but competitive cycling has taken hold in America only in recent years. It is now one of the fastest-growing of American sports, and part of its rising popularity has to do with the fact that—unlike distance running, which only *appears* to be democratic—cycling is truly a sport for Everyman. While a majority of people might find themselves, for reasons of overweight, sore joints, or inelastic tendons, unsuited to jogging, cycling in its wealth of events and kinder uses of the body can be healthfully and productively practiced by virtually everyone.

Even amid the unprecedented proliferation of exercise machines nowadays, the bicycle remains the ideal machine for the development of endurance, muscle speed and power, and motor agility. The basic geometry of the bicycle was perfected in the late 1890s and has changed very little since then. The evolution of the bicycle in this century has been mechanical in nature, and the development of lighter frames, more sophisticated gearing and parts, and high-pressure, narrow-gauged tires has resulted in important advances in the machine's speed potential. Just as there are many different types of modern bicycles—the upright, stiff, short-wheel-base track cycle; the springy, low-

slung, low-wheel-base touring cycle; the heavy-duty, knobby-tired, BMX off-road bike—there are many human body types and athletic abilities appropriate to maximizing the machines' various performance characteristics, both for racing and for recreational cycling.

THE CONTROL SYSTEM IN CYCLING

Reception

People tend to think of cycling as an all-or-nothing sport—something that either can or cannot be done—and while this is certainly true of *riding* a bicycle, staying balanced and upright on a moving machine is only the beginning of cycling as a sport.

While distance runners can afford to be more or less oblivious of the immediate environment, cyclists must have at all times a clear, three-dimensional, 360-degree picture of their surroundings, and of where their bicycles are and what they are doing within those surroundings. The cyclist's eyes and ears provide this picture. A racer in a pack uses dynamic visual acuity to create an accurate image of what is going on all around by quickly taking different visual readings—ahead, for what is coming up, and to the side and directly in front, for the constraints of the pack or for another bike's tire two inches away. This visual sense becomes critical for breaking out of and away from the pack, when a cyclist, like a race-car driver, must maneuver through and around other machines at high speed.

The three-dimensional picture created by dynamic visual acuity is supplemented by hearing, and this overall picture is perhaps even more important to the bike tourer or commuter than it is to the racer, whose pack environment is skillfully controlled. Tourers and commuters must use their ears to sense phasing differences and changes of pitch in traffic sounds in order to gauge the rate of closure of vehicles behind them. Without ever looking around, an experienced New York City bicycle commuter or messenger can judge, to within inches, the point at which a bus will pass; and such auditory acuity and integration in this environment is often a matter of life or death.

In both recreational and competitive cycling the balance provided by the inner ear serves the crucial and obvious function for the Control System of keeping the cyclist upright. This function becomes more sophisticated as the cyclist becomes more competent, enabling him to turn his head away from the direction in which he is going, and, in the case of the racer, to stay upright even as he bumps handlebars with other racers in a pack or blows a tire going downhill.

Abilities and Motor Learning

The inherent motor abilities required for competitive cycling are possessed by most people, though the motor agility found in the top sprint and criterium cyclists, which allows them to dart in and out of packs and into and through steep banked turns, is as highly developed as that found in any other sport. Learning how to ride a bicycle represents a steep jump in an individual's learning curve—a jump from not being able to do it at all to doing it. Later there can be significant progress along that curve, though it is made in subtler increments. A skillful bike rider is capable of very precise, exacting maneuvers, and cycling on its upper levels of performance requires a demanding set of motor skills. These skills become increasingly automatic as they are practiced, and are second nature to the racer, allowing him to divert his attention to the overall strategy of a particular race.

Americans have traditionally thought of bike racing as altogether an endurance sport, in which the paramount factor is physical performance. In fact, it is extremely intellectual in nature, with particular strategies carried out by employing groups of very precise tactics, which involve sudden accelerations, variously long bursts of speed, and considerable laying back, waiting for opportunities to present themselves. In the amount of strategy it involves, bike racing is very much like race-car driving, and as in that sport, the cyclist is able to determine tactics and to carry out winning strategies only to the degree that he understands the peculiar performance capacities and limitations of his machine's engine—in this case, his own body.

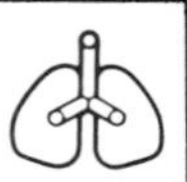

THE HEART-LUNG PACKAGE IN CYCLING

Compared with running or cross-country skiing, cycling is generally underrated as an aerobic sport. The fact is that heart size and lung capacity among top competitive cyclists rival those found among top cross-country skiers and distance runners.

The Heart

As we have seen, heart size is a closely correlated measure of maximum oxygen consumption, and the best cyclists tend to have large hearts. Though heart size can be increased through training, the volume overload on the heart is not so constant or so heavy in cycling as it is in cross-country skiing or crew, and therefore the large hearts found among competitive cyclists would appear to be genetically determined. While it is true that a large heart is a real asset to a cyclist and that cycling *can* be an extremely aerobic sport, only serious competitive and touring cyclists, as a rule, have conditioned their muscles well enough so that their heart size can really affect their cycling, or so that they can realize the true aerobic potential of the sport.

The Lungs

Since much of cycling is not steady-state endurance work, lung performance and capacity is critical. Cycling requires sudden bursts of energy, whether from a racer sprinting away from the pack or from a tourer at the bottom of a steep hill. Among bicycle racers minute-ventilations (the amount of air that can be moved in and out of the lungs in a minute) have been measured as high as 200 liters per minute, an exchange rate equal to that found in cross-country skiing and high-altitude climbing (though in cycling, breathing is not sustained at that level). In cross-country skiing and mountain climbing, numerous muscle groups share a continuous work load, but most of the work in cycling is done with the thigh muscles, resulting in less overall oxygen demand than is found in cross-country skiing, climbing, or crew, but producing enormous localized loads of lactic acid. This lactic-acid buildup in a cyclist's legs must be buffered and blown off in large quantities whenever he sprints; and it can, and often does, build to levels at which the muscles are forced to slow and finally to shut down. A competitive cyclist

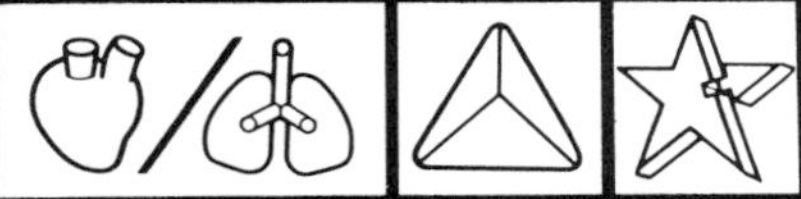

needs lungs as large as his frame will allow and very well trained respiratory muscles in order to perform the strenuous work of blowing off CO_2—work so demanding that it alone can require 10 percent of the body's total oxygen consumption. Fortunately, the position of the upper body in cycling (the forward lean onto the downturned bars) relieves the thorax of the weight of the arms and shoulders, and therefore allows the cyclist to breathe more deeply than can a skier or a runner, thereby effectively increasing whatever lung capacity he has.

Heart-Lung Power

The way an individual's heart-lung machine operates in cycling is closely linked to that individual's particular mix of strength and endurance muscle fibers. The heart-lung machine in a trained cyclist with a high percentage of endurance muscle fiber (such a cyclist is likely to be either a time trialist, a solo breakaway artist, a hill climber, or a long-distance tourer) is capable of delivering the large oxygen supply demanded of it over a long period of time. It is able to do this, first, because endurance fiber demands and uses more oxygen than sprint fiber; and, second, because endurance muscle fiber may be trained to higher anaerobic thresholds than sprint fiber—up to, in fact, 85 percent of an individual's maximum oxygen consumption. Since these anaerobic thresholds are considerably lower for sprint muscle fiber, the heart-lung machine in a cyclist with a high percentage of such fiber (such as the track, pursuit, or criterium sprinter) expends much of its energy in blowing off CO_2 during brief periods of intense exercise. The speed of oxygen delivery and the speed of recovery are equally important to the sprint cyclist and the endurance cyclist.

BODY COMPOSITION IN CYCLING

Somatotype and Skeleton

Like cross-country skiing, competitive and recreational cycling are done at mixed speeds over a variety of terrains, and there are different specific body sizes appropriate to different types of cycling. On somato charts, bicycle racers are seen to be mostly mesomorphic, with increasing muscularity in sprint com-

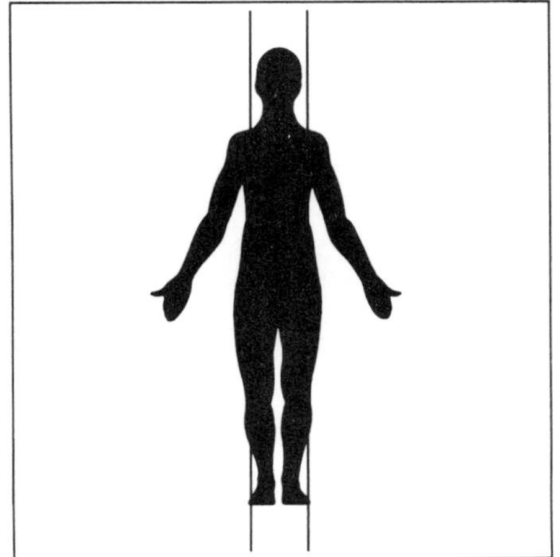

Cyclist: mesomorph; muscularity and leanness in proportion to event.

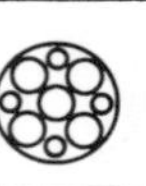

petitors, and less muscularity and more leanness (ectomorphy) in distance competitors. Although there is a considerable range in size between the light, short Colombian hill climber and the tall, muscular pursuit rider, that range comprises the intermediate segment of the size spectrum connecting all athletes from the jockey to the defensive end in football.

In a study conducted during the Montreal Olympics, track, or sprint, cyclists were found to have narrow hips, which, as in running, more directly transmit muscular power to acceleration; and distance cyclists were found to have wider hips, which rotate more and are therefore less efficient for sprinting. Up to 90 percent of a cyclist's energy is expended against wind resistance; it is therefore important to present as small and streamlined a front to the wind as possible for a given body mass, and from wind-tunnel tests we know that the ideal time trialist will have a small waist, narrow shoulders, and a deep but narrow chest (like John Howard's). Top cyclists also tend to have long, thin arms and forearms and long feet. Though one would expect such other physical features as a long back or long thighs to be important, the adjustable geometry of the bicycle compensates.

Muscle

In no other sport is muscle a more precise delimiter of the different categories of participation. One can divide cyclists into commuters, long-distance tourers, road-racing cyclists, time trialists, and track cyclists; the type of cyclist one is, is determined to a large degree (except in the case of the commuter) by the kind of muscles one has.

The track cyclist is a sprinter, and he must have considerable power and the ability to accelerate quickly. His muscles, therefore, will ideally contain a high percentage of sprint fiber, as much as 90 percent. For acceleration he needs large-diameter muscles in his legs, and Force-Speed Curves in these muscles that permit high power at high speeds. The sprinter also needs the highest pedaling cadence among cyclists (up to 120 RPMs). He can maintain it efficiently because his sprint muscle fiber operates at a lower energy cost at high cadences than does endurance fiber, and because, just like an automobile lugging along in fourth gear, a cyclist pedaling at less than a high cadence is unable to accelerate rapidly. High cadence is important to the sprint cyclist for a third reason as well: The greatest rhythmic power output of the leg muscles in cycling occurs at

	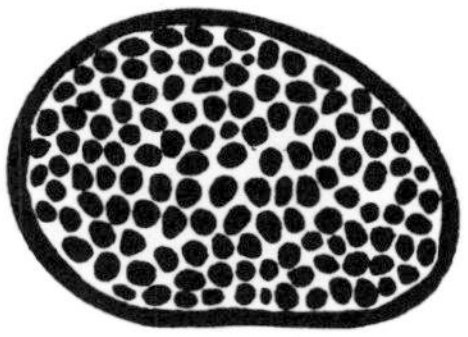	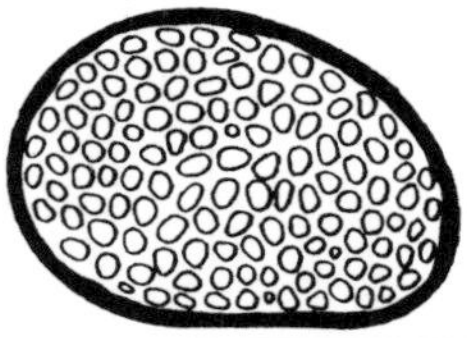
	Endurance	Sprint
Time Trialist	100% endurance	
Road Racer	70% endurance	30% sprint
Criterium	50% endurance	50% sprint
Track Pursuit	30% endurance	70% sprint

30 percent of their maximum contractions, at which point the blood supply to the muscles is compressed and restricted. Pedaling at a high cadence allows restrictions to blood flow to be relieved more often, and so the muscles remain well supplied with oxygen and the cyclist is able to do more work with less feeling of exertion.

The time trialist is the exact muscular opposite of the track rider. Because of the steady, continuous pace of racing from twenty minutes to twenty-four hours, a pace that requires no bursts of acceleration, the time trialist must have the highest possible percentage of endurance fiber, which often approaches 90 percent. He does not need large-diameter muscles, and almost certainly will be less muscular than the track cyclist. His endurance muscle fiber is more efficient at a lower pedaling cadence; and because he is not pedaling with peak muscular force, restrictions to blood flow in his legs are not a problem. Endurance fiber takes a longer time to develop maximum power in a given downstroke of the pedal than sprint fiber does, and the slower pedaling cadence of the time trialist allows this force to develop fully. Because of the extreme oxygen demands made by endurance fiber for performing at its limit, the success-

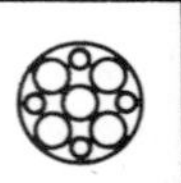

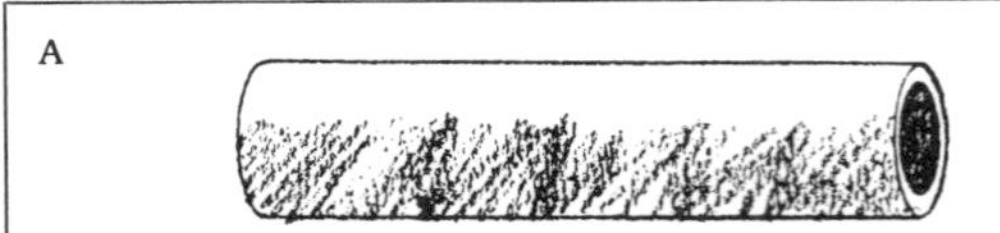

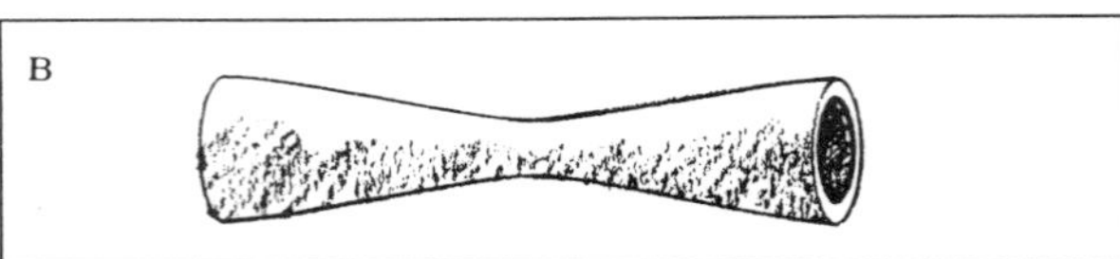

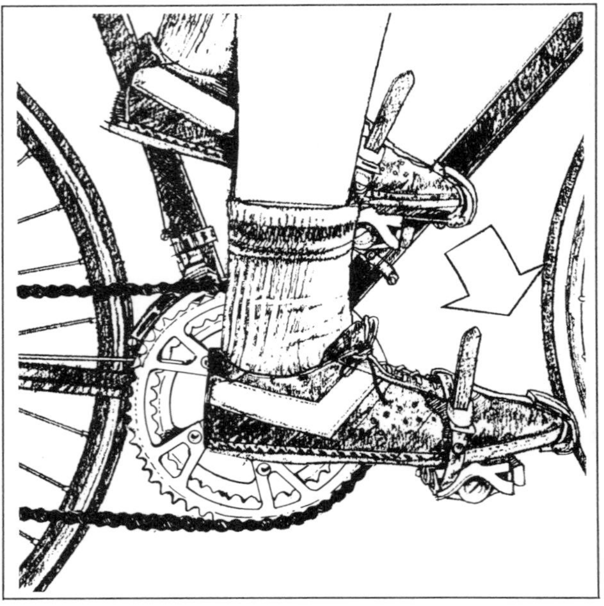

A. A high cadence, e.g., 100 RPM, allows fast return of blood flow and causes less compression of blood vessels coursing through the muscle. B. A low, lugging cadence, e.g., 50 RMP in a high gear causes some compression of blood vessels and delays the flow of blood for longer between pedal strokes.

ful time trialist must have a large heart and lungs, which along with trained endurance muscle fibers can deliver an anaerobic threshold that is very close to his maximum oxygen consumption.

The criterium racer is, by necessity, a mixture of the two extremes, needing as much as possible of the speed and acceleration of the pure sprinter, as well as some of the muscular endurance capacity of the trialist. A criterium course is often square, and typically no longer than a mile. Because racers usually travel the course in packs of up to fifty, there is a constant need in criterium racing for acceleration, both to keep up as the pack accordions out around corners and to break away during sprint laps.

Road racing, in contrast, is usually done on courses that average fifty to a hundred miles over highways and back roads, and in any typical road race there are three identifiable specialists: the sprinter, the hill climber, and the solo breakaway artist. The sprinter in road racing is usually a criterium specialist who doesn't require the high aerobic capacity of the time trialist because he spends much of the race in a pack, pedaling at a low aerobic work load and waiting for an opportunity to sprint. Typically he will have an equal mixture of sprint and endurance fiber. The good hill climber will be small, with a light frame; he will have a very high percentage of endurance muscle fiber in his legs, and a great deal of heart-lung power for his size. The solo breakaway cyclist has the endurance power of the time trialist but without the muscle power and speed of the track rider—his best chance to win a road race is to break away from the pack well before the finish (being careful not to drag along any sprinters in his draft) and to use his aerobic power to maintain his lead.

The long-distance tourer has no practical need for acceleration and, therefore, typically is best served by a high percentage of endurance muscle fiber and a fairly large and muscular frame for powering a relatively heavy bike and, often, forty pounds of gear. The tourer cycles at a moderate cadence and at the highest force for the lowest speed along the Force-Speed Curve. Though tourers are generally not taken seriously as racers, one of them, Lon Haldeman, in 1982 beat America's premier bike racer, John Howard, in a ten-day coast-to-coast cross-country race.

Although twenty-seven million Americans own bicycles, fewer than three thousand race them. For most people, then, the bicycle is a means of pleasurable recreation, exercise, and/or transportation (the bicycle remains the most energy-efficient means of self-propulsion ever built). Even for those of us who have no intention of racing, an understanding of the physical and mechanical requirements of racing can add greatly to our pleasure in any of the uses to which we put a bicycle. Most recreational cyclists are limited in their enjoyment of bicycle riding by their equipment and their pedaling cadence. An old, heavy, mechanically inefficient bike is simply not so much fun to use as a light, well-designed (but more expensive) modern bicycle—the racing versions of which allow today's bike riders to move 12 percent faster than cyclists could several decades ago. Even on the best-designed modern bicycle, a slow pedaling cadence of 40 to 50 RPMs can damage the joint surface of the kneecap; moreover, such a slow cadence does little to condition the muscles being used, and even less to maximize the pleasure potential of the bicycle.

The amount of muscle power a cyclist can exert continuously is a direct function of the amount of fuel left stored in the mus-

cles at a given time, and cyclists who are able to accumulate glycogen and conserve it by using it efficiently will consistently outperform those who can't.

Fat

Because the bicycle carries the body's weight in downhills and flats, the percentage of body fat is less important to the cyclist than it is to the runner—except in the case of the hill climber, who must carry whatever weight he has up hills. As former Tour de France winner Francesco Moser has said: "The first rule of training for hills is to be very light." Since fat is generally the only tissue that can be taken off, the competitive hill climber wants as low a percentage of it as possible—as low as 4 percent. Competitive values are 7 percent for men and 13 percent for women.

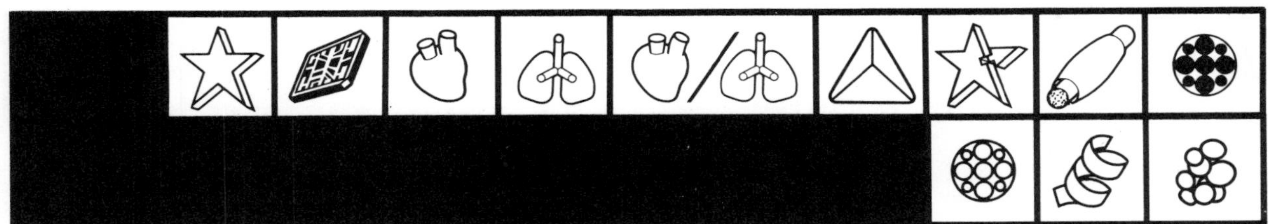

CROSS-COUNTRY SKIING

Cross-country skiing has evolved rapidly into the sport that, at high levels of performance, makes the most comprehensive demands on the human body.

Though skiing has been a means of cross-country travel for more than three thousand years, its real evolution into a sport began only in the 1920s. That evolution has occurred largely as a result of improvements in the sport's central piece of equipment, from the long, heavy wooden skis of the 1920s and before, the locomotion for which was provided by a single large pole, to the lighter-weight wooden skis of the 1940s and 1950s, on which it was possible to run but with limited gliding capacity, and finally to the modern ultra-light-weight fiberglass skis with plastic P-Tex bottoms. The very earliest cross-country technique relied heavily on upper-body strength, while the skis of the 1940s and 1950s made demands on the body similar to those of running (little upper-body strength, but considerable endurance strength in the legs). Modern cross-country skiing, done competently and at speed, requires both the upper-body strength characteristic of the very earliest skiing and the lower-body endurance strength of the later techniques.

The extraordinary demands made on the body by modern cross-country skiing are a direct result of the construction of the modern cross-country ski. P-Tex ski bottoms allow for much lower snow resistance than wood during the gliding phase of

skiing, and therefore much more speed. That increased speed occurs not only during downhills, but across flats and in uphills as well, making upper-body strength for poling critical. Downhill speeds in cross-country (as high as sixty-two miles per hour) now rival downhill speeds in Alpine skiing, and therefore the modern cross-country ski must track, carve, and turn. This is all made possible by fiberglass construction techniques that give a ski differing amounts of camber and stiffness throughout its length. The ease with which a ski turns is determined by the shape and softness of its shovel; the arc it carves in a turn is a function of the sidecut and the longitudinal stiffness of the ski's body; its bite, or "kick," in varying snow conditions (powder, corn, and so on) is determined by its camber; and its ability to track and hold a turn is determined by its resistance to torque and its cross-sectional stiffness. The technology of the modern cross-country ski combines these performance characteristics in a variety of sophisticated mixtures, resulting in skis so fast and maneuverable that in steep, mixed terrain they require of the skier a level of motor skills comparable to and occasionally surpassing those demanded of the Alpine skier. Moreover, keeping up with the speed potential of these skis involves tremendous upper-body work and a dynamic leg strength never required by wooden skis, and this combination of simultaneous upper- and lower-body activity places a greater work load on the heart-lung system than any other sport in the world.

THE CONTROL SYSTEM IN CROSS-COUNTRY SKIING

Bill Koch, the 1982 World Cup champion, is the physical prototype of the new cross-country ski racer; more than anything else, however, it is his motor genius at the sport that sets him apart from other racers. That motor genius is most apparent in the downhill phases of Koch's races, when he literally explodes down narrow, twisting, often icy tracks, seeming, like the best Alpine racers, to create more speed with every turn. Negotiating downhills well, whether on Bill Koch's level or on that of the weekend skier, is one of the ultimate challenges and pleasures of the sport—and it is a challenge and a pleasure that makes comprehensive demands on the Control System.

Reception, Anticipation, Abilities, and Motor Programs

Beginning ski tourers can be literally frozen into inaction by sudden drops and curves of the track and, without the ability to anticipate, often find themselves, particularly in downhills, just "holding on to their socks" to survive. The Control System of the cross-country novice in a downhill has the same sensory information coming into it from eyes, ears, and limbs as does the expert's, but the duffer has no developed motor program to respond to that information. With no ability to anticipate what is coming at him when his speed increases above what he is used to, his sense of timing is thrown off and he is forced to fall back on whatever genetic motor abilities he has, such as balance, simply to get down the hill in one piece. An expert skier on a downhill track parallel to the beginner's will have more sophisticated abilities available. He will begin the downhill by looking at it, to set up a series of visual markers at which various motor programs will have to be initiated. A sharp, icy turn to the left, for example, will require knee angulation and an appropriately applied weight transfer, such as a skating movement, onto the right ski. Through rapid shifts of his selective attention, which is tightly focused on visual input (specifically, depth perception, the identification of key markers, and the dynamic visual tracking between those markers), and on a kinesthetic feel for where each of his limbs is in preparation for the initiation of the next sequential motor program, the expert is able to stay ahead of himself on the track and to anticipate whatever may be required.

While downhills in cross-country are exciting, 90 percent of the skier's time is spent working on the flats and uphills, and while practically anyone can move around there, competent flats and uphill skiing involves a number of sophisticated motor programs. Most cross-country skiers simply walk across the snow on skis, using the poles, if at all, as an afterthought or to keep themselves from falling over; while the good skier on the flats and uphills is characterized by a fluid blend of strong, rhythmic poling, powerful kicks, and long glides. At any cross-country ski center, one sees proportionately very few of these good skiers. This is because, easy as it looks, competent cross-country skiing is really quite difficult and involves the same sort of intuitive jump from walking on the skis to kicking and gliding on them as is involved in the transition from the stem christie turn to the parallel turn in Alpine skiing.

A good cross-country stride begins with an explosive kick off one foot, which launches the skier's weight forward onto the gliding ski; the stride is given additional momentum by a poling action that accelerates into the glide so that the skier is precisely balanced over the gliding ski with his body at a forty-five-degree angle to it. The correct sequence, phasing, and force of this advanced motor program will serve the skier on any terrain and at any speed, in much the same way that good basic ground strokes serve the tennis player. Unfortunately, the same thing is true of the "snowshoe technique" of walking on skis, which a beginner may be tempted to adapt to varying terrains and speeds instead of making the difficult transition to a new, more effective, and enjoyable motor program.

Cross-country skiing has evolved into a truly thrilling sport that makes the highest possible demands on the heart and lungs. But in order for the participant to enjoy the true excitement of the sport and derive from it the great heart-lung exercise it can provide, good technique properly applied by the Control System is an absolute requirement.

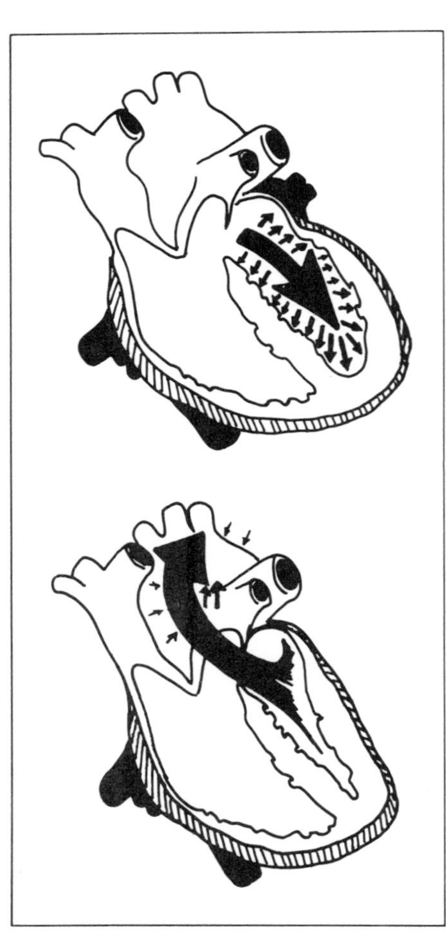

Highest preload, lowest afterload for cross-country skiing.

THE HEART-LUNG PACKAGE IN CROSS-COUNTRY SKIING

The Heart

Sven-Åke Lundbäck, the Swedish Olympic gold medal skier, has the highest oxygen consumption ever measured: ninety-four milliliters per kilogram. Oxygen consumption is a direct measure of the body's capacity for continuous exertion, but it is also a gauge of heart size, lung capacity, and the ability of muscles to extract oxygen delivered to them by the heart and lungs. At the world-class level of cross-country ski competition the human heart pumps more blood than it does in any other sport or at any other time. During such competition the trained heart is able to pump in excess of twenty-five quarts a minute, more than six times the amount pumped by a normal resting heart.

On any level of vigorous cross-country skiing done with proper technique, the heart performs a tremendous amount of work. The exercising muscles of the legs, arms, and trunk, acting as accessory pumps, force blood in a constant surge back to the heart, pre-loading it even before it contracts. Because a se-

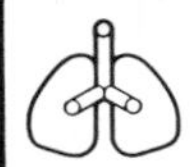

rious skier's heart is big, made so by constant volume overload, it can pump more blood than a smaller heart And, finally, just as this well-trained heart can load more fully, it can also empty more completely, and thereby meet the great blood-volume demands made by combined upper- and lower-body work. The heart of a serious cross-country skier is able to empty more completely than the heart of another athlete because of the multiple demands made on the various extremities in cross-country skiing and the subsequent reduction of resistance to blood flow into the vessels of these extremities. If this same skier were a runner or a cyclist, he would have a lower maximum oxygen consumption, even with the same size heart and lungs, because in technically correct cross-country skiing more muscles are offloading oxygen during exercise than in any other sport.

The Lungs

The lung capacity of great cross-country ski racers has sometimes been found to be in excess of seven quarts. This large capacity is necessary in a sport which, at advanced levels of competition, demands that competitors be able to breathe 160 liters of air in and out in one minute. Absolute lung capacity is important in cross-country skiing, but so is the ability to exhale quickly in order to maintain a high exchange rate: a world-class skier must be able to move those seven quarts of air in and out in less than three seconds, exhaling more than 80 percent of this volume in a single second. Cross-country skiing is the only sport in which performance at the top end is limited by the lungs—in serious competition the lungs *have* to operate at an extreme exchange rate for long periods of time. Though it is the lungs that make the exchange, it is the respiratory muscles that sustain heavy breathing, and these muscles must be as well trained in a cross-country racer as the thigh muscles of a cyclist or the calf muscles of a long-distance runner.

The second job of the lungs in exercise, in addition to oxygen exchanged, is the offloading of excess CO_2 created by the muscles. Cross-country skiers have to move a lot of air into and out of their lungs not only to bring oxygen in but also to exhale the considerable CO_2 produced by so many muscles exercising at the same time. As a skier increases his speed, he reaches points at which different muscles have recruited all their endurance fibers and have to begin employing sprint fibers. At these different thresholds, muscles begin to produce lactic acid, which when buffered by bicarbonate forms CO_2, which is transported

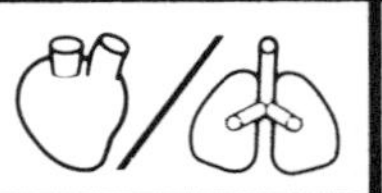

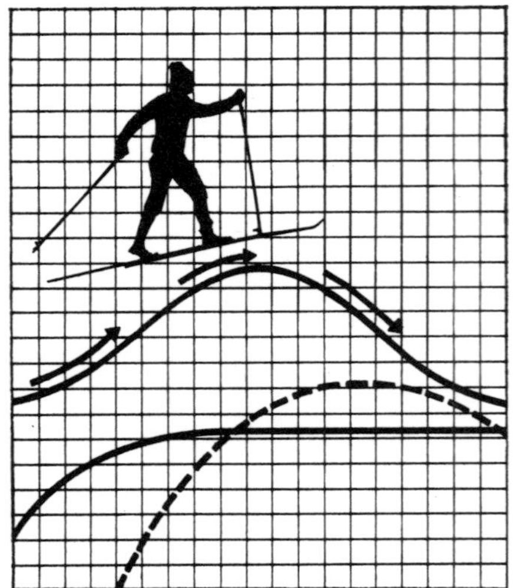

As skier reaches crest of long hill, O_2 consumption (solid line) increases in response to hill and remains steady to aid recovery. Increasing CO_2 levels (dotted line) must be blown off on downside of hill.

by the blood to the lungs in increasing amounts. The point at which the lungs increase their work to blow off the CO_2, rather than to supply oxygen, is the anaerobic threshold, and because top cross-country skiers must deal with so much lactic acid and excess CO_2, their anaerobic thresholds often occur close to their maximum aerobic capacities.

Heart-Lung Power

Because of the varying terrain over which it is performed, cross-country skiing, unlike long-distance running, is really not a steady-state endurance sport. Over and above sustaining a high level of expended energy, racers are required to put forth intense bursts of speed and power to climb hills, to pass other skiers, and to accelerate to the finish, and similar demands are made of the weekend tourer to climb hills and break new snow. During these bursts of energy the top athlete is distinguished by the heart-lung ability to meet the increased demand for oxygen quickly, and by the ability to blow off excess CO_2 quickly in recovery. If two equally competent recreational cross-country skiers were to race over one hill and to the top of the next, the winner would be the one who could more quickly meet the oxygen demand of the first hill and blow off CO_2 going down the backside—and thereby begin the second hill with a smaller oxygen deficit.

Before cross-country skiing became as dynamic as it is today, the winner of a race could be accurately predicted by VO_2 Max alone. This is no longer true: though a high VO_2 Max is still important to cross-country skiing, even more significant are technical ability, a high anaerobic threshold, the capacity to sustain heavy breathing, and the twin capacities to meet sharply increased oxygen demands quickly and to recover by blowing off excess CO_2 even more quickly.

BODY COMPOSITION IN CROSS-COUNTRY SKIING

Somatotype and Skeleton

Because of the varied terrains and snow conditions encountered in cross-country skiing, the sport accommodates a wide variety of body types. In cross-country racing alone every body type has its racecourse—the tall, lean Sven-Åke Lundbäck excels on uphills and in resistant snow, while the giant 220-pound Juha Mieto is practically unbeatable on fast, icy, level tracks.

Though overall body size can range in cross-country skiing from the small hill climber to the large klister skier, any given size must be matched by the size of the heart-lung engine driving it. A small, light skier with a large heart-lung capacity will have the advantages of maneuvering ability on tight tracks and less body weight to pull up hills. A large, heavily muscled skier, on the other hand, is likely to be underpowered by the heart and lungs for steep hill climbing, but has the advantage over the lighter skier of more upper-body strength and more weight to increase momentum in downhills and gliding. The ideal skier, in between these extremes, will have more than adequate heart-lung power for climbing, enough weight for gliding and downhill, and will have, besides, long thighs for long striding and long arms with strong shoulder girdles for good poling. This ideal combination of body composition on a somato chart would show an ectomesomorphic athlete, who combines height, leanness, and muscularity.

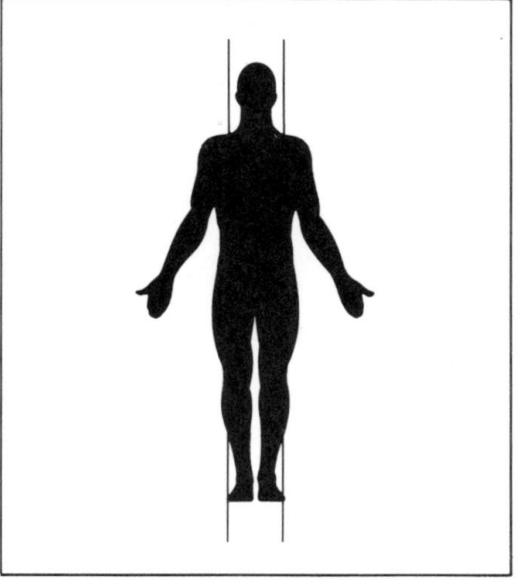

Cross-country skier: ectomesomorph who combines height, leanness, and muscularity; high center of gravity.

Muscle

There is really no single ideal combination of muscle fiber types for cross-country skiing because the demands of the sport are so varied. Someone with 90 percent sprint fiber in the thighs would do very well in a race over short, steep hills requiring frequent bursts of power and speed, but not so well on a course over long hills. An athlete with a very high percentage of endurance fiber in the thighs, on the other hand, will have a higher continuous speed capacity than the sprint fiber skier, but lower peak speed capacity. The first athlete will also have a higher VO_2 Max, given the same size heart and lungs as the sprint fiber skier, because endurance fiber has twelve times the capacity of sprint fiber to offload oxygen.

It is an advantage to any skier to have a high percentage of sprint fiber in the deltoids and triceps, because of the speed and power necessary for good poling. Poling occupies a large spectrum on the Force-Speed Curve because it begins, at pole plant, with high force and ends as the arm accelerates to speeds as high as 400 degrees per second.

It is also an important advantage for a cross-country skier to have a high percentage of sprint fiber in the calves and to have

large calves, since it is the speed and power of the calves that generate the force downward on the skis into the snow, so that the wax will bite and the skis will accelerate. In any sport there is likely to be a key muscle group that limits performance more than other muscles. The limiting muscle in much of cross-country skiing is the calf. In studies done with Bill Koch, it was discovered that his calves generated a downward force on the skis three times greater than that of other national team skiers. This downward force is a function not only of the fiber type and the diameter of the calf, but also of the extent to which it has been pre-stretched before it contracts. Any muscle has genetically determined elastic qualities, and the calf muscle of a good cross-country skier will have quite a bit of elasticity, allowing it to be pre-stretched, and therefore to store more elastic energy, during the compression when a skier sinks before kicking.

While cross-country skiing involves primarily the calf muscles, the quadriceps muscles of the thighs, and the deltoid and triceps muscles of the shoulders and arms, it engages many other muscle groups (more than any other sport, in fact), including the abdominal, lower-back, and gluteal muscles, and muscles in the chest and upper back. A well-trained muscle can store two and a half times more fuel in the form of sugar than can an untrained muscle, making good training critical in cross-country ski racing, where the distances covered can range up to ninety kilometers.

Fat

While it is true that today's cross-country skiers are more muscular than those of an earlier day, it is still important for any racer to be relatively light. Modern ski racers are able both to carry muscle and to keep their weights down by maintaining body-fat levels as low as those of top endurance runners (approximately 7 percent for men and 12 percent for women). Despite the severe cold in which much cross-country racing is performed (temperatures as low as −22°F. during the 1979 pre-Olympic Games at Lake Placid), extra body fat is not so desirable for insulation as is an extra layer of clothes. In fact, because of its level of exertion, cross-country skiing is known as the warmest sport of all—Juha Mieto completed the course at Lake Placid wearing only a single skin-tight suit and without gloves.

PART III

TESTING YOURSELF FOR SPORTSTALENT

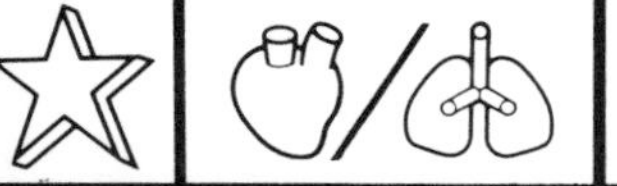

INTRODUCTION

The tests for sportstalent found in Part III have been gathered from a variety of sources: clinical medicine, exercise-physiology field testing, Olympic team testing, the Austrian and American ski teams, the U.S. Air Force, sportsvision testing centers, individual coaches and physiotherapists, and our own field-testing laboratory.

These tests are *not* designed to determine how well you presently perform at a sport (how fast you ski or swim or run, or how skillfully you windsurf), but rather what your underlying *aptitude* is for that sport. You could find here, for example, that you have great talent for Alpine skiing without ever having put on a ski boot. These tests measure inherent talent for a particular sport rather than previous experience or developed skills, and inherent talent is not at all the same thing as the capacity to participate in and enjoy that sport. It is perfectly possible to continue for the rest of your life participating in, enjoying, and even competing at a sport for which you have no talent whatsoever, and we wouldn't want these tests to discourage anyone from doing that. The tests are designed to give you an idea of your ultimate potential to excel at a sport, or a number of sports, *not* to direct you away from *any* athletic participation you enjoy. Having said that, however, we would like to repeat our belief that people do tend to enjoy things they do well more than things they do poorly, and to reaffirm that these tests have been brought together more to steer you toward new athletic enjoyments than to separate you from old ones.

It is possible to jump right into this book at this point and begin taking the tests without having read any of the preceding text, though we don't recommend doing so. If you do that you are likely to run into critical terms and concepts (both here and in Part IV) whose meanings aren't clear to you. In that event, we would suggest you go back to the appropriate sections of Parts I and II for clarification, or consult the Appendix. We would also suggest that a reading of those parts of the book will enlarge anyone's understanding of how whatever sportstalent he or she has can best be applied within a sport. No matter how good an athlete you are, a clear working image of how your body operates in sports will almost certainly make you a better one.

In this section we do not test every athletic component discussed in Parts I and II as being important to, or functional in, the performance of a sport. We test only those components and capacities that we consider *central* to the performance of a sport *and* that are not possessed more or less equally by almost everyone. Such psychological capacities as mental imagery and arousal, discussed at length in Part I, are considered by us to be sports tools that can be used by anyone who understands them, and for that reason they are not tested here. Psychological traits that often characterize athletes within a particular sport are not tested for two reasons: because we did not want to include psychological inventory testing (which is universally available through clinical psychologists), and because no given psychological trait or set of traits always characterizes athletes within a given sport.

Each of the tests for each of the sports measures a component or capacity that has been isolated and clearly identified as being vital to the performance of that sport; but *all* are field tests, designed to be done in your home or backyard and requiring no special equipment (except for a stationary bicycle, a fish scale, and a pair of calipers for measuring body fat). There are very precise, sophisticated laboratory tests for all the components and capacities tested here, and one of the numerous challenges of this book was to come up with field tests that would yield results as close in accuracy as possible to the results of corresponding laboratory tests. In some cases we have managed to do that; in some cases we have not. The Cooper Twelve-Minute-Run Test, the Vertical-Jump Test, and the Hexagonal-Obstacle Test, for example, yield accurate results when administered properly; the Lung-Volume Test, the Visual-Convergence Test, and a few others yield results that are indicative and qualitative rather than quantitatively characteristic. All the tests are designed to screen for individual elements or raw talent at a sport, not to make fine distinctions between the talents of already accomplished athletes.

Notes on Scoring

1. You will notice that a few of these tests are used for a number of different sports. The values representing the top scores, however, vary from sport to sport, depending on how great the demand made by the sport on the component or capacity tested. A top score on the Cooper Twelve-Minute-Run Test in Alpine skiing, for example, represents a smaller VO_2 Max than that for the top score on the same test for cross-country skiing, because less absolute aerobic power is demanded by Alpine skiing than by cross-country.

2. The empirical base for the scoring of some of these tests (that is, the total number of people who have been scored on them) is very large and well established; for some of the newer tests that base is necessarily smaller.

3. The scoring of these tests is calibrated for adults. Children and young adolescents are, of course, free to take the tests but we have not provided a separate scoring system for them here. Where we have felt it necessary (most notably in the areas of heart-lung power and muscular strength), we have provided separate scoring for men and women, though for the most part we have proceeded according to our belief that men and women are physically more equal than is popularly believed.

4. All the tests have been weighted individually to reflect our sense of how important to the performance of the sport is the component or capacity being tested. Additionally, each of the three general areas of testing (the Control System, the Heart-Lung Package, and Body Composition) has

a weighting (or degree of importance to the overall score for that sport) that varies from sport to sport and reflects the importance of that *area* of testing to the performance of the sport. The tests for the Control System components in tennis, for example, have a combined weighting of 70 percent (70 percent of your overall score for tennis comes from your results on the Control System tests for the sport), while in running, the Control System tests have a combined weighting of only 20 percent.

5. A scoring scale is given on the tabulation sheet at the end of the testing section for each sport. Your overall score for that sport, when located on the scale, represents the minimum level of play you are likely to reach in that sport.

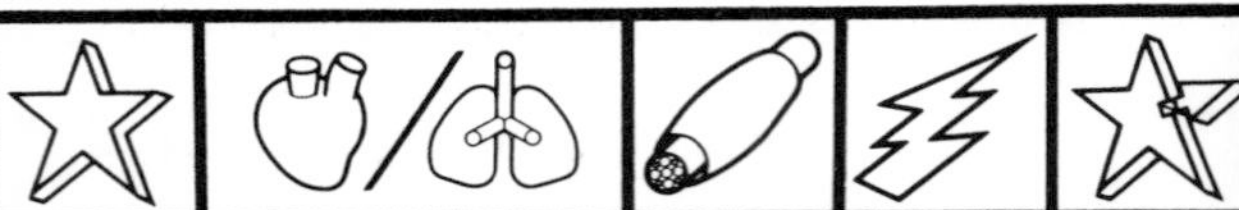

TESTING FOR ALPINE SKIING

As we said in the chapter on this sport, motor abilities are the most important components of talent in Alpine skiing, and the most significant of those abilities are agility, balance, and coordination. Another crucial Control System component of talent in Alpine skiing is the speed with which a person learns a new skill. Test 1, developed at the University of Innsbruck for the Austrian ski team, tests that speed of motor learning as well as the three basic underlying abilities. Test 2, developed by Warren Witherell, author of *How the Racers Ski*, also tests the motor abilities that underlie skiing talent, as well as quickness and anaerobic power in the legs.

Despite their overwhelming importance for determining Alpine skiing talent, the Control System tests have been given a relative significance of only 40 percent because the components of anaerobic power, flexibility, and muscle speed (a function of muscular dimensions and fiber type), which can contribute heavily to how well someone does on these tests, are tested separately under Body Composition. If you do poorly on Tests 1 and 2, it might be due less to a lack of abilities than to a lack of anaerobic power. If this is the case, you can improve your scores on those tests, and therefore your overall score for Alpine skiing, by developing more anaerobic power through training. Your scores on Tests 1 and 2 can also be improved by losing weight if you are overly fat. Dynamic visual acuity, also identified in the chapter on Alpine skiing as being a crucial Control System function, is not tested here because it is trainable and not genetic.

The heart-lung power necessary for Alpine skiing on all but the lowest levels of the sport is tested here by the Cooper Twelve-Minute-Run Test. Though aerobic capacity for any particular sport ideally should be tested within the context of that sport (aerobic capacity in Alpine skiing, for example, is most accurately determined by using special oxygen equipment while actually skiing), the Cooper Twelve-Minute Run is an effective general field test of an aerobic power that is largely transferable to skiing.

CHART 1. ALPINE SKIING

	Components tested	**Test**	**Relative importance of test to overall score**	
The Control System	Agility, coordination, balance, speed of motor learning, and anaerobic power in the legs	1. Hexagonal Obstacle	25%	40%
		2. Concrete-Block Jump	15%	
The Heart-Lung Package	VO_2 Max	3. Cooper Twelve-Minute Run	20%	
Body Composition	Anaerobic endurance strength in the legs	4. Wall Squat	8%	40%
	Leg explosiveness and muscle fiber type	5. Vertical Jump	10%	
	Center of gravity	6. Upper-Body/Lower-Body Proportion	7%	
	Degree to which knock-kneed	7. Knock-kneed–Bowlegged Spectrum	7%	
	Range of motion in hips	8. Hip Range of Motion	8%	
		Hip Flexion		
		External and Internal Hip Rotation (negative points only)		

TEST 1: HEXAGONAL OBSTACLE

Designed by the Austrians to determine Alpine skiing ability from age ten and modified by Dr. Charles Dillman of the U.S. Ski Team, the Hexagonal-Obstacle Test is the best single test there is for the kinds of agility, balance, and coordination required by Alpine skiing. To assess those abilities, take the test three times. Your best time of the three trials will determine your overall score in Table 1.

To evaluate your speed of motor learning, take the test twice more (for a total of five times). The difference between how fast you completed it the first time and how fast you finished it the fifth time will determine your score for speed of motor learning in Table 2.

All five repetitions of the test should be performed within a half-hour period, and you should not practice before performing the test the first time. If you botch a particular trial by knocking over a block or by not jumping the blocks in sequence, start the test over for that trial. You should count only the times for the trials completed successfully.

Certain people—maybe most—may not be able to perform this test at all as it is described here. If you can't complete the test with the blocks in place, take the test by jumping over the strips of tape only.

What You Will Need

To set up this test you will need a hard, flat surface and a minimum of twenty-five square feet of cleared area. You will also need a roll of two-inch masking tape, a stopwatch, and materials to construct your own version of the U.S. Ski Team Hexagonal-Obstacle Test shown in the illustration. You can use lumber, cardboard, Styrofoam, or other materials to construct the blocks, or sides; just make sure they are the proper height and that they form a safe construction. Side A should be thirteen inches high; side B, eight inches; side C, ten inches; side D, eight inches; side E, fourteen inches; and side F, eight inches.

Setting Up the Test

Draw a twenty-six-inch-per-side hexagon on the floor; then cover the lines with masking tape so that the outside edge of the tape delineates the outside of the hexagon. Then set up sides A through F on top of the tape, making sure again that the outsides of the blocks form the outside perimeter of the hexagon.

Taking the Test

Stand in the middle of the hexagon and face side F, as you must for the duration of the test. Either you or a tester must have a stopwatch, which is started on the command "Go." You begin by jumping with both feet over side A and immediately back into the hexagon. Then, continuing to face side F, jump over side B and back into the hexagon, side C and back in, side D and back in, side E and back in, and side F and back in, for one complete revolution. Make three full revolutions. When your feet enter the hexagon after jumping side F for the third time, the clock should be stopped and your time recorded. Take the best time for your first three uninterrupted performances to determine your overall score for the abilities test in Table 1. To find your score for motor-learning speed in Table 2, use the difference in the time it took you to complete the test between your first performance and your fifth.

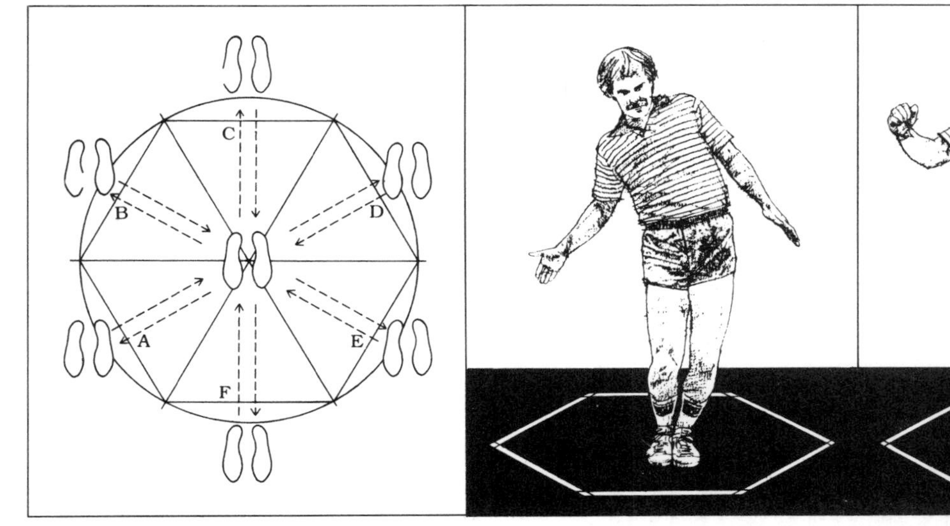

A = 13″ high; B = 8″ high; C = 10″ high; D = 8″ high; E = 14″ high; F = 8″ high

Bend legs slightly to bring knees over ball of foot.

TABLE 1. HEXAGONAL OBSTACLE

Best time with sides (*seconds*)		Points	Best time without sides (*seconds*)		Points
Men	**Women**		**Men**	**Women**	
16.0	16.0	15.0	9.0	9.0	10.0
17.4	18.0	13.5	10.1	10.6	9.0
18.8	20.0	12.0	11.2	12.2	8.0
20.2	22.0	10.5	12.3	13.8	7.0
21.6	24.0	9.0	13.4	15.4	6.0
23.0	26.0	7.5	14.5	17.0	5.0
24.4	28.0	6.0	15.6	18.6	4.0
25.8	30.0	4.5	16.7	20.2	3.0
27.2	32.0	3.0	17.8	21.8	2.0
28.6	34.0	1.5	18.9	23.4	1.0
30.0	36.0	0.0	20.0	25.0	0.0

TABLE 2. HEXAGONAL OBSTACLE

Men						Women					
Best time with sides	**Point value for difference in time between first performance and fifth with sides (*seconds*)**					**Best time with sides**	**Point value for difference in time between first performance and fifth with sides (*seconds*)**				
	10 Points	**8 Points**	**6 Points**	**4 Points**	**2 Points**		**10 points**	**8 points**	**6 points**	**4 points**	**2 points**
16.00	8.00	6.40	4.80	3.20	1.60	16.00	8.00	6.40	4.80	3.20	1.60
17.40	8.70	6.96	5.22	3.48	1.74	18.00	9.00	7.20	5.40	3.60	1.80
18.80	9.40	7.52	5.64	3.76	1.88	20.00	10.00	8.00	6.00	4.00	2.00
20.20	10.10	8.08	6.06	4.04	2.02	22.00	11.00	8.80	6.60	4.40	2.20
21.60	10.80	8.64	6.48	4.32	2.16	24.00	12.00	9.60	7.20	4.80	2.40
23.00	11.50	9.20	6.90	4.60	2.30	26.00	13.00	10.40	7.80	5.20	2.60
24.40	12.20	9.76	7.32	4.88	2.44	28.00	14.00	11.20	8.40	5.60	2.80
25.80	12.90	10.32	7.74	5.16	2.58	30.00	15.00	12.00	9.00	6.00	3.00
27.20	13.60	10.88	8.16	5.44	2.72	32.00	16.00	12.80	9.60	6.40	3.20
28.60	14.30	11.44	8.58	5.72	2.86	34.00	17.00	13.60	10.20	6.80	3.40
30.00	15.00	12.00	9.00	6.00	3.00	36.00	18.00	14.40	10.80	7.20	3.60
Best time without sides	**Point value for difference in time between first performance and fifth without sides (*seconds*)**					**Best time without sides**	**Point value for difference in time between first performance and fifth without sides (*seconds*)**				
	10 points	**8 points**	**6 points**	**4 points**	**2 points**		**10 points**	**8 points**	**6 points**	**4 points**	**2 points**
9.00	4.50	3.60	2.70	1.80	0.90	9.00	4.50	3.60	2.70	1.80	0.90
10.10	5.05	4.04	3.03	2.02	1.01	10.60	5.30	4.24	3.18	2.12	1.06
11.20	5.60	4.48	3.36	2.24	1.12	12.20	6.10	4.88	3.66	2.44	1.22
12.30	6.15	4.92	3.69	2.46	1.23	13.80	6.90	5.52	4.14	2.76	1.38
13.40	6.70	5.36	4.02	2.68	1.34	15.40	7.70	6.16	4.62	3.08	1.54
14.50	7.25	5.80	4.35	2.90	1.45	17.00	8.50	6.80	5.10	3.40	1.70
15.60	7.80	6.24	4.68	3.12	1.56	18.60	9.30	7.44	5.58	3.72	1.86
16.70	8.35	6.68	5.01	3.34	1.67	20.20	10.10	8.08	6.06	4.04	2.02
17.80	8.90	7.12	5.34	3.56	1.78	21.80	10.90	8.72	6.54	4.36	2.18
18.90	9.45	7.56	5.67	3.78	1.89	23.40	11.70	9.36	7.02	4.68	2.34
20.00	10.00	8.00	6.00	4.00	2.00	25.00	12.50	10.00	7.50	5.00	2.50

TEST 2: CONCRETE-BLOCK JUMP

This test was designed to identify Alpine skiing ability by Warren Witherell, until recently the head of Burke Mountain Ski Academy in Vermont and one of America's leading ski theoreticians. When Witherell was using this test at Burke Mountain, one of the country's premier high-school training academies for young ski racers, he found that every one of his skiers who went on to the Junior Nationals and/or the U.S. Ski Team did extremely well on this test. That finding indicates a very high correlation between good performance on the test and good underlying abilities for skiing.

What You Will Need

You will need the same cleared, flat area you used for Test 1, a stopwatch (a large clock with a second hand will do if you want to time yourself), and a standard concrete cinder block.

Taking the Test

You would do well to enlist a friend for this test, to time you and count your jumps. Lay the cinder block down with side (see illustration) facing upward. Stand with the concrete block at your side. Your friend should start the stopwatch on the command "Go." With both feet together, jump sideways over the concrete block, and then, as quickly as you can, back over it to your original position. Continue to jump over the block and back for forty seconds and have your friend count your jumps—each time you clear the block counts as one jump. If you miss a jump or you fall, you may start the test over again, but don't practice before taking it the first time. The total number of jumps from your *first* completed performance of the test will give you your score in Table 3.

TABLE 3. CONCRETE-BLOCK JUMP

Number of jumps		Points
Men	Women	
100	95	15.0
97	92	14.3
94	89	13.5
91	86	12.8
88	83	12.0
85	80	11.3
82	77	10.5
79	74	9.0
76	71	7.5
73	68	6.0
70	65	4.5
67	62	3.0
64	59	1.5

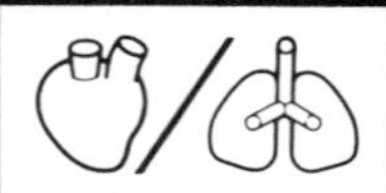

TEST 3: COOPER TWELVE-MINUTE RUN

The equipment necessary to test an individual's maximum oxygen consumption with laboratory accuracy costs upwards of fifty thousand dollars. This test was developed by Dr. Kenneth Cooper of the Cooper Aerobic Institute in Dallas, as a field-test alternative to laboratory testing, and it has the highest accuracy in measuring maximum oxygen consumption when running of any field test, its values correlating up to 90 percent with laboratory results. This test was designed by Dr. Cooper for men, but in 1977 its scoring system was adapted for women by Dr. Bud Getchell of Ball State University. Scoring for both men and women is provided in Table 4.

Maximum oxygen consumption differs in individuals from sport to sport, and the Cooper Test measures VO_2 Max specific to running. A large VO_2 Max in running, however, is transferable to skiing (if the individual has good technique and is in good shape for skiing); and a small running VO_2 Max would indicate that an individual should do some aerobic training (since VO_2 Max is improvable by up to 50 percent) before taking up skiing seriously.

If at the end of this test you are very winded, it was your heart and lungs that limited your maximum oxygen consumption; if your legs are burning, it was your muscles that limited you, either through lack of conditioning or because you have a high percentage of sprint muscle fiber.

Finally, if you don't like to run, don't want to, or for some reason can't, you may take the Astrand Bicycle Ergometer Test, described on pages 216–18, instead of this one. Scoring for that test is provided in Table 5.

What You Will Need

You should perform this test on a hard, level running surface (the ideal place is a measured high-school or college track). Your score is likely to be negatively affected if you run uphill, over uneven terrain, on soft ground or sand, or into a stiff head wind. If you perform the test on a road, as opposed to a measured track, you will need an accurate odometer to measure your distance after you have completed the run. You will also need a watch or a stopwatch to tell you when twelve minutes are up.

Taking the Test

You should be adequately warmed up before starting this test. Check the time on your watch or stopwatch and start running. Try to run *evenly*—avoiding sprints that will force you to slow down—and as fast as you can for twelve minutes exactly. If you are on a road, find a landmark to indicate where you stopped and measure with the odometer to the point from which you started, for your total distance covered; if you are on a track, calculate the distance in laps. That distance will give you your score in Table 4. Table

TABLE 4. COOPER TWELVE-MINUTE RUN

Distance run (*miles*)	**Points**	
	Men	**Women**
1 8/16		2.0
1 9/16		4.6
1 10/16		7.1
1 11/16		9.7
1 12/16	2.0	12.3
1 13/16	4.3	14.9
1 14/16	6.5	17.4
1 15/16	8.8	20.0
2	11.0	
2 1/16	13.3	
2 2/16	15.5	
2 3/16	17.8	
2 4/16	20.0	
2 5/16		
2 6/16		
2 7/16		
2 8/16		

5 will give you your score if you took the Astrand Bicycle Ergometer Test.

Be sure to warm down by jogging for at least half a mile after your run.

TABLE 5. ASTRAND BICYCLE ERGOMETER TEST

VO_2 Max	Points	
	Men	**Women**
74		
73		
72		
71		
70		
69		
68	20.0	
67	19.0	
66	18.0	
65	17.0	
64	16.0	
63	15.0	
62	14.0	
61	13.0	
60	12.0	
59	11.0	
58	10.0	20.0
57	9.0	19.0
56	8.0	18.0
55	7.0	17.5
54	6.0	17.0
53	5.0	16.0
52	4.0	15.0
51	3.0	14.0
50	2.0	13.0
49	1.0	12.0
48		11.0
47		10.0
46		9.0
45		8.0
44		7.0
43		6.0
42		5.0
41		
40		
39		

TEST 4: WALL SQUAT

This test measures the static anaerobic endurance strength of the thighs. The test has been a standard for a long time and is commonly used by skiers both as a measurement of thigh strength and as an effective method of training that strength. Without the use of expensive mechanical equipment it is very difficult to isolate the quadriceps muscles for strength testing of any kind, and as an accurate field test for the endurance strength of the quadriceps (absolutely necessary for ski racing and very important for all good skiing) the Wall-Squat Test is unequaled. Anaerobic endurance strength is quickly improved by training, and doing wall squats day after day will result in better and better scores on this test. Some young ski racers (among them the ambitious son of one of the authors of this book) through daily practice have been able to boost their times up to and over thirty minutes using both legs, but no skier, except perhaps a world-class downhill racer, really *needs* that much anaerobic endurance strength in the thighs. If you do well on this test by the standard given here, you have all the anaerobic endurance strength in the legs you need to ski well.

Anaerobic strength in the legs is crucial to success in competitive skiing. If you are seriously interested in ski racing, we suggest you also take the Bicycle Anaerobic Endurance Test (page 221) as an additional indicator of your ultimate anaerobic quadriceps strength.

What You Will Need

You will need a smooth wall, and since your feet will tend to slide out from you, either take the test barefoot or wear sneakers that grip the floor well. It is also a help to have a friend with a watch or stopwatch to time you, rather than trying to time yourself.

Taking the Test

Stand with your back flat against the wall, your feet on the ground and a hip-width apart. Slide your back down the wall and walk your feet out until your thighs form a ninety-degree angle with the wall and your calves a ninety-degree angle with the floor. Your feet should still be a hip-width apart. Now lift your left foot a couple of inches off the floor and hold it there. Have your friend time the total number of seconds you can remain supported only by your right leg, *without moving*. Now take the same test using only your left leg to support your weight, as you hold your right foot off the floor. Use your *lower*, or poorer, time of the two trials to determine your score in Table 6.

TABLE 6. WALL SQUAT

Time (*seconds*)		Points
Men	**Women**	
120	70	8.0
111	65	7.6
102	60	7.2
93	55	6.8
84	50	6.4
75	45	5.6
66	40	4.8
57	35	4.0
48	30	3.2
39	25	2.4
30	20	1.6
21	15	0.8

TEST 5: VERTICAL JUMP

The Vertical-Jump Test is an effective and accurate way of measuring overall leg explosiveness, which is of considerable significance to all ski racing and to expert recreational skiing. Good performance on this test indicates not only leg explosiveness but also its two underlying structural components: a high percentage of sprint muscle fiber in the legs, and large-diameter leg muscles. A high score on this test also indicates good multilimb coordination, another important requirement for skillful Alpine skiing.

If you do poorly on this test the chances are that you were unable to jump all the blocks in Test 1. If this is the case, go back and take Test 1 without the blocks. If you then score well, you simply lack explosiveness (and perhaps anaerobic power), not the more crucial motor abilities.

What You Will Need

For this test you will need a wall high enough to do the test against, a yardstick, and a friend on a stepladder.

Taking the Test

Face the wall, with both arms fully extended over your head, your fingers touching the highest point they can reach on the wall; the toes of your shoes should be touching the wall, and your heels should be flat on the floor. Extend the yardstick up the wall from the highest reach of your fingertips and have your friend on the stepladder hold it there. You should now have an exact measurement of three feet above your highest reach on the wall. Now, move back one foot from the wall and jump with legs together (without a running start), reaching as high over your head as you can with the hand nearest the wall, and touch the highest point you can reach on the yardstick. Have your friend tell you the height, in inches, that you reached. Do the test three times and take your highest *single* reach in inches to determine your score in Table 7.

Don't practice before taking the test, and if you should happen to reach above the yardstick on any of your jumps, don't worry about scoring yourself—just sign up on a national team.

TABLE 7. VERTICAL JUMP

Highest single reach (*inches*)		Points
Men	**Women**	
28.0	18.0	10.0
26.6	17.2	9.1
25.2	16.4	8.2
23.8	15.6	7.3
22.4	14.8	6.4
21.0	14.0	5.5
19.6	13.2	4.6
18.2	12.4	3.7
16.8	11.6	2.8
15.4	10.8	1.9
14.0	10.0	1.0

TEST 6: UPPER-BODY/ LOWER-BODY PROPORTION

This test incorporates measurements to determine how low or how high your center of gravity is. While a high center of gravity will not keep you from enjoying Alpine skiing, a low one is a definite advantage for skillful practice of the sport, and it is a fact that very few top recreational or competitive skiers have low, or short, sitting heights, and therefore high centers of gravity.

What You Will Need

You will need a friend, a yardstick, and a table sturdy enough and high enough off the ground for you to sit on without touching the floor with your feet. Also, you will need to know exactly how tall you are. (See Weight-to-Height Ratio [pages 187–89] for a method of measuring your height accurately.)

Taking the Test

Sit erect on the table with your feet dangling, your lower legs forming a right angle with your thighs, and your hands resting on your thighs. Be sure that your back is as straight as possible. Hold your head so that the bottom of your eye socket and the top of your ear opening are on a straight line. (Your friend can tell you when that line is straight, or parallel to the table.) Now take a deep breath and hold it while your friend measures from the highest point of your head (the "vertex"—see illustration) to the table. This measurement is known as your "sitting height." Your lower-body length is your sitting height subtracted from your overall height. To determine the ratio of your sitting height to your lower-body length, find the point in Table 8 at which your sitting height intersects with your overall height, and use that ratio to determine your score.

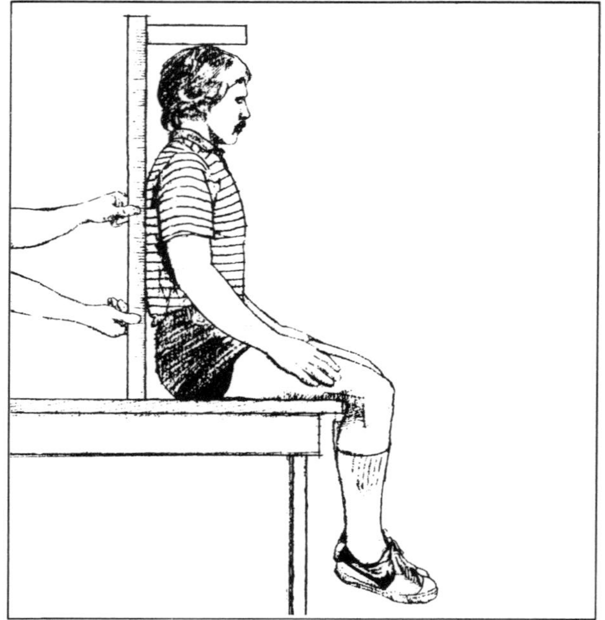

TABLE 8. UPPER-BODY/LOWER-BODY PROPORTION

Overall height (*inches*)	Sitting height (*inches*)																			
	26	**27**	**28**	**29**	**30**	**31**	**32**	**33**	**34**	**35**	**36**	**37**	**38**	**39**	**40**	**41**	**42**	**43**	**44**	**45**
54	0.9	1.0	1.1	1.2	1.3															
55	0.9	1.0	1.0	1.1	1.2	1.3														
56		0.9	1.0	1.1	1.2	1.2	1.3													
57		0.9	1.0	1.0	1.1	1.2	1.3													
58			0.9	1.0	1.1	1.1	1.2	1.3												
59			0.9	1.0	1.0	1.1	1.2	1.3												
60				0.9	1.0	1.1	1.1	1.2	1.3											
61				0.9	1.0	1.0	1.1	1.2	1.3											
62					0.9	1.0	1.1	1.1	1.2	1.3										
63					0.9	1.0	1.0	1.1	1.2	1.3										
64						0.9	1.0	1.1	1.1	1.2	1.3									
65						0.9	1.0	1.0	1.1	1.2	1.2									
66							0.9	1.0	1.1	1.1	1.2	1.3								
67							0.9	1.0	1.0	1.1	1.2	1.2	1.3							
68								0.9	1.0	1.1	1.1	1.2	1.3							
69								0.9	1.0	1.0	1.1	1.2	1.2	1.3						
70								0.9	0.9	1.0	1.1	1.1	1.2	1.3						
71									0.9	1.0	1.0	1.1	1.2	1.2	1.3					
72										0.9	1.0	1.1	1.1	1.2	1.3					
73										0.9	1.0	1.0	1.1	1.1	1.2	1.3				
74										0.9	0.9	1.0	1.1	1.1	1.2	1.2				
75											0.9	1.0	1.0	1.1	1.1	1.2	1.3			
76											0.9	0.9	1.0	1.1	1.1	1.2	1.2	1.3		
77												0.9	1.0	1.0	1.1	1.1	1.2	1.3		
78												0.9	1.0	1.0	1.1	1.1	1.2	1.2	1.3	
79													0.9	1.0	1.0	1.1	1.1	1.2	1.3	1.3
80													0.9	1.0	1.0	1.1	1.1	1.2	1.2	1.3

SCORING:

Ratio of sitting height to lower-body length (*inches*)	Points
1.3 or above	7
1.2	5
1.1	3
1.0	2
0.9	1

TEST 7: KNOCK-KNEED–BOWLEGGED SPECTRUM

This test measures the degree to which you are either knock-kneed or bowlegged. Since bowleggedness decreases the center of gravity, the condition would normally be assumed to be an advantage in Alpine skiing. But in fact it is much more of an advantage in skiing to be knock-kneed, since that condition automatically puts the knees over the inside, or carving, edges of the skis (while skiing in a neutral stance), allowing for quicker application of pressure to initiate turns. The more bowlegged you are, the more movement, and therefore time, is required to apply pressure to the skis' carving edges.

You are either knock-kneed or you are not, and the condition is not trainable. Both Mahre brothers and Ingemar Stenmark are among the many top skiers who are knock-kneed, and Warren Witherell has told us that he has very rarely seen a good ski racer who wasn't.

Although considerable bowleggedness can be remedied to some degree by boot cants, it is seriously counterproductive to the mechanics of good turns in Alpine skiing.

What You Will Need

All you will need for this test is a wall, a ruler or a measuring tape, and a friend to take the measurements.

Taking the Test

You should be barefoot and barelegged for this test. Stand with your back to the wall, feet slightly apart, and your leg muscles relaxed (*don't* try to bring your knees together). If you can't bring your feet together without your knees touching first, you are knock-kneed. If your feet come together at the same time your knees come together, you are neither knock-kneed nor bowlegged. If when your feet are brought together there is still a space between your knees, you are bowlegged.

If you find you are knock-kneed, hold your legs together, arrange your feet so they are exactly parallel, and have your friend measure the distance between your two inside anklebones. That distance in inches will give you your score in Table 9. If your feet and knees meet at the same time, use the value 0 in the table for your score. And if you find you are bowlegged, use the number of inches between the insides of your knee bones when your feet are together, and subtract the points indicated by that distance from your score.

TABLE 9. KNOCK-KNEED–BOWLEGGED SPECTRUM

Measurement (*inches*)	Points
1 ½ and above	7
1 ¼	6
1	5
¾	4
½	3
¼	2
0	1

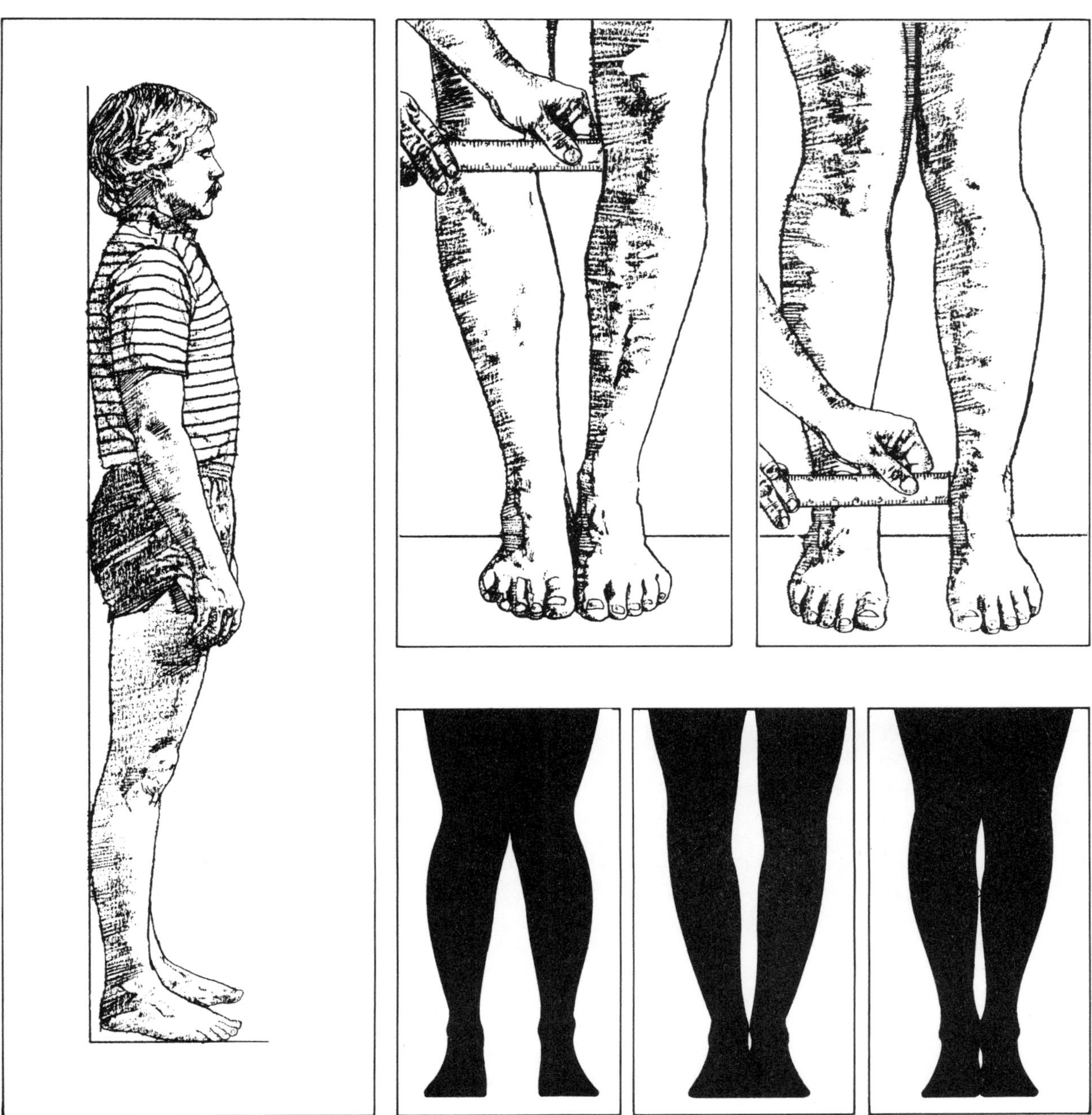

Note: Measure distance between knees from joint line to joint line; measure distance between ankles from ankle bone to ankle bone.

TEST 8: HIP RANGE OF MOTION

Angulation in skiing, or the ability to push the knees in toward the hill while leaning the upper body out away from the hill, is what allows a skier to make carved turns—and carved (as opposed to skidded) turns are the keys to good skiing, both recreational and competitive. The faster a skier moves and the shorter the radius of the turns, the more hip angulation is required to make the skis carve. The degree of hip angulation available to a particular skier is a function of how much range of motion he has in his hip joints; the amount of hip angulation he can employ at any given time is also a function of the strength of the flexor and extensor muscles in his hips. We are not testing that strength here, since flexion and extension strength in the hips is purely a matter of training, but rather your overall and maximum range of motion in the hips, which, leaving aside strength considerations, will determine your ability to angulate.

Unlike the knife-clasp-like joint of the knee, which is capable only of flexion and extension, the ball-and-socket joint of the hip can move from side to side as well as backward and forward. It can also rotate internally or externally, and does so every time you turn your foot in or out. Since there is a high correlation between hip flexion and Alpine skiing performance, we are testing that function of the hips' range of motion. Though there is no correlation between the internal and external hip rotation and skiing performance, a more limited than normal range of those motions does handicap a skier, particularly in the ability to angulate; therefore you will receive a negative score for the rotation test if your internal or external hip rotation has less than that normal range of motion.

What You Will Need

You will need a friend to watch you take the test.

Taking the Hip-Flexion Test

Lie on your back on the floor. Keeping your head, hands, back, and left leg flat on the floor, bring your right knee up as close to your chest as you can without bouncing. Now put your right leg back down and bring your left knee up toward your chest in the same way. Have your friend sit on the floor a distance away to note which of your upper legs remains farthest away from your chest and to make an approximation of the angle formed between that leg and your stomach. (See the illustration.) That angle will determine your score in Table 10.

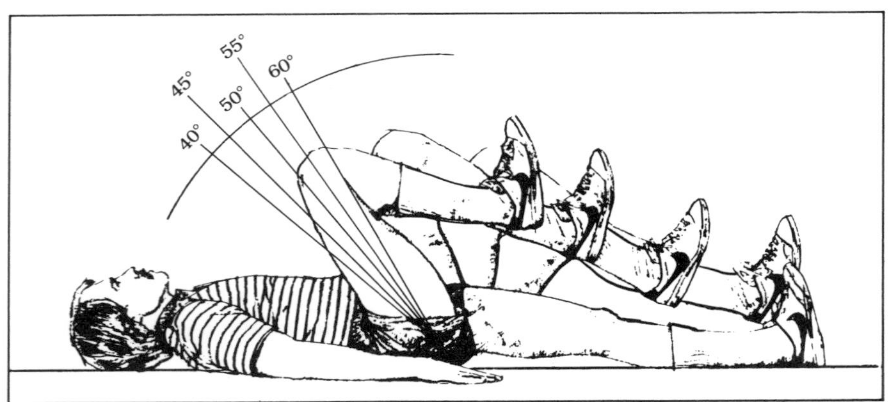

TABLE 10. HIP FLEXION

Angle (degrees)	Points
40	8
45	6
50	4
55	2
60	1

Taking the External- and Internal-Hip-Rotation Test

To test external hip rotation, stand, barefoot, with your heels together and your knees locked. Keeping your heels together, spread your feet away from each other as far as they will go, without walking them out or applying torque to your knees. There should be at least a ninety-degree (right) angle formed by your feet; if the angle is less than ninety degrees, deduct three points from your overall score in Alpine skiing.

To test internal hip rotation, stand with your feet together. Putting all your weight on your left leg, lift your right foot off the floor and let it dangle naturally and freely from your hip. Now turn the toes of your right foot in toward the ball of your left foot as far as you can, keeping your right leg under you and your hips facing forward, and put the right foot back down on the floor. Note the angle now created between your right foot and your left foot. (You can either judge this angle or measure it with a protractor.) Now repeat the test with your left foot by starting from the beginning with your feet together. If the test with either foot produces an angle between your two feet of less than forty-five degrees, deduct three points from your overall score for Alpine skiing.

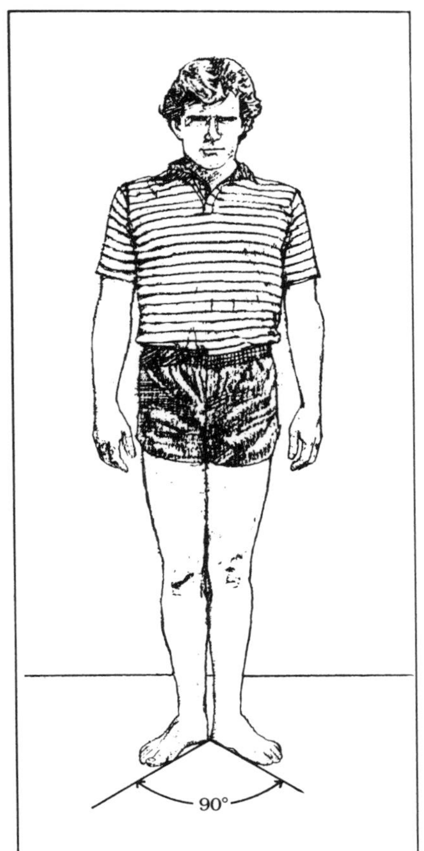

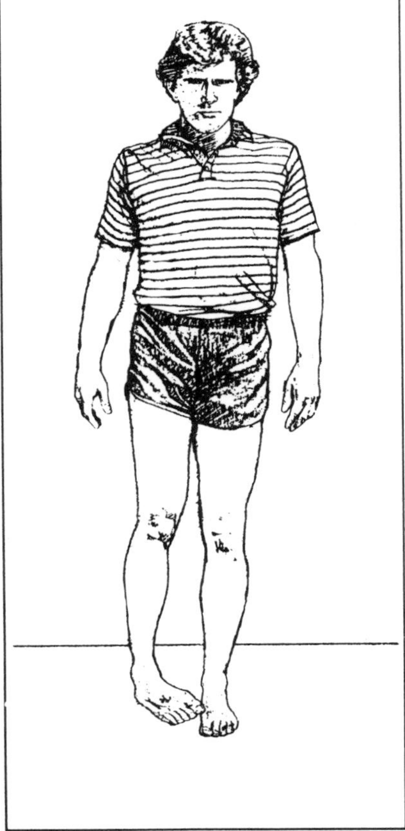

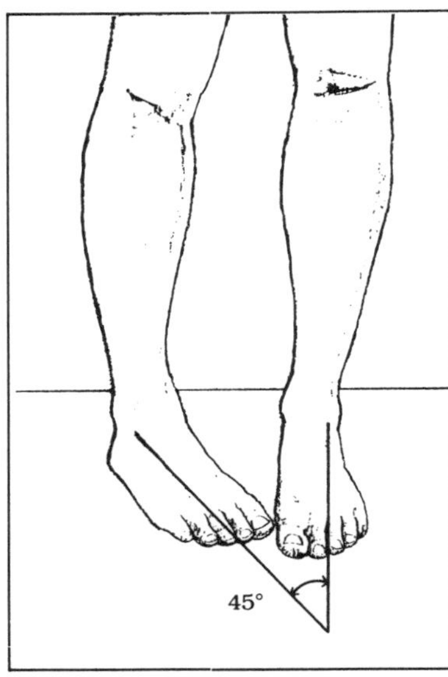

TESTING FOR TENNIS

Your strokes, the timing of those strokes, and the agility and quickness that get you to the ball in time to make your strokes are 95 percent of your tennis game. The leg explosiveness that makes for court quickness in tennis, and a complete range of motion in the shoulders and hips that allows for good racquet readiness and follow-through, are tested here under Body Composition and given a combined weight, or value, of 30 percent, just under a third of the overall value of the tests, a percentage that reflects the paramount importance of the Control System in tennis.

The good vision, anticipation and reaction time, agility, and smooth, powerful strokes that most accurately characterize the world's best tennis players are all functions of the Control System. In the first six tests we are looking for the underlying structures of these Control System abilities rather than for specific demonstrations of them on the court, and therefore there are no tests that require the use of a tennis racquet. Any tennis stroke requires coordinated multilimb movement, control precision, and aiming, which together define the stroke's effectiveness and consistency. The tennis serve can be closely approximated with an overhand throwing motion, which, like the serve, mobilizes the entire body behind a specific arm movement to produce both velocity and accuracy—and so an overhand-throwing test (page 167) is used to assess the effectiveness of the Control System structure underlying your serving motion. We are not testing separately the coordinative structures that serve as the basis for the forehand and backhand strokes, because the ability to put the entire body behind an arm motion is already tested in the serving-motion test, and because no single underhand throwing motion has been identified as being central to those strokes.

The science of sportsvision has made major advances in the last few years and there are extremely sophisticated and accurate laboratory measurements of the vision components we test here (as there are also for anticipation and reaction time). The vision tests here, like our tests for anticipation and reaction time, are field tests, but they will indicate the gross effectiveness of the Control System structures underlying tennis-related vision, timing, and reaction time.

We are not testing overall height, though being tall can be a real advantage in tennis, because a good player can and does adapt his game to whatever height he has. While a tall player will likely tend toward a serve-and-volley game to take advantage of his height and reach, a short player who is quick and agile will more likely tend toward a court-covering, retrieving game. Moreover, we are not testing upper-body strength—though such strength is often believed to be important to good tennis—because there is no particular muscle group that *has* to be strong in order for an individual to play tennis well, and because, given good strokes, modern racquet technology allows a player to overcome almost any upper-body muscular weakness with a proper choice of racquet. Finally, there are no heart-lung package tests because the average tennis point lasts only three seconds and even points played by world-class players rarely last longer than twenty or thirty seconds, meaning that no limiting aerobic demand is made by the sport.

CHART 2. TENNIS

	Components tested	**Test**	**Relative importance of test to overall score**	
The Control System	Visual convergence	1. Toothpick-Straw Convergence	10%	70%
	Visual binocularity	2. String-and-Button Binocularity	10%	
	Reaction time with choice	3. Latham Yardstick Reaction Time	10%	
	Anticipation	4. Yardstick Anticipation	10%	
	Agility	5. Hexagon	15%	
	Control precision, multilimb coordination, aiming	6. Nerf Ball Stroke-Structure	15%	
Body Composition	Explosiveness	7. Vertical Jump	15%	30%
	Hip range of motion	8. Internal/External Hip Rotation	8%	
	Shoulder range of motion	9. Shoulder Range of Motion	7%	

TEST 1: TOOTHPICK-STRAW CONVERGENCE

Sportsvision experts now believe that naturally convergent vision allows tennis players who have it to concentrate visually on the ball more intensely and for longer periods of time than can players without it, because their eye muscles converge easily and without strain. Naturally convergent vision, therefore, is a major asset to any tennis player.

We are assuming in both this test and the following one that you have healthy, normal vision with good corrected visual acuity. If you want to test your overall visual acuity, the National Society for the Prevention of Blindness has made available a home acuity test that may be ordered through the mail (see Appendix), or you can visit an ophthalmologist.

What You Will Need

You will need a toothpick, a standard drinking straw, and a friend with a ruler.

Taking the Test

While sitting down, hold the straw at one end with one hand and the toothpick at one end with the other hand. Bring the straw and toothpick together at eye level and one inch from the bridge of your nose (have your friend measure this distance with the ruler and watch to make sure you don't extend the toothpick and straw farther than an inch from the bridge of your nose), and try to stick the toothpick into the straw by focusing your eyes on them. You are not allowed to touch your face with either hand, or to touch the toothpick and straw together more than once, and your hands and elbows must be held away from your body. You get only one chance at this test at the one-inch distance. If you put the toothpick into the straw at that distance, you earn ten points (see Table 11). If you fail at the one-inch distance, repeat the test while holding the toothpick and straw three inches from the bridge of your nose; if you put the toothpick into the straw at that distance, you earn five points. If you cannot perform the test at three inches, you score no points.

Try to focus on the straw.

TABLE 11. TOOTHPICK-STRAW CONVERGENCE

	Points
Success at 1 inch	10
Success at 3 inches	5

TEST 2: STRING-AND-BUTTON BINOCULARITY

Visual binocularity is the ability to focus clearly on an object with both eyes simultaneously. The only way to judge accurately an approaching ball's exact distance from your body is to triangulate the ball in space by focusing on it with both eyes; binocularity allows you to do that. Along with good visual convergence, binocularity provides a player with multiple tracking points along a ball's trajectory, which when integrated by the Control System tell the player when and where the ball will arrive at the point of intended impact and allow him to ready the proper motor program for stroke production in advance.

Binocularity is critical for playing good tennis. Many good club players who spend thousands of dollars on lessons and equipment find that their game becomes blocked at certain points; quite often those blocks are due to an absence of binocular vision. For the same reason, other players can get absolutely nowhere at all with the sport.

You either have binocular vision or you don't; this is, therefore, an all-or-nothing test: you receive ten points if you perform it successfully, and no points if you don't. If you fail this test, have your eyes examined by an ophthalmologist.

What You Will Need

You will need a piece of white string (about four feet long), a shirt button, and a ruler or tape measure.

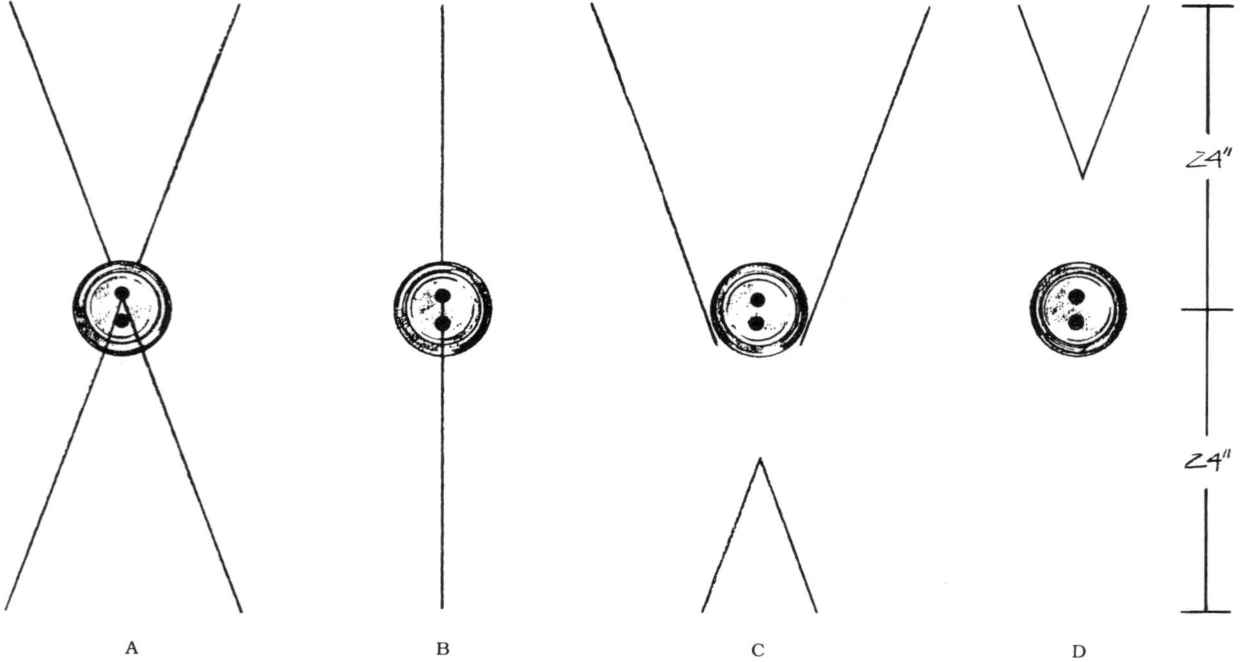

Taking the Test

Sit on a chair and tie one end of the string to a doorknob or drawer handle—something solid and at eye level. Thread the button onto the string and slide it along so that it is twenty-four inches from your face, a distance you should measure with the ruler. Lay the unfixed end of the string across your forefinger and rest it on the tip of your nose. Now look down the string and focus both eyes on the button. What you should see in order to receive a score for this test is reproduced in Illustration A. If what you see is reproduced in Illustration B, you have no binocular vision. If what you see is reproduced in Illustration C, you will project an approaching tennis ball ahead of its actual location and therefore will have a tendency to hit early. If what you see is reproduced in Illustration D, you will project an approaching ball behind its actual location and therefore will have a tendency to hit late. Take a score of ten points in Table 12 *only* if what you see matches what is shown in Illustration A.

TABLE 12. STRING-AND-BUTTON BINOCULARITY

	Points
Strings meet in button	10
Only 1 string	0
Strings meet before button	0
Strings meet after button	0

TEST 3: LATHAM YARDSTICK REACTION TIME

Tennis is a hand/eye sport, and one of the best measurements of hand/eye coordination is the timed response to a visual stimulus, known as reaction time. Reaction time in human beings usually averages around 170 milliseconds, which incorporates the time required to register a stimulus visually, to prepare a motor program, and to initiate a movement. This time will be lengthened if there is a choice of responses to the stimulus, or if more than one stimulus is presented at a time. Reaction time to a given stimulus may be considerably shortened if the stimulus is accurately anticipated, by virtue of training, and among people with naturally fast Control Systems. Athletes who are known to have "quick hands" or "quick feet" are athletes with extraordinarily quick reactions to the stimuli presented by their sports, and though reaction time within a given sport is trainable, some athletes—such as hockey's Wayne Gretzky, for example—are simply born with phenomenally quick reactions, an enormous advantage in any hand/eye sport.

In the laboratory, reaction times are measured, in milliseconds, by sophisticated and expensive electronic timing devices. In this field test, your reaction time will be measured in inches on the yardsticks, the millisecond value for which has been incorporated into Table 13 by adapting Galileo's principle that two objects, regardless of their individual weights, will fall at the same speed and rate of acceleration. Inches in this test, in other words, equal time.

Two yardsticks are used to incorporate choice into the test and thereby to simulate the sort of "choice reaction time" active in tennis, and also to diminish the effect of anticipation. You should *not* try to anticipate which yardstick will be dropped, but react only to one of the two being dropped. If you do try to anticipate which yard-

stick will be dropped, the test will not yield an accurate measure of your reaction time (that is, the test will show reaction time as faster than it really is if you anticipate correctly, and slower than it really is if you anticipate incorrectly).

What You Will Need

You will need a chair, a narrow table or desk, two yardsticks, and a friend to administer the test.

Taking the Test

Sit at the table or desk with your forearms lying flat and your hands held as shown in the illustration. It is very important that you not move your hands off the table during the test, and that you keep your thumbs and forefingers absolutely level throughout. Have your friend stand in front of you, holding the two yardsticks at their thirty-six-inch ends and above your hands. (Your friend may want to stand on a chair to do this.) To position the yardsticks correctly for the test, your friend should steady their bottom ends on your thumbs, then move those ends into the gaps created by your thumbs and forefingers, so that the ends of the yardsticks are horizontal with the tops of your fingers. Your friend can drop either yardstick (never both at the same time), waiting at least a second and no more than ten seconds to drop it after you say you are ready for the trial. Your friend should try to keep you guessing as to which yardstick will drop each time and exactly

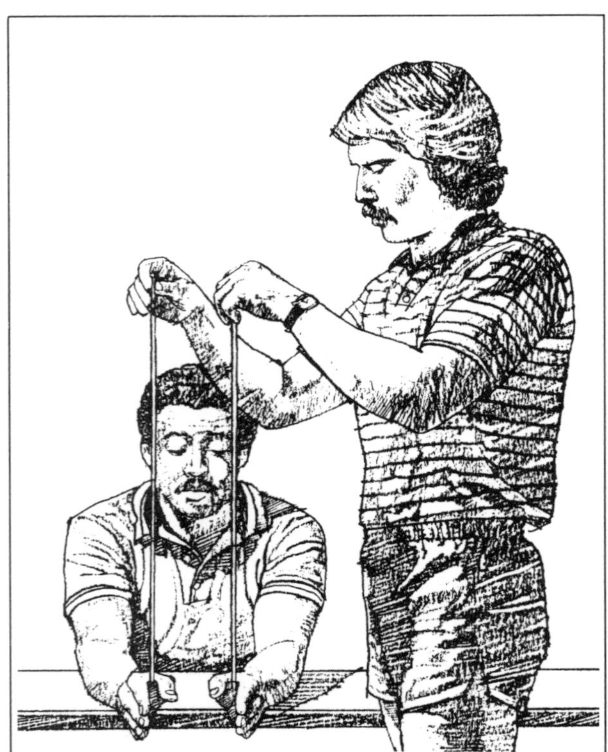

Remember to keep your fingers clear of the sticks.

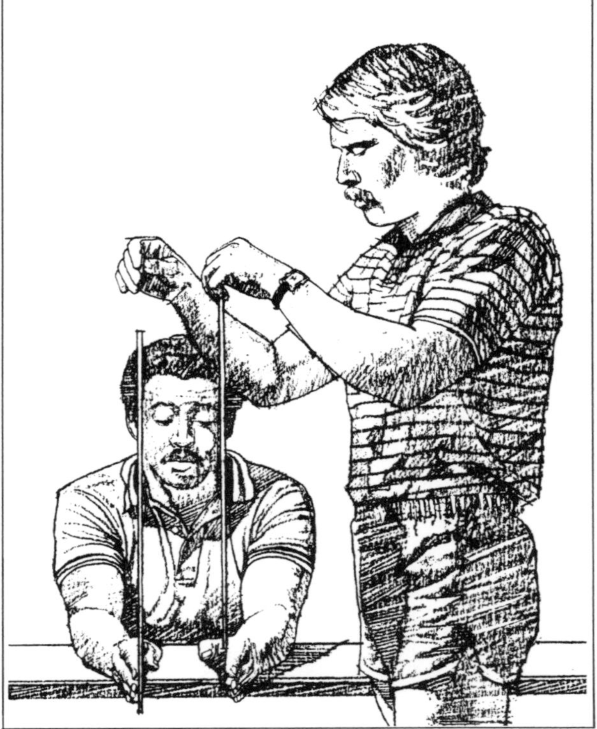

Don't try to guess—wait until the stick falls.

when it will drop within the nine-second limit.

Don't practice before taking this test. You should take ten trials with each hand. Your score for each trial will be exactly where, in inches, the tops of your thumb and forefinger catch the yardstick. For your score on the test, take your best trial with either hand, and use that figure to find your test score in Table 13.

TABLE 13. LATHAM YARDSTICK REACTION TIME

Caught at how many inches (best trial)	Points
5	10
6	9
7	8
8	7
9	6
10	5
11	4
12	3
13	2
14	1
15	0

TEST 4: YARDSTICK ANTICIPATION

Experiments have shown that some very good tennis players can return shots to which they are totally blinded as the approaching ball crosses the net. They are able to do this by virtue of highly honed anticipation. Good anticipation, commonly thought of as good timing, is even more central to playing tennis well than is quick reaction time, since good anticipation will allow a player to pre-program a response to any shot well enough in advance so that even with poor reaction time the return can be made. Most tennis experts we have consulted believe that good anticipation and quick reaction time are generally found together in an individual, but not always. In fact, one world-class tennis player we know of has phenomenally good anticipation and a very slow reaction time. Anticipation is highly trainable, and if you found in the preceding test that you have a slow reaction time, you can make up for that fact in your tennis game by working on your anticipation.

What You Will Need

The same setup required in the preceding test is necessary, but for this test, mark a single yardstick clearly in red at its twenty-inch line.

Taking the Test

Sit as you did for Test 3 but with your hand placed three inches from the far edge of the table or desk (see illustration). Your friend should position the yardstick at a height level with the tops of your thumb and forefinger and less than an inch from the edge of the table or desk. Your friend should drop the yardstick, waiting between one and ten seconds to drop it after you say you are ready for the trial. When the yardstick falls, you should slide your hand outward along

the table or desk (don't lift your hand from the surface) and catch it between your thumb and forefinger at a point on the yardstick as close to the red mark as you can.

Don't practice before taking the test. Take five trials with either hand, and the score for each of those trials will be the number of inches and fractions of inches between the tops of your fingers and the twenty-inch line on the yardstick. Take your best trial with either hand, and use that figure to find your score in Table 14.

TABLE 14. YARDSTICK ANTICIPATION

Inches early or late (best trial)	Points
0.0	10
0.5	9
1.0	8
1.5	7
2.0	6
2.5	5
3.0	4
3.5	3
4.0	2
4.5	1
5.0	0

Keep your hands clear. Keep your eye on the red mark.

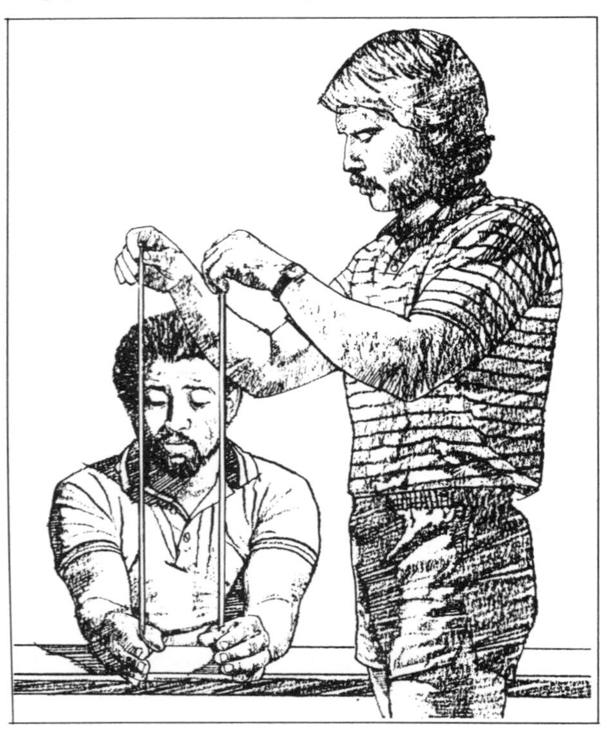

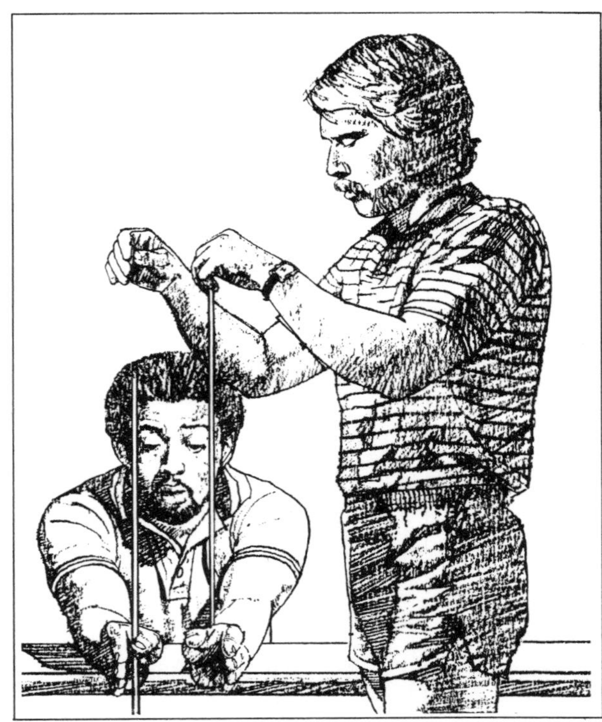

TEST 5: HEXAGON

This test is a variation of the Hexagonal-Obstacle Test developed by the Austrians to determine Alpine skiing ability in individuals from age ten on. Generally, the test measures agility, balance, and gross body coordination, abilities important to all three skill sports treated in this book; specifically, it is used here to measure foot quickness in changing direction backward, forward, and laterally while facing in one direction (toward the net), and the ability to stabilize the body quickly between those changes of direction. Agility in both cases is crucial to good court movement and to providing a correctly positioned and solid platform from which to stroke.

Do not practice before taking this test. Take it three times within a twenty-minute period, add the total number of seconds for all three trials, and divide that number by 3 for your average time, which will give you your score in Table 15.

What You Will Need

Lay out a hexagon as instructed on page 144. No blocks are used in this test.

Taking the Test

Perform the test as instructed on page 144. Your overall score for the test is determined in Table 15 from your average time for your first three uninterrupted performances.

TABLE 15. HEXAGON

Average time (*seconds*)		Points
Men	**Women**	
9.0	9.0	15.0
10.1	10.6	13.7
11.2	12.2	12.3
12.3	13.8	11.0
13.4	15.4	9.6
14.5	17.0	8.3
15.6	18.6	6.9
16.7	20.2	5.6
17.8	21.8	4.2
18.9	23.4	2.9
20.0	25.0	1.5

TEST 6: NERF BALL STROKE-STRUCTURE

This test assesses the structure of coordinated, multilimb movement, consistent control precision, and aiming ability that together underlie the serving stroke in tennis. The movement used here to simulate and assess that stroke is an overhand throwing motion, and while no such motion underlies the forehand and backhand strokes, the motion does have in common with those strokes the ability to mobilize the entire momentum of the body behind a single movement of the arm to produce both accuracy and velocity. Therefore, the test may serve as a rough measure of those aspects of the Control System's effectiveness in the production of the forehand and backhand strokes as well as of the serve.

It is important that you *not* try to take this test by throwing only with your arm or wrist. You should put your whole body into the motion, the way a baseball pitcher does. Throwing in this way is a more common motion to some people than to others (it is more common to men, for example, than it is, as a rule, to women). Those people will have an advantage in this test, just as they will likely have more natural potential serving ability than will people to whom overhand throwing is an unaccustomed motion.

What You Will Need

You may take this test on a level lawn, in a cleared area of a parking lot, or on a level section of road, and there should be no wind when you take it. You will need a standard round Nerf ball (it is about four inches in diameter), a square two feet on each side, laid out on the ground with sticks or tape, a measuring tape, and a friend to help you with the test.

Taking the Test

Measure off forty feet from the center of the target square if you are a man, and thirty feet if you are a woman. You must throw from behind that point. Have your friend stand beside the target square. Take five practice throws, trying to throw the Nerf ball into the square and putting your entire body behind each throw. For the test, take fifteen throws, again putting your entire body behind each one. To score (see Table 16), award yourself one point for each time your friend sees the ball land inside the square on the fly (bouncing or rolling the ball in doesn't count). You will also receive a point if the ball hits the tape or sticks marking off your square. If you repeatedly can't reach the box with your throw, you may move five feet closer.

Put your whole body into it.

TABLE 16. NERF BALL STROKE-STRUCTURE

Number of balls in center of square	Points
15	15
14	14
13	13
12	12
11	11
10	10
9	9
8	8
7	7
6	6
5	5
4	4
3	3
2	2
1	1
0	0

TEST 7: VERTICAL JUMP

A ball you can't get to in tennis is a ball you can't hit, no matter how good your strokes or the other components of your game. Court quickness is a function of the speed generated in the first two steps you take toward a ball—the steps that break your inertia and get your body mass moving. That speed is generated by the explosive power of the upper and lower legs, which is tested here.

What You Will Need

The equipment needed for this test is listed on page 151.

Taking the Test

Proceed as instructed on page 151. Don't practice before taking the test. Do the test three times and take your highest *single* reach in inches. To determine your score, find the point in Table 17 at which that number of inches intersects with your body weight.

TABLE 17. VERTICAL JUMP

Highest single reach (*inches*)	Weight (*pounds*)																	
	80	**90**	**100**	**110**	**120**	**130**	**140**	**150**	**160**	**170**	**180**	**190**	**200**	**220**	**240**	**260**	**280**	**300**
8	53	60	67	73	80	87	93	100	107	113	120	127	133	147	160	173	187	200
10	67	75	83	92	100	108	117	125	133	142	150	158	167	183	200	217	233	250
12	80	90	100	110	120	130	140	150	160	170	180	190	200	220	240	260	280	300
14	93	105	117	128	140	152	163	175	187	198	210	222	233	257	280	303	327	350
16	107	120	133	147	160	173	187	200	213	227	240	253	267	293	320	347	373	400
18	120	135	150	165	180	195	210	225	240	255	270	285	300	330	360	390	420	450
20	133	150	167	183	200	217	233	250	267	283	300	317	333	367	400	433	467	500
22	147	165	183	202	220	238	257	275	293	312	330	348	367	403	440	477	513	550
24	160	180	200	220	240	260	280	300	320	340	360	380	400	440	480	520	560	600
26	173	195	217	238	260	282	303	325	347	368	390	412	433	477	520	563	607	650
28	187	210	233	257	280	303	327	350	373	397	420	443	467	513	560	607	653	700
30	200	225	250	275	300	325	350	375	400	425	450	475	500	550	600	650	700	750
32	213	240	267	293	320	347	373	400	427	453	480	507	533	587	640	693	747	800
34	227	255	283	312	340	368	397	425	453	482	510	538	567	623	680	737	793	850
36	240	270	300	330	360	390	420	450	480	510	540	570	600	660	720	780	840	900
38	253	285	317	348	380	412	443	475	507	538	570	602	633	697	760	823	887	950
40	267	300	333	367	400	433	467	500	533	567	600	633	667	733	800	867	933	—

SCORING:

Men	Women	Points
360	220	15.0
342 or above	207 or above	13.5
324 " "	193 " "	12.0
307 " "	180	10.5
289 " "	167	9.0
271 " "	153 " "	7.5
253	140	6.0
236 " "	127	4.5
218 " "	113	3.0
200	100	1.5

TEST 8: INTERNAL/EXTERNAL HIP ROTATION

A full range of motion in the hips and shoulders is absolutely essential to getting the racquet back and to following through completely in the proper production of the serve and of the forehand and backhand ground strokes. Though any one of these three strokes *can* be hit if the racquet is not taken fully back and/or without full follow through, they cannot be hit consistently and with the power and accuracy allowed by complete strokes. This test and Test 9 measure those ranges of motion in your hips and shoulders that are essential to producing such strokes.

Taking the Test

The test is the same as that on page 157. Follow the instructions given there and award yourself four points if the angle formed by your feet for the internal-rotation test is more than forty-five degrees, and another four points if the angle formed by your feet for the external-rotation test is greater than ninety degrees.

TEST 9: SHOULDER RANGE OF MOTION

Taking the Test

While standing, put the hand of your playing arm behind your neck, with the fingers pointed down between your shoulder blades and your palm lying flat against your back. Now bring your other hand up behind your back, palm outward, as far as it will comfortably go, and work the fingers of your playing hand as far down your back toward the other hand as you can get them. If you can touch your two middle fingers together, work the middle finger of your playing hand as far as you can into the palm of your other hand. For your score, look for the illustration that most exactly depicts the position your two hands finally achieve in relation to each other. (You might want to have a friend determine that position for you.)

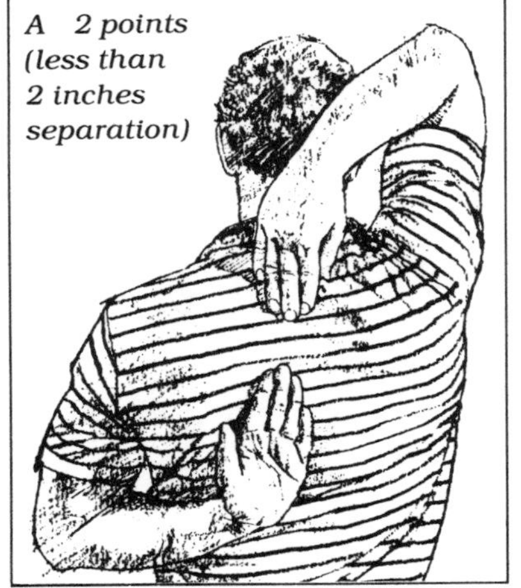
A 2 points (less than 2 inches separation)

B 3 points

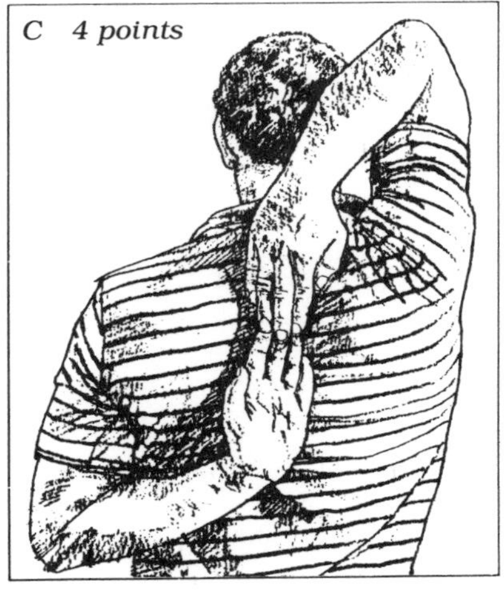
C 4 points

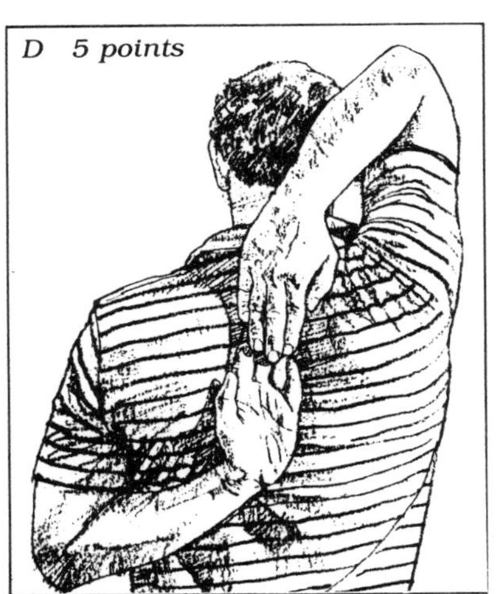
D 5 points

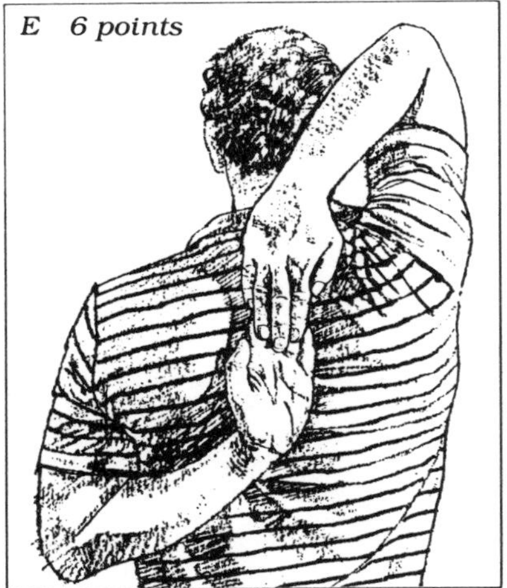
E 6 points

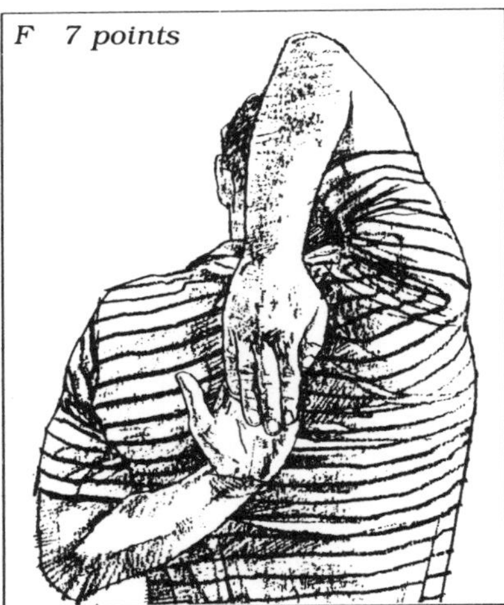
F 7 points

TESTING FOR WINDSURFING

Of the sports covered in this book, windsurfing is probably the one that the smallest number of people have tried. Even more than tennis and Alpine skiing, it is almost entirely a skill sport, a sport of the Control System, and that fact is reflected in the relative importance or value given to the tests here. The underlying abilities of agility, balance, and coordination, along with a quick motor-learning capacity, are the most important components of talent at windsurfing. Good dynamic visual acuity is also important, but is not tested here because it is so highly trainable.

There are no tests here for the Heart-Lung Package because the aerobic demands made by windsurfing can be met by practically any healthy person. As for the balance of the tests for this sport, an individual's natural ability at windsurfing is appreciably enlarged if he or she has a low center of gravity, is slightly knock-kneed, and has a body weight that is not more than 10 percent fat. There are not more Body Composition tests here because the equipment used in windsurfing is so easily adaptable to different body types: a heavy windsurfer can get a board with more than the usual flotation, for example, and a very tall windsurfer can get a larger than average sail or a higher than average boom.

Though the talent being tested here is talent for windsurfing in general, the sport breaks into a number of competitive events involving varying requirements of an individual's skills. The underlying motor abilities tested in Test 1, for example, while important for all windsurfing, are far more important in big ocean surf than they are on a calm lake. Conversely, someone with only fair to good agility but with excellent balance might not perform well in big surf but might do very well in flat-water triangle races.

CHART 3. WINDSURFING

	Components tested	**Test**	**Relative importance of test to overall score**	
The Control System	Agility, coordination, speed of motor learning	1. Hexagon	40%	80%
	Static balance	2. Blind-Stork Balance	20%	
	Stabilization, dynamic balance	3. Balance Stabilization	20%	
Body Composition	Center of gravity	4. Upper-Body/Lower-Body Proportion	10%	20%
	Degree to which knock-kneed	5. Knock-kneed–Bowlegged Spectrum	10%	
	Percentage of body fat	6. Caliper Body-Fat-Percentage Measurement (negative points only)		

TEST 1: HEXAGON

This test is a variation of the Hexagonal-Obstacle Test developed by the Austrians to determine Alpine skiing ability in individuals from age ten on. Specifically, this test measures agility, balance, and gross body coordination—abilities as important to windsurfing as they are to skiing. This variation of the Hexagonal-Obstacle Test does away with the blocks, or sides, used in the ski test, because constant retraction of the legs is not necessary in windsurfing.

Take the test three times. The average time for the three trials will give you your overall score in Table 18. To test your speed of motor learning, take the test twice more, for a total of five times—the difference between how fast you did it the first time and how fast you did it the fifth time will provide your score for speed of motor learning in Table 19. All five repetitions of the test should be performed within a half-hour period, and you should not practice before performing the test for the first time.

What You Will Need

See page 144. (You will not need the blocks.)

Taking the Test

Perform the test as instructed on page 144. Determine your overall score for the abilities test in Table 18 from your average time for your first three uninterrupted performances of the test. Find your score for motor-learning speed in Table 19 by using the difference in time it took you to complete the test between your first performance and your fifth.

TABLE 18. HEXAGON

Average time (*seconds*)		Points
Men	Women	
9.0	9.0	30.0
10.1	10.6	27.5
11.2	12.2	25.0
12.3	13.8	22.5
13.4	15.4	20.0
14.5	17.0	17.5
15.6	18.6	15.0
16.7	20.2	12.5
17.8	21.8	10.0
18.9	23.4	7.5
20.0	25.0	5.0

TABLE 19. HEXAGON

Men						Women					
Average time	Point value for difference in time (*seconds*)					Average time	Point value for difference in time (*seconds*)				
	10 points	8 points	6 points	4 points	2 points		10 points	8 points	6 points	4 points	2 points
9.00	4.50	3.60	2.70	1.80	0.90	9.00	4.50	3.60	2.70	1.80	0.90
10.10	5.05	4.04	3.03	2.02	1.01	10.60	5.30	4.24	3.18	2.12	1.06
11.20	5.60	4.48	3.36	2.24	1.12	12.20	6.10	4.88	3.66	2.44	1.22
12.30	6.15	4.92	3.69	2.46	1.23	13.80	6.90	5.52	4.14	2.76	1.38
13.40	6.70	5.36	4.02	2.68	1.34	15.40	7.70	6.16	4.62	3.08	1.54
14.50	7.25	5.80	4.35	2.90	1.45	17.00	8.50	6.80	5.10	3.40	1.70
15.60	7.80	6.24	4.68	3.12	1.56	18.60	9.30	7.44	5.58	3.72	1.86
16.70	8.35	6.68	5.01	3.34	1.67	20.20	10.10	8.08	6.06	4.04	2.02
17.80	8.90	7.12	5.34	3.56	1.78	21.80	10.90	8.72	6.54	4.36	2.18
18.90	9.45	7.56	5.67	3.78	1.89	23.40	11.70	9.36	7.02	4.68	2.34
20.00	10.00	8.00	6.00	4.00	2.00	25.00	12.50	10.00	7.50	5.00	2.50

TEST 2: BLIND-STORK BALANCE

This test is the best we've found for reducing balance—a crucial ability for good windsurfing—to its most important components. You may notice that you begin to lurch a few seconds into this test. Any movement of the head produced by lurching will cause the inner ears to begin discharging messages to the cerebellum; the more sensitive the reception of your inner ears to shifts in position of your head, and the better your cerebellar integration, the better your balance will be on this test. The test is done with your eyes closed in order to avoid the substantial positional information provided by the eyes, which, along with other information from the limb receptors, helps to keep us upright but has nothing to do with the core, gyroscopic balance function of the inner ear. Some degree of balance was tested in the preceding test. This is a "super-balance" test, and some people may not be able to score on it at all.

Keep your leg well out to the side and don't peek.

What You Will Need

You will need a friend with a stopwatch.

Taking the Test

Take this test wearing sneakers—the results won't be as good if you do it barefoot—and standing on a hard surface. Stand on your dominant leg (the leg you kick with) and put your other foot on the knee of your weighted leg (see illustration). Put your hands on your hips and close your eyes. Your friend should start timing you as soon as your eyes are closed. The test is over when you take your hands off your hips or your foot off your knee, or when you move your weighted foot from its original position on the floor. (You may shift around on the foot, so long as it doesn't move.) Take the test three times within five minutes and use your single best time to find your score in Table 20.

TABLE 20. BLIND-STORK BALANCE

Men		Women	
Best time (*seconds*)	**Points**	**Best time (*seconds*)**	**Points**
60	20	35	20
55	18	30	17
50	16	25	14
45	14	20	11
40	12	15	8
35	10	10	4
30	8	5	2
25	6		
20	4		
15	3		
10	2		

TEST 3: BALANCE STABILIZATION

Windsurfing requires dynamic, as well as static, balance—or the ability to constantly restabilize the body on a shifting platform. This test, developed on the island of Maui by Dr. Arnot, tests that ability.

What You Will Need

You will need a friend with a stopwatch.

Taking the Test

Do this test on a slick floor. Wear socks. Start in the same body position you assumed for Test 2—hands on hips, standing on your dominant leg, with the unweighted foot on the knee of your weighted leg. Keep your eyes open throughout the test. Have your friend start the stopwatch. After five seconds your friend should tell you to turn. Turn 180 degrees to your right by swiveling on the ball of your foot. After five more seconds, again on the command to turn, turn back to your original position. Keep turning every five seconds until your unweighted foot comes off your knee or until your hands come off your hips. The total number of seconds you last will give you your score in Table 21.

TABLE 21. BALANCE STABILIZATION

Number of seconds		Points
Men	Women	
110	105.0	20.0
103	97.5	18.6
96	90.0	17.2
89	82.5	15.8
82	75.0	14.4
75	67.5	13.0
68	60.0	11.6
61	52.5	10.2
54	45.0	8.8
47	37.5	7.4
40	30.0	6.0
33	22.5	4.6
26	15.0	3.2
19	7.5	1.8

TEST 4: UPPER-BODY/ LOWER-BODY PROPORTION

If you are a tall person, you may have noticed in the two previous tests that once you begin to lose your balance the weight of your height above your center of gravity contributes substantially to that loss of balance and makes it more difficult for you to recover than it would be for someone with a lower center of gravity. A low center of gravity, therefore, is a stabilizing asset in windsurfing, as it is in any kind of sailing.

TABLE 22. UPPER-BODY/LOWER-BODY PROPORTION

Overall height (*inches*)	Sitting height (*inches*)																			
	26	**27**	**28**	**29**	**30**	**31**	**32**	**33**	**34**	**35**	**36**	**37**	**38**	**39**	**40**	**41**	**42**	**43**	**44**	**45**
54	0.9	1.0	1.1	1.2	1.3															
55	0.9	1.0	1.0	1.1	1.2	1.3														
56		0.9	1.0	1.1	1.2	1.2	1.3													
57		0.9	1.0	1.0	1.1	1.2	1.3													
58			0.9	1.0	1.1	1.1	1.2	1.3												
59			0.9	1.0	1.0	1.1	1.2	1.3												
60				0.9	1.0	1.1	1.1	1.2	1.3											
61				0.9	1.0	1.0	1.1	1.2	1.3											
62					0.9	1.0	1.1	1.1	1.2	1.3										
63					0.9	1.0	1.0	1.1	1.2	1.3										
64						0.9	1.0	1.1	1.1	1.2	1.3									
65						0.9	1.0	1.0	1.1	1.2	1.2									
66							0.9	1.0	1.1	1.1	1.2	1.3								
67							0.9	1.0	1.0	1.1	1.2	1.2	1.3							
68								0.9	1.0	1.1	1.1	1.2	1.3							
69								0.9	1.0	1.0	1.1	1.2	1.2	1.3						
70								0.9	0.9	1.0	1.1	1.1	1.2	1.3						
71									0.9	1.0	1.0	1.1	1.2	1.2	1.3					
72										0.9	1.0	1.1	1.1	1.2	1.3					
73										0.9	1.0	1.0	1.1	1.1	1.2	1.3				
74										0.9	0.9	1.0	1.1	1.1	1.2	1.2				
75											0.9	1.0	1.0	1.1	1.1	1.2	1.3			
76											0.9	0.9	1.0	1.1	1.1	1.2	1.2	1.3		
77												0.9	1.0	1.0	1.1	1.1	1.2	1.3		
78												0.9	1.0	1.0	1.1	1.1	1.2	1.2	1.3	
79													0.9	1.0	1.0	1.1	1.1	1.2	1.3	1.3
80													0.9	1.0	1.0	1.1	1.1	1.2	1.2	1.3

SCORING:

Ratio of sitting height to lower-body length (*inches*)	Points
1.3 or above	10.0
1.2	5.7
1.1	4.3
1.0	2.9
0.9	1.4

What You Will Need

You will need the same equipment as indicated on page 152.

Taking the Test

Proceed with this test as indicated on page 152. Locate the point in Table 22 at which your sitting height intersects with your overall height, and use that ratio to determine your score.

TEST 5: KNOCK-KNEED–BOWLEGGED SPECTRUM

In Alpine skiing it is an advantage to be slightly knock-kneed, because that condition automatically and naturally puts the knees over the inside, or carving, edges of the skis, allowing for quicker applications of pressure in the initiation of turns. Being knock-kneed provides a similar advantage in windsurfing, where turns are also initiated by the application of pressure to the turning, or carving, edge of the board. This test measures the degree to which you are either knock-kneed or bowlegged. The latter condition, while it might slightly lower an individual's center of gravity, is a marked disadvantage in making the quick, linked turns that are necessary in advanced windsurfing.

What You Will Need

The same materials as those indicated on page 154 are necessary.

Taking the Test

Proceed with the test as indicated on page 154. If you find you are knock-kneed, hold your knees together, arrange your feet so they are exactly parallel, and have your friend measure the distance between your two inside anklebones. That distance in inches will give you your score in Table 23. If your feet and knees meet at the same time, use the value 0 in the table to determine your score. And if you find you are bowlegged, use the number of inches left between the insides of your knee bones when your feet are together, and subtract the points indicated by that distance from your score.

TABLE 23. KNOCK-KNEED–BOWLEGGED SPECTRUM

Measurement (*inches*)	Points
1 ½ and above	10.0
1 ¼	8.6
1	7.2
¾	5.7
½	4.3
¼	2.9
0	1.4

TEST 6: CALIPER BODY-FAT-PERCENTAGE MEASUREMENT

For the quickness and agility necessary to the sport, and because less body weight on a standard board means more speed, a windsurfer wants as low a percentage of body fat as possible. The only accurate way to measure that percentage outside a laboratory is with calipers, and since all athletes should want to keep an accurate running measurement of their percentages of body fat, we suggest here, as in the body-fat tests for the other sports in this book, that you borrow a pair of laboratory calipers, or purchase a pair of inexpensive plastic ones, with which to take that measurement on a regular basis. (See Appendix for information on ordering calipers.)

The tables used here are for a general population, and people with specialized fat stores in only one or two specific parts of the body may get a slightly inaccurate overall score.

What You Will Need

A pair of calipers.

Taking the Test

Measuring yourself with calipers for body fat takes some practice. If you know a physiologist, sports physician, trainer, or coach with experience in doing it, ask him or her to help you; if not, practice with the calipers for a while before taking the test. See the illustrations (page 180) for the measurement sites. This test is best done standing and with no clothes on. For the thigh test, ideally the legs should be elevated on the step of a staircase, or about eight inches.

Measure yourself at each of the sites with the calipers in the following way: With the forefinger and thumb of your left hand pinch a fold of skin at the site and lift it away from the muscle. Place

the calipers on the fold just below your fingers and let them settle there for about five seconds before taking the reading. Add the readings from all measurement sites together and use that total to find your percentage of body fat in Table 24 if you are a man; that percentage will give you your score for this test in Table 26. Women should use Table 25 and find their score in Table 26.

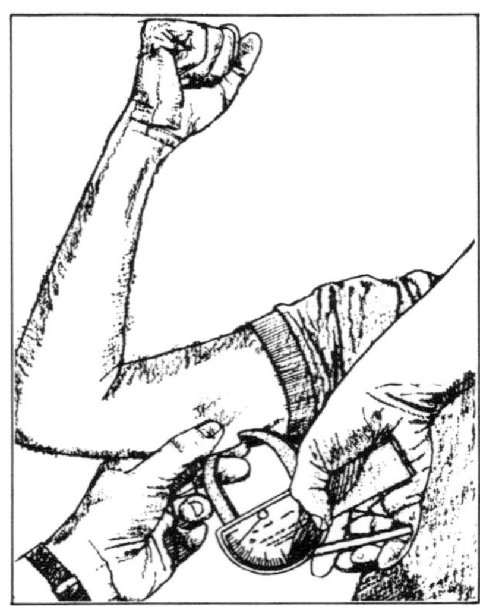

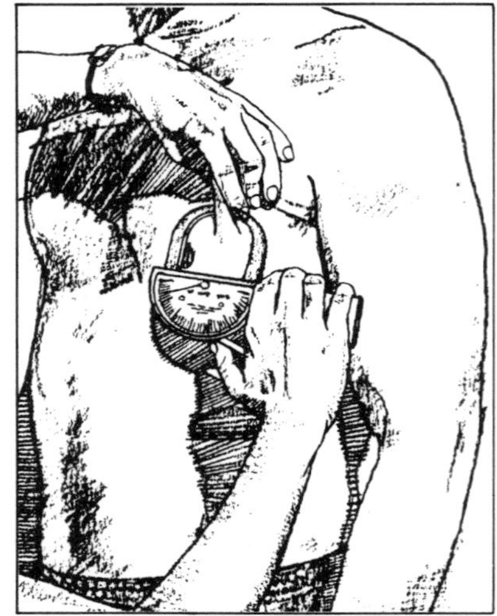

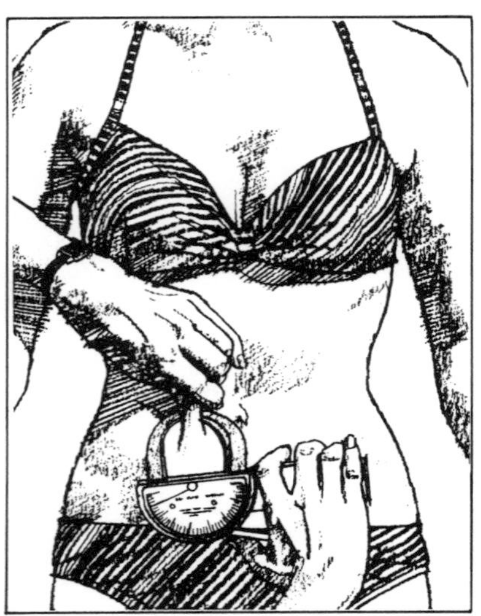

TABLE 26. CALIPER BODY-FAT-PERCENTAGE MEASUREMENT

Body-fat percentage		(Negative) points
Men	**Women**	
9.1	15.0	0
10.0	15.8	−1
11.0 or above	16.5	−2
12.1 " "	17.4	−3
13.3	18.2	−4
14.7	19.1	−5
16.1	20.1	−7
17.7	21.1	−8
19.5 " "	22.2 or above	−9
21.5	23.3 " "	−10
23.6	24.4	−11
26.0	25.7	−12
28.6	26.9	−13
31.4	28.3	−14
34.6 " "	29.7	−15

TABLE 24. CALIPER BODY-FAT-PERCENTAGE MEASUREMENT

	Men								
Sum of skin folds (*millimeters*)	**Age to the last year**								
	Under 22	**23–27**	**28–32**	**33–37**	**38–42**	**43–47**	**48–52**	**53–57**	**Over 58**
8–10	1.3	1.8	2.3	2.9	3.4	3.9	4.5	5.0	5.5
11–13	2.2	2.8	3.3	3.9	4.4	4.9	5.5	6.0	6.5
14–16	3.2	3.8	4.3	4.8	5.4	5.9	6.4	7.0	7.5
17–19	4.2	4.7	5.3	5.8	6.3	6.9	7.4	8.0	8.5
20–22	5.1	5.7	6.2	6.8	7.3	7.9	8.4	8.9	9.5
23–25	6.1	6.6	7.2	7.7	8.3	8.8	9.4	9.9	10.5
26–28	7.0	7.6	8.1	8.7	9.2	9.8	10.3	10.9	11.4
29–31	8.0	8.5	9.1	9.6	10.2	10.7	11.3	11.8	12.4
32–34	8.9	9.4	10.0	10.5	11.1	11.6	12.2	12.8	13.3
35–37	9.8	10.4	10.9	11.5	12.0	12.6	13.1	13.7	14.3
38–40	10.7	11.3	11.8	12.4	12.9	13.5	14.1	14.6	15.2
41–43	11.6	12.2	12.7	13.3	13.8	14.4	15.0	15.5	16.1
44–46	12.5	13.1	13.6	14.2	14.7	15.3	15.9	16.4	17.0
47–49	13.4	13.9	14.5	15.1	15.6	16.2	16.8	17.3	17.9
50–52	14.3	14.8	15.4	15.9	16.5	17.1	17.6	18.2	18.8
53–55	15.1	15.7	16.2	16.8	17.4	17.9	18.5	18.1	19.7
56–58	16.0	16.5	17.1	17.7	18.2	18.8	19.4	20.0	20.5
59–61	16.9	17.4	17.9	18.5	19.1	19.7	20.2	20.8	21.4
62–64	17.6	18.2	18.8	19.4	19.9	20.5	21.1	21.7	22.2
65–67	18.5	19.0	19.6	20.2	20.8	21.3	21.9	22.5	23.1
68–70	19.3	19.9	20.4	21.0	21.6	22.2	22.7	23.3	23.9
71–73	20.1	20.7	21.2	21.8	22.4	23.0	23.6	24.1	24.7
74–76	20.9	21.5	22.0	22.6	23.2	23.8	24.4	25.0	25.5
77–79	21.7	22.2	22.8	23.4	24.0	24.6	25.2	25.8	26.3
80–82	22.4	23.0	23.6	24.2	24.8	25.4	25.9	26.5	27.1
83–85	23.2	23.8	24.4	25.0	25.5	26.1	26.7	27.3	27.9
86–88	24.0	24.5	25.1	25.7	26.3	26.9	27.5	28.1	28.7
89–91	24.7	25.3	25.9	25.5	27.1	27.6	28.2	28.8	29.4
92–94	25.4	26.0	26.6	27.2	27.8	28.4	29.0	29.6	30.2
95–97	26.1	16.7	27.3	27.9	28.5	29.1	29.7	30.3	30.9
98–100	26.9	27.4	28.0	28.6	29.2	29.8	30.4	31.0	31.6
101–103	27.5	28.1	28.7	29.3	29.9	30.5	31.1	31.7	32.3
104–106	28.2	28.8	29.4	30.0	30.6	31.2	31.8	32.4	33.0
107–109	28.9	29.5	30.1	30.7	31.3	31.9	32.5	33.1	33.7
110–112	29.6	30.2	30.8	31.4	32.0	32.6	33.2	33.8	34.4
113–115	30.2	30.8	31.4	32.0	32.6	33.2	33.8	34.5	35.1
116–118	30.9	31.5	32.1	32.7	33.3	33.9	34.5	35.1	35.7
119–121	31.5	32.1	32.7	33.3	33.9	34.5	35.1	35.7	36.4
122–124	32.1	32.7	33.3	33.9	34.5	35.1	35.8	36.4	37.0
125–127	32.7	33.3	33.9	34.5	35.1	35.8	36.4	37.0	37.6

TABLE 25. CALIPER BODY-FAT-PERCENTAGE MEASUREMENT

	Women								
Sum of skin folds (*millimeters*)	**Age to the last year**								
	Under 22	**23–27**	**28–32**	**33–37**	**38–42**	**43–47**	**48–52**	**53–57**	**Over 58**
23–25	9.7	9.9	10.2	10.4	10.7	10.9	11.2	11.4	11.7
26–28	11.0	11.2	11.5	11.7	12.0	12.3	12.5	12.7	13.0
29–31	12.3	12.5	12.8	13.0	13.3	13.5	13.8	14.0	14.3
32–34	13.6	13.8	14.0	14.3	14.5	14.8	15.0	15.3	15.5
35–37	14.8	15.0	15.3	15.5	15.8	16.0	16.3	16.5	16.8
38–40	16.0	16.3	16.5	16.7	17.0	17.2	17.5	17.7	18.0
41–43	17.2	17.4	17.7	17.9	18.2	18.4	18.7	18.9	19.2
44–46	18.3	18.6	18.8	19.1	19.3	19.6	19.8	20.1	20.3
47–49	19.5	19.7	20.0	20.2	20.5	20.7	21.0	21.2	21.5
50–52	20.6	20.8	21.1	21.3	21.6	21.8	22.1	22.3	22.6
53–55	21.7	21.9	22.1	22.4	22.6	22.9	23.1	23.4	23.6
56–58	22.7	23.0	23.2	23.4	23.7	23.9	24.2	24.4	24.7
59–61	23.7	24.0	24.2	24.5	24.7	25.0	25.2	25.5	25.7
62–64	24.7	25.0	25.2	25.5	35.7	26.0	26.7	26.4	26.7
65–67	25.7	25.9	26.2	26.4	26.7	26.9	27.2	27.4	27.7
68–70	26.6	26.9	27.1	27.4	27.6	27.9	28.1	28.4	28.6
71–73	27.5	27.8	28.0	28.3	28.5	28.8	28.0	29.3	29.5
74–76	28.4	28.7	28.9	29.2	29.4	29.7	29.9	30.2	30.4
77–79	29.3	29.5	29.8	30.0	30.3	30.5	30.8	31.0	31.3
80–82	30.1	30.4	30.6	30.9	31.1	31.4	31.6	31.9	32.1
83–85	30.9	31.2	31.4	31.7	31.9	32.2	32.4	32.7	32.9
86–88	31.7	32.0	32.2	32.5	32.7	32.9	33.2	33.4	33.7
89–91	32.5	32.7	33.0	33.2	33.5	33.7	33.9	34.2	34.4
92–94	33.2	33.4	33.7	33.9	34.2	34.4	34.7	34.9	35.2
95–97	33.9	34.1	34.4	34.6	34.9	35.1	35.4	35.6	35.9
98–100	34.6	34.8	35.1	35.3	35.5	35.8	36.0	36.3	36.5
101–103	35.3	35.4	35.7	35.9	36.2	36.4	36.7	36.9	37.2
104–106	35.8	36.1	36.3	36.6	36.8	37.1	37.3	37.5	37.8
107–109	36.4	36.7	36.9	37.1	37.4	37.6	37.9	38.1	38.4
110–112	37.0	37.2	37.5	37.7	38.0	38.2	38.5	38.7	38.9
113–115	37.5	37.8	38.0	38.2	38.5	38.7	39.0	39.2	39.5
116–118	38.0	38.3	38.5	38.8	39.0	39.3	39.5	39.7	40.0
119–121	38.5	38.7	39.0	39.2	39.5	39.7	40.0	40.2	40.5
122–124	39.0	39.2	39.4	39.7	39.9	40.2	40.4	40.7	40.9
125–127	39.4	39.6	39.9	40.1	40.4	40.6	40.9	41.1	41.4
128–130	39.8	40.0	40.3	40.5	40.8	41.0	41.3	41.5	41.8

TESTING FOR RUNNING

A long stride for a given length of leg is a significant requirement for successful competitive or recreational running. The length of an individual's running stride is determined by a basic imprint in that individual's nervous system—an imprint that is largely genetic but can be deepened by training. In Test 1 we are determining natural stride length at a given speed, but that length is often difficult to assess accurately in individuals with no previous running experience. If you have never run before and do poorly on the Stride-Length Test, you may find that after a few weeks of regular running, as you become stronger, you will uncover your natural stride and therefore improve your score on this test. Length of stride is the Control System's major contribution to an individual's running style. In all middle- and long-distance running (running at distances greater than a mile, through marathon distances, and farther, the kinds of running dealt with in this book), if two competing runners are equally strong in frame, heart-lung power, and technique, the length of stride will determine which of them is the faster.

Maximum oxygen consumption, the measure of heart-lung power, determines the potential upper limit of performance for middle- and long-distance runners. If your score on the Cooper Twelve-Minute-Run Test is in the middle to low-middle range and you have not run or trained aerobically before, that score can be improved by training. Training can increase VO_2 Max by

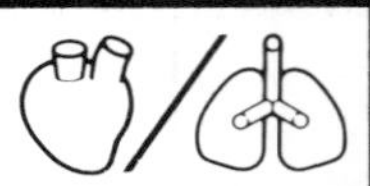

only 30 percent, however—so if your score here is very low, whether you have run before or not, you probably don't have the heart-lung power for successful middle- or long-distance running. Your anaerobic threshold, which represents the percentage of your VO_2 Max that is available to you, is not tested here because it is so highly trainable; it is discussed instead in the running section of Part IV, where speed of recovery is also discussed.

Body Composition comprises the largest group of tests for talent in running because the body is your sole piece of equipment in running and its parts supply not only all your locomotion but all your shock-absorption capacity as well, making the design of those parts, and their overall configuration, crucial. Effective running is done in a single forward plane; all forces that carry parts of the body out of that plane are inefficient, and some, through constant repetition, are physically damaging. Out-of-plane movements in running can be up and down, rotational, or side to side. While most of these movements, such as up-and-down bobbing of the body, excessive hip rotation, or excessive side-to-side movement of the arms, are merely inefficient, certain other out-of-plane movements (as well as certain in-plane movements for which there is not enough shock-absorption capacity) can result in serious injury when repeated over and over as they usually are in running, and so we have added a section on "fatal flaws" to the Body Composition tests. These three tests will neither add to nor subtract from your overall sportstalent score for running, but if you find that you have one or more of these fatal running flaws we strongly recommend that you either take up another sport or limit your running to very short distances (several miles), regardless of how well you score on the running tests.

Not everyone is suited to medium- and long-distance running, but almost everyone can do *some* kind of running safely and enjoyably. If you have one or more of the fatal running flaws, you can still run short distances. If you have a low VO_2 Max and a high percentage of sprint muscle fiber, and especially if you weigh more than three pounds per inch of body height, you should also consider running short distances, at mixed speeds, and over varied terrain.

CHART 4. RUNNING

	Components tested	**Test**	**Relative importance of test to overall score**
The Control System	Motor ability (stride length)	1. Stride Length	20%
The Heart-Lung Package	VO_2 Max	2. Cooper Twelve-Minute Run	38%
Body Composition	Height-weight ratio	3. Weight-to-Height Ratio	15% } 42%
	Width of hips	4. Width of Hips	10% } 42%
	Leg Length	5. Upper-Body/Lower-Body Proportion	10% } 42%
	Hamstring flexibility	6. Hamstring Looseness	7% } 42%
	Percentage of body fat	7. Caliper Body-Fat-Percentage Measurement (negative points only)	
	Muscle fiber type	8. Vertical Jump	
Fatal Flaws	External hip rotation	9. External Hip Rotation	} no score
	Cavus foot	10. Cavus Foot	} no score
	Leg malalignment	11. Leg Malalignment	} no score

TEST 1: STRIDE LENGTH

This test was developed by Dr. Arnot in the spring of 1981 in Kona, Hawaii, while he was covering the Iron Man Triathlon for ABC's *Wide World of Sports*, as a method of assessing both a runner's speed at a particular point on the course and how well that runner's stride was holding up. The values are taken from top U.S. track stars; surprisingly, there is no variation in the optimal stride length due to height or leg length.

What You Will Need

You will need a measured 100-yard section of a flat, hard road or track. Mark both the start and the finish of the section with tape or chalk so that it is clearly visible. You will also need two friends, one positioned at the start of the 100-yard stretch, the other at its finish. The second friend will need a stopwatch.

Taking the Test

You shouldn't sprint through this test or in any other way change your normal medium- or long-distance-running style. The measured 100-yard test section should be just that, a section of a longer run—a sort of speed trap, over which you should run unselfconsciously, as though it were just a segment of a longer run—a 440- or 880-yard run on the track.

Start running well before the measured 100-yard test section begins, and be sure you are warmed up before starting. Run at a smooth medium- or long-distance speed. As soon as any part of your body crosses the start line of the test section your friend there should drop an arm, signaling the person at the end of the test section to start the stopwatch. Begin counting your strides the first time either foot hits the ground after your body passes the start line, and count each time that same foot hits the ground through the finish. As soon as any part of your body crosses the finish line, your friend there should stop the stopwatch and note your time through the test section. For your score on this test, find your time and number of strides in Table 27(a) if you are a long-distance runner, or in Table 27(b) if you are a middle-distance runner. You must complete the test within 16.6 seconds.

TABLE 27. STRIDE LENGTH

	Time for 100 yards (*seconds*)					
	14.1–16.6		**12.2–14.1**		**10.8–12.2**	
	Strides	**Points**	**Strides**	**Points**	**Strides**	**Points**
(a) Long-distance runners (3,000, 5,000 and 10,000 meters)	57	5	50	10	48	10
	53	10	48	15	46	15
	51	20	47	20	45	20
	48	20	45	20	43	20
	45	20	43	20	41	20
	43	15	42	15	40	15
	41	15	41	15	38	15
(b) Middle-distance runners (800 and 1,500 meters)	51	5	50	10	43	10
	49	10	47	15	42	15
	46	15	45	20	41	20
	44	20	42	20	41	20
	42	20	41	20	40	20
	40	15	38	15	40	20
	39	15	37	15	39	20

TEST 2: COOPER TWELVE-MINUTE RUN

This test was developed by Dr. Kenneth Cooper as a field test for measuring VO_2 Max in running, and it remains the best non-laboratory method for doing that. Dr. Cooper's test was designed for men only, but in 1977 its scoring system was adapted for women by Dr. Bud Getchell of Ball State University.

What You Will Need

See page 148 for the prerequisites for this test.

Taking the Test

Follow the instructions given on page 148, and calculate the total distance covered. That distance will give you your score in Table 28. Be sure to warm down by jogging for at least half a mile after you run.

TABLE 28. COOPER TWELVE-MINUTE RUN

Distance run (*miles*)	Points	
	Men	Women
1 8/16		3.8
1 9/16		8.1
1 10/16		12.4
1 11/16		16.6
1 12/16	3.8	20.9
1 13/16	6.7	25.2
1 14/16	9.5	29.5
1 15/16	12.4	33.7
2	15.2	38.0
2 1/16	18.1	
2 2/16	20.9	
2 3/16	23.8	
2 4/16	26.6	
2 5/16	29.5	
2 6/16	32.3	
2 7/16	35.2	
2 8/16	38.0	
2 9/16		
2 10/16		

TEST 3: WEIGHT-TO-HEIGHT RATIO

A relatively light frame is necessary for anyone who wants to run seriously at middle and long distances. A light frame in running means less wear and tear on the mechanical parts of the body, less body surface area to resist wind, and a lighter overall load to be driven by the heart-lung machine. Lightness of frame is relative to body height, of course, so here we are testing the *ratio* of your weight to your height, using two pounds per inch of body height as the ideal ratio for middle- and long-distance runners.

Regardless of what your weight-to-height ratio is, however, too much height is a disadvantage in running because it necessarily adds to a runner's wind resistance, and too little height is a disadvantage because very short people lack the overall leg length necessary for long striding.

What You Will Need

You will need an accurate scale, a tape measure, a friend to measure your height, a large hard-backed book, and a wall.

Taking the Test

Weigh yourself without clothes and round off your weight to the nearest pound. Now have your friend measure your exact height. To do this you should stand, barefoot, with your heels, calves, buttocks, back, and head touching the wall. Hold your head so that the top of your ear opening and the lower bone of your eye socket form a line parallel to the floor. Take a deep breath and hold it. Now have your friend place the book's spine against the wall above your head and lower the book until it rests squarely on the

top of your head. Have your friend mark the bottom of the book's spine on the wall, and measure from the floor to that point for your height. To determine your score, refer to Table 29 and find the point at which your weight and height intersect.

TABLE 29. WEIGHT-TO-HEIGHT RATIO

Height (*inches*)	Weight (*pounds*)																			
	90	**95**	**100**	**105**	**110**	**115**	**120**	**125**	**130**	**135**	**140**	**145**	**150**	**155**	**160**	**165**	**170**	**175**	**180**	**185**
56	13	13	13	13	13	13	10	9	8	7	6	6	5	4	3	2	1	0	0	0
57	13	13	13	13	13	13	10	10	9	8	7	6	5	5	3	3	2	1	0	0
58	13	13	13	13	13	13	13	10	9	8	7	6	6	5	4	3	2	1	0	0
59	13	13	13	13	13	13	13	10	9	9	8	7	6	5	4	4	3	2	1	0
60	13	13	13	13	13	13	13	13	10	9	8	7	6	6	5	4	3	2	3	1
61	13	13	13	13	13	13	13	13	10	9	9	8	7	6	5	4	4	3	2	1
62	13	13	13	13	13	13	13	13	13	10	9	8	7	6	6	5	4	3	2	2
63	13	13	13	13	13	13	13	13	13	10	9	8	8	7	6	5	5	4	3	2
64	13	13	13	13	13	13	13	13	13	12	12	11	10	9	8	8	7	6	5	5
65	15	15	15	15	15	15	15	15	15	15	12	11	10	10	9	8	7	7	6	5
66	15	15	15	15	15	15	15	15	15	15	12	12	11	10	9	8	8	7	6	5
67	15	15	15	15	15	15	15	15	15	15	15	12	11	10	10	9	8	7	7	6
68	15	15	15	15	15	15	15	15	15	15	15	12	11	11	10	9	8	8	7	6
69	15	15	15	15	15	15	15	15	15	15	15	12	12	11	10	10	9	8	7	7
70	15	15	15	15	15	15	15	15	15	15	15	15	12	11	11	10	9	8	8	7
71	15	15	15	15	15	15	15	15	15	15	15	15	12	12	11	10	10	9	8	7
72	15	15	15	15	15	15	15	15	15	15	15	15	15	12	11	11	10	9	8	8
73	13	13	13	13	13	13	13	13	13	13	13	13	13	12	12	11	10	10	9	8
74	13	13	13	13	13	13	13	13	13	13	13	13	13	13	12	11	11	10	9	9
75	13	13	13	13	13	13	13	13	13	13	13	13	13	13	10	9	9	8	7	7
76	13	13	13	13	13	13	13	13	13	13	13	13	13	13	10	10	9	8	8	7

190	195	200	205	210	215	220	225	230	235
0	0	0	0	0	0	0	0	0	0
0	0	0	0	0	0	0	0	0	0
0	0	0	0	0	0	0	0	0	0
0	0	0	0	0	0	0	0	0	0
0	0	0	0	0	0	0	0	0	0
0	0	0	0	0	0	0	0	0	0
1	0	0	0	0	0	0	0	0	0
1	1	0	0	0	0	0	0	0	0
4	3	2	1	1	0	0	0	0	0
4	3	3	2	2	0	0	0	0	0
5	4	3	2	2	1	0	0	0	0
5	4	4	1	2	1	1	0	0	0
6	5	4	1	1	2	1	0	0	0
6	5	5	4	1	2	2	1	0	0
6	6	5	4	3	3	2	1	1	0
7	6	5	5	4	3	3	2	1	1
7	6	6	5	4	4	3	2	2	1
7	7	6	5	5	4	3	3	2	1
8	7	6	6	5	4	4	3	2	1
6	5	5	3	3	2	2	1	1	0
6	6	5	4	4	3	3	2	1	1

TEST 4: WIDTH OF HIPS

All good competitive runners have narrow hips, regardless of the distances they run in competition. Narrow hips are an absolute requirement for successful competitive running, and a substantial asset in recreational running, because they allow less out-of-plane rotation, and because they allow the runner's legs to track a straighter line, since less lateral movement is required to bring the legs in under the body with each stride.

What You Will Need

You will need a friend to help with the measurements, and a yardstick (preferably metal).

Taking the Test

Stand with your heels together. Hold the yardstick across your waist with the narrow edge touching the skin. Slide the yardstick down your waist until it rests on the tops of your two hipbones. Suck in your belly and hold the yardstick tight against your abdomen. Measure the distance between the two points on the tops of your

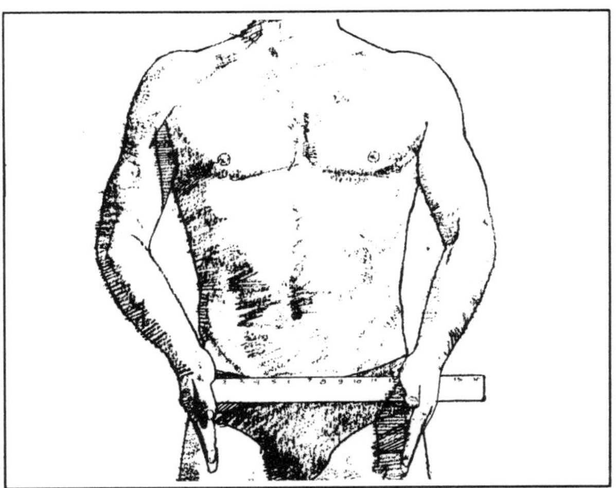

Flatten your stomach.

hipbones that are the farthest apart (see illustration on page 189). That distance in inches will give you your score in Table 30.

This test is scientifically done by using calipers. If you are pregnant or overweight, you may have difficulty in accurately testing your hip width as suggested here and may have better luck using makeshift calipers, like those shown at left. The calipers can be constructed easily by overlapping two T-squares on a carpenter's rule, so that a right angle exists at each end of the rule.

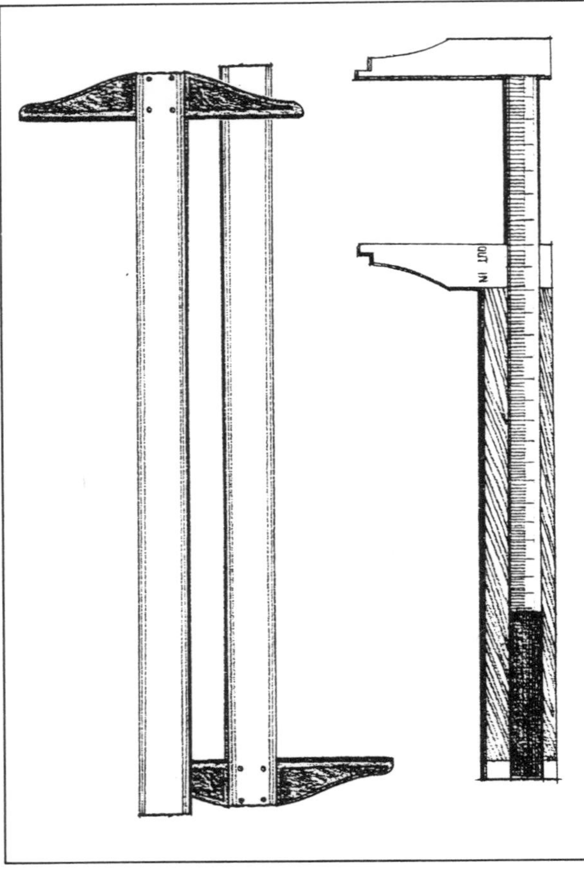

T-squares can be adapted to function as makeshift calipers.

TABLE 30. WIDTH OF HIPS

Men		Women	
Hip width (*inches*)	**Points**	**Hip width (*inches*)**	**Points**
9.00	10.00	9.00	10.00
9.10	9.67	9.10	9.75
9.20	9.33	9.20	9.50
9.30	9.00	9.30	9.25
9.40	8.67	9.40	9.00
9.50	8.33	9.50	8.75
9.60	8.00	9.60	8.50
9.70	7.67	9.70	8.25
9.80	7.33	9.80	8.00
9.90	7.00	9.90	7.75
10.00	6.67	10.00	7.50
10.10	6.33	10.10	7.25
10.20	6.00	10.20	7.00
10.30	5.67	10.30	6.75
10.40	5.33	10.40	6.50
10.50	5.00	10.50	6.25
10.60	4.67	10.60	5.75
10.70	4.33	10.70	5.25
10.80	4.00	10.80	4.75
10.90	3.67	10.90	4.25
11.00	3.33	11.00	3.75
11.10	3.00	11.10	3.25
11.20	2.67	11.20	2.75
11.30	2.33	11.30	2.25
11.40	2.00	11.40	1.75
11.50	1.67	11.50	1.25
11.60	1.33	11.60	0.75
11.70	1.00	11.70	0.25
11.80	0.67	11.80	0.00

TEST 5: UPPER-BODY/ LOWER-BODY PROPORTION

All good middle- and long-distance runners have legs that are long in proportion to their upper-body length. Bill Rodgers, for example, at an overall height of five feet eight inches, has a thirty-three-inch inseam, or a leg length that you might expect to find on a six-foot-tall man. This test measures how long your legs are in proportion to your overall height.

What You Will Need

The materials needed for this test are listed on page 152.

Taking the Test

Follow the directions given on page 152. The ratio of your sitting height to your lower-body length in inches, tabulated in Table 8 on page 153, will translate here into your score in Table 31.

TABLE 31. UPPER-BODY/ LOWER-BODY PROPORTION

Men		Women	
Ratio of sitting height to lower-body length (*inches*)	**Points**	**Ratio of sitting height to lower-body length (*inches*)**	**Points**
0.9 or below	10	1.0 or below	10
1.0	8	1.1	5
1.1	4	1.2	0
1.2	0		

TEST 6: HAMSTRING LOOSENESS

The ability to move the thighs forward easily in long strides while running, and to continue to do so, stride after stride, is a function of flexible hamstring muscles. Though flexibility in the hamstrings can be improved by stretching, it cannot be improved much, and runners with naturally loose hamstrings have a real advantage over runners with naturally tight ones, particularly after all the muscles in the legs have begun to tighten owing to continued contraction during a long run or a race.

Taking the Test

Stand, barefoot, on a hard surface, with your feet a hip-width apart. Bend over at the waist, locking your knees and letting your arms drop toward the ground. *Don't bounce,* but do push your hands as far toward the floor as your hamstrings will allow. (You are not doing the test properly if you don't feel a burning in the backs of your legs.) Look at the illustrations to determine your score in Table 32.

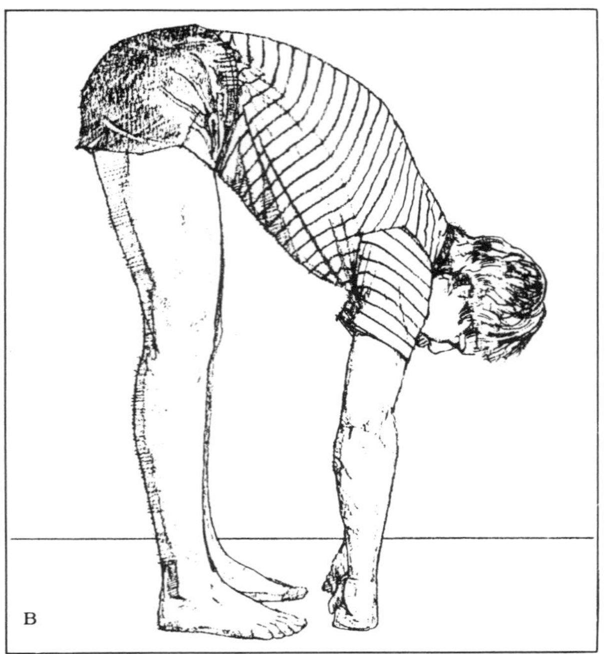
B

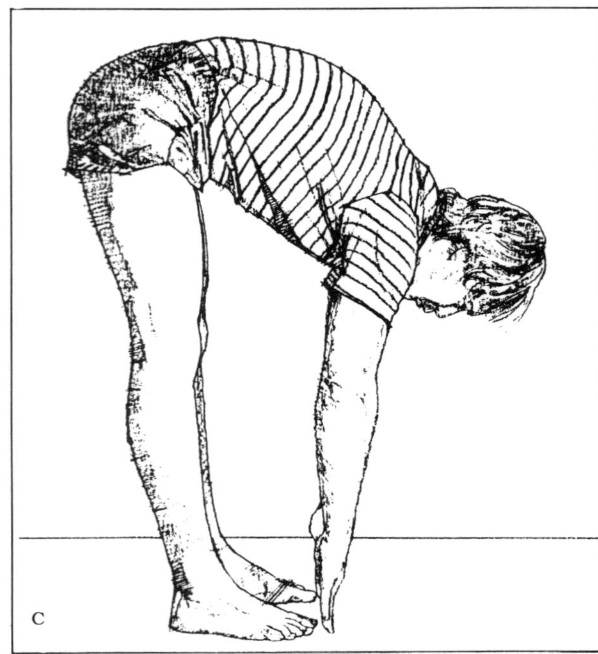
C

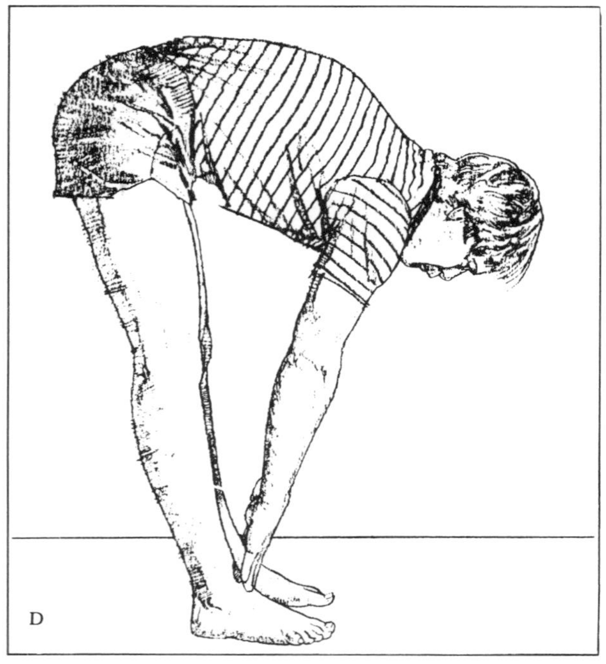
D

TABLE 32. HAMSTRING LOOSENESS

Position	Points
Palms touch floor (A)	7
Metacarpal-phalangeal joint touches floor (B)	6
Distal phalanx touches floor	5
Fingertip touches floor (C)	4
Fingertip touches toes	3
Fingertip touches any part of foot	2
Fingertip touches ankle (D)	1

TEST 7: CALIPER BODY-FAT-PERCENTAGE MEASUREMENT

Bodies are composed of fat, bone, muscle, and residual tissues such as the liver, kidneys, and lungs. The only one of these elements that can be radically diminished to lower the body's weight is fat, and since middle- and long-distance runners want to be as light as possible without sacrificing functional muscle mass, they can afford very little fat—less, in fact, than athletes in any other sport.

Outside the research laboratory there is no perfectly accurate way of measuring body-fat percentages. Some ways, however, are more accurate than others. The ladies' magazine "pinch-an-inch" method is so inaccurate, albeit easy to administer, that we have not used it here. If you are truly interested in sports you will likely want to keep accurate, long-term gauges of your percentage of body fat, and to do that we suggest you send away for (or borrow) a pair of inexpensive plastic calipers. (See the Appendix for information on ordering these.) Caliper measurements are even more accurate than underwater-submersion tests for body-fat percentages because differences in bone densities and intestinal gas contents can increase or decrease the natural buoyancy of the body.

The tables we use are for a general population, and people who have specialized fat stores in only one or two specific parts of the body may get a slightly inaccurate overall score. However, with the calipers, they will be able to monitor the size of these fat stores. In fact, the calipers will provide a much more accurate gauge of the transference from fatness to fitness than a bathroom scale will.

What You Will Need

A pair of calipers.

Taking the Test

Proceed with measurements as indicated on page 179. Add together the readings from all measurement sites and use the total to find your percentage of body fat in Table 24 if you are a man, or in Table 25 if you are a woman. Locate that percentage in Table 33 to determine your score for this test.

TABLE 33. CALIPER BODY-FAT-PERCENTAGE MEASUREMENT

Body-fat percentage		(Negative) points
Men	**Women**	
5.8	11.0	0
6.4	11.7	−1
7.0	12.3	−2
7.7	12.8	−3
8.5	13.5	−4
9.1	14.3	−5
10.2	14.8	−7
11.3	15.5	−8
12.4	16.5	−9
13.7	17.2	−10
15.0	18.2	−11
16.5	19.1	−12
18.2	19.8	−13
20.0	20.7	−14
22.0	22.1	−15

TEST 8: VERTICAL JUMP

The Vertical-Jump Test measures overall leg explosiveness, which is largely a function of muscle fiber type in the legs. Middle- and long-distance runners need a high percentage of endurance fiber in their legs. Though some sprint muscle fiber there can be useful in the kick phases of races, too much of it renders a runner's legs incapable of the aerobic work they must perform for successful middle- and long-distance running. Unfortunately, short of a tissue biopsy, there is no test to determine your percentage of sprint muscle fiber exactly, and the results of this particular test are only significant if your score is extremely high. For that reason your score here should not be totaled into your overall sportstalent score in running, but should instead be thought of as a personal guideline.

If your score here is in the low to medium range, it means very little to your potential as a middle- or long-distance runner. If your score is in the high range, it may mean that you should concentrate on running short middle-distances, where your sprint fiber can be utilized best. If you score ten points on this test, you have an extremely high percentage of sprint fiber in your legs, which is a fine athletic gift but one not suited to middle- and long-distance running. No matter how well you may have done on the other running tests, if you find here that you have an extremely high percentage of sprint fiber in your legs, we recommend that you consider taking up sprinting or one of the sports that require explosiveness, such as basketball or tennis, in order to make the most of that rare and valuable physical asset.

What You Will Need

The materials necessary for this test are listed on page 151.

Taking the Test

Proceed with the test, following the instructions on page 151. To determine your score, find your highest *single* reach in inches in Table 34.

TABLE 34. VERTICAL JUMP

Highest single reach (*inches*)			Points
	Men	Women	
Sprint	28.0	18.0	10.0
	26.6	17.2	9.1
	25.2	16.4	8.2
Middle distance	23.8	15.6	7.3
	22.4	14.8	6.4
	21.0	14.0	5.5
	19.6	13.2	4.6
Long distance	18.2	12.4	3.7
	16.8	11.6	2.8
	15.4	10.8	1.9
	14.0	10.0	1.0

FATAL FLAWS IN RUNNING

Not everyone is suited to middle- and long-distance running, and there are certain genetic anatomical flaws that make it a debilitating form of exercise for some people. There are also, of course, medical disabilities, such as a weak heart or missing cartilage in the knee, that make it inadvisable to take up running as a sport, and anyone with any doubts about his or her health, as well as anyone over thirty-five years old, should consult with a physician before beginning to run. However, we assume here that you are a medically normal individual, curious about your talent for running. Regardless of how you have scored on the previous tests, we recommend that you also take the three following tests to discover whether or not you may have one of the three primary anatomical flaws that, if present singly or in combination, and notwithstanding your talent for the sport, may indicate either that you should run only short distances or that you should consider taking up another aerobic sport, such as swimming or cycling.

These tests are not quantified with scores because you either have one or more of these syndromes or you don't, and therefore how you do here will not affect your overall score for sports-talent in running. If you find that you do have one or more of these fatal flaws, however, and are intent on running anyway, we suggest that you see an orthopedist who specializes in sports medicine for detailed advice.

TEST 9: EXTERNAL HIP ROTATION

Any severe limitation on the ability of the hips to rotate, particularly outwardly, will seriously limit the mechanics of running and make an individual susceptible to leg and hip injuries. This test measures the external-rotation capacity of the hips.

Taking the Test

Proceed with the test as indicated on page 157. If the angle formed is smaller than ninety degrees, your external hip rotation is severely limited for middle- and long-distance running.

TEST 10: CAVUS FOOT

Injury can result in running if your foot is either too flexible or not flexible enough in its lateral movement. Too much flexibility may be rectified by strengthening exercises, special shoes, or orthotics, but nothing can be done for a foot with too little lateral flexibility. That condition is known as cavus foot, and though it can provide a substantial speed advantage in short-distance running, it constitutes a serious, injury-producing flaw for middle- and long-distance runners. This test will let you know whether or not you have a cavus foot.

What You Will Need

You will need a can of baby powder or talcum powder and a smooth floor, preferably dark in color.

Taking the Test

You should be barefoot. Sprinkle the powder generously onto a small area of the floor and step onto it with both feet. Stand normally for a moment in the powder but do not roll your feet in it; then step back out of the powder, and look at the footprints you have made. If only your heels and the balls of your feet have made a print (if there is no print made by either your arch or your toes) you have cavus feet.

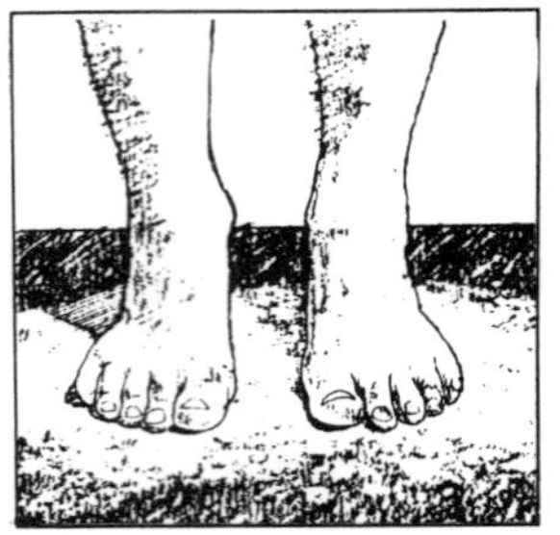

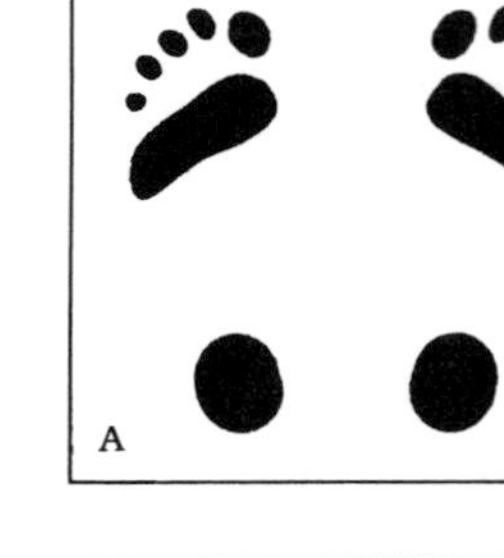

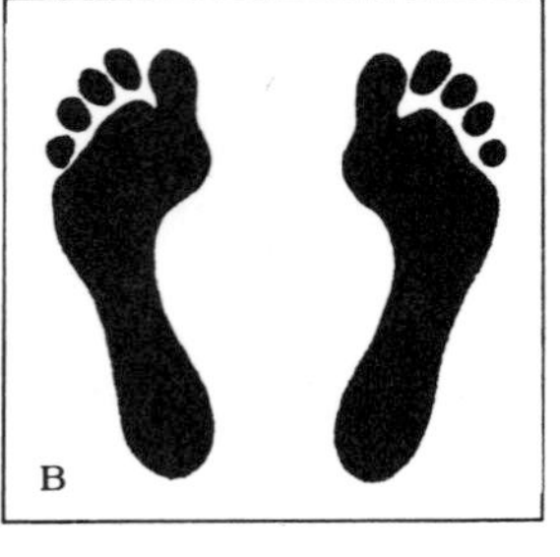

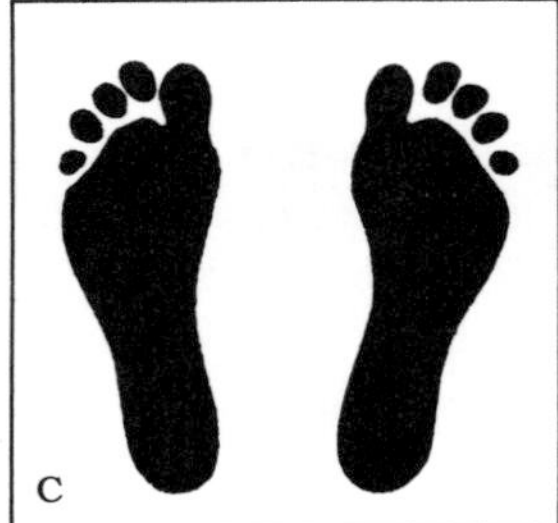

A = Cavus feet
B = High-arch feet
C = "Flat" feet

TEST 11: LEG MALALIGNMENT

The forces generated by running should propel the body along a single forward plane. When any part of the skeleton is substantially out of alignment with that plane, running becomes not only inefficient but potentially damaging to the maligned part of the skeleton. There are a number of leg malalignments that can cause serious problems to the middle- or long-distance runner. If you are either very knock-kneed or very bowlegged, a lot of running is likely to lead to leg injury. A third problem producing malalignment is the one known as tibial torsion (found in a person who is duckfooted or pigeon-toed), which creates torque up through the bones of the lower leg each time the foot strikes the ground in running. This condition is tested here.

Taking the Test

Stand on a flat, hard surface with your feet a hip-width apart. (It is a help to be standing on a board floor, so that you can use the lines between the boards to help align the knees.) Transfer all your weight onto one foot; lift the other foot off the floor and let it dangle naturally. Using your hands, line up the unweighted knee so that it is pointed directly forward; then step back down onto that foot. Now look at the alignment between your foot and your knee: if the toes of your foot are more than twenty degrees inside or outside the plane of your knee, then your knee and foot are seriously misaligned. Repeat the test with your other leg. If you have more than twenty degrees of malalignment in either leg, you are very likely to injure yourself with any substantial amount of middle- or long-distance running.

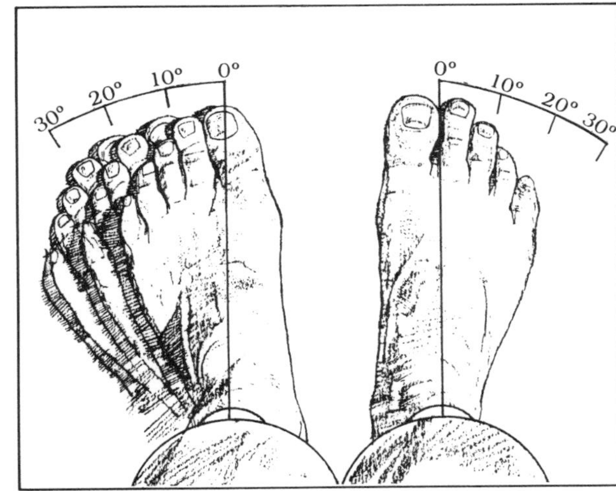

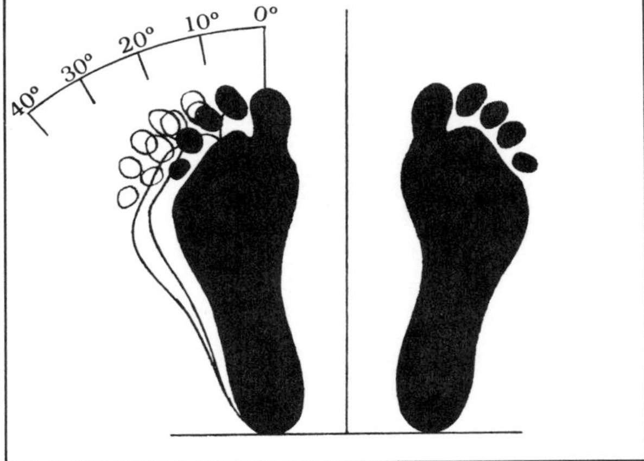

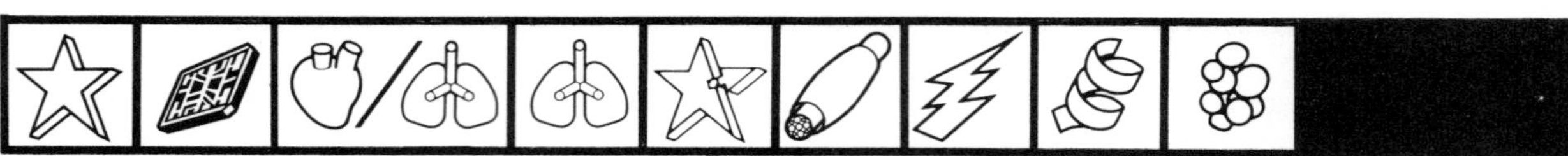

TESTING FOR SWIMMING

The single most important component of talent for swimming is good stroke mechanics. The mechanical effectiveness of an individual's swimming stroke is a function of that individual's Control System, and though a good stroke can be made better by training and coaching, the basic feel for the water that is the *sine qua non* of good strokes cannot be developed or taught—individuals either have that feel or they don't.

The mechanical effectiveness of a given stroke can be measured both by how far it causes the body to travel through the water and by its absolute force of propulsion. Test 1 measures the number of strokes required to travel a given distance (and therefore the distance of travel per stroke), and Test 5 measures the absolute force generated by the stroke, along with upper-body strength. Reflecting the paramount importance of good stroke mechanics, these two tests have a combined weight of 43 percent, or nearly half the total for swimming. We have chosen the freestyle stroke for testing because it is the most widely practiced and most efficient of all strokes.

Maximum oxygen consumption is tested here by the Cooper Twelve-Minute-Run Test because it is the most practical field test we know of for VO_2 Max, and because any in-the-water field assessment of VO_2 Max for swimming can be negatively and unfairly affected if the individual being tested has poor strokes (that individual may use as much as five times the energy to swim at the same speed as a swimmer with good strokes). There is a very accurate laboratory method of measuring VO_2 Max in swimming, a method involving the use of a flume and expensive oxygen-consumption-measurement gear, the values for which are not affected by inefficient strokes, but this test is administered in only a few places.

A large lung volume is critical in swimming. Water naturally constricts the lungs, so that normally small lungs will hold even less air underwater. Large lungs, therefore, make more usable air available to a swimmer as well as adding to buoyancy. If you did well on the Cooper Twelve-Minute-Run Test, your lungs are large enough for good swimming. But if you are not a runner it is possible that you could do poorly on the Cooper Test and still have large lungs. We have, therefore, incorporated a separate test for lung size, to be taken only if you scored fewer than twenty points on the Cooper Test.

Though certain frame dimensions are important enough in swimming to warrant being tested here, little relative weight or value is given to them because the *effect* of most of those dimensions is made apparent in other tests within this section.

CHART 5. SWIMMING

	Components tested	**Test**	**Relative importance of test to overall score**	
The Control System	Stroke mechanics	1. Stroke Distance	28%	
The Heart-Lung Package	VO_2 Max	2. Cooper Twelve-Minute Run	30%	
	Lung size	3. Lung Volume	10% (Up to 10% can be given here if individual being tested receives less than 20 points as a score on Test 2)	
Body Composition	Frame proportions: hand length, elbow width, shoulder width, forearm girth, upper-arm girth, thigh girth, hip width	4. Measurement of Bodily Proportions	7%	42% (Tests 4–8)
	Stroke force and peak upper-body power	5. Fish-Scale Stroke Power	15%	
	Leg explosiveness	6. Vertical Jump	10%	
	Range of motion in shoulders	7. Shoulder Range of Motion	5%	
	Range of motion in ankles	8. Ankle Range of Motion	5%	
	Percentage of body fat	9. Caliper Body-Fat-Percentage Measurement (negative points only for short- to middle-distance swimmers)		

TEST 1: STROKE DISTANCE

This test measures a simple knowledge of results: how far your body travels in the water per stroke—the greater that distance, the more effective the mechanics of the stroke producing it. The results of this test will not tell you why you do or do not have good stroke mechanics, only whether or not you have them. While a good effort at this test is expected, the speed at which you swim is not crucial to the results of the test—just swim evenly, and as fast as you comfortably can.

What You Will Need

You should take this test in a standard twenty-five-yard pool; if one isn't available to you, mark off a twenty-five-yard stretch of a larger pool, or a lake, or the ocean. You will need a friend to count your strokes.

Taking the Test

It is important to swim as straight a line as possible for this test. If you take it somewhere other than in a pool with lanes, get a friend to stand at the end of the twenty-five-yard course and swim directly at him. Start from as close to a horizontal, freestyle position in the water as possible, floating on your stomach. Your friend should give you the command to "Go." Swim freestyle, evenly, and as fast as you comfortably can, until your hand either touches the other end of the twenty-five-yard pool or crosses a twenty-five-yard marker in a larger pool, a lake, or the ocean. Either you or your friend should count your exact number of strokes through the twenty-five yards, a stroke being counted each time either arm comes up out of the water. The number of your strokes will give you your score in Table 35.

TABLE 35. STROKE DISTANCE

Number of strokes	Points
20.0	28.00
21.0	26.32
22.1	24.64
23.2	22.96
24.3	21.28
25.5	19.60
26.8	17.92
28.1	16.24
29.5	14.56
31.0	12.88
32.6	11.20
34.2	9.52
35.9	7.84
37.7	6.16
39.6	4.48
41.6	2.80

TEST 2: COOPER TWELVE-MINUTE RUN

Other than expensive laboratory testing, the Cooper Test is the best method we know of for measuring VO_2 Max, and though the Cooper measure is not specifically and precisely transferable to swimming, a large part of an individual's VO_2 Max, as established by this test, can be adapted to swimming.

A high score on this test means that you have the aerobic capacity for swimming at any level. But a low score shouldn't necessarily be discouraging, since VO_2 Max is improvable up to 50 percent, and since a good score here depends on being able to run and being somewhat accustomed to doing it.

What You Will Need

See page 148 for the prerequisites for this test.

Taking the Test

Follow the instructions given on page 148, and calculate the total distance covered. That distance will give you your score in Table 36. Be sure to warm down by jogging for at least half a mile after you run.

TABLE 36. COOPER TWELVE-MINUTE RUN

Distance run (*miles*)	**Points**	
	Men	**Women**
1 8/16		3.0
1 9/16		6.9
1 10/16		10.7
1 11/16		14.6
1 12/16	3.0	18.4
1 13/16	6.4	22.3
1 14/16	9.8	26.1
1 15/16	13.1	30.0
2	16.5	
2 1/16	19.9	
2 2/16	23.3	
2 3/16	26.6	
2 4/16	30.0	
2 5/16		
2 6/16		
2 7/16		

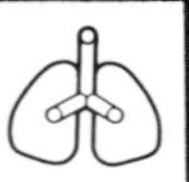

TEST 3: LUNG VOLUME

This test measures (with less than laboratory accuracy) the functional volume of the lungs. That volume is important for the sport, and if a swimmer or a potential swimmer wants a precise measure of lung volume, standard pulmonary-function tests are routinely available in doctors' offices, industrial clinics, and clinical laboratories.

What You Will Need

You will need a plastic bag with a two-gallon capacity, a one-quart measuring cup, and a funnel.

Taking the Test

The bag should be air-free. Make a tube or neck at the top of the bag, with an opening that will fit snugly over your mouth. Take as deep a breath as you possibly can and exhale as completely as possible into the bag (really push out every bit of air from your lungs). Now twist the top of the bag to close it, and slide your hand down its neck to the point at which the bag is fully expanded. Force the funnel down through your closed hand and into the bag, keeping your hand firmly in place on the bag's neck. Now pour water from the one-quart measuring cup into the bag, measuring the number of pints you pour, until the bag is filled to the same level at which it was filled with your breath, or up to your hand on the bag's neck. In Table 37, locate the point at which the number of pints of water required to fill the bag to that level intersects with your weight, and use that value to determine your score.

TABLE 37. LUNG VOLUME

Number of pints	80	90	100	110	120	130
4.0	52.0	46.3	41.6	37.9	34.7	32.0
4.5	58.6	52.0	46.8	42.6	39.0	36.0
5.0	65.1	57.8	52.0	47.3	43.4	40.0
5.5	71.6	63.6	57.3	52.0	47.7	44.0
6.0	78.1	69.4	62.5	56.8	52.0	48.0
6.5		75.2	67.7	61.5	56.4	52.0
7.0			72.9	66.2	60.7	56.1
7.5				71.0	65.1	60.1
8.0				75.7	69.4	64.1
8.5					73.7	68.1
9.0					78.1	72.1
9.5						76.1
10.0						
10.5						
11.0						
11.5						
12.0						
12.5						
13.0						
13.5						
14.0						
14.5						
15.0						
15.5						
16.0						
16.5						
17.0						
17.5						
18.0						

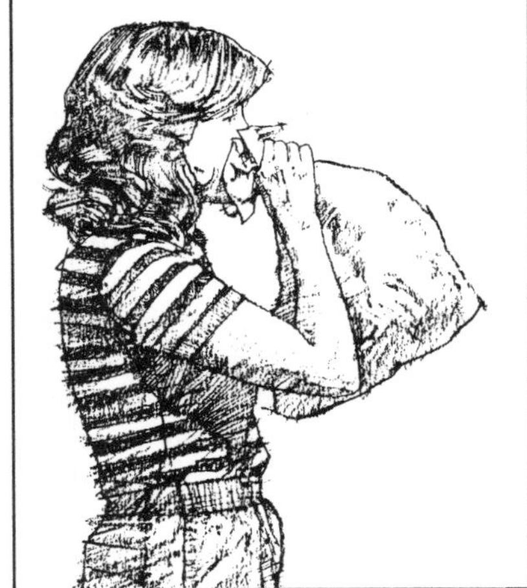

Exhale fully into a completely empty bag.

Weight (*pounds*)											
140	**150**	**160**	**170**	**180**	**190**	**200**	**210**	**220**	**230**	**240**	**250**
29.7	27.8	26.0	24.5	23.1	21.9	20.8	19.8	18.9	18.1	17.3	16.7
33.5	31.2	29.3	27.6	26.0	24.7	23.4	22.3	21.3	20.4	19.5	18.7
37.2	34.7	32.5	30.6	28.9	27.4	26.0	24.8	23.7	22.6	21.7	20.8
40.9	38.2	35.8	33.7	31.8	30.1	28.6	27.3	26.0	24.9	23.9	22.9
44.6	41.6	39.0	36.7	34.7	32.9	31.2	29.7	28.4	27.2	26.0	25.0
48.3	45.1	42.3	39.8	37.6	35.6	33.8	32.2	30.8	29.4	28.2	27.1
52.0	48.6	45.5	42.9	40.5	38.4	36.4	34.7	33.1	31.7	30.4	29.1
55.8	52.0	48.8	45.9	43.4	41.1	39.0	37.2	35.5	33.9	32.5	31.2
59.5	55.5	52.0	49.0	46.3	43.8	41.6	39.7	37.9	36.2	34.7	33.3
63.2	59.0	55.3	52.0	49.2	46.6	44.2	42.1	40.2	38.5	36.9	35.4
66.9	62.5	58.6	55.1	52.0	49.3	46.8	44.6	42.6	40.7	39.0	37.5
70.6	65.9	61.8	58.2	54.9	52.0	49.4	47.1	45.0	43.0	41.2	39.6
74.4	69.4	65.1	61.2	57.8	54.8	52.0	49.6	47.3	45.3	43.4	41.6
78.1	72.9	68.3	64.3	60.7	57.5	54.7	52.0	49.7	47.5	45.5	43.7
	76.3	71.6	67.4	63.6	60.3	57.3	54.5	52.0	49.8	47.7	45.8
	79.8	74.8	70.4	66.5	63.0	59.9	57.0	54.4	52.0	49.9	47.9
		78.1	73.5	69.4	65.7	62.5	59.5	56.8	54.3	52.0	50.0
		81.3	76.5	72.3	68.5	65.1	62.0	59.1	56.6	54.2	52.0
		84.6	79.6	75.2	71.2	67.7	64.4	61.5	58.8	56.4	54.1
		87.8	82.7	78.1	74.0	70.3	66.9	63.9	61.1	58.6	56.2
					76.7	72.9	69.4	66.2	63.4	60.7	58.3
					79.4	75.5	71.9	68.6	65.6	62.9	60.4
					82.2	78.1	74.4	71.0	67.9	65.1	62.5
						80.7	76.8	73.3	70.2	67.2	64.5
							79.3	75.7	72.4	69.4	66.6
							81.8	78.1	74.7	71.6	68.7
									76.9	73.7	70.8
									79.2	75.9	72.9
										78.1	75.0

SCORING:

Pints expelled per body weight		**Points**
Men	**Women**	
70.4	58.2	10
68.6	56.8	9
67.2	55.8	8
65.9	54.8	7
64.5	54.1	6
63.4	52.0	5
62.0	50.0	4
60.7	49.9	3
59.5	49.3	2
58.3	48.3	1

TEST 4: MEASUREMENT OF BODILY PROPORTIONS

In swimming, where the body is not only the means of locomotion but functions as a sort of craft as well, certain bodily proportions that add to its overall speed and efficiency of movement through the water have significance in and of themselves for good performance. The measurements you will take here will be scored against those taken of Olympic swimmers in Montreal in 1976 by Lindsay Carter. The parts of the body measured here are the ones found by Mr. Carter to deviate most from the norm among swimmers; they are, therefore, assumed to have the most isolatable significance in the mechanics of swimming. To anyone who has looked even casually at Olympic swimmers, it is apparent that they tend to have wide shoulders, muscular arms, long hands, and narrow thighs and hips. It is no accident that swimmers are built this way—competitive swimming demands that they be. The measurements here will let you know how closely your swimming-significant proportions match theirs. You get a total of only seven points for matching the Olympic standards because the effect of all those proportions together will count for you in other swimming tests, and because without good stroke mechanics, a high VO_2 Max, and substantial muscular power, those proportions alone will not make you a good swimmer.

What You Will Need

You will need a friend to help you take the measurements, a yardstick, a pen, a tape measure, and, for the elbow measurement, two foot-long sections of two-by-four-inch board. (Make sure the ends of each board are squared off.)

Taking the Test

Take each of these measurements on bare skin, and measure carefully. Award yourself one point for each measurement that falls at or between the minimum and maximum Olympic standards given in Table 38.

1. *Hand Length:* Place either hand on a piece of lined, legal-pad paper, with your fingers perpendicular to the lines on the paper. Make a mark on the paper at the top of your middle finger, and another at the bottom of your wristbone, at the base of your thumb (see illustration). Draw a line through each of the marks all the way across the width of the paper, keeping your lines parallel to the lines on the paper. Now measure the distance between the two lines you drew. That distance is the length of your hand.

2. *Elbow Width:* Lay your upper arm flat on a table and raise your forearm so that it forms a right angle to the table. Bring the two pieces of two-by-four board in as close as you can get them to either side of your elbow and line up the ends of the boards with the front edge of the table (see illustration). You should push the two boards together so that they are touching the bone (not just the skin) on either side of the elbow. Now slide your elbow out from between the boards without moving them and measure the distance between the two inside edges of the board. That distance is the width of your elbow.

3. *Shoulder Width:* Sit relaxed in a chair with your back straight. From behind you, your friend should locate the outermost extremity of each of your shoulder bones (they are at the very ends of your clavicle) and mark those points with a pen or marker. Now have your friend use the tape measure to determine the distance between those two points by laying the tape across the top of your chest and under your neck. That distance is your shoulder width.

4. *Forearm Girth:* Extend your right arm straight

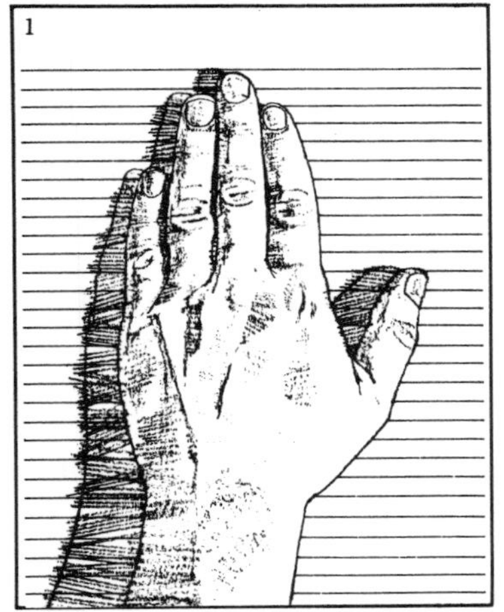
1

2

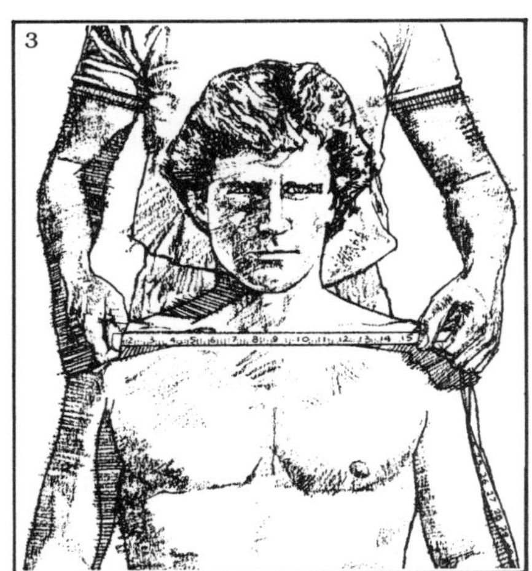
3

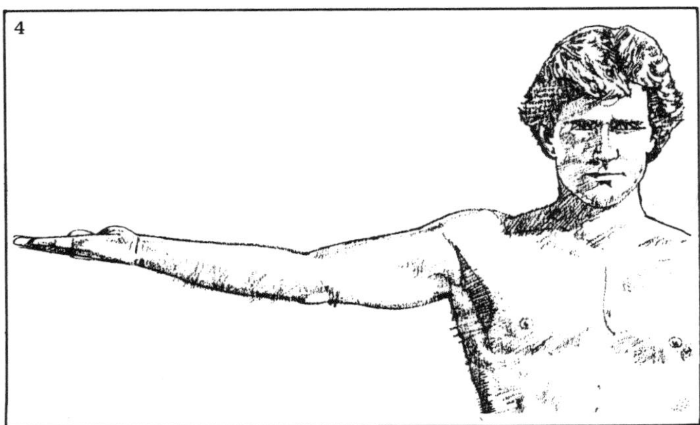
4

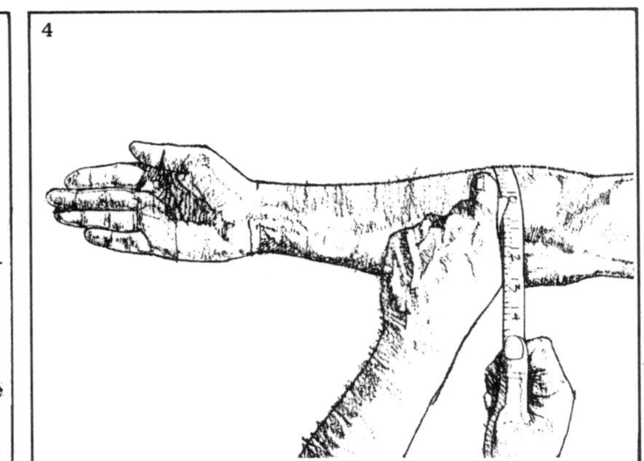
4

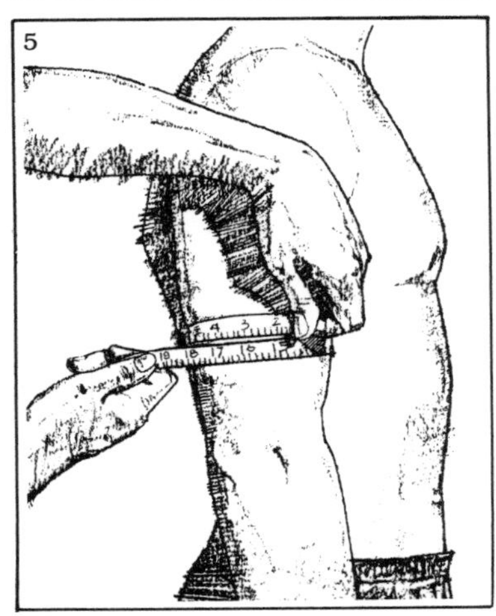
5

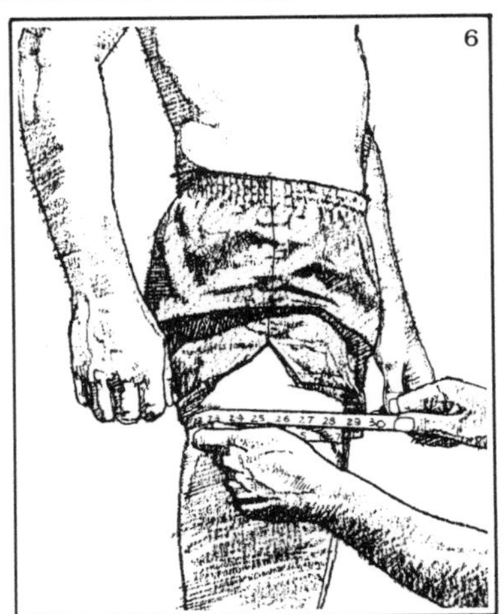
6

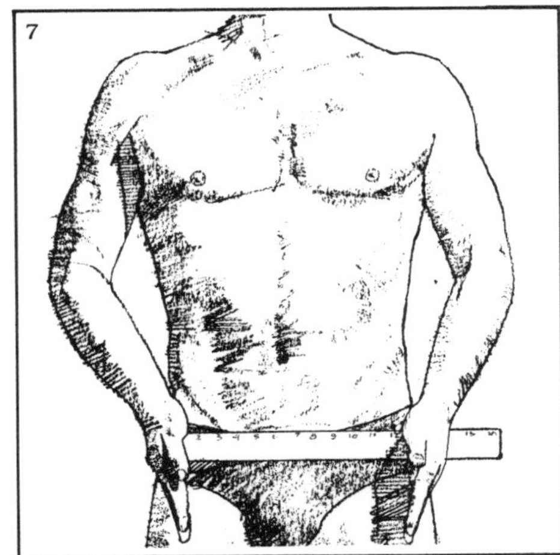
7

out from your body, your palm facing upward and your fingers extended (see illustrations). Have your friend measure with the tape the girth of your forearm at its widest point and when it is fully relaxed.

5. *Upper-Arm Girth:* Stand with your right arm hanging loose and relaxed at your side. Your friend should measure the girth of your upper arm at a point halfway between your shoulder bone and your elbow.

6. *Thigh Girth:* Stand with your feet slightly apart, your weight evenly distributed on both feet, and your thighs fully relaxed. Have your friend measure the girth of your right thigh at a point one-half inch below your gluteal, or buttocks, fold (see illustration).

7. *Hip Width:* Stand with your heels together. Hold the yardstick across your waist, with the narrow edge touching the skin. Slide the yardstick down your waist until it rests on the tops of your two hipbones. Suck your belly in and hold the yardstick tight against your abdomen. To determine your hip width, measure the distance between the two points on the tops of your hipbones that are the farthest apart (see illustration).

TABLE 38. MEASUREMENT OF BODILY PROPORTIONS

	Olympic standard measurements (*inches*)			
	Men		Women	
	Minimum	Maximum	Minimum	Maximum
Hand length	7.5	8.3	6.9	7.8
Elbow width	2.7	3.0	2.4	2.6
Shoulder width	15.4	16.8	14.0	15.2
Forearm girth (relaxed)	10.2	11.4	8.9	9.9
Upper-arm girth (relaxed)	11.2	12.9	10.0	11.5
Thigh girth (relaxed)	20.3	23.3	19.5	22.1
Hip width	10.1	11.9	9.8	11.2

TEST 5: FISH-SCALE STROKE POWER

Modern swimmers are as good as they are, and records in the various events are now set and reset as often as they are, largely because of weight training. Swimmers are faster than ever before because they are stronger, and this is particularly true of American women. The force exerted by a swimmer's stroke against the water is partly a function of effective stroke mechanics and partly a function of how strong the swimmer is in the upper body. This test measures both that part of stroke mechanics which accounts for the force of propulsion, and the maximum, or peak, upper-body power that can be generated by a single stroke—a power that is trainable to a degree, and to a degree a genetic function of muscle fiber type and innervation. Raw upper-body power can be tested in a number of ways, but as it applies to swimming it is best tested, as it is here, in the water.

What You Will Need

For this test you will need to borrow or buy (see Appendix for details on buying) a spring-loaded fish scale graduated in ounces and pounds up to fifty pounds. The scale should have a hook at one end and a handle at the other. You will also need a pool or other body of water in which to take the test, a friend, some nonstretching cord or rope, and a bandanna.

Taking the Test

Tie the bandanna snugly around both your ankles and attach one end of a thirty-foot-long section of cord to the bandanna. Tie the other end of the cord to the hook of the scale. Have your friend tie another piece of cord to the handle of the scale and fix the other end of that piece (it shouldn't be more than a foot long) to something absolutely solid on a bank or on the side of a pool (see illustration). As they extend toward you, both pieces of cord and the scale should be level with your body when it is horizontal in the water. Have your friend kneel or sit in a position from

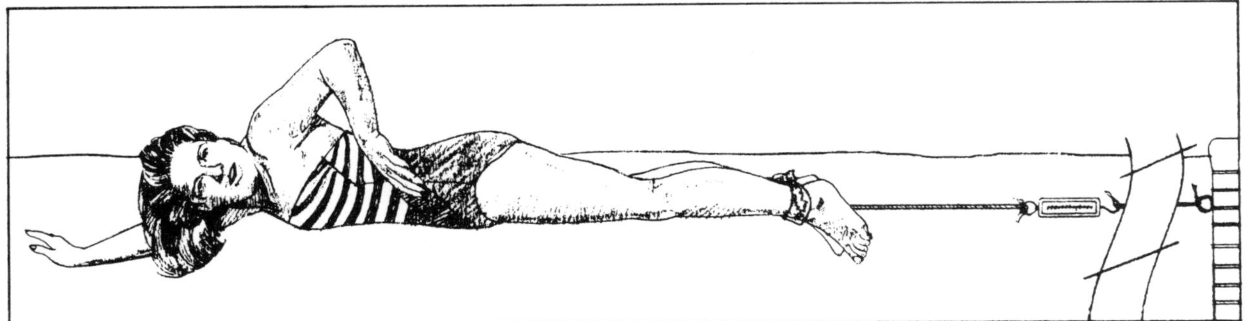

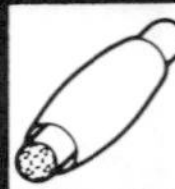

which he or she can see the face of the scale. Let your legs trail out behind you in the water and keep them motionless throughout the test. In a freestyle position take ten strokes with each arm, pulling against the scale and exerting as much power as you can on each stroke. Your friend should note the single highest reading to which you are able to pull the marker on the scale at any time during your twenty strokes, and that reading in pounds will give you your score in Table 39.

TABLE 39. FISH-SCALE STROKE POWER

Fish-scale reading (*pounds*)		Points
Men	**Women**	
60.0	45.0	15.0
57.0	42.8	14.4
54.2	40.6	13.7
51.4	38.6	13.1
48.9	36.7	12.4
46.4	34.8	11.8
44.1	33.1	11.1
41.9	31.4	10.5
39.8	29.9	9.9
37.8	28.4	9.2
35.9	26.9	8.6
34.1	25.6	7.9
32.4	24.3	7.3
30.8	23.1	6.6
29.3	21.9	6.0
27.8	20.8	5.4
26.4	19.8	4.7
25.1	18.8	4.1
23.8	17.9	3.4
22.6	17.0	2.8
21.5	16.1	2.1
20.4	15.3	1.5

TEST 6: VERTICAL JUMP

According to swim coach Doc Counsilman, good performance on this test indicates a high degree of the overall muscular explosiveness that characterizes good sprint swimmers. If you do *extremely* well at this test, you are likely to be too fatigable for competitive swimming and training at long distances. If you do poorly here, you are probably better suited for middle- or long-distance swimming than for sprinting.

What You Will Need

The materials necessary for this test are listed on page 151.

Taking the Test

Follow the instructions given on page 151. Don't practice before taking the test. Do the test three times and take your highest *single* reach in inches to determine your score in Table 40.

TABLE 40. VERTICAL JUMP

Highest single reach (*inches*)		Points
Men	**Women**	
26	15	10
25	14	9
24	13	8
23	12	7
22	11	6
21	10	5
20	9	4
19	8	3
18	7	2
17	6	1

TEST 7: SHOULDER RANGE OF MOTION

Though swimmers are generally thought of as having great overall flexibility, there are really only two joints, the shoulder and the ankle, whose range of motion is a necessary prerequisite of good stroke mechanics, and all the best swimmers have a complete range of motion in the shoulders. This test is used by Doc Counsilman to determine shoulder range of motion in his swimmers.

What You Will Need

You will need a friend with a yardstick, and a broomstick.

Taking the Test

Lie on your chest with your chin on the floor and your arms stretched out in front of you at shoulder width. Grasp the broomstick in both hands, and without bending either your wrists or your elbows, and without raising your head off the ground, lift the broomstick as high off the floor as you can and have your friend measure that distance. That distance in inches will give you your score in Table 41.

Raise your arms as high as you can.

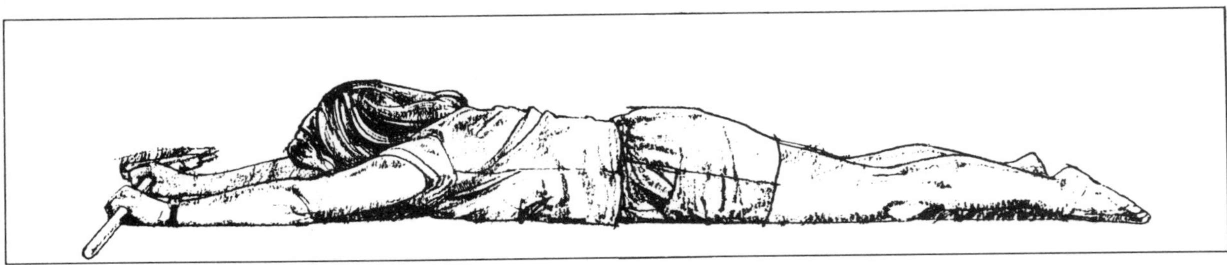

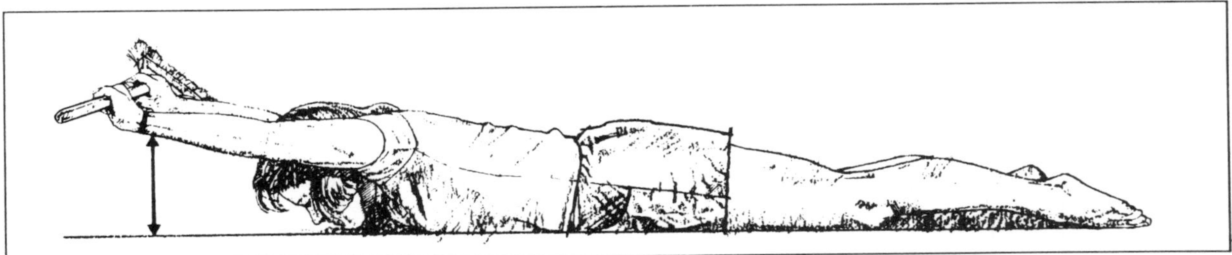

TABLE 41.
SHOULDER RANGE OF MOTION

Inches from floor		Points
Men	**Women**	
22	19	5
18	16	4
14	13	3
10	9	2
6	4	1

TEST 8: ANKLE RANGE OF MOTION

For the flutter kick to be maximally effective, the foot must be capable of being extended at the ankle joint, so that it and the leg are in the same horizontal plane. This test, also used by Doc Counsilman, measures the ankle's range of motion.

What You Will Need

You will need a friend and a ruler.

Taking the Test

Lie on your back on the floor with your legs extended. Point the toes of your right foot and extend them outward and downward as far as you can. Have your friend measure the distance between the bottom of your big toe and the floor. That distance in inches will give you your score in Table 42.

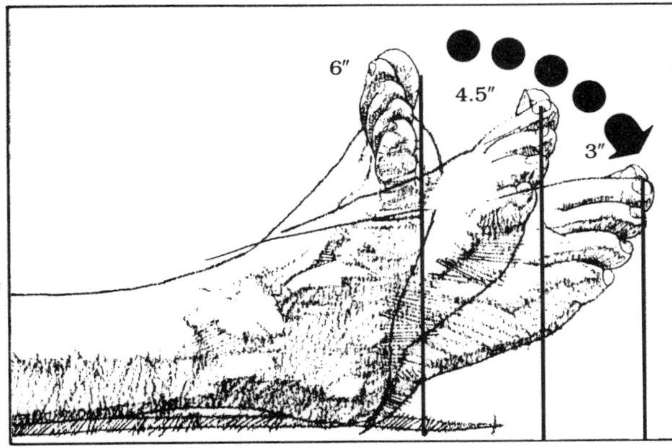

Press hard for maximum score.

TABLE 42. ANKLE RANGE OF MOTION

Inches off floor		Points
Men	**Women**	
2.5	1.5	5
3.0	2.0	5
3.5	2.5	4
4.0	3.0	3
4.5	3.5	2
5.0	4.0	2
5.5	4.5	1
6.0	5.0	1

TEST 9: CALIPER BODY-FAT-PERCENTAGE MEASUREMENT

The ideal percentage of body fat in swimmers increases from short- to long-distance events. Sprinters will ideally have less than 10 percent body fat, while ultra-long-distance swimmers may have as much as 30 percent. For the short to middle distances that most people swim competitively and recreationally, an ideal is around 7.5 percent body fat for men and 15.5 percent for women. The only accurate way to measure that percentage outside a laboratory is with calipers, and since all athletes should want to keep an accurate running measure of their percentage of body fat, we suggest here, as in the body-fat tests for the other sports, that you borrow a pair of laboratory calipers or purchase a pair of inexpensive plastic ones with which to take that measurement on a regular basis. (See Appendix for information on ordering calipers.)

The tables used in this book are for a general population, and people with specialized fat stores in only one or two specific parts of the body may get a slightly inaccurate overall score.

What You Will Need

A pair of calipers.

Taking the Test

Proceed with measurements as indicated on page 179. Add together the readings from all measurement sites and use that total to find your percentage of body fat in Table 24 if you are a man, or in Table 25 if you are a woman. Locate that percentage in Table 43 to determine your score for this test.

TABLE 43. CALIPER BODY-FAT-PERCENTAGE MEASUREMENT

Body-fat percentage		(Negative) points
Men	Women	
7.5	15.5	0
8.3	16.3	−1
9.1	17.2	−2
10.0	17.9	−3
11.1	18.8	−4
12.2	19.8	−5
13.3	20.8	−7
14.7	21.8	−8
16.1	22.9	−9
17.7	24.0	−10
19.4	25.2	−11
21.4	26.6	−12
23.4	27.8	−13
25.9	29.2	−14
28.5	30.6	−15

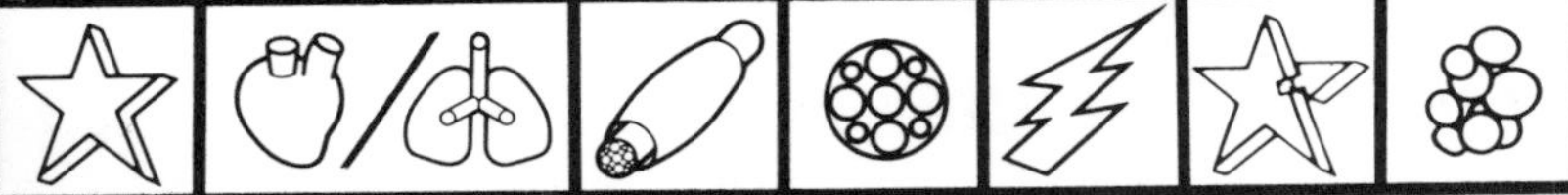

TESTING FOR CYCLING

Test 1 in this section requires a bicycle, and Tests 2 through 4 require a stationary bicycle, one with graduated work-load designations in either watts or KPMs. (See Appendix for appropriate makes and models of stationary bikes.) This stationary bicycle is one of only three pieces of specialized equipment required for the testing in this book, and it is absolutely necessary. The agility and balance, VO_2 Max, leg explosiveness, and anaerobic endurance peculiar to cycling can be tested effectively only on a bicycle, for much the same reasons that stroke mechanics and power in swimming can be tested effectively only in the water. Though we realize that very few people own stationary bicycles, they are so widely available in gyms, YMCAs, corporate-fitness centers, and rehabilitation facilities across the country that access to one should not be too difficult.

Competitive cycling is divided into a number of events, each of which makes somewhat different demands on the cyclist. Generally speaking, track, pursuit, and criterium events require high explosiveness and excellent agility, whereas aerobic power is the primary requisite for road events and time trials. In addition to indicating your overall potential talent for cycling, your results on the tests here can be patterned to indicate which type of competitive cycling you are best suited for. All talent components tested here are significant for serious recreational cyclists, regardless of what implications they might have individually for competitive cyclists.

As is reflected in the more or less even weighting among the three categories of testing here, serious cycling is a system of exercise complete unto itself, requiring and developing agility and other motor skills, aerobic fitness, and muscular power and speed.

CHART 6. CYCLING

	Components tested	**Test**	**Relative importance of test to overall score**	
The Control System	Agility, balance, multilimb coordination	1. Bicycle Agility	10%	
The Heart-Lung Package	VO_2 Max	2. Astrand Bicycle Ergometer	40%	
Body Composition	Leg explosiveness and muscle fiber type	3. U.S. National Team Bicycle Sprint	20%	50%
	Lower-body anaerobic endurance	4. Bicycle Anaerobic Endurance	20%	
	Height-weight ratio, frontal surface area, overall height	5. Weight-Height Chart	5%	
	Width of shoulders	6. Width of Shoulders	2%	
	Width of hips	7. Width of Hips	3%	
	Percentage of body fat	8. Caliper Body-Fat-Percentage Measurement (negative points only)		

TEST 1: BICYCLE AGILITY

Agility and balance on a moving bicycle are crucial Control System abilities for the competitive cyclist, who must constantly maneuver his bike in and out of turns and the flow of other bicycles. Those abilities are also important to recreational cyclists, particularly in traffic, off the road, and whenever cycling at slow speeds, since the gyroscopic effect created by a bicycle's moving wheels makes it more stable at higher speeds. To enjoy cycling, whether recreational or competitive, and to be good at it, a cyclist must have well-developed riding skills, and chief among these are the agility and moving balance tested here. During this test you will never be in a position of static balance; your "sense of balance" should provide you with a shifting, ongoing sense of where your body should be in order to remain upright on the bike, and your agility should allow you to make the corrections necessary to achieve and maintain those positions. Be careful when you take this test: don't use a bike with a seat or a top bar too high for you, don't tighten traps on the pedals, and, if you lose your balance, *don't* turn the handlebars suddenly to one side or the other in an attempt to regain it.

What You Will Need

You will need a bicycle and five empty one-gallon plastic bottles set up (preferably in an empty parking lot) in the configuration pictured in the illustration. You will also need a friend with a stopwatch to time you.

Taking the Test

Start at the starting line (Position A), with one foot on the ground and the other foot on a pedal. When your friend says "Go," ride the course, going around the bottles according to the diagram, three full times. When you cross the start-finish line for the third time, your friend should stop the watch for your time. You may take two practice runs before your three time trials. Only count time-trial runs in which you do not miss a turn or knock down a bottle. Take your best single time and use it to find your score in Table 44.

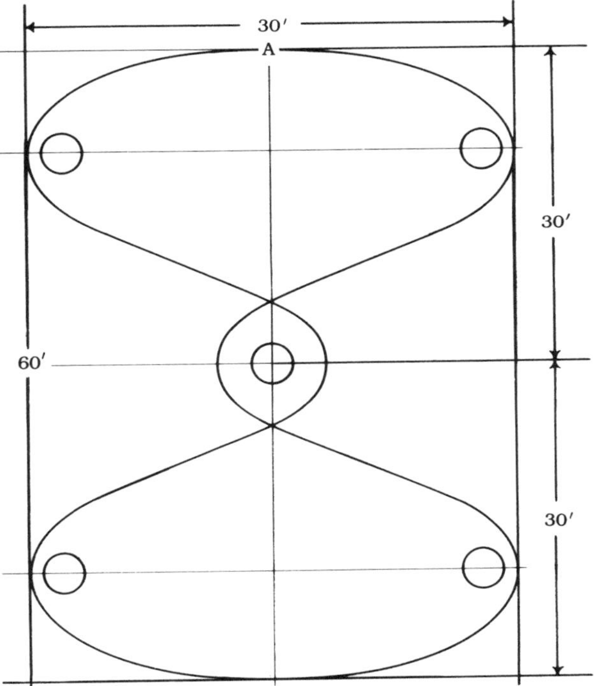

TABLE 44.
BICYCLE AGILITY

Best time (*seconds*)	Points
35.0	10
36.8	9
38.6	8
40.5	7
42.5	6
44.7	5
46.9	4
49.2	3
51.7	2
54.3	1
57.0	0

TEST 2: ASTRAND BICYCLE ERGOMETER

This is a standard test for maximum oxygen consumption in cycling. It was developed by Per-Olof Astrand, the godfather of modern exercise physiology, and has been in use around the world for more than twenty years. The basis for the test is the linear relationship between heart rate and maximum oxygen consumption that is established at any work load over 50 percent of VO_2 Max. Your VO_2 Max is determined here by plotting your heart rate against your final work load. Taken with laboratory oxygen-consumption equipment, this test is an extremely accurate determinant of VO_2 Max; taken without such equipment as a field test, it is still an excellent indicator of heart-lung power, as well as a practical method of monitoring your aerobic process in cycling.

TABLE 45. ASTRAND BICYCLE ERGOMETER TEST

Men											
	Maximal oxygen uptake (*liters per minute*)						**Maximal oxygen uptake (*liters per minute*)**				
Heart rate	**300 KPM/ min 50W**	**600 KPM/ min 100W**	**900 KPM/ min 150W**	**1,200 KPM/ min 200W**	**1,500 KPM/ min 250W**	**Heart rate**	**300 KPM/ min 50W**	**600 KPM/ min 100W**	**900 KPM/ min 150W**	**1,200 KPM/ min 200W**	**1,500 KPM/ min 250W**
120	2.2	3.5	4.8			148		2.4	3.2	4.3	5.4
121	2.2	3.4	4.7			149		2.3	3.2	4.3	5.4
122	2.2	3.4	4.6			150		2.3	3.2	4.2	5.3
123	2.1	3.4	4.6			151		2.3	3.1	4.2	5.2
124	2.1	3.3	4.5	6.0		152		2.3	3.1	4.1	5.2
125	2.0	3.2	4.4	5.9		153		2.2	3.0	4.1	5.1
126	2.0	3.2	4.4	5.8		154		2.2	3.0	4.0	5.1
127	2.0	3.1	4.3	5.7		155		2.2	3.0	4.0	5.0
128	2.0	3.1	4.2	5.6		156		2.2	2.9	4.0	5.0
129	1.9	3.0	4.2	5.6		157		2.1	2.9	3.9	4.9
130	1.9	3.0	4.1	5.5		158		2.1	2.9	3.9	4.9
131	1.9	2.9	4.0	5.4		159		2.1	2.8	3.8	4.8
132	1.8	2.9	4.0	5.3		160		2.1	2.8	3.8	4.8
133	1.8	2.8	3.9	5.3		161		2.0	2.8	3.7	4.7
134	1.8	2.8	3.9	5.2		162		2.0	2.8	3.7	4.6
135	1.7	2.8	3.8	5.1		163		2.0	2.8	3.7	4.6
136	1.7	2.7	3.8	5.0		164		2.0	2.7	3.6	4.5
137	1.7	2.7	3.7	5.0		165		2.0	2.7	3.6	4.5
138	1.6	2.7	3.7	4.9		166		1.9	2.7	3.6	4.5
139	1.6	2.6	3.6	4.8		167		1.9	2.6	3.5	4.4
140	1.6	2.6	3.6	4.8	6.0	168		1.9	2.6	3.5	4.4
141		2.6	3.5	4.7	5.9	169		1.9	2.6	3.5	4.3
142		2.5	3.5	4.6	5.8	170		1.8	2.6	3.4	4.3
143		2.5	3.4	4.6	5.7						
144		2.5	3.4	4.5	5.7						
145		2.4	3.4	4.5	5.6						
146		2.4	3.3	4.4	5.6						
147		2.4	3.3	4.4	5.5						

This test assumes that you have a healthy, vigorous heart; if you don't, see a doctor before taking it. You should not be sick when you take the test; and you should not have just eaten, or drunk any alcohol, or exercised heavily. The laboratory version of this test is normally monitored by a trained technician. Though this version is a field test, if you have a friend who is a doctor, a nurse, or a trained exercise technician, ask him or her to administer the test.

What You Will Need

You will need a stationary bicycle, a method of taking your pulse (either a friend with a stopwatch or a heartbeat monitor), and a clock or watch with a minute hand. Your results will most likely be better if you take the test on a stationary bicycle set up as a racing bike, with traps on the pedals, a racing seat, and lowered racing-type handlebars.

Women

	Maximal oxygen uptake (*liters per minute*)						**Maximal oxygen uptake (*liters per minute*)**				
Heart rate	**300 KPM/ min 50W**	**450 KPM/ min 75W**	**600 KPM/ min 100W**	**750 KPM/ min 125W**	**900 KPM/ min 150W**	**Heart rate**	**300 KPM/ min 50W**	**450 KPM/ min 75W**	**600 KPM/ min 100W**	**750 KPM/ min 125W**	**900 KPM/ min 150W**
120	2.6	3.4	4.1	4.8		148	1.6	2.1	2.6	3.1	3.6
121	2.5	3.3	4.0	4.8		149		2.1	2.6	3.0	3.5
122	2.5	3.2	3.9	4.7		150		2.0	2.5	3.0	3.5
123	2.4	3.1	3.9	4.6		151		2.0	2.5	3.0	3.4
124	2.4	3.1	3.8	4.5		152		2.0	2.5	2.9	3.4
125	2.3	3.0	3.7	4.4		153		2.0	2.4	2.9	3.3
126	2.3	3.0	3.6	4.3		154		2.0	2.4	2.8	3.3
127	2.2	2.9	3.5	4.2		155		1.9	2.4	2.8	3.2
128	2.2	2.8	3.5	4.2	4.8	156		1.9	2.3	2.8	3.2
129	2.2	2.8	3.4	4.1	4.8	157		1.9	2.3	2.7	3.2
130	2.1	2.7	3.4	4.0	4.7	158		1.8	2.3	2.7	3.1
131	2.1	2.7	3.4	4.0	4.6	159		1.8	2.2	2.7	3.1
132	2.0	2.7	3.3	3.9	4.5	160		1.8	2.2	2.6	3.0
133	2.0	2.6	3.2	3.8	4.4	161		1.8	2.2	2.6	3.0
134	2.0	2.6	3.2	3.8	4.4	162		1.8	2.2	2.6	3.0
135	2.0	2.6	3.1	3.7	4.3	163		1.7	2.2	2.6	2.9
136	1.9	2.5	3.1	3.6	4.2	164		1.7	2.1	2.5	2.9
137	1.9	2.5	3.0	3.6	4.2	165		1.7	2.1	2.5	2.9
138	1.8	2.4	3.0	3.5	4.1	166		1.7	2.1	2.5	2.8
139	1.8	2.4	2.9	3.5	4.0	167		1.6	2.1	2.4	2.8
140	1.8	2.4	2.8	3.4	4.0	168		1.6	2.0	2.4	2.8
141	1.8	2.3	2.8	3.4	3.9	169		1.6	2.0	2.4	2.8
142	1.7	2.3	2.8	3.3	3.9	170		1.6	2.0	2.4	2.7
143	1.7	2.2	2.7	3.3	3.8						
144	1.7	2.2	2.7	3.2	3.8						
145	1.6	2.2	2.7	3.2	3.7						
146	1.6	2.2	2.6	3.2	3.7						
147	1.6	2.1	2.6	3.1	3.6						

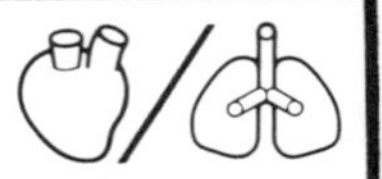

Taking the Test

Get on the bike and start pedaling at 60 RPMs (one complete revolution of the wheel per second, the standard pedaling cadence for this test). Turn the bike's work load up to the number of watts (for example, 50, 150, or 200) or KPMs (300, 600, 900, or 1,200) at which you feel you could pedal for five or ten minutes comfortably. After you have warmed up for a couple of minutes, either you or your friend should start timing the test. Pedal for six minutes at 60 RPMs and at the same work load established during your warm-up, and have your pulse taken sometime during the last minute of pedaling. Use that pulse rate along with your work-load setting in watts or KPMs to find your maximal oxygen uptake (in liters per minute) in Table 45. Then, in Table 46, match that value (in the left-hand column) with your weight (at the top of the table) to obtain your VO_2 Max. Use that value to calculate your score in Table 47. (If your pulse rate during the test is not more than 150 beats per minute, turn the work load of the bike up 50 watts and take the test again without stopping your pedaling.)

TABLE 46. ASTRAND BICYCLE ERGOMETER TEST

Maximal oxygen uptake (liters per minute)	Weight (pounds)																				
	80	**85**	**90**	**95**	**100**	**105**	**110**	**115**	**120**	**125**	**130**	**135**	**140**	**145**	**150**	**155**	**160**	**165**	**170**	**175**	**180**
2.0	56	51	49	47	43	42	40	38	36	35	34	33	31	30	29	29	27	27	26	25	24
2.2	61	56	54	51	48	46	44	42	40	39	37	36	34	33	32	31	30	29	29	28	27
2.4	67	62	59	56	52	50	48	46	44	42	41	39	38	36	35	34	33	32	31	30	29
2.6	72	67	63	60	57	54	52	50	47	46	44	43	41	39	38	37	36	35	34	33	32
2.8	78	72	68	65	61	58	56	54	51	49	47	46	44	42	41	40	38	37	36	35	34
3.0	83	77	73	70	65	63	60	58	55	53	51	49	47	45	44	43	41	40	39	38	37
3.2		82	78	74	70	67	64	62	58	56	54	52	50	48	47	46	44	43	42	40	39
3.4			83	79	74	71	68	65	62	60	58	56	53	52	50	49	47	45	44	43	41
3.6				84	78	75	72	69	65	63	61	59	56	55	53	51	49	48	47	45	44
3.8					83	79	76	73	69	67	64	62	59	58	56	54	52	51	49	48	46
4.0						83	80	77	73	70	68	66	63	61	59	57	55	53	52	50	49
4.2							84	81	76	74	71	69	66	64	62	60	58	56	55	53	51
4.4								85	80	77	75	72	69	67	65	63	60	59	57	55	54
4.6									84	81	78	75	72	70	68	66	63	61	60	58	56
4.8										84	81	79	75	73	71	69	66	64	62	60	59
5.0											85	82	78	76	74	71	68	67	65	63	61
5.2												85	81	79	76	74	71	69	68	65	63
5.4													84	82	79	77	74	72	70	68	66
5.6														85	82	80	77	75	73	70	68
5.8															85	83	79	77	75	73	71
6.0																86	82	80	78	75	73
6.2																	85	83	81	78	76

185	190	195	200	205	210	215	220	225	230	235	240	245	250	255	260
24	23	22	22	22	21	20	20	20	19	19	18	18	18	17	17
26	26	25	24	24	23	22	22	22	21	21	20	20	19	19	19
29	28	27	26	26	25	24	24	24	23	22	22	22	21	21	20
31	30	29	29	28	27	27	26	25	25	24	24	23	23	22	22
33	33	31	31	30	29	29	28	27	27	26	26	25	25	24	24
36	35	34	33	32	32	31	30	29	29	28	28	27	26	26	25
38	37	36	35	34	34	33	32	31	30	30	29	29	28	28	27
40	40	38	37	37	36	35	34	33	32	32	31	31	30	29	29
43	42	40	40	39	38	37	36	35	34	34	33	32	32	31	31
45	44	43	42	41	40	39	38	37	36	36	35	34	33	33	32
48	47	45	44	43	42	41	40	39	38	37	37	36	35	34	34
50	49	47	46	45	44	43	42	41	40	39	39	38	37	36	36
52	51	49	48	47	46	45	44	43	42	41	40	40	39	38	37
55	53	52	51	49	48	47	46	45	44	43	42	41	40	40	39
57	56	54	53	52	51	49	48	47	46	45	44	43	42	41	41
60	58	56	55	54	53	51	50	49	48	47	46	45	44	43	42
62	60	58	57	56	55	53	52	51	50	49	48	47	46	45	44
64	63	61	59	58	57	55	54	53	51	50	50	49	47	47	46
67	65	63	62	60	59	57	56	55	53	52	51	50	49	48	47
69	67	65	64	62	61	59	58	57	55	54	53	52	51	50	49
71	70	67	66	65	63	61	60	59	57	56	55	54	53	52	51
74	72	70	68	67	65	63	62	61	59	58	57	56	54	53	53

TABLE 47. ASTRAND BICYCLE ERGOMETER TEST

VO_2 Max	Points	
	Men	Women
74	40	
73	39	
72	38	
71	36	
70	35	
69	34	
68	32	
67	31	
66	30	
65	29	
64	28	
63	26	
62	25	
61	24	
60	23	40
59	21	38
58	20	36
57	19	35
56	18	33
55	16	32
54	15	30
53	14	28
52	13	26
51	12	24
50	10	23
49	9	21
48	8	20
47	6	18
46	5	16
45	4	14
44		12
43		11
42		9
41		8
40		6
39		4

TEST 3: U.S. NATIONAL TEAM BICYCLE SPRINT

One of the greatest natural gifts any cyclist can have is the largely genetic ability to accelerate quickly and powerfully. This test, adapted from a National Team cycling test developed by Ed Burke, the team's chief physiologist, measures that ability. A very good result on this test will indicate a high percentage of sprint muscle fiber in your legs, and might, therefore, also indicate to a competitive (or potentially competitive) cyclist a talent for track, pursuit, or criterium events. A high percentage of sprint fiber in the legs is also a real asset to a road racer—allowing him to spring away from other racers—as long as he has enough endurance to hang in the pack.

What You Will Need

You will need a stationary bike, a friend with a stopwatch, and, to do as well as possible on this test, a great deal of motivation.

Taking the Test

Set the work load of the bike at 100 watts (600 KPMs) if you are a man, and 50 watts (300 KPMs) if you are a woman, and warm up for a couple of minutes at that work load, pedaling at a cadence of about 60 RPMs. To start the test, have your friend tell you to "Go" when your left (or right) foot reaches its full downstroke, or six-o'clock, position. Pedal as fast as you possibly can—really dig for effort here—and have your friend time how long it takes you to complete thirty revolutions. (Your friend should count your revolutions, one revolution being completed each time your foot comes back to the six-o'clock position after the test begins; after thirty revolutions your friend should stop the watch.) Your time in seconds (the time it took you to do the thirty revolutions) will give you your score in Table 48.

TABLE 48. U.S. NATIONAL TEAM BICYCLE SPRINT

Time (*seconds*)	Points
6.0	20
6.5	18
7.0	17
7.5	15
8.0	13
8.5	12
9.0	10
9.5	8
10.0	7
10.5	5
11.0	3
11.5	2
12.0	0

TEST 4: BICYCLE ANAEROBIC ENDURANCE

This test measures anaerobic endurance power in the legs—the power that allows a competitive cyclist to sustain a breakaway and a recreational cyclist to climb hills anaerobically. Anaerobic power in the legs is a major asset to any cyclist, particularly when it is matched with a high VO_2 Max. While it is sprint power that is employed to accelerate a cyclist to overdrive speed, it is anaerobic endurance power that keeps him there for any length of time; and it is the usable percentage of VO_2 Max that gives any cyclist, competitive or recreational, his baseline cruise speed, from which overdrive is achieved and sustained.

What You Will Need

You will need a stationary bike, a metronome (see Appendix), and a friend with a stopwatch.

Taking the Test

Set the metronome at 100 beats per minute and start cycling at that cadence (timing your pedaling so that your left, or right, foot reaches its full downstroke on each click of the metronome). The work load of the bike should be set at zero. After warming up in this way for a couple of minutes, have your friend abruptly turn the power setting on the bike up to 200 watts (3,200 KPMs) if you are a man, and 150 watts (2,400 KPMs) if you are a woman, and immediately begin timing the test. While your friend is timing you, he should be watching your pedaling cadence. When your foot comes around for three quarters of a full circle or less per beat of the metronome (in other words, when your cadence falls to 75 RPMs or under), your friend should stop the clock. Your time for the test in seconds will give you your score in Table 49.

TABLE 49.
BICYCLE ANAEROBIC ENDURANCE

Time (*seconds*)		Points
Men (3,200 KPM)	**Women (2,400 KPM)**	
75	75	20
71	71	19
67	67	18
63	63	17
59	59	16
55	55	15
51	51	14
47	47	13
43	43	12
39	39	11
35	35	10
31	31	9
27	27	8
23	23	7
19	19	6
15	15	5

TEST 5: WEIGHT-HEIGHT CHART

Up to 90 percent of the total physical work of cycling on flats and in downhills is work done to overcome wind resistance, and in uphills most of the work of cycling is expended in pulling the weight of the body and the bike up the hills. Obviously, then, a cyclist is well served by a frontal surface area that offers as little resistance to the wind as possible, and, power considerations being equal, by as light a body weight as possible for a given height. Being too tall, no matter what your weight-to-height ratio, is a disadvantage in cycling because it diminishes your ability to draft and because it raises your center of gravity relative to the bicycle. Table 50 will give you one score that simultaneously evaluates your frontal surface area (which is approximated by your weight-height ratio), your weight in proportion to your height, and your height alone.

Taking the Test

Determine your weight by weighing yourself, unclothed, on an accurate scale, and your height, measured as described in Running Test 3 (page 187). Locate the point at which these measurements intersect in Table 50 to determine your score.

TABLE 50. WEIGHT-HEIGHT CHART

Height (*inches*)	Weight (*pounds*)																						
	90	**95**	**100**	**105**	**110**	**115**	**120**	**125**	**130**	**135**	**140**	**145**	**150**	**155**	**160**	**165**	**170**	**175**	**180**	**185**	**190**	**195**	**200**
56	5	5	5	5	5	5	5	5	4	2	1	1	0	0									
57	5	5	5	5	5	5	5	5	4	2	1	1	1	0									
58	5	5	5	5	5	5	5	5	5	4	2	1	1	0									
59	5	5	5	5	5	5	5	5	5	4	2	1	1	1	0	0	0	0	0	0	0	0	0
60	5	5	5	5	5	5	5	5	5	4	4	2	1	1	0	0	0	0	0	0	0	0	0
61	5	5	5	5	5	5	5	5	5	5	4	2	1	1	1	0	0	0	0	0	0	0	0
62	5	5	5	5	5	5	5	5	5	5	4	4	2	1	1	0	0	0	0	0	0	0	0
63	5	5	5	5	5	5	5	5	5	5	5	4	2	1	1	1	0	0	0	0	0	0	0
64	5	5	5	5	5	5	5	5	5	5	5	4	4	2	1	1	0	0	0	0	0	0	0
65	5	5	5	5	5	5	5	5	5	5	5	5	4	2	1	1	1	0	0	0	0	0	0
66	5	5	5	5	5	5	5	5	5	5	5	5	4	4	2	1	1	0	0	0	0	0	0
67	5	5	5	5	5	5	5	5	5	5	5	5	5	4	2	1	1	1	0	0	0	0	0
68	5	5	5	5	5	5	5	5	5	5	5	5	5	4	2	2	1	1	1	0	0	0	0
69	5	5	5	5	5	5	5	5	5	5	5	5	5	5	4	2	1	1	1	0	0	0	0
70	5	5	5	5	5	5	5	5	5	5	5	5	5	5	4	2	2	1	1	1	0	0	0
71	5	5	5	5	5	5	5	5	5	5	5	5	5	5	4	4	2	1	1	1	0	0	0
72	4	4	4	4	4	4	4	4	4	4	4	4	4	4	4	4	2	2	1	1	1	0	0
73	4	4	4	4	4	4	4	4	4	4	5	4	4	4	4	4	4	2	1	1	1	0	0
74	3	3	3	3	3	3	3	3	3	3	3	3	3	3	3	3	4	2	2	1	1	1	0
75	3	3	3	3	3	3	3	3	3	3	3	3	3	3	3	3	4	4	2	1	1	1	0
76	3	3	3	3	3	3	3	3	3	3	3	3	3	3	3	3	3	4	2	2	1	1	1

TEST 6: WIDTH OF SHOULDERS

The width of your shoulders is an indicator of the breadth of your upper body and therefore of your overall frontal surface area above the bicycle. While cyclists are helped by large hearts and lungs, those organs are better enclosed in deep, narrow chests than in wide, wind-resistant ones.

What You Will Need

You will need a friend with a measuring tape.

Taking the Test

Sit relaxed in a chair with your back straight. From behind you, your friend should locate the outermost extremity of each of your shoulder bones (they are at the very ends of your clavicle) and mark those points with a pen or marker. Now have your friend use the tape measure to measure the distance between those two points, laying out the tape across the top of your chest and under your neck. Use that distance in inches to determine your score in Table 51.

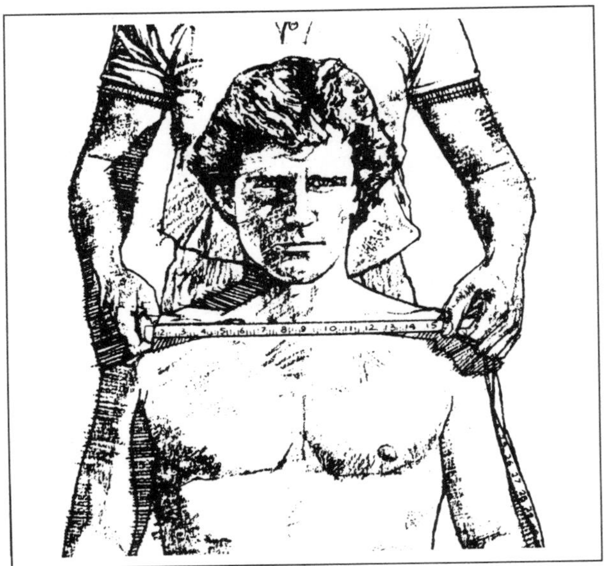

TABLE 51. WIDTH OF SHOULDERS

Shoulder width (*inches*)	**Points**
14 or more	2.0
15	1.5
16 or less	1.0

TEST 7: WIDTH OF HIPS

The width of your hips is an indicator of your lower-body frontal surface area. Also, and more important in cycling, the width of your hips determines how much rotational movement in your hip joints is created by pedaling: the narrower your hips, the less rotational movement is created, and therefore the more direct and effective the drive train producing the force exerted on the pedals. As direct as possible a transfer of force onto the pedals is always important in cycling, but it is of particular significance during acceleration and in sprints.

What You Will Need

The equipment needed for this test is given on page 189.

Taking the Test

Follow the instructions given on page 189 (note also the special instructions for homemade calipers). The distance measured in inches will give you your score in Table 52.

TABLE 52. WIDTH OF HIPS

Hip width (*inches*)	Points
10 or less	3.0
11	2.5
12 or more	2.0

TEST 8: CALIPER BODY-FAT-PERCENTAGE MEASUREMENT

It is critical to good performance for a cyclist to be as light as possible for a given height without sacrificing the muscular strength necessary for the sport, which means that he or she can carry very little fat. The ideal body-fat percentages for competitive cyclists are 7 percent for men and 12 percent for women, which are comparable to the ideal percentages for cross-country skiing and running, though, owing to the mechanical efficiency of the bicycle, one's percentage of fat is somewhat less important in cycling than in the other two sports.

The only accurate way to measure that percentage outside a laboratory is with calipers, and since all athletes should want to keep accurate running measurements of their body-fat percentages, we suggest here, as in the body-fat tests for the other sports, that you borrow a pair of laboratory calipers or purchase a pair of inexpensive plastic ones with which to take that measurement on a regular basis. (See Appendix for information on ordering calipers.)

The tables used in this book are for a general population, and people with specialized fat stores in only one or two specific parts of the body may get a slightly inaccurate overall score.

What You Will Need

A pair of calipers.

Taking the Test

Proceed with measurements as indicated on page 179. Add together the readings from all measurement sites and use the total to find your percentage of body fat in Table 24 if you are a man, or in Table 25 if you are a woman. That percentage will give you your score for this test in Table 53.

TABLE 53. CALIPER BODY-FAT-PERCENTAGE MEASUREMENT

Body-fat percentage		(Negative) points
Men	**Women**	
6.7	13.4	0
7.4	14.1	−1
8.1	14.8	−2
8.9	15.5	−3
9.8	16.3	−4
10.8	17.1	−5
11.9	18.0	−7
13.1	18.9	−8
14.4	19.8	−9
15.8	20.8	−10
17.4	21.8	−11
19.1	22.9	−12
21.0	24.1	−13
23.1	25.3	−14
25.4	26.5	−15

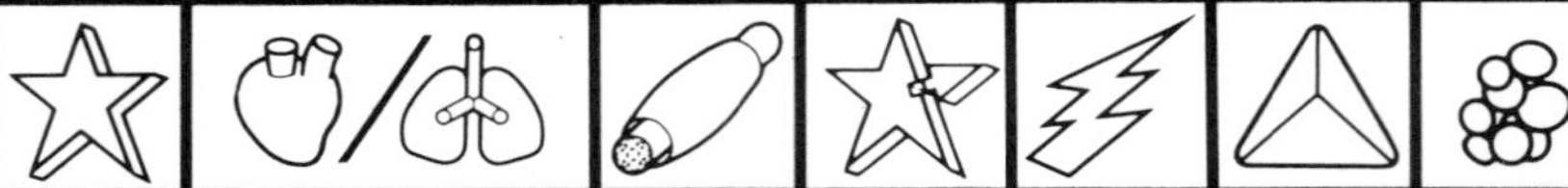

TESTING FOR CROSS-COUNTRY SKIING

No sport has been more thoroughly examined by the science of exercise physiology than cross-country skiing, whose birthplace, Scandinavia, is also the birthplace of that science. One reason cross-country skiing holds such high fascination for sports scientists is that it places higher physiological demands on the body than any other sport. The new techniques and equipment of cross-country skiing have added the requirements of technical ability and considerable anaerobic strength in both the upper and lower body to the highest aerobic requirements. The weighting of our tests reflects the fact that, important as aerobic power is to the sport, it is no longer possible, as it once was, to predict the winners of races on their VO_2 Max alone. Nonaerobic capacities now form a crucial segment of overall aptitude for cross-country skiing.

It should be noted that we are *not* testing the ability to walk on Nordic skis over a snow-covered golf course. Almost any healthy individual, even one with no talent whatsoever for the sport, can cross-country ski for some exercise and enjoyment of the winter landscape. Instead, as in the other testing sections of this book, we are testing an aptitude for the more advanced recreational practices of the sport and/or for potential competitive talent.

CHART 7. CROSS-COUNTRY SKIING

	Components tested	Test	Relative importance of test to overall score
The Control System	Agility, multilimb coordination	1. U.S. Nordic Ski Team Agility Run	15% } 30%
	Balance	2. Blind-Stork Balance	15%
The Heart-Lung Package	VO_2 Max	3. Cooper Twelve-Minute Run	45%
Body Composition	Upper-body poling force and power endurance	4. Teardrop Push-up	5% } 25%
	Leg length	5. Upper-Body/Lower-Body Proportion	5%
	Leg explosiveness	6. Vertical Jump	7%
	Calf speed and anaerobic endurance	7. Calf Raise	8%
	Percentage of body fat	8. Caliper-Body-Fat Percentage Measurement (negative points only)	

TEST 1: U.S. NORDIC SKI TEAM AGILITY RUN

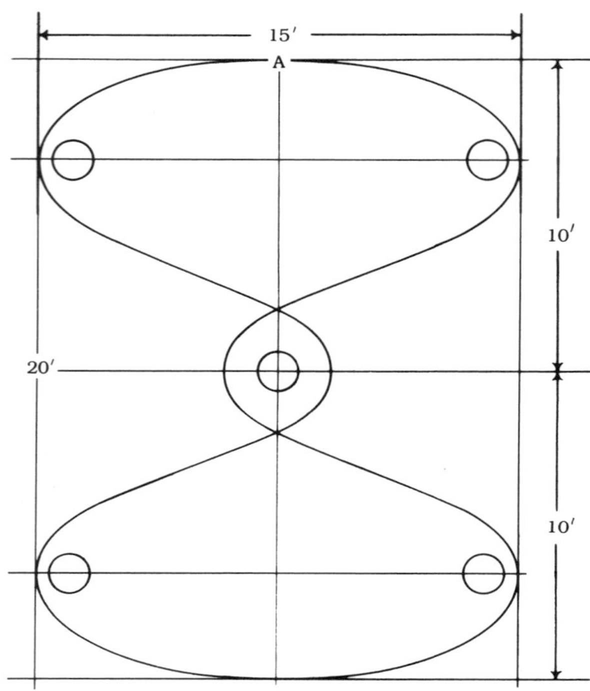

The agility and multilimb coordination necessary to make turns off a narrow platform and to stabilize the body instantly between those turns are crucial Control System functions in cross-country skiing. This standard agility drill, which is administered to young skiers by the U.S. Nordic Ski Team, is designed to measure the underlying abilities of agility and multilimb coordination in turning quickly and stabilizing without losing speed. Though these abilities are largely genetic, your score on this test can be measurably improved with practice.

What You Will Need

You will need a hard, flat surface and a cleared area at least twenty feet long and fifteen feet wide. You will also need five empty one-gallon plastic bottles and a friend with a stopwatch.

Taking the Test

Set up the plastic bottles according to the illustration. Get into a semicrouched position at the start line (Position A). At the command "Go," run the course in the designated pattern *three times around* as fast as you can without knocking over any of the bottles; if you do knock over a bottle, start the test over again. Take two practice runs and then two time trials (count only time trials during which no bottle is knocked over). Each time trial should take you around the course three times, and your friend should stop the watch as soon as you cross the start-finish line for the third time. Use your best time to determine your score in Table 54.

TABLE 54. U.S. NORDIC SKI TEAM AGILITY RUN

Best time (*seconds*)	Points
18.5	15.0
20.0	13.5
21.5	12.0
23.0	10.5
24.5	9.0
26.0	7.5
27.5	6.0
29.0	4.5
30.5	3.0
32.0	1.5
33.5	0.0

TEST 2: BLIND-STORK BALANCE

In both competitive and recreational cross-country skiing, good balance is even more of a requirement than it is in Alpine skiing, since Nordic skis are considerably narrower than Alpine skis, Nordic boots provide little or no lateral support for the ankles, and a Nordic skier, moving correctly, is usually balanced over only one foot at a time. The Blind-Stork Balance Test is the best we know for reducing balance to its single most important component: the sensitivity of the inner ear. With no positional information coming in through the eyes, the gyroscopic function of the inner ear, which provides our "sense of balance," is isolated and forced to operate without the considerable benefit of supplementary visual information.

What You Will Need

See page 175 for the prerequisites for this test.

Taking the Test

Follow the instructions given on page 175. Take all six tests within a period of ten minutes, and use your single best time on either leg to find your score in Table 55. (If your times on one leg are considerably shorter than those on the other, you should work on improving your balance on that leg.)

TABLE 55. BLIND-STORK BALANCE

Men		Women	
Best time (*seconds*)	**Points**	**Best time (*seconds*)**	**Points**
60	15.0	35	15.0
55	13.7	30	12.8
50	12.3	25	10.5
45	11.0	20	8.3
40	9.6	15	6.0
35	8.3	10	3.8
30	6.9	5	1.5
25	5.6		
20	4.2		
15	2.9		
10	1.5		

TEST 3: COOPER TWELVE-MINUTE RUN

At Dr. Arnot's sports-medicine training center in Lake Placid, New York, during a U.S. Ski Team testing camp in 1979, a number of sophisticated laboratory tests were devised to assess the tremendous aerobic work done by cross-country ski racers—aerobic work that is greater than that for any other sport because of the simultaneous activity of many muscle groups in cross-country skiing. These tests for VO_2 Max in cross-country skiing measured heavy uphill leg work, striding, and the upper-body work of poling—all done simultaneously. Unfortunately, such tests are possible only under laboratory conditions and there is no field test for VO_2 Max specific to skiing. The Cooper Twelve-Minute-Run Test, however, does provide an adequate assessment of overall aerobic power, and the experience of the U.S. Nordic Ski Team would indicate that so long as an individual has sufficient arm and shoulder strength to pole effectively, that strength can be developed into aerobic upper-body power through training.

What You Will Need

See page 148 for the prerequisites for this test.

Taking the Test

Follow the instructions given on page 148, and calculate the total distance covered. That distance will give you your score in Table 56. Be sure to warm down by jogging for at least half a mile after you run.

TABLE 56. COOPER TWELVE-MINUTE RUN

Distance run (*miles*)	**Points**	
	Men	**Women**
1 6/16		4.5
1 7/16		9.0
1 8/16		13.5
1 9/16		18.0
1 10/16	4.5	22.5
1 11/16	7.4	27.0
1 12/16	10.3	31.5
1 13/16	13.2	36.0
1 14/16	16.1	40.5
1 15/16	19.0	45.0
2	21.9	
2 1/16	24.7	
2 2/16	27.6	
2 3/16	30.5	
2 4/16	33.4	
2 5/16	36.3	
2 6/16	39.2	
2 7/16	42.1	
2 8/16	45.0	
2 9/16		
2 10/16		

TEST 4: TEARDROP PUSH-UP

In filmed analyses of the pre–Olympic Games in Lake Placid in 1979, it was found that very few of the women competitors had the shoulder and arm strength for effective poling up hills, where body momentum was slowing and poling became crucial to speed maintenance. In the same analyses, arm strength and muscle speed were found to be deficient in many of the male competitors as well. On the upper levels of recreational cross-country skiing, as well as in competition, strong poling is crucial to effective technique, and is an important contributor to the upper-body-training effect that can be derived from cross-country skiing. The great majority of recreational skiers do only isometric work in their poling, by simply sticking the pole into the snow, holding on to it, and skiing past it. At pole plant, the dynamic work of good poling is begun at high force and low speed by the deltoid muscles of the shoulder, and it is completed at increasing speed (up to 400 degrees per second, one of the fastest repetitive movements in all of sports) and decreasing force by the triceps muscles in the rear of the arms. The strength of those two muscle groups, the deltoids and the triceps, and their anaerobic endurance capacity are tested here.

If you find that you can't do this test at all

Keep hands together and back straight.

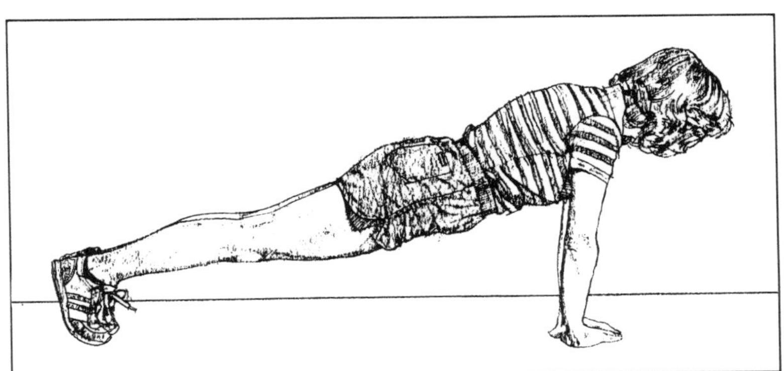

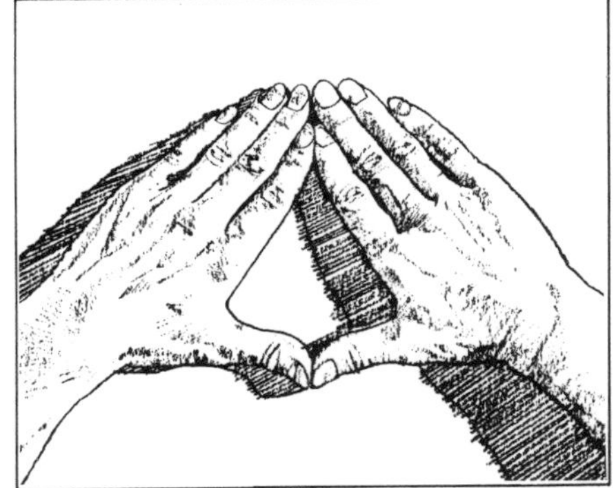

(and many people can't), don't conclude that you shouldn't ski or that you don't have potential for the sport. Arm- and shoulder-strength training can help you to realize your potential, improve your technique, and enjoy your skiing more.

Taking the Test

This test is a variation of the standard push-up. It is important in testing triceps and deltoid strength (as opposed to pectoral strength) to do this variation exactly as described, *without cheating*. Lie flat on the floor or ground, face down, with your feet together. Put your forefingers and thumbs together so that they form a teardrop shape (see illustration). Holding your hands together in this way, put them under your chest, so that your nipples rest on your thumb bones. Drop your head so that your nose touches the floor, and lift your knees off the floor. Now push yourself up to a full extension of your arms, keeping your back and hips in an absolutely flat, locked plane as you push upward. Don't squirm upward or raise your shoulders before your hips. Do as many of these push-ups as you can in thirty seconds; the number you do will give you your score in Table 57.

TABLE 57. TEARDROP PUSH-UP

Number of push-ups	Points
35	5.0
30	4.3
25	3.6
20	2.9
15	2.2
10	1.5
5	0.7
0	0.0

TEST 5: UPPER-BODY/ LOWER-BODY PROPORTION

The length of your stride in cross-country skiing, as in running, is the final measure of your technical ability. That length is a function of the force applied to the skis, the force of poling, and the length of your legs, as well as of your overall technique. The longer your legs, the farther you can step on skis, and—with proper poling, proper technique, and the correct force supplied to the skis—the longer your stride will be. This test measures the overall length of your legs, and it should be remembered that your legs may be long in proportion to your body height.

What You Will Need

You will need the equipment indicated on page 152.

Taking the Test

Proceed with this test as directed on page 152. The ratio of your sitting height to your lower-body length, as determined from Table 8, will give you your score in Table 58.

TABLE 58. UPPER-BODY/ LOWER-BODY PROPORTION

Ratio of sitting height to lower-body length	Points
0.9	5
1.0	3
1.1	1

TEST 6: VERTICAL JUMP

The Vertical-Jump Test is included here to test the ability to apply substantial leg muscular force quickly, a critical ability in some kinds of cross-country skiing. There are fine cross-country ski racers with a large percentage of endurance muscle fiber in their legs and therefore limited explosiveness. These skiers generally have a very high VO_2 Max and long, even, tireless strides. Other skiers, like Bill Koch, have a higher percentage of sprint muscle fiber in their legs, and therefore more explosiveness and acceleration. With the development of modern equipment and techniques, and with the increase in technical difficulty of courses, leg explosiveness has become more and more important to racers, and it is a desirable characteristic for any recreational skier. This test measures the explosiveness of both the quadriceps muscles of the thigh, which are crucial to hill climbing, and the gastrocnemius muscles of the calf, the rate-limiting muscle group for the application of force onto the skis in all of cross-country skiing.

What You Will Need

The equipment needed for this test is listed on page 151.

Taking the Test

Proceed as instructed on page 151. Don't practice before taking the test. Do the test three times and take your highest *single* reach in inches to determine your score in Table 59.

TABLE 59. VERTICAL JUMP

Highest single reach (*inches*)		Points
Men	**Women**	
26.0	18.0	7
24.6	17.2	6
23.2	16.4	5
21.8	15.6	4
20.4	14.8	3
19.0	14.0	2
17.6	13.2	1
16.2	12.4	0

TEST 7: CALF RAISE

The rate-limiting muscle in cross-country skiing is the gastrocnemius muscle of the calf, which exerts push-off power onto the snow through the ski. High-speed computerized motion analysis has shown that the top cross-country racers have incredibly fast foot extension on push-off, with angular velocities of up to 371 degrees per second. This extension is accomplished by the calf muscles, which must be not only fast, but powerful and durable as well, in order to lift the full weight of the body over and over again at a high speed.

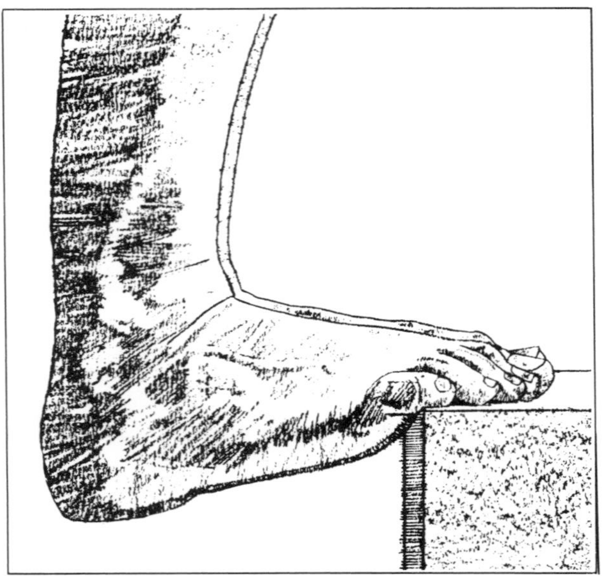

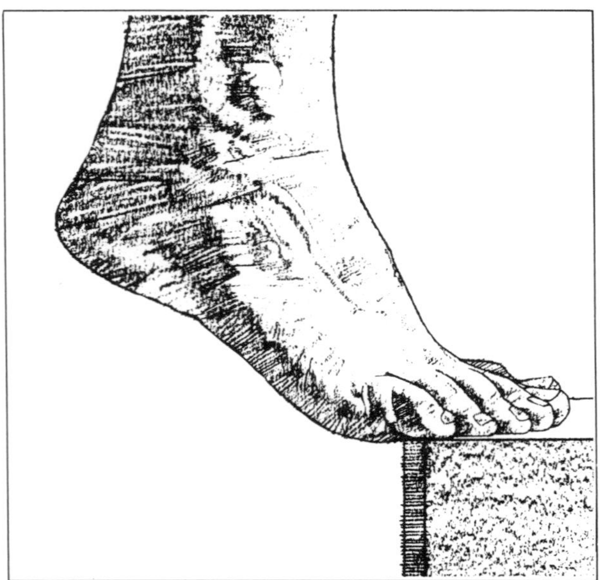

Extend fully. Don't bounce.

What You Will Need

You will need a block of wood, three to four inches deep by a couple of feet long, and a friend with a stopwatch.

Taking the Test

Take this test on your dominant leg. Stand, barefoot, on the block of wood on the ball of your foot, so that your heel can touch the ground. Put your hands on a wall or some other solid object at chest level to steady yourself, but don't use them to help pull yourself up. When your friend says "Go," stand up on your tiptoes, then let your heels fall back down, below the plane of your toes, for one repetition. Do as many repetitions as you can *in good form* (without bouncing and with full range of motion) in thirty seconds. That number of repetitions will give you your score in Table 60.

TABLE 60. CALF RAISE

Number of calf raises	Points
44	8
40	7
36	6
32	5
28	4
24	3
20	2
16	1

TEST 8: CALIPER BODY-FAT-PERCENTAGE MEASUREMENT

Whatever your degree of explosiveness and anaerobic power in cross-country skiing, those values can be improved by carrying as little body fat as possible, especially for uphills and in cold, new snow. The ideal percentage of body fat for cross-country skiers is around 7 percent for men and 12 percent for women, one of the lowest ideal ranges in sports. The only accurate way to measure that percentage outside a laboratory is with calipers, and since all athletes should want to keep accurate running measurements of their percentages of body fat, we suggest here, as in the body-fat tests for the other sports in this book, that you borrow a pair of laboratory calipers or purchase a pair of inexpensive plastic ones with which to take those measurements on a regular basis. (See Appendix for information on ordering calipers.)

The tables used here are for a general population, and people with specialized fat stores in only one or two specific parts of the body may get a slightly inaccurate overall score.

What You Will Need

A pair of calipers.

Taking the Test

Proceed with measurements as indicated on page 179. Add together the readings from all measurement sites and use the total to find your percentage of body fat in Table 24 if you are a man, or in Table 25 if you are a woman. That percentage will give you your score for this test in Table 61.

TABLE 61. CALIPER BODY-FAT-PERCENTAGE MEASUREMENT

Body-fat percentage		(Negative) points
Men	**Women**	
7.0	12.0	0
7.7	12.6	−1
8.5	13.2	−2
9.3	13.9	−3
10.2	14.6	−4
11.3	15.3	−5
12.4	16.1	−7
13.6	16.9	−8
15.0	17.7	−9
16.5	18.6	−10
18.2	19.5	−11
20.0	20.5	−12
22.0	21.6	−13
24.2	22.6	−14
26.6	23.8	−15

PART IV

INTERPRETING YOUR TEST RESULTS AND MAXIMIZING YOUR SPORTSTALENTS

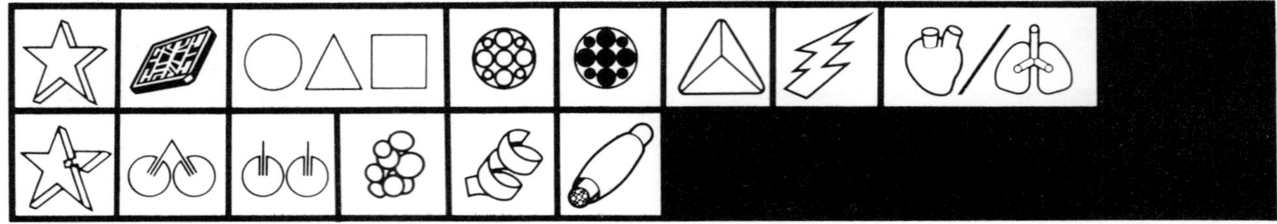

INTRODUCTION

Part IV is designed to help you interpret your results on the tests in Part III, to maximize what talents you found you had, and to compensate for whatever sports-talent deficits you discovered. It is also designed, through an overall interpretation of your test results, to give you a picture of yourself as an athlete—an "X ray" of your assets and liabilities in a particular sport that can allow you to devise an effective, personalized strategy for competition that makes the most of your strengths and compensates for your weaknesses.

This is not a training section per se, though some general and specific training information and advice is given for each of the sports. It would require at least seven separate volumes to treat adequately the training for seven sports, and there are already many good training books available for each of the sports we deal with. A list of what we consider to be the best of these can be found in the appropriate sections of the Appendix.

Each of the seven sections in Part IV is divided according to the abilities and physical components tested in Part III. We have tried to provide an interpretation of any result you might have had on every test given for every sport, and those results can and should be very helpful in and of themselves for indicating your individual strengths and weaknesses in a particular sport and, therefore, for indicating where and how your performance can be improved. If you scored very well on a particular test, we tell you how you can best maximize the ability or physical component tested, and—where appropriate—how you can continue to improve it. If you had a poor score on a particular test, we tell you how the ability or physical component tested can be improved, if it can be, and how you can best compensate if it cannot.

More valuable to you than an interpretation of your individual test results is the composite image of yourself as an athlete that you will form when you have a clear understanding of your *overall* results on the tests for any of the seven sports. This image can help you to devise a personalized strategy for a sport—an approach that maximizes your strengths and minimizes your weaknesses, and allows you to play and compete at your full potential.

Let's assume, for example, that you are a tennis player who was taught—and has played for years with some success—a steady baseline retrieval game. And let's assume that you find in the tennis tests that you have very good leg explosiveness, quick reaction time, good anticipation and agility, and good stroke mechanics for the serve. When taken as a *whole*, such results would indicate that you have extraordinary potential as a serve-and-volley player. By using those results—and the new image you can construct of yourself from them—to give yourself confidence in changing from a baseline to a serve-and-volley game, you will play better tennis and derive more enjoyment from the sport.

Finally, we will not attempt to tell you everything you could do to improve your performance at any one of the seven sports. As in the testing section, we focus here on those abilities and physical components that we consider central to the performance of each of the sports. This is a book about differences—not similarities—among athletes or potential athletes. If we assume that an ability or physical component (wrist and forearm strength in tennis, for example) can be developed to a degree adequate for the sport by virtually anyone, and/or if we consider that development not *essential* to good performance at the sport, we do not address that ability or physical component.

  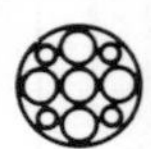

ALPINE SKIING

THE CONTROL SYSTEM

AGILITY, COORDINATION, BALANCE, SPEED OF MOTOR LEARNING, AND ANAEROBIC POWER IN THE LEGS. If your score was 13 or above on both the Hexagonal-Obstacle Test and the Concrete-Block Jump Test, you have the necessary agility, coordination, and balance to be an excellent Alpine skier. In Austria such a score on Test 1 alone, whether you knew how to ski or not, would mark you as a top potential Alpine skier and would classify you as developable by the Austrian National Ski Team. If you also scored well (8 or above) on the speed-of-motor-learning section of Test 1, you could learn to adapt your good motor abilities to skiing (as well as to other agility sports) relatively quickly and easily.

If you had to take down the blocks to complete the Hexagonal-Obstacle Test and then scored 6 or above on the test, check your results on Test 5, the Vertical-Jump Test, to determine whether or not you lack the necessary leg explosiveness to have completed Test 1 with the blocks in place; if those results were good, the chances are that your deficit is one of agility, specifically the in-the-air deftness and precision of movement that characterize great slalom skiers.

If you scored very well on Test 1 but did not score well on the

Concrete-Block Jump Test, it is likely that you lack anaerobic power in your legs. Good anaerobic power in the legs is extremely important to all ski racers; if you race, or plan to, and if you found on this test that your anaerobic leg power is deficient, you should develop that power by using this test as a drill, along with other anaerobic-power-training routines such as stair running, hill running, agility runs, and so on. You should also use this test as a method of monitoring your progress.

Conversely, if you scored well on the Concrete-Block Jump Test but poorly on the Hexagonal-Obstacle Test, you have good anaerobic power in the legs, as well as good balance and the ability to stabilize your body quickly, but you are lacking in agility. Agility is a structural trait that underlies a number of important skills in skiing. It is very difficult to develop agility if you don't have it, and any improvement of as much as 20 percent is almost unheard of. The fact that you have little natural ability doesn't mean you can't ski well, or even expertly; it does mean that you will have to build your skiing skills from the ground up, without benefit of the substantial foundation provided by good agility.

If you scored below 3 both on Test 1 without the blocks and on Test 2—and we assume that you were in reasonably good condition when you took those tests—anything more advanced than intermediate recreational skiing is likely to be difficult for you.

Few motor programs are harder to create than those that are central to Alpine skiing. The reason testing for Alpine skiing talent is so widely practiced in Europe is that it is far easier to produce a good skier by finding someone with all the natural building-block motor abilities already in place and to develop skiing skills in that individual than it is to try to inculcate the proper motor programs. A learning recreational skier or ski racer with great natural motor ability does not have to be so dependent on the standard body-position references used (often poorly) by instructors and coaches trying to convey accurate images of correctness; the talented beginner can rely to a much larger extent on natural abilities—what Warren Witherell calls a "genius for the game"—to feel the always unique circumstances of a given turn and to find the most efficient way to make the skis carve through it.

The very best skiers are always those with great natural motor abilities for the sport. Much of what they do on skis cannot be

taught, and yet the ways in which they use their skis as tools form the standards from which the images of correctness for skiing are drawn. These superb athletes intuitively form their own images of correctness—by skiing, in competition, and by watching expert skiers and racers. These people tend to be enthusiastic students of movement, often beginning when they are quite young, and almost always have an uncanny ability to analyze precisely what a top racer or recreational skier is doing on the snow and to transfer the biomechanical information gleaned from that analysis to their own skiing. The best way for these "natural skiers" to improve is to spend as much snowtime as possible around champions. A good mechanical understanding of how skis sit in and turn through the snow is also helpful, as is good race-coaching—though no coach except the most brilliantly analytical is likely to be able to do much more for a natural skier than to advise on tactics and to point out the best line through a course.

There are people without great motor abilities who make themselves into first-rate skiers. These skiers always have phenomenal analytical ability, but because they don't have equally phenomenal motor abilities they are not able to transfer to their skiing all that they learn from their analyses. By virtue of discipline, intelligence, and hard work, and by skiing precisely and avoiding mistakes, some of these people, of whom Billy Kidd is a example, can often use a simple, basic style to beat more talented skiers.

Finally, there are skiers—the majority of us—who possess neither great natural motor abilities nor great natural capacity to analyze movement; we must work hard to learn to ski expertly. With neither the supporting foundation of super motor abilities on which to build skiing skills nor the intuitive analytical ability to form exact and accurate images of correctness, we have to dissect the various skiing skills (or have them dissected for us) into their basic components and learn those components one or two at a time. We work at these components (smooth unweighting and the transfer of weight onto the new turning ski, for example) over and over, with no apparent progress, and then suddenly they "come to us" with an almost audible click. Once one of these components has "clicked," we can go on to the next one within the skill, and then the next, until we have thoroughly learned the skill and formed a solid motor program for it. Though this course is considerably slower than that by which the natural athlete or the natural analyzer pro-

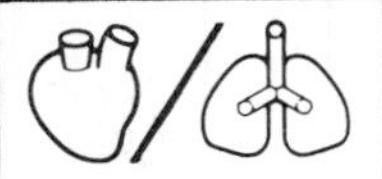

ceeds, it can yield certain motor programs for the sport that are just as effective as those formed by talent and/or skillful analysis.

Of all the methods now available for improving your skiing, the most effective by far (albeit impractical for a lot of people) is attendance at a ski-racing camp. Not only is a recreational skier more likely to develop proper images of correctness at a good camp than anywhere else because of the opportunity to watch top racers, but racing tends to *force* you to ski correctly while much recreational skiing does not, and good racing coaches are probably best equipped to analyze and correct practical skiing deficiencies.

In the future, computerized motion-analysis equipment and microcomputerized electronic-feedback training devices will likely shorten and facilitate considerably the process of learning to ski for even the clumsiest of us. Already in use as prototypes are electronic muscle sensors that announce through audible signals the intensity and sequence of muscle activity; joint-position sensors; and ski-boot pressure sensors that let a skier know exactly where his or her foot pressure is being applied.

THE HEART-LUNG PACKAGE

MAXIMUM OXYGEN CONSUMPTION. If you scored 17 or above on the Cooper Twelve-Minute-Run Test or on the Astrand Bicycle Ergometer Test, you have considerable aerobic power, more than enough for any recreational or competitive form of Alpine skiing. Up to 80 percent of all the energy requirements of Alpine skiing are aerobic, and a lot of aerobic power will allow you to race or to ski very long runs of moguls or deep powder without tiring as a result of a buildup of lactic acid in your muscles. The best way for you to adapt your large VO_2 Max to the sport is by skiing long, nonstop, physically demanding runs that tax that VO_2 Max as much as possible. If your mountain doesn't offer such runs, strenuous cross-country skiing will provide fine adjunctive aerobic training for Alpine skiing.

If you scored between 10 and 16 on the Cooper Test or on the Bicycle Ergometer Test, you have good aerobic power that can be made even better for your skiing by cycling (especially criterium), speed roller-skating, and running natural intervals (see Maximum Oxygen Consumption in the Running section, page

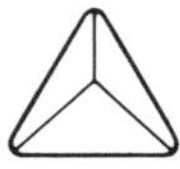

258) and obstacle courses. While skiing, you should push yourself to ski long runs, nonstop, and you should supplement your training with some strenuous cross-country work.

If you scored below 8 on the Cooper Test or on the Bicycle Ergometer Test and are aerobically trained, you don't have much aerobic power and will be able to ski hard without muscle fatigue for substantially shorter distances than someone with a larger VO_2 Max could. If you are a racer or would-be racer, you can best compensate for your small VO_2 Max by building up the anaerobic strength in your legs. If you are in this scoring range and are untrained aerobically, the aerobic training mentioned above will never give you a very large VO_2 Max, but it can increase what you have by up to 50 percent. To maximize your talent for Alpine skiing you should make an effort to effect that increase.

BODY COMPOSITION

ANAEROBIC ENDURANCE STRENGTH IN THE LEGS. If you scored 4 or above on the Wall-Squat Test, you have the isometric holding strength in the thighs to carve long, sharp, chattering, high-speed turns in all snow conditions, and to hold a tuck for as long as you will ever need to.

If you scored below 2 on this test and are a serious recreational skier, a bump skier, or a racer or potential racer, you should build up the anaerobic endurance strength in your legs to the point at which you can score 4 or above. To build both static and dynamic endurance strength in the legs you should do a variety of exercises, including resistance-strength training, running obstacle and dry-land slalom courses, and concrete-block jumps. This test may be used by itself as a drill to build isometric leg strength and as a gauge to measure your progress.

LEG EXPLOSIVENESS AND MUSCLE FIBER TYPE. If your score on the Vertical-Jump Test was 7 or above, you have the necessary muscle speed and explosiveness for any type or level of Alpine skiing. Leg explosiveness is a major asset for both competitive and expert recreational skiers. If you have it, you will want to be able to use it consistently over the course of an entire race or through an entire mogul field. Check your score on Test 2 to determine how durable your explosiveness is, and if you didn't do well, make sure your training includes power-endurance work both on and off the slope, *particularly* if you have a small VO_2 Max, since, in that event, your anaerobic leg power is all the more important to your skiing.

If your score on this test was between 4 and 6, you have good leg explosiveness for skiing. Here, as in the scoring range above, you should make certain that explosiveness is as durable as possible by training for power endurance. Most world-class skiers have a more or less even mixture of endurance and sprint muscle fiber in their thighs, and therefore, as a rule, have vertical jumps of less than twenty-six inches. They perform most of the work of their racing aerobically, and use their usually considerable anaerobic power and leg explosiveness to squeeze extra speed out of every turn.

If your score on this test was lower than 2, you have little leg explosiveness. Leg explosiveness is virtually unimprovable, and it is extremely difficult for those with little of it to improve their anaerobic power. A large VO_2 Max and the ability to use a high percentage of it are really the only compensations in ski racing for having little leg explosiveness.

CENTER OF GRAVITY. If your score on Test 6 was 3 or above, you have a low center of gravity for your height, and that fact will be of benefit to your skiing, particularly if you race. If you don't have a low center of gravity, it is not an extreme liability, but you will want to keep yourself consistently well balanced over your skis (particularly if you have poor agility), since you have more top-heavy weight to recover when you lose your balance than does a skier with a low center of gravity.

KNOCK-KNEED. If you are knock-kneed, you will be able to hit your edges more quickly and easily than someone who is not knock-kneed or is bowlegged, particularly if you have narrow hips. If you are not knock-kneed or are bowlegged, cants will get your knees centered over your inside edges; however, the linkage they provide is not so mechanically effective as that provided to a person who is naturally knock-kneed.

RANGE OF MOTION IN THE HIPS. If you scored 6 or above on the Hip-Flexion Test and had no negative points on the External- and Internal-Hip-Rotation Test, you have a full range of motion in your hips, which will allow you to move laterally from the

hips to either side of your skis for effective edge sets. Even if you do have a full hip range of motion, as shown by these tests, you will want that range to be fully functional. If you find you have a sticking point in your hips, you should increase your flexibility through that point with hip-flexibility exercises that also increase the muscular strength of your hips.

If your score on the Hip-Flexion Test was lower than 2, and/or if you had negative points on the External- and Internal-Hip-Rotation Test, your range of hip motion is limited. If you are older than eleven, there is no way that range of motion can be significantly increased. A limited range of motion in the hips, unless it is serious, will not have any major negative impact on your skiing, but you would do well to make sure that what range of motion you do have is fully available to you by doing hip-flexibility exercises and by training the muscular strength of your hips through the limits of your range of motion.

ALPINE SKIING

Test	Measures	Your score	Top score
1. Hexagonal Obstacle	Agility	20	25
2. Concrete-Block Jump	Agility	10	15
3. Cooper Twelve-Minute Run	Heart and lung	15	20
4. Wall Squat	Power endurance	5	8
5. Vertical Jump	Leg explosiveness	5	10
6. Upper-Body/Lower-Body Proportion	Center of gravity	2	7
7. Knock-kneed–Bowlegged Spectrum	Knock-kneedness	3	7
8. Hip Range of Motion	Hip flexion	4	8
Total		64	100

100 Olympic champion	50 Nastar Gold
90 World Cup circuit	40 Strong recreational
80 National team	30 Danger to others
70 Regional team	20 Danger to self
60 Club racer	10 National security risk

TENNIS

THE CONTROL SYSTEM

VISUAL CONVERGENCE. If you were able to put the toothpick into the straw at one inch from the bridge of your nose in Test 1, you have excellent visual-convergence ability—which means that you will be able to follow a tennis ball a long way in toward your racquet, and to do so repeatedly over a long period of time without strain.

If you were able to put the toothpick into the straw at three inches from the bridge of your nose, but not from one inch, you have average convergence ability, and that ability can be improved with special eye exercises (ask your ophthalmologist about such exercises).

If you were unable to put the straw into the toothpick from either the one- or the three-inch distance, and you have an overall visual acuity corrected to at least 20/30, your convergence ability is below average. Before you embark on a convergence-training program you should have your eyes thoroughly checked by an ophthalmologist to make sure you don't have an organic visual defect. If you don't, the chances are good that you can improve your convergence ability with the types of exercises referred to above. Anyone with average to less than average visual-convergence ability will not be able to follow the ball well, and will tire visually in trying to do so. The ability, therefore, is well worth developing.

VISUAL BINOCULARITY. If in Test 2 you saw what appeared to be two strings crossing each other in an "X" exactly at the button, you have better than average visual binocularity while focusing on a stationary object. A tennis ball in play is a moving object, however, and you may or may not be able to adapt your static binocularity to judge accurately a moving ball's exact speed and distance from you. The only available training aids for developing dynamic visual acuity are aids that operate in a single plane and therefore are not adequate for training three-dimensional binocularity. The only really adequate training for adapting your good binocularity to tennis is actually to play the game.

If in Test 2 you saw what appeared to be two strings crossing in front of the button, it means you will see an approaching object as being closer to you than it really is, and therefore you will tend to hit a tennis ball early. If in the test you saw what appeared to be two strings crossing behind the button, you will see an approaching object as being farther away from you than it really is, and therefore you will tend to hit a tennis ball late. In either case, you can compensate for your lack of natural accurate binocularity while staring at a fixed object by using this test as a training drill. In the first case, while staring at the button, you should try to relax your eyes and let the two strings "back up" to cross inside the button. In the second case, you should try to concentrate on bringing your focus closer until the two strings "move up" to cross inside the button. This and other training drills contained in a number of books (see the Appendix for titles) and also available from sportsvision centers can improve your binocularity considerably. If you don't want to bother with the exercises, recognize in your game that your vision is consistently causing you to hit either early or late and adjust your effector anticipation accordingly, by hitting either later for an early swing or earlier for a late one.

Finally, if in Test 2 you saw only a single string going through the button, you have no visual binocularity, and you should have your eyes checked for organic defects by an ophthalmologist. The best compensation in tennis for a complete lack of binocularity is experience in playing the game, experience wide enough to allow you to judge accurately how far away an approaching ball is by its trajectory and apparent size.

REACTION TIME WITH CHOICE. If your score on Test 3 was 8 or above, you have excellent reaction time, and that quickness of reaction will be extremely valuable to you, particularly at the net, once you have adapted your quick reactions to the demands of the game. You can achieve this easily through good coaching and/or drills specifically designed to sharpen reaction times in tennis. (A number of such drills can be found in books recommended in the Appendix.)

If your score was between 5 and 7 on Test 3, you have good reactions, and since reaction time is highly specific to a particular set of stimuli, you may train yourself to have very quick reactions in tennis. Reaction time comprises the time required to register a stimulus, the time required to choose an appropriate motor program, and the time required to implement the motor program. Register time cannot be improved. Experience with the game can improve motor-program-choice time, and movement time can be improved by good coaching, by the drills referred to above, and by playing with a light, fast racquet.

If your score was below 4 on this test and you find that you do in fact have slow reactions while playing tennis, and particularly if you also have a low score on the Vertical-Jump Test, you can best compensate for your lack of quickness by developing a baseline, placement game and by avoiding the net.

ANTICIPATION. If you scored 7 or above on the Yardstick-Anticipation Test, you have very good anticipation, and once that has been adapted to tennis it can make up considerably for slow reaction time. In combination with quick reaction time, good anticipation in tennis is perhaps the most important natural asset you can have. Good anticipation in tennis amounts to knowing in advance where a hit ball is going to go. Part of that knowledge is provided by the convergence and binocularity abilities of the eyes as they identify the ball's trajectory; the rest is provided by an accurate recall of thousands of ball trajectories seen and traced in your visual memory. The anticipation tested in Test 4 is two dimensional; in order for it to be effectively adapted to tennis, depth perception must be added to it, and the best ways to improve it are to sharpen your visual convergence and binocularity abilities, to build a broad base of experience with the game, and to make a concentrated effort to capture visually and memorize as much of each ball's trajectory as possible.

Anticipation in tennis is highly improvable. If you scored below 4 on Test 4 and know through your scores on Tests 1 and 2 that you have no visual hindrance to your anticipation, you should work according to the suggestions above to improve it.

AGILITY. If you scored a perfect 15 on the Hexagon Test, you have excellent agility, and if you also have good leg explosiveness, as determined in Test 7, there should be very few balls you can't get to once your agility has been adapted to the footwork of tennis.

If you scored between 8 and 12 on the Hexagon Test, you have good potential agility in tennis, and it can be improved further by using this test as a drill, and by learning and practicing good footwork.

If you scored below 6 here, you will likely never have very good agility on a tennis court, but you can partially compensate for that fact with well-developed footwork and good anticipation.

CONTROL PRECISION, MULTILIMB COORDINATION, AIMING. If you scored 12 or above on Test 6, you have the necessary Control System components to coordinate your leg drive and body mass behind a single, precise, rate-controlled arm motion to produce both velocity and accuracy of aim. These components are directly active in both the serve and the overhead, and if you have them to any appreciable degree, you will have an advantage in forming good motor programs for the forehand and backhand strokes as well. If your score was 12 or above, the chances are good that you now have, or could develop, very good tennis strokes.

If you scored between 8 and 11 on the test, you have good control precision, multilimb-coordination, and aiming motor abilities, which will be an advantage to you in developing good tennis strokes.

If you scored under 5 on the test, you have very poor abilities underlying the serve and overhead.

This test is purely diagnostic. You either have the abilities it measures or you don't, and while those abilities are active in the serve and overhead and relate to the forehand and backhand, not having them does not mean you can't develop those strokes. Your performance of any skill will be helped if you have the underlying structural abilities that are integral to it, but after a motor program for the skill has been formed, and as it is practiced, those abilities in and of themselves become less and less important, and the refinement and versatility of adaptation of the motor program become more and more important.

Central to good motor programs for tennis strokes are accurate images of correctness, or images of how the strokes ideally should be made. The person with good natural abilities can easily form those accurate images of correctness by developing a feel for the strokes and by reinforcing that feel by observing good players and with coaching. Someone with few or no natural abilities can also form accurate images of correctness, but to do so generally requires an analytical rather than an intuitive approach. An analytical approach is now possible only via videotapes, films, books, watching other players, and various kinds of instruction—all of which can and often do fail to build a three-dimensionally correct image. A number of more effective analytical methods are being developed using microtechnology, and should be available in the near future as actual training tools rather than bulky, laboratory-confined equipment. Prototypes are already available of EMG devices that trace muscular activity, courtside computerized motion analyzers, and electronic tennis racquets that analyze and feed back information on racquet-ball impact. Analytical advances such as these could soon revolutionize the democratization of tennis, by making the formation of images of correctness far easier for players who have few of the abilities that underlie the skills of the sport.

BODY COMPOSITION

EXPLOSIVENESS. If your score on the Vertical-Jump Test was 15, you have tremendous leg explosiveness—a great athletic gift that will enable you to overcome a number of other deficiencies in your overall talent for tennis by allowing you to get to the ball more quickly than most people, and to cover the entire court once your tennis footwork is refined.

If your score on this test was between 10 and 14, you have the necessary explosiveness for good court quickness and coverage, particularly if you have good agility, too.

If your score was below 6 on Test 7, you can best compensate for your lack of explosiveness by developing your anticipation and your tennis footwork and by trying to avoid getting badly out of position on the court as you play.

Any amount of explosiveness is useful to a tennis player only up to the point at which he or she becomes fatigued. Therefore, regardless of how much explosiveness you have, you can make it more functional by doing natural interval training—taking regular thirty- to forty-five-minute runs that combine recovery jogging with sprints and hill work. Explosiveness is largely ge-

netic but can be slightly improved by using this test as a drill and/or by performing such exercises as jumping quarter-squats.

HIP AND SHOULDER RANGE OF MOTION. If you scored 4 on both Tests 8 and 9, you have sufficient range of motion in your hips and shoulders to allow for full natural windup and follow-through in all of your tennis strokes.

If your score was 2 or under on Test 8, your hips' range of motion is limited. Though that can't be increased after age eleven, you can ensure full functional use of the range you possess by doing hip-flexibility exercises regularly. Such exercises will also be helpful to an individual who has a wide range of motion in the hips but some sticking point within that range beyond which he or she can move only with difficulty.

If your score was 2 or under on Test 9, you have a limited range of motion in your shoulders, which can and should be increased by means of flexibility exercises. As is always true, the muscles around a joint should be trained for strength concurrently with training the joint itself for flexibility.

TENNIS

Test	Measures	Your score	Top score
1. Toothpick-Straw Convergence	Convergence	5	10
2. String-and-Button Binocularity	Binocularity	0	10
3. Latham Yardstick Reaction Time	Reaction time	10	10
4. Yardstick Anticipation	Anticipation	10	10
5. Hexagon	Agility	10	15
6. Nerf Ball Stroke-Structure	Control precision	10	15
7. Vertical Jump	Explosiveness	15	15
8. Internal/External Hip Rotation	Hip flexion	8	8
9. Shoulder Range of Motion	Shoulder flexion	7	7
Total		75	100

100 Grand Slam	50 Class B club player
90 Wimbledon champ	40 Class C club player
80 Internationally ranked	30 Novice
70 Regional champion	20 Racquet best used for flyswatting
60 Class A club player	10 Hits self with racquet

WINDSURFING

THE CONTROL SYSTEM

AGILITY, COORDINATION, AND SPEED OF MOTOR LEARNING. If you scored a perfect 30 on the Hexagon Test, you have the motor abilities necessary to windsurf at any level of the sport. A perfect score on this test might also indicate that you have an opportunity to really star at windsurfing in big surf and big winds, the form of the sport we believe to be both its cutting edge and its future.

Your speed-of-motor-learning score on this test will indicate how quickly you are likely to learn to windsurf, but with perseverance and good instruction, even someone with a very poor motor-learning score *can* learn the sport. Your score on the abilities section of the test should serve as an overall indicator of the degree to which you possess the motor abilities that are most central to good performance. A score of between 15 and 20 would indicate adequate to good abilities, and individuals with such abilities, while they might never be brilliant at the sport, can become quite expert. Those with poor to fair motor abilities can, honestly, enjoy no such expectation, though they can learn to windsurf and can learn to enjoy the sport on a recreational level. If your score was fair to good on this test, and you did well on the two following balance tests, it is possible that triangle

racing, with its emphasis on balance rather than agility, might be a good competitive option for you.

Though the raw motor abilities that underlie the skills you need for windsurfing are not very trainable, the skills themselves can be improved. Therefore, no matter how well or poorly you did on the Hexagon Test, we don't recommend that you try to improve at windsurfing through dry-land agility or coordination training, but rather that you buy a good book on the sport (see the Appendix for titles), choose some of the skills from it that demand the most of your agility and coordination, and practice those skills on a board in the water. Linking increasingly difficult skills together in increasingly difficult wind and wave conditions is the only way you can really become expert at windsurfing. As you master these specific skills, and as you learn more about the characteristics of winds and waves, your developing anticipation for different combinations of circumstances and your increasingly sophisticated motor programs will allow you to rely less and less on raw motor ability.

A well-formed image of correctness is crucial to motor learning in windsurfing, and such an image is best formed by imitating experts, since it is very difficult to take verbal or written instructions into the water with you. Therefore, if you want to become good at the sport quickly, we recommend that you learn or practice it in the company of good windsurfers.

STATIC BALANCE. Static balance is a very important skill in windsurfing, beginning with the moment you first try to stand on the board in the water and continuing through the sophisticated requirements of keeping yourself upright in waves when there is little or no supporting wind. If you scored 15 on Test 2, you have excellent genetic balance, and it will serve you well in windsurfing. If your score was below 4, you can best improve your static balance in windsurfing by balancing on a board in the water, or by practicing this test and the one following it, or by trying other balance drills such as beam- or rope-walking.

STABILIZATION AND DYNAMIC BALANCE. The agility required to keep your balance on a moving board while constantly reacting with movements of your own to the forces of water and wind is central to windsurfing, as is the related ability to stabilize your body between movements with small, precise balance corrections. These abilities are most dramatically called for in such high-skill maneuvers as the duck-jibe, in which the windsurfer throws the sail forward and ducks under it in order to turn through the wind. When you first start doing duck-jibes and jump-turns, you have no motor programs for those maneuvers, and your ability to perform them at all is directly dependent on your dynamic balance and your ability to stabilize yourself between movements. Without good dynamic balance and stabilization, a windsurfer at any level will spend a good deal of time in the water.

Dynamic balance and stabilization are improvable, and if you scored under 12 on the Balance-Stabilization Test, we recommend that you work on improving those abilities by practicing this test and/or the various maneuvers that require those abilities.

BODY COMPOSITION

CENTER OF GRAVITY. If you have a low center of gravity, it is less easy to lose your balance and easier to regain it; thus, you have a real advantage in windsurfing. If you find through Test 4 that you have a high center of gravity, you can compensate somewhat by bending at the knees and ankles during critical maneuvers, but you will still be top-heavy and therefore will have more weight to recover if you do lose your balance than will someone with a low center of gravity.

KNOCK-KNEED. You are either knock-kneed or you are not. If you are, you can apply turning pressure to the board with your legs more quickly and with better leverage than someone who is not. Skiers who are knock-kneed enjoy a similar advantage, and some skiers who are not knock-kneed or are bowlegged have compensating cants built onto the boot plates of their skis. If you find in Test 5 that you are bowlegged, you may want to consider having cants built onto the surface of your board. Though canting will allow you to make sharp turns more quickly, it won't fully compensate for the fact that you are not naturally knock-kneed.

PERCENTAGE OF BODY FAT. In a sport that requires as much agility as windsurfing does, fat is nothing but a hindrance. If you had points taken off your overall score as a result of the Caliper Body-Fat-Percentage Test, we suggest you lose some fat in order to maximize whatever talent you may have for the sport.

WINDSURFING

Test	Measures	Score: Your	Score: Top
1. Hexagon	Agility	35	40
2. Blind-Stork Balance	Static balance	15	20
3. Balance Stabilization	Dynamic balance	15	20
4. Upper-Body/ Lower-Body Proportion	Center of gravity	9	10
5. Knock-kneed–Bowlegged Spectrum	Knock-kneedness	5	10
6. Caliper Body-Fat-Percentage Measurement	Body fat	−2	−10
Total		77	90

100 Hurricane speed demon
90 Tidal-wave-jump star
80 Maui slalom champ
70 Nor' easter speedster
60 Triangle course king
50 Pond sailor
40 Pool sailor
30 Best when becalmed
20 Floats on windsurfer
10 Suns on windsurfer

RUNNING

THE CONTROL SYSTEM

MOTOR ABILITY: STRIDE LENGTH. The stride length tested in Test 1 is the final outcome of a runner's technique. If you scored 20 on this test, the most important technical component of your running, your stride length, is the same as that found among Olympic runners. The stride lengths of those Olympic runners were measured with high-speed cameras that also allowed for computerized analysis of the other important components of their techniques. No such analysis is possible here, and while with a score of 20 on Test 1 you do have the ideal length of stride for middle- and long-distance running, you may also have some mechanical deficiencies in your running technique that can be improved—such deficiencies as too much vertical rise, improper landing under your center of gravity, head bobbing, incorrect arm movements, or excess rotation in the hips. If you scored 20 on Test 1, you have real talent for middle- and/or long-distance running, and to learn whether or not your technique can be further improved, you should have a computerized motion analysis of it done, or have it evaluated by a good running coach.

If you scored under 15 on this test, it is because your running stride is either too long or too short. If your stride length is too short, it may be because you are anatomically restricted from a longer stride by short legs or genetically tight hamstrings. If either of these restrictions is present (you will know whether or not this is true from your results on Tests 5 and 6, respectively), there is virtually nothing you can do to lengthen your natural stride. A short stride may also be due to poor conditioning and/or to poor technique. If your stride is short and you do well on Tests 5 and 6 but are untrained, the chances are that your short stride is due, at least in good part, to poor conditioning, and you should take Test 1 again after you have reached fifteen to twenty miles of running a week on a good training program. If your stride is short and you did well on Tests 5 and 6 and are reasonably well conditioned, then your problems are technical and can probably be diagnosed and corrected by a good coach. The most common technical problems are inadequate foot thrust at push-off, too much vertical bobbing at the expense of forward speed, too much hip rotation, and too much extraneous upper-body movement.

If you found in Test 1 that your stride is too long, you are overstriding in your running. Overstriding occurs when you reach out too far in front of your center of gravity with the forward foot—a practice that can be mechanically harmful to the foot or knee—or when you increase the thrust off the push-off foot—which wastes energy. You can correct either of these technical mistakes when they are accurately diagnosed by videotape, computerized motion analysis, or a good coach—either by landing with the forward foot directly underneath your center of gravity or by decreasing the thrust off the push-off foot. Overstriding is considerably easier to correct than understriding, once the cause has been isolated and understood.

Until recently it was believed that a runner's most efficient stride length at a given running speed was whatever felt most natural or comfortable at that speed. Recently, however, it has been discovered through computerized motion analysis that a runner's natural stride length is not always biomechanically the most efficient; and studies at Pennsylvania State University have demonstrated that a runner can adapt to a stride length that is more mechanically correct than his or her natural one, and within a matter of weeks be running naturally at the improved stride length at no increased energy cost.

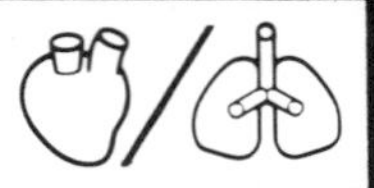

THE HEART-LUNG PACKAGE

MAXIMUM OXYGEN CONSUMPTION. If you scored 32 or above on Test 2, the Cooper Twelve-Minute-Run Test, you have the heart-lung power necessary to be an excellent competitive middle- or long-distance runner. Your concerns should be, first, that you are running with as much mechanical efficiency as possible and, second, that you are *using* as much as possible of your high VO_2 Max.

The usable portion of any individual's VO_2 Max is limited by the threshold at which lactic acid begins to accumulate rapidly. This threshold, known as the anaerobic threshold (AT), varies among individuals, from a very restricting 40 percent of VO_2 Max to 90 percent. The best distance runners have not only a very high VO_2 Max, but a very high anaerobic threshold as well, a combination that allows them to *use* practically all of their considerable aerobic power.

If you scored 32 or above on the Cooper Test you are a talented runner, and if you are currently training for serious middle- or long-distance competition, you are undoubtedly running between fifty and a hundred miles a week. You can raise your anaerobic threshold by giving over part of that training volume to tempo training, or running for six miles twice a week at race pace (that is, running evenly for six miles as fast as you can). Though an individual's anaerobic threshold can accurately be determined only in a laboratory, it is generally found around the race pace at which that individual can run for six miles, and the threshold can be raised by running twice a week at or near that point. You don't want to do tempo training more than twice a week because, even for the best runners, around seventy-two hours are required between AT workouts for the leg muscles to recover sufficiently their fuel and buffering sources.

The most important part of any middle- or long-distance runner's training is AT training. For elite middle- and long-distance runners a further "hardening" is accomplished through speed training, such as Frank Shorter's quarter-mile repeats or Albert Salazar's mile repeats. This hardening, which comes through running repeatedly at speeds faster than race pace for short distances, strengthens a runner's form by making it more efficient; it also prepares the runner for faster race paces as the AT increases, speeds up oxygen delivery time, serves as excellent strength training, and provides the individual with a race "kick." This kind of speed training is most valuable to the best runners, whose anaerobic thresholds are already up around 90 percent of a very high VO_2 Max.

If you did not score well on the Cooper Test, either you haven't run much (or at all) before or, if you do run, you have inadequate heart-lung power for the sport.

If you have never trained for middle- or long-distance running, a low score on this test might reflect only that lack of experience, and you could get a more accurate measurement of your aerobic power for running by taking the test again after six weeks of training. If after that time you score considerably better on the test, remember that your VO_2 Max is still improvable, and may improve overall—over the course of six years if you are an adolescent, or two and a half years if you are an adult—by as much as 50 percent.

VO_2 Max responds best to sustained aerobic demand: either to low-intensity demand during long training sessions or, more dramatically, to high-intensity, short-duration demand. If you are not yet a good competitive runner, your primary training goal should be to work up to an adequate training volume without injury. This goal is best achieved by adding low-intensity mileage slowly and gradually, and forgoing any high-intensity speed or hill training until you have a solid, safe training volume established as a base. When starting from scratch, it takes years to construct such a base in running—as opposed to swimming—because the shock-absorbing capacities of tendons and ligaments have to be built up along with muscular endurance and aerobic power. There are many good books now available, some of them by top American coaches and runners, that include detailed programs for safely building a training volume. (A list of some of those books is included in the Appendix.)

If you *have* trained for running and do poorly on the Cooper Test, it could be that (1) you have a very high percentage of sprint fiber in your legs (a fact that can be determined in Test 8); (2) you have very inefficient running mechanics (which you would have learned from Test 1); or (3) your heart and/or lungs are too small for running at competitive speeds, or are too small for your weight.

BODY COMPOSITION

HEIGHT-WEIGHT RATIO. All the best middle- and long-distance runners have height-weight ratios of about one inch of body height to two pounds of body weight. Such a light frame suffers less impact from running and is ideal if springier than a heavier frame. It also requires less heart-lung power and less muscular thrusting power from the legs. If you weigh around two and a half pounds per inch of body height, you can run very well at middle or long distances, but you will never break any records. If you weigh three or more pounds per inch of body height, you may be *able* to run middle or long distances, but you will never run very well at those distances and your body will take substantial punishment if you run regularly. If your weight-to-height ratio is three to one or higher, you are really not properly built for middle- or long-distance running, and if you want to run at those distances you should lose weight. If you don't want to—or can't—and still want to run, you should confine yourself to jogging speeds and to distances of one to three miles so as not to aggravate preexisting cartilage damage or microfractures of the underlying bone.

WIDTH OF HIPS. The width of your hips is fixed. If you have wide hips and want to run middle and long distances, you should build up the lower trunk muscles in your hips and waist to limit your hip rotation and, particularly if you are a woman, develop your quadriceps muscles to keep your kneecaps from floating out of line as you run.

LEG LENGTH. The length of your legs is fixed, and there is no way to compensate in middle- or long-distance running for the disadvantage of having legs that are too short for good stride length.

TABLE 62

	Men						
Distance	**100 meters**	**800 meters**	**Mile**	**5,000 meters**	**10,000 meters**	**10 miles**	**Marathon**
World record time	9.93	1:41.73	3:47.33	13:00.41	27:22	46:00	2:08:13
Individual time	9.93	1:42	3:47	13:00	27:00	46:00	2:08
	10.92	1:52	4:11	14:18	29:42	50:36	2:21
	11.92	2:02	4:37	15:36	32:24	55:12	2:34
	12.91	2:12	5:06	16:54	35:06	59:48	2:46
	13.90	2:22	5:38	18:12	37:48	64:24	2:59
	14.80	2:32	6:10	19:22	40:14	68:32	3:11

HAMSTRING FLEXIBILITY. Even if you have an ideal leg length for middle- or long-distance running, your running stride will be restricted at both push-off and during forward leg drive by hamstrings that are too tight. Such muscles restrict the mechanical components of a stride and its fluidity. Overall flexibility in the hamstrings can be improved some, but not much. If your score on Test 6 indicates that you have tight hamstrings, you can make them somewhat more flexible through long-held, static stretchings of the muscles—the kind that stretch muscles, not joints, and build strength as well as flexibility in the muscles, protecting them against injury throughout their range of motion.

Your hamstrings tighten naturally with running. Stretching them back to normal after a run should not be confused with stretching to increase their flexibility.

PERCENTAGE OF BODY FAT. The ideal percentages of body fat for middle- and long-distance runners are around 5.8 percent for men and 11.1 percent for women. If you have more fat than this, you can considerably improve your heart-lung power and your power-to-weight ratio for leg thrust by losing some of it. People often believe that they will automatically lose fat when they start to run, but in fact the low intensity and short distances of beginning running burn very few calories. If you are just starting to run, don't expect to lose any substantial amount of fat and don't try to force such a loss until you have built up your training volume to twenty miles a week or more. Neither should you diet while running to the point where you rob yourself of the carbohydrates necessary to run at the speeds and distances you want.

Women						Men and women
100 meters	**800 meters**	**Mile**	**5,000 meters**	**10,000 meters**	**Marathon**	**Percent of world record time**
10.79	1:53.28	4:17.4	15:08.2	31:35.02	2:22:43	
10.79	1:53	4:17	15:08	31:35	2:22	100%
11.87	2:05	4:43	16:39	34:45	2:36	110%
12.95	2:16	5:09	18:10	37:54	2:50	120%
14.03	2:27	5:35	19:41	41:04	3:05	130%
15.11	2:39	6:00	21:11	44:13	3:19	140%
16.08	2:49	6:24	22:33	47:04	3:32	149%

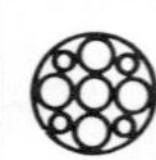

MUSCLE FIBER TYPE. If you scored 10 on the Vertical-Jump Test, you very likely have too much sprint fiber in your legs to run successfully at long distances, and if you jumped higher than thirty inches (for men) or twenty inches (for women), you may not be able to run at those distances at all. Virtually no world-class long-distance runner in training has ever jumped higher than thirteen and a half inches on this test.

If you scored between 6 and 8 on this test and did well on the Cooper Test, you should have good "kick" as a middle-distance runner. There is no way to tell from this test how much endurance fiber you have in your legs, but we have provided a chart (Table 62) from which, by checking your own best times at certain distances against the world record times at those distances, you can get some idea of your endurance and sprint capabilities.

FATAL FLAWS. If you found that you have one or more of the three anatomical flaws tested in Tests 9, 10, and 11, you should bear in mind that each of them *can* cause a runner serious orthopedic injury. You can have one of these faults to a minor degree and run in spite of it—for example, by running on grass and for relatively short distances at relatively low speeds—without injuring yourself; but if one or more of them are present to anything more than a minor degree, you should check with a doctor before you run, and/or take up another aerobic sport.

RUNNING

Test	Measures	Your score	Top score
1. Stride Length	Motor ability	20	20
2. Cooper Twelve-Minute Run	Heart and lung	10	38
3. Weight-to-Height Ratio	Height-weight ratio	15	15
4. Width of Hips	Power endurance	5	10
5. Upper-Body/Lower-Body Proportion	Leg length	5	10
6. Hamstring Looseness	Hamstring flexion	7	7
7. Caliper Body-Fat-Percentage Measurement	Body fat		−10
8. Vertical Jump	Leg explosiveness		
Total		62	90

100 Boston Marathon winner	50 Completes 5 kilometers
90 2:45 runner	40 2-mile jogger
80 3:00 runner	30 Runs around the block
70 34-minute 10 kilometers	20 Walks to get the paper
60 Completes 10 kilometers	10 Has dog fetch paper

SWIMMING

THE CONTROL SYSTEM

STROKE MECHANICS. The stroke mechanics tested in the Stroke-Distance Test are the final outcome of a swimmer's technique, combining a subtle, unteachable "feel for the water" with the inherent ability to make that "feel" work mechanically. As Indiana University swim coach Doc Counsilman says, "Natural swimming ability is basically an inherent factor, beyond the influence of the coach or teacher."

If you scored 20 or above on this test, you have fine natural stroke mechanics and are potentially a very talented swimmer. That potential can probably be maximized by working with a good coach.

If you scored between 15 and 20 on this test, your stroke mechanics are good, and proper coaching (along with a fundamental understanding of the mechanical principles involved in the sport, an understanding that can be gained from a number of books listed in the Appendix) is very likely to make them better by improving your image of correctness.

If you scored 12 or below on this test, either you have very little experience with swimming or you are in poor condition. If you are now poorly conditioned, training will likely improve your swimming and give you a more accurate measure of your stroke mechanics. Similarly, if you have done very little swim-

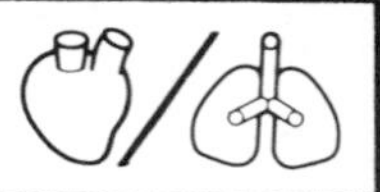

ming, your score will likely improve after you have become more familiar with the sport. If you do swim regularly and are in relatively good condition and your score on this test was 12 or below, you can, of course, swim for pleasure and exercise but you should probably not set your competitive sights too high. Again, the science of biomechanics has made possible major improvements in even the poorest of natural strokes through good coaching.

THE HEART-LUNG PACKAGE

MAXIMUM OXYGEN CONSUMPTION. Even though the Cooper Twelve-Minute Run tests VO_2 Max for running, not swimming, much of whatever VO_2 Max you have for running is transferable to swimming, and any swimming test for VO_2 Max would necessarily have to test for stroke mechanics, too, and might thereby potentially obscure a high VO_2 Max in a swimmer with poor strokes.

If you scored 24 or above on the Cooper Test, whether or not you now swim, you have all the aerobic power you need for any kind of competitive or recreational participation. If you have a high VO_2 Max and don't swim competitively now but would like to, use your results on Tests 5 and 6 as an indication of whether you are better suited to short- or long-distance events. You can adapt your considerable aerobic power for running to swimming by establishing a solid training-volume base, swimming at a comfortable pace from one-quarter to one-half mile a day in the beginning of the season and increasing to two or three miles a day by the end of the season. (Top competitive swimmers will work up to seven-plus miles a day at the height of the season.) Swimming distributes the work load and stresses on the body even better than cycling does, and far better than running, making it possible for swimmers to build up to a high volume of training relatively quickly during a season. If after your aerobic training base has been built you want to speed your oxygen delivery and raise your anaerobic threshold to make more of your large VO_2 Max available to you, you should begin swimming fast middle distances. A good training routine at this point would be periodically to swim two hundred meters as fast as you can five times consecutively with just enough of a rest between each one to let your heart rate get down below one hundred beats per minute.

The training advice above would also apply if your score on the Cooper Test was between 10 and 14. If your score was under

that and you have trained at running, you don't have much VO_2 Max to transfer to swimming, and if you found on Tests 1, 5, and 6 that you have those components of talent for the sport, you should concentrate your competitive efforts on sprint events. If, with a small VO_2 Max, you did well on Test 1 and not particularly well on Tests 5 and 6, you may be well suited for long-distance swimming (in which a higher than average percentage of body fat is actually an advantage).

If you had a low score on the Cooper Test and do no aerobic training whatever, it is impossible to determine your true effective VO_2 Max for running and therefore impossible to evaluate it for swimming. For this reason we have included the Lung-Volume Test (Test 3).

If your score on Test 3 was 7 or above, you have the necessary lung capacity to support a high VO_2 Max. If your score was under 3, you don't have such lung capacity; neither do you have sufficient lung volume to afford much buoyancy in the water or to blow off effectively the CO_2 that builds up in the blood during short- and middle-distance events.

BODY COMPOSITION

FRAME PROPORTIONS. The seven frame proportions given as ideal for swimmers in Test 4 were taken from Olympic standards. The width of your hips, elbows, and shoulders and the length of your hands are all fixed measurements. Though having the ideal measurements in these places is an advantage in competitive swimming, a good coach can adapt stroke mechanics to whatever measurements you have as well as to how you lie in the water.

The girth of the forearms and upper arms of Olympic swimmers reflects large muscle masses, and therefore strength, in those areas. If your arm size does not meet these ideal measurements, you can increase your upper- and lower-arm girth with weight training. Thigh girth among Olympic freestyle swimmers is reflective of muscle mass that is not developed to large proportions because, aside from the dive and the flip-turn, there are few demands for upper-leg power in freestyle. Thighs that are substantially larger than the Olympic standard, whether because of too much fat or too much muscle, can be reduced to that standard, either by diet and exercise in the first case, or by exercising less for bulk and more for muscle speed in the second.

STROKE FORCE AND PEAK UPPER-BODY POWER. If you scored 10 or above on the Fish-Scale Stroke-Power Test, you have sufficient upper-body strength for virtually any level of competitive swimming. A high score on this test should also indicate good stroke mechanics. If you have a high score here and an average to low score on Test 1, you are extraordinarily powerful and could score even higher on this test with good strokes.

If you scored between 4 and 6 on the Fish-Scale Test, you could have plenty of upper-body strength but very bad strokes, in which case your score on the test, and your swimming in general, would go up if you improved your strokes. If your score on Test 1, however, was good, then you need upper-body strength training, as does anyone whose score on this test was below 4. According to Doc Counsilman, the key dry-land exercises for building effective upper-body strength for swimming are these: elbow extensions, supine straight-arm pullovers, arm rotators, wrist curls, and jumping quarter-squats. (A description of these exercises, along with much good training advice, can be had from Counsilman's *Competitive Swimming Manual.*) Counsilman warns against trying to build strength for swimming with an entire body-building routine, saying that much of the bulk gained by such a routine is, in effect, just extra baggage to be hauled through the water. Since swimmers are best served by fast—as opposed to bulky—muscle, Counsilman also suggests that dry-land resistance exercises be performed at high speed and high resistance, using either free weights or (ideally) isokinetic machines rather than traditional weight-training machinery. Such training provides the necessary upper-body strength and muscular speed for sprinting, which, after over-distance and middle-distance training, is the third tier of all competitive swim training.

TABLE 63

Distance (*meters*)	**Men**					
	50	**100**	**200**	**400**	**800**	**1,500**
World record time	22.54	49.36	1:47.87	3:48.32	7:52.33	14:54.75
Individual time	22.54	49.36	1:48	3:48	7:52	14:55
	24.79	54.30	1:59	4:11	8:40	16:24
	27.05	59.23	2:09	4:34	9:27	17:54
	29.30	64.17	2:20	4:57	10:14	19:23
	31.56	69.10	2:31	5:20	11:01	20:53
	33.58	73.55	2:41	5:40	11:44	22:13

LEG EXPLOSIVENESS. Your score on the Vertical-Jump Test is a measure of your sprint potential in swimming. According to Doc Counsilman, everything else (such as stroke mechanics) being equal, an individual's score on this test is accurately reflective of the competitive distances that individual is best suited to swim. If your score on this test was 10, you are best suited for sprint distances of between 50 and 100 meters. If your score was above 10, you have a very high percentage of sprint fiber, are easily fatigable, and probably cannot tolerate large amounts of over-distance training. If your score here was below 4, you are best suited for long distances of 400 meters and more. And if your score was between 6 and 8, you probably should concentrate competitively on middle distances and long sprints. As in the previous section, we've included a chart (Table 63) that allows you to compare your own best times at certain distances with world record times at those distances.

Besides indicating the competitive distances you are best suited for, your score on this test will also suggest the general type of training regime you should undertake to maximize your ability at those distances. Any training program for competitive swimming is a mixture of long-distance, middle-distance, and sprint training; your score here will give a general indication of what the proportions of that mixture should be. For specific training programs, we suggest you consult Doc Counsilman's *Competitive Swimming Manual* (see Appendix).

The leg explosiveness tested in the Vertical-Jump Test plays a very important role in making good dives and flip-turns, and this explosiveness can be improved somewhat by training on isokinetic machinery and/or by doing jumping quarter-squats.

SHOULDER RANGE OF MOTION. If your score on Test 7 was 5, you have excellent shoulder flexibility, which in freestyle will al-

Women						**Men and women**
50	**100**	**200**	**400**	**800**	**1,500**	**Percent of world record time**
25.69	54.79	1:58.23	4:06.28	8:24.62	16:04.49	
25.69	54.79	1:58	4:06	8:25	16:04	100%
28.26	60.27	2:10	4:31	9:15	17:41	110%
30.83	65.75	2:22	4:56	10:06	19:17	120%
33.40	71.23	2:34	5:20	10:56	20:54	130%
35.97	76.71	2:46	5:45	11:46	22:30	140%
38.28	81.64	2:56	6:07	12:32	23:57	149%

low you to recover your arms over the water easily and economically. If your score was under 3, you should increase your shoulder flexibility in order to avoid the drag-producing excess body roll and/or flat-arm recovery that are the usual compensations in a freestyle stroke for too little flexibility in the shoulders. Shoulder flexibility for swimming can best be improved with the horizontal and vertical isometric stretching exercises recommended in Counsilman's book; and with work, that flexibility can be improved quite a bit.

ANKLE RANGE O MOTION. If your score on Test 8 was 5, you have all the ankle flexibility you need to effect maximum backward thrust against the water in your flutter kick. If your score was under 3, you should try to increase your ankle flexibility for freestyle by use of ankle-range-of-motion exercises, such as the ones described in Counsilman's book.

PERCENTAGE OF BODY FAT. While 7.5 percent body fat for men and 15.5 percent for women are the ideal percentages for short- to middle-distance competitive swimmers, a little more will not negatively affect recreational swimmers, and long-distance or competitive swimmers can effectively carry up to 30 percent fat. If you want to swim competitively at short to middle distances, your body fat should be at the ideal percentage for your sex, as reflected by the scoring of Test 9.

SWIMMING

Test	Measures	Your score	Top score
1. Stroke Distance	Stroke mechanics	20	28
2. Cooper Twelve-Minute Run	Heart and lung	18	30
3. Lung Volume	Lung	7	10
4. Measurement of Bodily Proportions	Body proportions	5	7
5. Fish-scale Stroke Power	Upper-body power	13	15
6. Vertical Jump	Explosiveness	8	10
7. Shoulder Range of Motion	Shoulder flexion	3	5
8. Ankle Range of Motion	Ankle flexion	3	5
9. Caliper Body-Fat-Percentage Measurement	Body fat	−4	−10
Total		73	90

100 Gold medalist	50 Surfer
90 Olympic team	40 Lifeguard
80 National team	30 Kids' pool
70 Regional champ	20 Pool chair
60 Local hotshot	10 Pool chaise longue

CYCLING

THE CONTROL SYSTEM

AGILITY, BALANCE, MULTILIMB COORDINATION. Though practically everyone has enough motor ability to ride a bicycle, competitive and good recreational cycling require considerable bike-handling skills—not possessed by everyone—that have as their underlying structural components better than ordinary agility, balance, and multilimb coordination. If you scored 8 on the Bicycle-Agility Test, you have enough underlying motor ability to develop excellent bike-handling skills very easily. Those skills can be acquired, with more or less difficulty, by virtually everyone, and *should* be acquired by anyone who plans to ride a bicycle out of his or her own driveway. If your score was under 3 on this test, you will endanger yourself and other people by cycling wherever there is traffic or pedestrians, and any score under 5 should suggest that you work on building your bike-handling skills by using this test as a drill before you do much cycling. These skills are so crucial to safety on a bike that competitive cyclists with a notable lack of them, even cyclists who win races, are often held back from advancement by Cycling Federation officials for the safety of the pack.

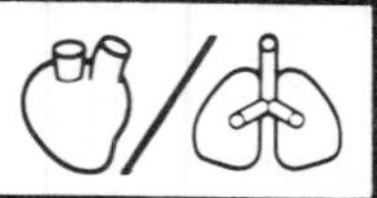

THE HEART-LUNG PACKAGE

MAXIMUM OXYGEN CONSUMPTION. If you scored 35 on the Astrand Bicycle Ergometer Test, you have an aerobic capacity equal to that of the top international bicycle racers, and thus the aerobic potential to be a world-class cyclist. The amount of your aerobic potential available to you is limited by your anaerobic threshold, and how well you are able to keep up with the pack will depend on how far up you are able to train your AT. Any serious competitive cyclist will want to train at a minimum volume of 200 miles a week and build up to the 400-plus miles per week of world-class competitors. To increase your anaerobic threshold, a certain amount of this training should be given over to time trials. Specifically, twice a week you should cycle a 20- to 25-mile time trial (as fast as you can go for that distance at an even pace). If you follow this program regularly over the course of a training season, once your base miles are in, you can increase your AT from the 50 percent of VO_2 Max normal for casual racers to the 90 percent often found among top competitors. If you scored 35 on the Ergometer Test, you have an extraordinary VO_2 Max, and it is well worth the training effort to build up your AT as high as you can get it in order to maximize the use of that large VO_2 Max. With a high usable percentage of a large VO_2 Max, you can become an excellent time trialist and a first-rate road-racing team member. If you also have the kick and the anaerobic endurance tested in Tests 3 and 4, you could win road races, and could likely compete successfully at criterium, the most popular form of bike racing in America.

If you scored under 35 on Test 2, remember that your VO_2 Max is improvable by up to 50 percent, and if your score was between 16 and 32, and you have not previously trained at cycling, you do have the aerobic potential to become an excellent competitive cyclist. Because the muscles used in cycling are so specific for that sport, it is possible that an individual who had never cycled could have a poor score on this test and a very good score on the Cooper Twelve-Minute-Run Test, which measures VO_2 Max in running. Ninety percent of that aerobic capacity for running is transferable to cycling, and such an individual, after specific training for cycling, could radically improve his score.

The best way to train to improve your VO_2 Max in cycling is to put in hours on a bicycle. When you commence training, you should start—as top competitors do when beginning a training season—with long-duration, low-intensity bike rides. The major mistake made by many athletes coming into cycling from other sports is to begin their training by riding at too-high gear settings and too-low RPMs, a practice that tires the muscles early and is counterproductive to building the long-distance base necessary for good aerobic training. Because of the slight amount of stress imposed on the body by cycling, the sport allows an individual to put in great volumes of training early without risk of injury, and doing so is the best way to build your aerobic base.

If you have trained seriously at cycling and scored under 10 on Test 2, or if you have never trained at the sport and scored under 6, you lack the aerobic power to cycle fast for long periods of time, and you should not expect to be able to compete successfully at any form of road racing. You can, of course, enjoy recreational cycling, or you could take up touring. If you want to improve your VO_2 Max, you can do so by up to half of its present capacity by training according to the methods discussed above.

BODY COMPOSITION

LEG EXPLOSIVENESS AND MUSCLE FIBER TYPE. If you had a score of 20 on the Bicycle Sprint Test, you have tremendous leg explosiveness, one of the most valuable assets a cyclist can have and the one most sought after by National Team coaches. Leg explosiveness will serve you very well in any kind of bicycle racing, and if you also have a high VO_2 Max, you are superbly equipped for road and track events.

Leg explosiveness is not very improvable, but it can be bettered somewhat (by 5 to 10 percent), and if you scored under 12 on this test and are serious about racing, you should make an effort to improve your leg explosiveness by practicing this test and/or by sprinting on a bicycle, since sprint ability plays a major role in bicycle racing. If you have very little leg explosiveness but have highly developed aerobic power, you can compensate by tiring sprinters before the finish on long, aerobically demanding pulls and by otherwise employing strategies designed to keep those sprinters off your wheel.

LOWER-BODY ANAEROBIC ENDURANCE. Leg explosiveness determines a cyclist's ability to accelerate; anaerobic endurance in the legs, tested in Test 4, determines how long the cyclist can

sustain an overdrive speed beyond the anaerobic threshold. If you have a score of 20 on this test, you have excellent anaerobic power and will be able to maintain breakaways and long field-sprints.

Underlying and, to some degree, determining anaerobic power is muscle fiber type. If you have a high percentage of endurance fiber in your legs, anaerobic endurance power there can be improved only with difficulty, whereas a high percentage of sprint fiber in your legs makes anaerobic endurance power easily trainable and improvable. The best compensation for a lack of anaerobic endurance power, as it is for a deficit of leg explosiveness, is well-developed aerobic power, which will partially make up for little or no overdrive with a relatively fast overall cruising speed.

A cyclist should not start training for anaerobic endurance until he has established a good base of volume training and has already begun to push up his AT. At that point anaerobic endurance is best developed by interval training, or training that periodically (two or three times a week) forces the cyclist to extend himself anaerobically at varying speeds over varying intervals of time. Since cycling is an interval sport, this kind of training is central. There are a number of good books and one excellent periodical that provide detailed information and advice on interval training, and they are listed in the Appendix. If you race often enough, you can use your races, or portions of them, as the European racers do, for your interval training. You can also use the Bicycle Anaerobic Endurance Test as an interval-training method.

HEIGHT-WEIGHT RATIO, FRONTAL SURFACE AREA, AND OVERALL HEIGHT. If you are tall and/or have a large frontal surface area, you can compensate for those competitive cycling disadvantages by drafting behind people who are also tall and/or broad enough to provide you with a full windshield, and by denying drafting shelter to other racers. A general method of compensation for having a large frontal surface area is to assume and hold as low an aerodynamic body position on the bike as possible.

If the ratio of your weight to your height is more than three pounds per inch, you will be at a real disadvantage in cycling up hills, whether competitively or recreationally. Your weight will compensate somewhat for this disadvantage on downhill stretches by adding to your overall momentum, but on the whole, the higher the ratio of power to weight, the better, and most top cyclists have a very low percentage of body fat and carry very little upper-body muscle mass.

WIDTH OF SHOULDERS. The width of your shoulders, like your height, is a fixed measurement that influences your overall frontal surface area. If you have wide shoulders, you can compensate by riding as low as possible over your bike.

WIDTH OF HIPS. The width of your hips is another fixed measurement. Narrow hips allow you a more direct transfer of power to the pedals than wide ones, but during acceleration you can partially compensate for having wide hips by shifting your body weight laterally and rotating your hips over the pedal on each downstroke while standing.

PERCENTAGE OF BODY FAT. The ideal percentages of body fat for competitive cyclists are 6.7 percent for men and 13.4 percent for women. If you have a higher percentage of fat than that, you are carrying unnecessary baggage up hills, and if you are serious about your cycling you should train down to, or very near, the ideal percentage. You can do this fairly easily in the early stages of your training by adding a few extra miles to your daily training volume; later in your training, time-trialing or racing is as effective a method as any for losing fat.

CYCLING

Test	Measures	Your score	Top score
1. Bicycle Agility	Agility	9	10
2. Astrand Bicycle Ergometer	Heart and lung	35	40
3. U.S. National Team Bicycle Sprint	Leg explosiveness	15	20
4. Bicycle Anaerobic Endurance	Sprint endurance	15	20
5. Weight-Height Chart	Height-weight ratio	5	5
6. Width of Shoulders	Shoulder width	2	2
7. Width of Hips	Hip width	1	3
8. Caliper Body-Fat-Percentage Measurement	Body fat	−4	−10
Total		78	90

100 Gold medalist	50 Cat III racer
90 Tour de France	40 Heavy touring
80 Olympic team	30 Commuter
70 National team	20 Training wheels
60 Cat II racer	10 Tricycle

CROSS-COUNTRY SKIING

THE CONTROL SYSTEM

AGILITY, MULTILIMB COORDINATION. On any level of cross-country skiing beyond simply walking over the snow on skis, agility and coordination are crucial abilities, because they enable the skier to negotiate turns and corners and icy downhills from the narrow, unstable leverage base provided by Nordic skis. If you scored 15 on the U.S. Nordic Ski Team Agility Run Test, you have excellent agility and multilimb coordination, and if you already ski, those abilities are evident. If you don't already ski cross-country, those abilities should allow you to develop quickly a high level of skill, though your dry-land agility and coordination will have to be adapted to skis and snow. You will adapt most quickly if you tackle courses with downhills and tight turns that demand a lot of your coordination and agility, and if you concentrate on "working" turns rather than just sliding through them.

If you scored under 7 on Test 1, whether you already ski cross-country or not, you will have no problem skiing flat, tracked courses, but you could make your skiing much more challenging and enjoyable by improving your agility and coordination. In the summer, those abilities can be improved with dry-land drills, such as this test. In the winter, you can set up agility courses for yourself on the snow that require sudden, well-coordinated movements, or practice running slalom gates on an easy Alpine slope using cross-country skis.

BALANCE. Given the narrowness of Nordic skis and the lack of lateral support provided by cross-country boots, it is not surprising that good balance is so important in cross-country skiing. Test 2 is a sort of "super-balance" test, an all-or-nothing test. If you scored 13 or above on it, your balance is superb and will serve you well in your skiing. If your score was 8 or under, your skiing will be improved by improving your balance, which you can do by practicing this test or another balance drill, such as beam- or ropewalking.

THE HEART-LUNG PACKAGE

MAXIMUM OXYGEN CONSUMPTION. A high VO_2 Max for running is easily transferable to skiing (in fact, it is apt to be higher for skiing, once your arms have been developed), and therefore a score of 30 or above on the Cooper Twelve-Minute-Run Test would indicate that you have all the aerobic power you need for cross-country skiing. You can improve that aerobic power by adding heavy arm work to your lower-body aerobic training. Specifically, in the off-season, you should be roller-skiing or speed-hiking with poles to adapt your large VO_2 Max to cross-country skiing and to enlarge it even further.

To be able to use a large VO_2 Max effectively in cross-country skiing, you have to be able to get to it quickly (by means of good oxygen-delivery speed), to tax a high percentage of it (by means of a high anaerobic threshold), and to recover quickly from a heavy lactic-acid load (which is most likely to be created in steep hill work). For serious competitive cross-country ski racers, aerobic training of the upper and lower body simultaneously should go on all year—through skiing in the winter and through roller-skiing and/or speed-hiking with poles in the off-season. To lift the anaerobic threshold, at least two days a week of this training should be given over to tempo, steady-state, race-pace training at distances of ten to twelve kilometers. Once your anaerobic threshold is up to 70 or 80 percent of your VO_2 Max, you should begin interval training to speed up oxygen

delivery and recovery. Cross-country skiing is naturally an interval sport, and your training should proceed from short, low-intensity intervals to longer, higher-intensity ones, using the terrain to help determine the intervals by going from short, shallow hills to long, steep ones. From the beginning of the season through the end, two days a week should be given over to interval training for the expert, and one day per week for the intermediate skier, with the difficulty of the intervals increasing throughout the season. Interval training should not be done on the same days you do your AT training. During interval training it is important not to stop and glide at the end of the interval (for example, at the top of the hill); you should continue to work. The downhill will automatically drop your work load below your AT, and by continuing to exert yourself you will prevent built-up lactic acid from shutting down muscle by being blown off, and you will speed your overall recovery from the interval.

If you scored 18 or below on the Cooper Test and are a trained runner or cross-country skier, you have limited aerobic power for cross-country skiing. You should work on maximizing what VO_2 Max you have, according to the suggestions above, and should you want to compete at cross-country ski racing, you should assess your other talent components for the sport, determined in the other tests, and decide on the basis of that assessment what type of racing you are best suited for. If, for example, you are very powerful in the upper body, your strength can make up for a small VO_2 Max on a flat course and in klister conditions.

If you scored 18 or below on the Cooper Test and are not trained at either running or cross-country skiing, remember that proper training can improve your VO_2 Max by up to 50 percent. The best way to train your VO_2 Max for cross-country skiing is by skiing in the winter, and by roller-skiing or speed-hiking with poles during the off-season. Your goal when you first begin training should be to build up comfortably to around twenty miles of low-intensity skiing per week if you are sedentary, and up to around forty if you are active, concentrating on improving your technique while you are developing this volume. Once you have comfortably established such a training volume, you can begin doing tempo work to bring up your AT. Any interval training should be seen as a method of strengthening your form, since such training will have little effect on your skiing until you have a high AT. In each succeeding season, you should plan on increasing your training volume by 15 to 20 percent, up to the eighty-plus miles per week put in by top racers, and on increasing your tempo and interval training in proportion to that volume. The most important single principle in training your VO_2 Max for cross-country skiing is that upper- and lower-body aerobic work should always be done simultaneously, so that VO_2 Max may be effectively enlarged for the sport.

BODY COMPOSITION

UPPER-BODY POLING FORCE AND POWER ENDURANCE. The poling force and power endurance generated by the deltoid muscles of the shoulders and the triceps muscles at the rear of the arms are both highly trainable. The poling motion in cross-country skiing begins with high force applied by the deltoids and ends with low-force, high-speed work by the triceps. The Teardrop Push-up Test simulates that combination of effort and also tests for the power endurance of the two muscle groups.

If your score on this test was 4 or above, you have the necessary muscular force, speed, and power endurance for competitive cross-country poling. If your score was between 2 and 4, you should be doing heavy poling work in training to build endurance, with high-force plants and high-speed follow-throughs on increasingly steep hills.

If you couldn't perform any of these push-ups and your score, therefore, was zero, you will need some resistance weight training before you will be able to pole effectively. Military presses, lateral dumbbell raises, triceps dips and presses, and standard push-ups are all good resistance exercises for building the strength of the deltoids and triceps.

LEG LENGTH. If you scored 3 on Test 5, you have long legs for your body height, and they will make it easy for you to develop a naturally long stride in cross-country skiing. If you did not score well on this test, you can compensate in your skiing for your lack of leg length by exerting more power during your kick and by poling more forcefully to increase the length of your stride, though both these activities require more effort.

LEG EXPLOSIVENESS. Good leg explosiveness can compensate in cross-country skiing both for having short legs and for having a low VO_2 Max. In combination with long legs and a high VO_2 Max, leg explosiveness is a terrific asset, allowing a skier explosiveness in coming out of turns and the ability to sprint

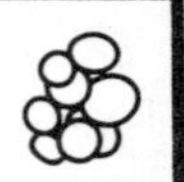

over hills and pass other skiers. If your score on the Vertical-Jump Test was 3 or below, you don't have much leg explosiveness, and your best way to compensate in cross-country ski racing will be to develop as high an AT as you can and to use it to hold a fast overall pace. You would also do well to choose courses with long, steep hills to discourage sprinters, and to race as often as possible in cold, new snow.

CALF SPEED AND ANAEROBIC ENDURANCE. If you scored 7 or above on Test 7, you have the same muscular speed in your calf (or speed of ankle flexion), and the anaerobic endurance to support that speed, as top world-class cross-country ski racers. If you started fast and slowed during the test, your anaerobic endurance is deficient; and if you were slow throughout the test, you don't have much speed in your calves. Both the endurance and strength of the calves are trainable (though the absolute speed of the muscle when loaded is limited genetically), and this test is a good way to train those qualities. Pliometrics, a training system used by the U.S. Ski Team, is also a good method for training anaerobic endurance.

PERCENTAGE OF BODY FAT. If you had points subtracted here, your uphill skiing will suffer from the extra body fat you are carrying, and if you are a serious recreational skier or a competitor, you should work at getting down to the 7 percent body fat for men or 12 percent for women that is considered ideal for the sport.

CROSS-COUNTRY SKIING

Test	Measures	Your score	Top score
1. U.S. Nordic Team Skiing Agility Run	Agility	12	15
2. Blind-Stork Balance	Balance	13	15
3. Cooper Twelve-Minute Run	Heart and Lung	44	45
4. Teardrop Push-up	Arm power	4	5
5. Upper-Body/Lower-Body Proportion	Leg length	5	5
6. Vertical Jump	Explosiveness	6	7
7. Calf Raise	Calf power	7	8
8. Caliper Body-Fat-Percentage Measurement	Body fat	0	−10
Total		91	90

100 World champion	50 Citizen racer
90 Olympic team	40 Day tourer
80 National team	30 Backyard hacker
70 Regional champ	20 Armchair skier
60 Local hotshot	10 Bowler

PART V

IDENTIFYING AND DEVELOPING SPORTSTALENT IN CHILDREN AND ADOLESCENTS

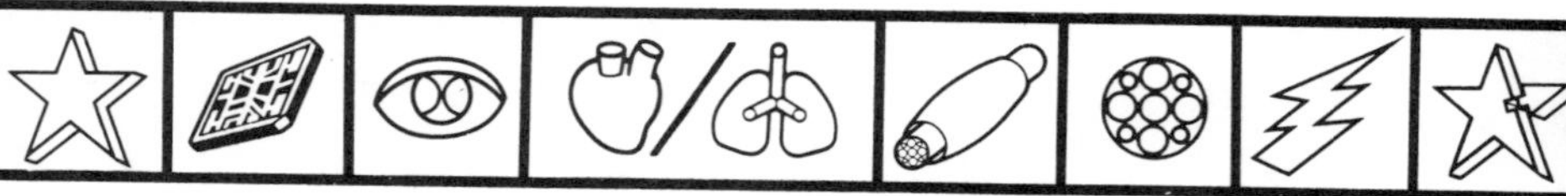

INTRODUCTION

Up to this point, we have addressed ourselves to adults: to men and women over eighteen or nineteen years old. Sportstalent in children and adolescents is a special subject, so special and heretofore so largely unexamined that an entire volume would be required to do it justice. Rather than make a sketchy attempt at that volume here, we will discuss in general terms the application to children and adolescents of some of this book's underlying premises.

We will also offer some advice, since we believe that children have been victimized both by the democratic, laissez-faire sports system of this country and by the enforced sports-participation programs of Eastern Europe, notably of East Germany.

Sportselection has been widely practiced in East Germany since 1960—the year that country decided to make an all-out national effort to excel in the Olympic Games—as a method of recognizing, nurturing, and rewarding exceptional athletic talent in young people. By identifying talented young athletes and then sending them to year-round sports camps for state-of-the-art, scientifically supervised training, East Germany has achieved phenomenal athletic success. But as successful as this method has proved to be for developing national sportstalent, and though it has made available even to very young children a level of scientifically informed training not always available even to national-level athletes in many U.S. sports, it has also made the competitive interests of the country the ultimate goal of those children's participation in sports, and that approach is simply too authoritarian for most of us.

Although the problems with organized sports confronting American children are altogether different from those facing children in East Germany and other Eastern European countries, they are, to our way of thinking, every bit as serious. In eschewing the highly scientific and selective East German approach, this country has developed instead a sports system that more often than not fits a child to a sport on the basis of parental selection, of subjective selection by coaches (which is too often based on the wrong criteria, such as early physical maturity and personality), and of convenience.

Such a system has a number of serious liabilities. Children selected for sports in the ways mentioned above may very well wind up in sports for which they are simply not well equipped and/or which they do not enjoy. Such children can, and often do, develop a distaste for sports so intense that it carries over into adulthood and sometimes prevents them from ever again participating in athletics. Similarly, many adults in America are no longer athletically active because of an injury suffered in a childhood sport (football is the major offender) for which they had neither aptitude nor enthusiasm, or which they began playing before they were physically mature enough for it.

A much larger percentage of Americans are not athletically active as adults because as children they were not selected for sports at all. These people might have had talent for a sport that was not easily available to them; they might have been embarrassed out of sports early by a phys ed instructor who was cruel in pointing out a lack of demonstrated ability; or they might have had some sportstalent that went unrecognized by themselves and others, either because they were not physically mature enough for the sport at that time or because they never had an opportunity to play it.

Such a system also tends to encourage the creation and perpetuation of sports myths—that eating meat and potatoes before a football game is good for you, that water intake should be restricted during heavy exercise, and so on. Perhaps the most pervasive and damaging of these myths, and the one centrally addressed in this book, is that all athletes are created equal. This myth can lead children to knock their brains out, almost literally, trying to do things they can't, to become discouraged, and to form negative self-images.

In short, the sports system in the United States has too often unnecessarily introduced children to physical and emotional trauma and to the dispiriting concept of failure at a time in their lives when they most need success, and in an arena of their lives that can and should be entered and played in joyfully and freely.

We would like to see a sports system for children in this country that is as scientifically informed as East Germany's but that *encourages*, rather than recruits, participation—and that deserves participation. We believe that the primary principle behind encouraging as broad a spectrum of participation as possible in such a program should be that of individuation—of matching a child to the right sport at the right time of the child's life. To compete successfully, happily, and safely at a given sport, a child must be completely equipped, both physically and emotionally, for that competition. Part of the reason sports competition for children has developed such a bad reputation among many Americans since the 1930s is that our guidelines for determining when and if a child is so equipped have been inadequate at best, and at worst, completely inappropriate. Coaches and parents (and children themselves) have determined childhood preparedness for competition at a sport—and continue to do so—on the basis of age, size, biological maturity, personality, economic or social status, and the competitive zeal of parents. In fact, *none* of these guidelines is an effective determiner of a child's readiness to learn, or preparedness to compete at, a sport.

A child's basic equipment for competing in a given sport at a given time in that youngster's life embodies two factors: the child's genetic constitution as it has been developed or trained to that point, and the prerequisite athletic skills that he or she has acquired to that point. Regardless of a child's age, height, weight, personality, or whatever, sending that child into competition at a sport for which he or she has not developed either the necessary skills or the necessary physical capacities is tantamount to sending a hockey goalie into play without a glove, a face mask, or a stick.

The age at which a child becomes ready to learn and equipped to compete at a given sport varies from sport to sport and from child to child, but overall athletic development can be divided generally into two stages: the skill-acquisition years of infancy through puberty, and the heart-lung-muscle-development years of adolescence. Understanding how a child can and should develop during these stages is an absolute necessity for any parent or coach who would see that child safely, happily, and productively introduced to sports competition. Understanding these developmental stages will also allow a parent or coach to recognize the various components of sportstalent in a child as they are revealed during the processes of maturation, skill acquisition, and training.

THE SKILL-ACQUISITION YEARS

Motor-skill acquisition begins virtually on the day of birth. A newborn infant already possesses certain reflexes and innate motor patterns of movement that begin immediately to be adapted to specific functions. The very first effectively coordinated movements made by an infant, such as grasping, reaching, and sucking, constitute the first motor skills acquired by that individual, and are the subunits or basic building blocks of all future motor programs. The infant acquires more and more of these skills and begins to link them together in different ways and to substitute one for another in order to create new patterns of effective movement that afford a choice of responses to different stimuli. The motivation to pick up hundreds of basic motor skills, and to experiment with those skills by forming different combinations in increasingly complex patterns, is in direct proportion to the amount, quality, and kind of stimulation the infant receives.

If you are a parent, read that last sentence again—its implications for parents are enormous. During the first two years of life more primary motor skills are acquired than at any other time, and many experts believe that *all* the primary motor skills an individual will ever have are acquired by age four. (New skills acquired after that age, these experts believe, are just modifications and new combinations of primary skills.) The more effectively and comprehensively a child is stimulated during the first

two to four years of life, the greater the number and sophistication of motor skills that child will develop within the context of his or her genetic endowment.

This book is about sports, and the sports-related significance of what we have just said is this: *if you want your child to have a chance at uncovering all of his or her genetic athletic ability, you should begin creating a proper environment of stimulation for that child as soon as possible after he or she is born.*

But the early development of motor skills has significance in areas other than sports, and is every bit as important as the development of cognitive skills to the overall development of the brain. Variety and sophistication of motor skills are required in activities as disparate as flying an airplane, ballet dancing, sculpting, and watchmaking; and a person without such variety and sophistication will be unable to uncover whatever motor abilities he or she might have in a broad spectrum of human activities. No parent wants a child to go through life physically clumsy, or to be made to suffer a negative self-image because of awkwardness, or to be blocked from being able to do things, athletic and otherwise, that require coordination and physical deftness. Yet very few American parents make any real effort to develop motor skills in their children, particularly at the time in their children's lives when that development is most important. Between birth and four years of age is the time in a child's life when parents can and should do a substantial amount to ensure that the child develops a large number of increasingly sophisticated motor skills.

Every child goes through a normal, orderly developmental sequence in the acquisition of basic motor skills, and that sequence can't be changed. Children have to be able to sit up before they can pivot without falling, before they can bear their full standing weight, before they can stand while holding on to furniture, before they can walk with assistance—and they must do *all* these things, in sequence, before they can finally walk. Children progress through a given motor-skill sequence at different speeds of learning, and chronological age has very little to do with when a skill can be attained: readiness is the key to skill attainment. To learn a new motor skill (for example, standing while holding on to furniture), children must have mastered the prerequisite skill subordinate to it, their sensory and motor systems must be mature enough to perform the new skill, and they must *want* to learn it. *You cannot teach children a new skill before they have met the three criteria of readiness to learn the skill.* Children simply cannot walk, for example, no matter how

much you encourage them to, if they have not learned the skills prerequisite to walking, or if the spinal cord is not sufficiently developed, or if they are overly cautious and don't want to walk.

What all this means for parents who want to help a child develop a large number of sophisticated motor skills is that readiness is everything. Certain basic sequences of motor development cannot be hurried, and instead of trying to rush a very young child through a sequence of motor skills toward a particular goal, such as walking or throwing a ball, wise parents will take advantage of each level of skill acquisition as it comes, making sure that the child learns as wide a variety of skills on that level as possible, *whether or not* they are part of the sequence leading to the particular desired goal. These parents will also make the sequential progression from one skill to the next as easy as possible for the child by breaking down each new skill into components that are both appetizing to the child and easy to digest.

To create the proper environment for the best possible development of a child's motor skills, parents should have some scientific understanding of the child's physiological development, and must spend creative time with the child, breaking down skills into enticing units of movement and awareness that will hold the child's interest and attention. Unfortunately, there is no program or formal set of specifications for doing this effec-

Creative crib toys develop hand/eye coordination. Rolling a ball toward the child develops visual tracking.

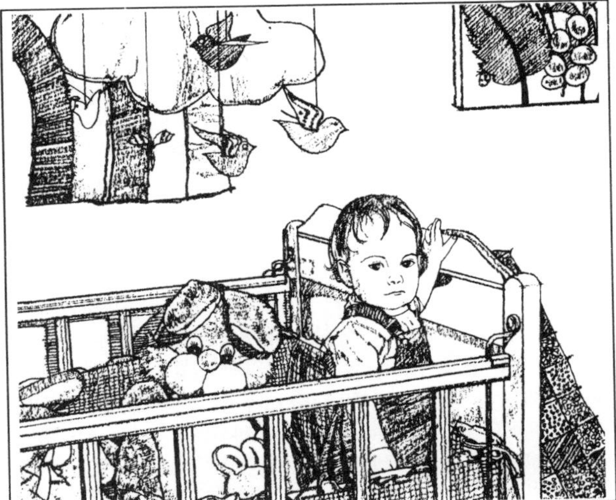

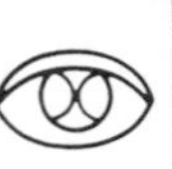

tively—it is up to your intuition and imagination as parents. We can, however, offer a few suggestions. With the proper stimulation, even infants can begin to develop hand/eye coordination and visual-tracking skills. The development of those skills has recently been made considerably easier by the appearance of some very creative crib toys that develop hand/eye coordination, increasingly fine motor control, and visual tracking, and that are designed for the progressive stages of a child's development. Parents can encourage visual-tracking ability in infants by moving a held ball slowly back and forth across the crib and in and out of a baby's range of vision, and, once a child is able to sit up outside the crib, by rolling a beach ball toward the child and encouraging him or her to track the ball and to stop it with a hand. These visual exercises will help to lead the child later to smooth visual tracking and accurate, full convergence—skills that are important to a variety of sports.

What we are really suggesting is not that parents occasionally push individual exercises and learning toys at small children, but that they create an overall *environment* for their children that will interest them early on in movement and awareness. Successful athletic prodigies tend to come from family environments in which the joy of graceful, effective movement is an integral, necessary part of life, just as successful prodigies in other fields such as art and music tend to come from environments in which those artistic pursuits are part of the normal life of the family. Such environments are created most naturally and best when what the parents want for a child coincides with their own activities and enthusiasms, and when the stimulation provided by the environment is not so much force-fed as just a naturally occurring part of what the child is exposed to.

Just as there are certain antecedent skills that must be learned before they are linked together in the motor program for walking, so there are discrete antecedent skills underlying the finished motor programs for all sports that must be learned before those motor programs can be formed. In some sports, such as gymnastics and soccer, there are neatly defined packages of skills for each stage of development toward the finished motor programs for those sports, packages that lend themselves to being easily broken down and taught to even very young children. Because gymnastics develops whole-body, multilimb coordination and balance, children from eighteen months to two and older can benefit greatly from carefully supervised gymnastics courses, regardless of whether or not they continue to pursue the sport. Similarly, the drills of soccer can provide excellent

The building blocks of batting. Have the child begin by hitting a stationary ball; then track and hit a ball rolling in the ground. Finally, hit the ball in flight.

development of agility, anticipation, reaction time, and eye/limb coordination in children from a very early age. These drills can be practiced with a kickball or a beach ball even by children as young as two or three.

Many an American child's first failure in life occurs on a baseball field. Traditionally, a child who performs well immediately at baseball is perceived as being a "natural athlete," while a child who does not is often perceived as lacking athletic talent altogether. As often as not, both of these traditional perceptions are wrong. The entry-level motor programs for baseball of catching, throwing, and hitting are very complex. None of them has been effectively broken down into packages of antecedent skills that are easily learnable through drills such as those used to teach the skills of soccer and gymnastics. For this reason, many kids come into baseball with none of those motor programs very well developed—which doesn't necessarily imply anything about their ultimate potential for the sport. Others, some of whom might not ultimately be good baseball players, come into the sport with one or more of those motor programs already developed through practice, and immediately outperform those kids who have not developed motor programs for the sport.

Despite the fact that baseball motor programs have not been formally and effectively broken down into packages of antecedent skills, parents can facilitate a child's entry into baseball by creatively working with the child on some of the sport's building-block skills, such as tracking, anticipation, aiming, and swinging a bat. These skills should be practiced one at a time, well within the child's abilities and attention span, and

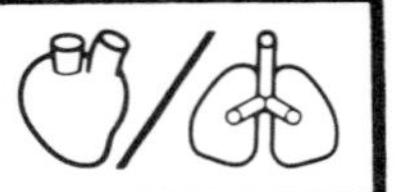

their development should always be met by the reward of approval. Young children are usually unable to track a thrown ball's trajectory sufficiently well to be able to hit it in the air. An example of the creative approach we are advocating for the development in a young child of good motor programs is to begin building the child's motor program for batting by having him or her hit rolled kickballs or beach balls with a stick or short bat, thus reducing a complex three-dimensional task to a performable two-dimensional one.

At some point in the process of motor-skill development, usually beginning around the age of seven, a child begins putting acquired skills to work in the actual performance of a sport. The transition from drills and practice for a sport to actual play happens by means of a process known as "spontaneous cuing," by which a child begins spontaneously to select skills from those already amassed in order to respond to real sports situations without the need for external directions. At this point, if the child is *ready* for the transition, skilled movement becomes sport.

It is advisable that children try a variety of sports, once the prerequisite skills are acquired. After about ten years of age, at the latest, the acquisition of basic skills becomes considerably more difficult and less spontaneous. The early combining and recombining of skills into motor programs for a variety of sports gives a child the large library of motor programs and the agility at using them that characterize all good athletes. Some of the sports that develop particularly useful motor programs among preadolescent children, and/or that should be taken up at a young age for successful competition at them later, are Alpine skiing, racquet sports, figure skating (both for itself and as an excellent preparation for hockey), soccer, gymnastics, baseball, basketball, football, diving, water-skiing, and roller-skating.

Aerobic sports will offer no muscular- or heart-lung-training effect to a child until just before the onset of puberty, but their skills can be developed by young children, and certain of these aerobic sports (such as swimming, cross-country skiing, and cycling) *must* be practiced early by youngsters who want to compete successfully at them later. While it is crucial for a child who wants to compete at swimming, for example, to develop early on the skills and motor programs central to that sport, it is almost equally important that that child not work exclusively at building just those skills and motor programs, but practice a variety of sports during the skill-acquisition years. Swimming or running for hours is *not* productive ath-

letic activity for a preadolescent child, and in fact does nothing but waste good skill-acquisition time. Children who believe they may want to take up cross-country skiing seriously should concentrate on building good motor programs for the sport during their skill-acquisition years by doing agility drills and running slalom courses, and should not waste time on aerobic volume or hill training. Similarly, potential cyclists are much better served in their preadolescent years by the fun of BMX dirt-bike cycling than they are by putting in a lot of miles on the road.

THE AEROBIC- AND MUSCLE-DEVELOPMENT YEARS

Until the time of the maximum growth spurt (the year during which a child gains the most height), most children have all the heart-lung power they need for their relatively small bodies. Until this time, which may come anywhere between ten and fourteen years old, there is very little difference in heart-lung power and muscular strength between boys and girls. In fact, Tracy Caulkins, one of America's premier female swimmers, regularly beat boys of her own age and older until her early teens.

Beginning with the year before a child's maximum growth spurt and lasting until the child's late teens, the period generally thought of as adolescence is the prime time in an individual's life for the development of aerobic power. The heart-lung package is more responsive to aerobic training during this period than at any other time in a person's life, and aerobic-training time not taken advantage of during this period can never be fully made up for later. Though the heart-lung package of an adolescent girl is just as responsive to aerobic training as that of an adolescent boy, studies have shown that aerobic capacities achieved by males during this period are, on average, 25 percent larger than those achieved by females. It has always been assumed that females are genetically limited from achieving aerobic capacities as large as those achieved by males, and in fact the extra fat that women are genetically obliged to carry

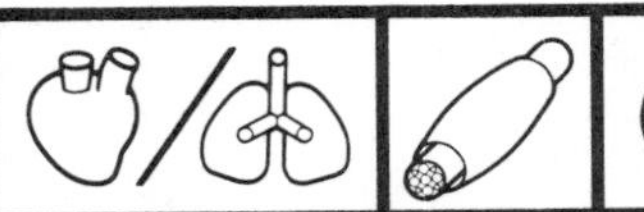

does diminish the amount of heart-lung power available to them proportionate to their weight. But there is recent evidence (including the 1983 Boston Marathon female winner Joan Benoit's measured VO_2 Max of seventy-eight milliliters per kilogram, a VO_2 Max larger than that of many male runners, including Frank Shorter) that much of the difference between males and females in ultimate aerobic capacity is not genetic, but due to the facts that, traditionally, more men train aerobically than women and that they train harder and begin earlier.

A child who wants to compete at any of the aerobic sports (except for running) should begin practice at the skills of that sport early enough so that they are well learned by age ten. Before the child's maximum-growth-spurt year, he or she should be doing a reasonable amount of volume training at the sport. As a child enters that maximum-growth-spurt year, and on beyond that year up through the late teens, the volume of training should be carefully increased (by no more than 20 percent a year) and managed according to sound training principles, like those offered by the training books listed in the Appendix.

The development of muscular strength and anaerobic power appropriate to a child's size almost always lags behind that child's maximum growth spurt, sometimes by as much as two years. For this reason, a young adolescent should concentrate on building a broad volume base of aerobic training at a sport before any high-intensity strength training, anaerobic threshold training, or interval training is begun. As we have said before, for any aerobic sport a competitor needs first to have developed aerobic power before adding on the overdrive capacity of a high AT, muscular strength, and anaerobic power. As an example, a good marathon runner may have attained a large VO_2 Max by age eighteen, but it will likely be another three or four years, at least, before that runner can add to his or her large VO_2 Max the high AT and the hardening results of interval training necessary to bring his or her times down to the levels required to win major races.

It should be mentioned here that, where children are concerned, middle- and long-distance running is in a different category from the other aerobic sports. Because of their relatively high centers of gravity and their relatively short legs, children cannot develop finished skills for running, as they can for the other aerobic sports, before their maximum-growth-spurt years. For that reason, and because they can get no training effect from running, and because it is possible that their sen-

sitive growth plates can be damaged by the impact of running, it is not advisable for children to begin endurance running before reaching their maximum-growth-spurt years.

Few people realize how long it takes to develop a first-rate endurance athlete properly. Greg LeMond, probably the finest cyclist ever produced in this country, and who is now, in his early twenties, a top European racing pro, would not consider racing in the Tour de France, Europe's top endurance cycling event, until recently, because he felt he had not reached his maximum endurance potential. The world's top rowers and cross-country ski racers don't reach their aerobic peaks until their mid- to late twenties; and at that point in their career, many wish that they had spent more time and energy in their youth on developing skills.

Any youngster who wants to train seriously for competition at an aerobic sport would do well to view that training as a sort of pyramid that takes a long time to construct correctly. Good skills should form the base of the pyramid, onto which, when the time is right, should be laid a number of years of solid aerobic volume training. Only after these large foundation blocks are in place should the pyramid be built upward with AT training, anaerobic power training, and, finally, muscular strength training.

The development of muscular strength in American children and adolescents for athletic purposes is widely misunderstood and mispracticed. Weight-room strength training is often thought of and encouraged as a general sports panacea in this country, while it is not in Europe. In Europe, in fact, very little if any weight-room strength training is practiced by young endurance athletes, who choose, rather, to build what muscular strength they do build, when they are biologically ready to do so, through interval training at their actual sports.

Before puberty a child can get very little, if any, training effect from lifting weights, and therefore the practice is essentially a waste of time. Additionally, from childhood through late adolescence the growth plates in a child's limbs are not completely closed, and they can be damaged at any time into the late teens by maximum-resistance weight training. For this reason, the highly practical and scientific East German coaches (as well as many other European coaches) refuse to let their athletes do *any* high-resistance weight training (training with heavy weights) until they are eighteen or over.

High-resistance weight training does play an important role in the overall training for some sports, particularly for football—where it can be credited with having raised the quality of competition over the past ten to fifteen years and with having drastically reduced certain kinds of injuries, particularly neck injuries and shoulder separations. But even for football, for the reasons mentioned earlier, we advise against high-resistance weight training for children before they are sixteen or seventeen; if they want to lift weights, we suggest that before they are sixteen or seventeen they learn the skills involved in weight lifting and work on developing muscle speed and endurance by doing high-repetition, low- to medium-resistance weight training under the supervision of a qualified trainer or coach. The sole exception to this is protective strength—for example, the neck strength so important to football players.

By and large, for most nonaerobic sports other than football, the field events, and wrestling—all of which require considerable low-speed, high-resistance strength—anyone (child, adolescent, or adult) is better served in building muscular strength for a sport, where possible, by actual practice at the sport rather than by weight training. This is also true of all the aerobic sports except swimming.

Low- to medium-resistance, high-speed, isokinetic weight training has been responsible, in large part, for the dramatic worldwide improvement in competitive swimmers, especially women, over the past fifteen to twenty years. Probably because swimming provides less natural resistance to the body's forward progress than any other aerobic sport, it offers the least within-the-sport opportunity for resistance strength training, and weight training has proved to be a very effective substitute. Thus weight training for swimmers should begin fairly early—by age twelve or thirteen—since the entire maturation of a competitive swimmer is by necessity a quick one and national champions are often only in their mid-teens. But weight training should be confined to the high-speed, low- to medium-resistance variety mentioned above.

A final reason why children and adolescents should be careful in their employment of weight training as a method of developing muscular strength for sports is that too often a young person's tendons, ligaments, and cartilage are not sufficiently developed to handle the torque generated in certain movements by the sort of excessive muscular strength obtained through the use of weights.

IDENTIFYING SPORTSTALENT IN CHILDREN AND ADOLESCENTS

Sportselection, or the process of identifying and nurturing sports aptitude in children, has been widely practiced in Eastern European countries for years. Rumania's success with gymnastics, Czechoslovakia's with tennis, and East Germany's with crew, swimming, the luge, and the marathon—to name just a few examples—can be largely attributed to the use of sportselection in those countries. Despite these successes, sportselection is largely an unknown science in the United States, and while we are not crazy about some of the implications of that science as it is practiced in Eastern Europe, we do believe that sportstalent should be recognized and encouraged in children, by parents if not by the state, since that talent is an important part of a child's overall potential, and one that deserves recognition and encouragement as much as any other.

We began this section with a discussion of sportstalent development because in most cases, and particularly during the skill-acquisition years, the development of sportstalent precedes its recognition: in most cases both development and time are required to reveal sports potential in children. The age at which aptitude for a particular sport becomes apparent in a child varies from sport to sport, and, more often than not, that aptitude reveals itself a little at a time over a period of years. In Eastern Europe the most important components of talent for a particular sport are singled out and tested in children as soon

as they can be detected. Explosiveness, for example—the most crucial component of talent for sprinting—is tested among five-year-old children by using EMG tests to look for a specific pattern of muscular recruitment that first becomes apparent at around that age. If a five-year-old is found to have leg explosiveness and can apply it in a synchronous, coordinated pattern of muscle recruitment, that child is automatically identified as a potential sprinter.

The Eastern Europeans also attempt to identify talent for swimming among five-year-olds by looking at certain frame dimensions, particularly the size of the hands and feet, and at the effectiveness of a child's stroke mechanics. And children in these countries are selected at very young ages for high-skill sports, such as gymnastics and figure skating, that *have* to be begun, and specialized in, early by anyone who expects to compete on a world-class level. In the case of gymnastics, a five-year-old's motor skills and underlying motor abilities for the sport are assessed, and since coaching and nurturing a young gymnast to world-class competition is an expensive, time-consuming procedure, the five-year-old is also tested for height potential to determine whether or not he or she will ultimately be too tall for the sport.

In America at present, we have neither the developed methods nor the desire to identify sportstalent among very young children. Here, the earliest age at which sports aptitude is traditionally identified is around ten, when a child possesses all the basic motor skills he or she will ever have and, more than likely, has already begun to apply those skills in a variety of sports. If you are the parent of a child who is around ten years old and either you or the child is curious about his or her talent for a particular sport, we recommend that you consult with a top coach in your area, who may very well have a personal, empirically developed system for recognizing talent and will likely know about available scientific talent-testing for the sport (such as the U.S. Ski Team Alpine Motor Skills Test).

Children who are not athletically skillful enough (or who do not want) to begin or to continue competition at the skill sports have a new chance at athletics through the aerobic sports when they enter adolescence. These children—as well as those who *choose* to participate, or continue, in aerobic sports—can have their overall aerobic potential assessed when they are a year or so into adolescence, through available laboratory tests for maximum oxygen consumption, heart size, and lung capacity. Determining the specific aerobic sport for which an adolescent with

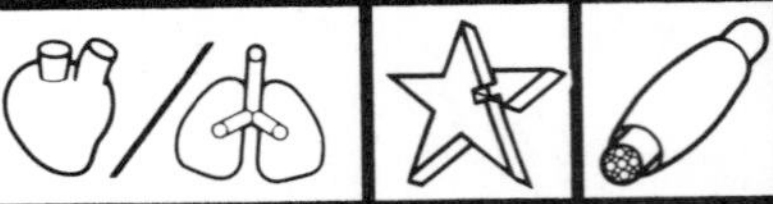

good aerobic potential is likely to be best suited is a matter of evaluating the elements of body composition discussed in Part I of this book—elements such as overall body size, muscle fiber type, height-to-weight ratio, and upper-body/lower-body proportion.

Unfortunately, there is at present no comprehensive and organized testing system available in this country for identifying either aerobic or skill sportstalent in children and adolescents—though there will be before long, both in the form of Sportslab testing facilities and in a forthcoming book on the subject by the present authors.

A GLOSSARY OF IMPORTANT TERMS

after-loading: After-loading is the amount of resistance encountered by the heart as it pumps blood. Decreased after-load, a function of good aerobic training, is the minimum resistance encountered in the aorta to the heart's effort to expel blood.

anaerobic threshold (AT): A person's anaerobic threshold is the percentage of his or her VO_2 Max that can be utilized over a prolonged period of time. This threshold, or "puff-point"—beyond which an individual becomes increasingly short of breath—occurs as a result of rapid lactic acid buildup.

anticipation (receptor and effector): Anticipation is the attempt by an athlete to guess exactly when and where something will arrive or occur (e.g., when and where a hit tennis ball will arrive at a player's racquet, or when and where a football lineman will move). Receptor anticipation attempts to gauge an object's arrival; effector anticipation attempts to meet that arrival with the appropriate physical action.

arousal: Arousal is a quantitative measure of the degree to which the brain is stimulated at any given time. In sports it is the measure of how "up" or "psyched" an athlete is for a particular performance.

binocularity: Binocularity is the visual ability to fix an object in space by focusing both eyes on it simultaneously.

Computerized Motion Analysis (CMA): Computerized Motion Analysis is currently the most precise method available for determining a knowledge of performance in sports. CMA uses a computer to trace the speed and movement of the torso and limbs during sports performance and to compare the data with ideal standards of performance.

convergence: Convergence is the visual ability that allows the eyes to focus precisely and repeatedly without fatigue on an object (such as a tennis ball) that approaches the eyes quickly from far away to close up.

dynamic visual acuity: Dynamic visual acuity is the ability of the eyes either to focus precisely and quickly on a variety of objects and to fix those objects in space, or to take accurate sequential visual fixes on a single moving object.

elasticity: Elasticity is the measure of a muscle's inherent springiness.

endurance muscle fiber: Endurance muscle fiber is characterized by its resistance to fatigue and relative lack of speed and power.

Force-Speed Curve: The Force-Speed Curve describes a particular muscle's overall performance, designating that muscle's maximum power at any specific speed.

joint looseness: Joint looseness is the measurement of a joint's end-range of motion. If you have elastic muscles, the more joint looseness in a particular part of the body, the more flexible that part of the body is.

knowledge of performance (KP): Knowledge of performance is an assessment of *how* a specific athletic result is achieved. Such an assessment is made by analyzing the various biomechanical forces that produced the result.

knowledge of result (KR): Knowledge of result is an objective assessment of the outcome of a physical movement. In sports a knowledge of result can be either qualitative (e.g., a tennis serve was either in or out, a basketball goes through the hoop or it doesn't) or quantitative (e.g., a baseball is hit three hundred and seven feet, a runner's stride length is 1.92 meters).

lactic acid: Lactic acid is a chemical byproduct of exercise. As it increases in concentration, it causes muscles first to grow tired and finally to quit working.

Maximum Oxygen Consumption (VO_2 Max): Maximum Oxygen Consumption is a measure of the oxygen transport capacity of an individual's heart and lungs, as well as of the ability of specific muscles to off-load and burn the oxygen delivered to them.

motor abilities: Motor abilities are innate, inherited traits that determine an individual's coordination, balance, agility, and speed of reactions.

motor learning: Motor learning is the acquisition of new motor skills and the building of new motor programs.

motor programs: A motor program is composed of a specific number of motor skills linked together in a particular order and executed in unvarying sequence.

motor skills: Motor skills, which are based on underlying motor abilities, are the learned, functional components of coordinated movement. Any complex athletic movement, such as swinging a tennis racquet, is composed of a number of discrete motor skills.

pre-loading: Pre-loading is the stretching of the muscles in the heart's main chamber by forcing a large volume of blood into that chamber. Pre-loading is a function of good aerobic training.

receptors (exteroceptive and proprioceptive): Receptors are bodily sensors that collect positional data. Exteroceptive receptors, such as the eyes, locate objects in space; proprioceptive receptors, such as the specialized nerve endings in the various joints of the body, tell us where different parts of the body are in relation to each other and how those parts are moving.

selective attention: Selective attention is the function of the Control System that allows it to focus exclusively on a specific range of sensory input being supplied by the receptors.

somatotype: A somatotype is a specific index that reflects an individual's leanness, fatness, and muscularity.

sprint muscle fiber: Sprint muscle fiber is characterized by high speed, power, and quick fatigability.

standard of correctness: A standard of correctness is a mental image of how to perform a physical act or movement. That image can be either appropriate or inappropriate.

SPECIAL TESTING EQUIPMENT

Calipers:
There are several good, inexpensive plastic calipers available by mail order. The McGaw plastic caliper can be ordered from the McGaw Laboratories, a Division of American Hospital Supply Corporation, Irvine, California 92714. The Ross plastic caliper can be ordered from the Ross Laboratories, a Division of Abbott Laboratories, P.O. Box 8617, Montreal, Canada H3C3P3. The state-of-the-art SKYNDEX Electronic Body Fat Calculator can be ordered from Caldwell, Justiss & Company, Inc., P.O. Box 520, Fayetteville, Arkansas 72702.

Fish scale:
The best fish scale for measuring stroke power in swimming is the Chatillion 50 lb. × 8 oz. graduated scale. It can be ordered from the Orvis Company, Manchester, Vermont 05254.

Home Vision Test:
Two excellent home tests for overall visual acuity are "The Home Eye Test for Adults" and "The Home Eye Test for Pre-schoolers." Both are available from the National Society to Prevent Blindness, 79 Madison Avenue, New York, New York 10016. Include one dollar for postage and handling.

Metronomes:
Metronomes can be bought at most music stores. Their prices start at about twenty-three dollars for a key-wound Franz model, and Seth Thomas, Seiko, and Toc-Tale are other good brands to consider. For certain of the tests in cycling we recommend using a metronome for measuring cadence. This can also be accomplished by using a small bicycle computer that provides a digital readout of cadence; these computers can be bought for as little as twenty dollars.

Stationary Bicycles:
The two best stationary bicycles for measuring work output are the Warren E. Collins Bicycle Ergometer and the Monarch Bicycle Ergometer. There are other adequate bicycle ergometers, but when choosing one, make sure that it is capable of measuring workloads in either watts or KPMs.

BIBLIOGRAPHY

Books

Adams, J. A., *Human Memory*. New York: McGraw-Hill, 1967.

Adams, J. A., *Learning and Memory: An Introduction*. Homewood, Ill.: Dorsey, 1976.

Bergh, Ulf, *Physiology of Cross-Country Ski Racing*. Champaign, Ill.: Human Kinetics Publishers, 1982.

Braden, Vic, and Bill Bruns, *Vic Braden's Tennis for the Future*. Boston: Little, Brown, 1977.

Brock, Greg, *How Road Racers Train*. Los Altos, Calif.: Track and Field News Press, 1980.

Burke, Ed, et al., *Inside the Cyclist*. Brattleboro, Vt.: Velo-News, 1975.

Counsilman, James E., *Competitive Swimming Manual*. Bloomington, Ind.: Counsilman Co., Inc., 1977.

Counsilman, James E., *The Science of Swimming*. Englewood Cliffs, N.J.: Prentice-Hall, 1968.

Deutsch, Georg, and Sally P. Springer, *Left Brain, Right Brain*. San Francisco: W. H. Freeman, 1981.

Eriksson, Bengt, M.D., and Bengt Furberg, M.D., *International Series on Sports Sciences: Swimming Medicine, IV*. Baltimore, Md.: University Park Press, 1978.

Faria, Irvin E., *Cycling Physiology for the Serious Cyclist*. Springfield, Ill.: Charles C Thomas, 1978.

Fixx, James F., *The Complete Book of Running*. New York: Random House, 1977.

Fleishman, E. A., *The Structure and Measurement of Physical Fitness*. Englewood Cliffs, N.J.: Prentice-Hall, 1964.

Gallwey, Timothy W., *The Inner Game of Tennis*. New York: Bantam, 1974.

Gilbert, Doug, *The Miracle Machine*. New York: Coward, McCann, & Geoghegan, 1980.

Holt, Kenneth (ed.), *Movement and Child Development*. New York: Spastics International Medical Publications, 1975.

Illingworth, Ronald S., *The Development of the Infant and Young Child*. New York: Churchill Livingstone, 1980.

Jarver, Jess (ed.), *Long Distances*. Los Altos, Calif.: Track and Field News Press, 1980.

Joubert, Georges, and Jean Vuarnet, *How to Ski the New French Way*. New York: Dial Press, 1967.

Karner, Richard S., and Lorraine Dusky, *Total Vision*. New York: A & W Visual Library, 1978.

Kendall, Philip C., and Stephen D. Hollon, *Cognitive Behavioral Interventions: Theory, Research, and Procedures*. New York: Academic Press, 1979.

Kolin, Michael J., and Denise De La Rosa, *The Custom Bicycle*. Emmaus, Pa.: Rodale Press, 1979.

Martens, Rainer, *Joy and Sadness in Children's Sports*. Champaign, Ill.: Human Kinetics Publishers, 1978.

Martens, Rainer, *Sport Competition Anxiety Test.* Champaign, Ill.: Human Kinetics Publishers, 1982.

Martens, Rainer, et al., *Coaching Young Athletes.* Champaign, Ill.: Human Kinetics Publishers, 1981.

Matheny, Fred, *Beginning Bicycle Racing.* Brattleboro, Vt.: Velo-News, 1980.

Neisser, U., *Cognitive Psychology.* New York: Appleton-Century-Crofts, 1967.

Norman, D. A., *Memory and Attention.* New York: John Wiley, 1976.

Orlick, Terry, *In Pursuit of Excellence.* Champaign, Ill.: Human Kinetics Publishers, 1980.

Ruch, Theodore, and Harry D. Patton, *Physiology and Biophysics.* Philadelphia, Pa.: W. B. Saunders, 1982.

Ryan, Allan J., M.D., *The Physician and Sportsmedicine Guide to Running.* New York: McGraw-Hill, 1980.

Schmidt, Richard A., *Motor Control and Learning—A Behavioral Emphasis.* Champaign, Ill.: Human Kinetics Publishers, 1982.

Seefeldt, V., and J. Haubenstricker, *History and Current Status of Motor Performance Study.* East Lansing, Mich.: Michigan State University. Unpublished manuscript, 1973.

Shepherd, Roy J., M.D., *Physical Activity and Growth.* Chicago, Ill.: Year Book Medical Publishers, 1982.

Shepherd, Roy J., M.D., *Physiology and Biochemistry of Exercise.* New York: Praeger, 1982.

Southmayd, William, M.D., and Marshall Hoffman, *Sportshealth.* New York: Quick Fox, 1981.

Squires, Bill, and Raymond Krise, *Improving Your Running.* Brattleboro, Vt.: Stephan Greene Press, 1982.

Stanciu, Ulrich, and Reinhart Winkler, *This Is Windsurfing.* Boston, Mass.: Sail Books, 1979.

Struna, Monika, and Connie Church, *Self Massage.* New York: Simon & Schuster, 1983.

Tutko, Thomas, and Umberto Tosi, *Sports Psyching.* Los Angeles: J. P. Tarcher, 1976.

Witherell, Warren, *How the Racers Ski.* New York: W. W. Norton, 1972.

Articles

Adams, J. A., "An Evaluation of Test Items Measuring Motor Abilities," Research Report AFPTRC-TN-56-55, 1956.

Atkinson, R. C., and R. A. Shiffren, "The Control of Short-Term Memory," *Scientific American*, 1971, pp. 82–90.

Barclay, C. R., and K. M. Newall, "Children's Processing of Information in Motor Skill Acquisition," *Journal of Experimental Child Psychology*, 1980, pp. 98–108.

Beaulieu, John E., "Developing a Stretching Program," *The Physician and Sportsmedicine*, November 1981, pp. 59–69.

Belanger, A. Y., and A. J. McComas, "Extent of Motor Unit Activation During Effort," *Journal of Applied Physiology*, 1981, pp. 1131–35.

Bennett, Frederick M., et al., "Dynamics of Ventilatory Response to Exercise in Humans," *Journal of Applied Physiology*, 1981, pp. 194–201.

Bliss, J. C., et al., "Information Available in Brief Tactile Presentation," *Perception and Psychophysics*, 1966, pp. 273–83.

Bosco, C., et al., "Effect of Elastic Energy and Myoelectrical Potentiation of Triceps Surae During Stretch Shortening Cycle Exercise," *International Journal of Sports Medicine*, 1982, pp. 137–40.

Bronson, G., "The Hierarchical Organization of the Central Nervous System: Implications for Learning Processes and Critical Periods in Early Development," *Behavioral Science*, 1965, pp. 7–25.

Brown, I. D., and R. M. Schiffren, "Measuring the Spare Mental Capacity of Car Drivers by a Subsidiary Auditory Task," *Ergonomics*, 1962, pp. 247–50.

Buono, Michael J., et al., "The Effect of an Acute Bout

of Exercise on Selected Pulmonary Function Measurements," *Medicine and Science in Sports and Exercise*, 1981, pp. 290–93.

Butts, Nancy Kay, "Physiological Profile of High School Female Cross-Country Runners," *The Physician and Sportsmedicine*, November 1982, pp. 103–12.

Cantwell, John Davis, M.D., "Rhythms of Runners," *The Physician and Sportsmedicine*, March 1981, pp. 69–81.

Cavanagh, Peter R., and Keith R. Williams, "The Effect of Stride Length Variation on Oxygen Uptake During Distance Running," *Medicine and Science in Sports and Exercise*, 1982, pp. 30–35.

Clement, D. B., and J. E. Taunton, "A Survey of Overuse Running Injuries," *The Physician and Sportsmedicine*, May 1981, pp. 47–58.

Conley, Douglas, et al., "Training for Aerobic Capacity and Economy," *The Physician and Sportsmedicine*, April 1981, pp. 107–14.

Conley, Douglas L., and Gary S. Krahenbuhl, "Running Economy and Distance Running Performance of Highly Trained Athletes," *Medicine and Science in Sports and Exercise*, 1980, pp. 357–60.

Craig, B. W., et al., "Adaptation of Fat Cells to Exercise: Response of Glucose Uptake and Oxidation to Insulin," *Journal of Applied Physiology*, 1981, pp. 1500–1506.

Dicker, Scott G., et al., "Respiratory and Heart Rate Responses to Tethered Controlled Frequency Breathing Swimming," *Medicine and Science in Sports and Exercise*, 1980, pp. 20–23.

DiMarco, Anthony F., et al., "Effects on Breathing of Selective Restriction of Movement of the Rib Cage and Abdomen," *Journal of Applied Physiology*, 1981, pp. 412–20.

Fardy, Paul S., "Isometric Exercise and the Cardiovascular System," *The Physician and Sportsmedicine*, September 1981, pp. 43–46.

Fleishman, Edwin A., "Toward a Taxonomy of Human Performance," *American Psychologist*, December 1975, pp. 1127–49.

Hagberg, J. M., et al., "Effect of Pedaling Rate on Submaximal Exercise Responses of Competitive Cyclists," *Journal of Applied Physiology*, 1981, pp. 447–51.

Katch, Frank, et al., "The Underweight Female," *The Physician and Sportsmedicine*, December 1980, pp. 55–60.

Katch, Victor L., et al., "Biological Variability in Maximum Aerobic Power," *Medicine and Science in Sports and Exercise*, 1982, pp. 21–25.

Klapp, S. T., "Short-Term Memory As a Response-Preparation State," *Memory and Cognition*, 1976, pp. 721–29.

Klapp, S. T., "Response Programming, As Assessed by Reaction Time, Does Not Establish Commands for Particular Muscles," *Journal of Motor Behavior*, 1977, pp. 301–12.

Krissoff, William B., M.D., "Runner's Injuries," *The Physician and Sportsmedicine*, December 1979, pp. 53–64.

Liang, Isabella, et al., "Effect of Exercise Conditioning on Coronary Resistance," *Journal of Applied Physiology*, 1982, pp. 631–36.

Malina, R. M., "Adolescent Changes in Size, Build, Composition and Performance," *Human Biology*, 1974, pp. 117–31.

Malina, R. M., "Anthropometric Correlates of Strength and Motor Performance," *Exercise and Sports Science Reviews*, 1975, pp. 249–74.

Martin, Bruce J., et al., "Control of Breathing During Prolonged Exercise," *Journal of Applied Physiology*, 1981, pp. 27–31.

Martin, Bruce J., and Joel M. Stager, "Ventilatory Endurance in Athletes and Non-Athletes," *Medicine and Science in Sports and Exercise*, 1981, pp. 21–26.

Menapace, Francis J., et al., "Left Ventricle Size in Competitive Weight Lifters: An Echocardiographic Study," *Medicine and Science in Sports and Exercise*, 1982, pp. 72–75.

Moore, Marjorie A., and Robert S. Hutton, "Electromyographic Investigation of Muscle Stretching Techniques," *Medicine and Science in Sports and Exercise*, 1980, pp. 322–29.

Moore, Mike, "Percent Body Fat Testing: A Two Edged Sword," *The Physician and Sportsmedicine*, December 1980, pp. 79–81.

Moore, Mike, "What Are We Learning from Road Races?," *The Physician and Sportsmedicine*, August 1982, pp. 151–57.

Moutz, Alfred, et al., "Flexibility as a Predictor of Knee Injuries in College Football Players," *The Physician and Sportsmedicine*, July 1982, pp. 93–97.

Murase, Yutaka, et al., "Longitudinal Study of Aerobic Power in Superior Junior Athletes," *Medicine and*

Science in Sports and Exercise, 1981, pp. 180–84.

Noble, Bates, et al., "Diagnosis and Treatment of Iliotibial Band Tightness in Runners," *The Physician and Sportsmedicine*, April 1982, pp. 67–74.

Peronnet, François, "Echocardiography and the Athlete's Heart," *The Physician and Sportsmedicine*, May 1981, pp. 103–12.

Pesmen, Curtis, "The Athletic Eye," *Esquire*, March 1983, pp. 19–21.

Rothstein, A. L., and R. K. Arnold, "Bridging the Gap: Application of Research on Videotape Feedback and Bowling," *Motor Skills: Theory into Practice*, 1976, pp. 185–90.

Roussos, Charis, M.D., and Peter T. Macklem, M.D., "The Respiratory Muscles," *The New England Journal of Medicine*, September 1982, pp. 786–97.

Ryan, Alan J., M.D., "Heart Size and Sports," *The Physician and Sportsmedicine*, August 1980, pp. 29–38.

Sapega, Alex A., et al., "Biophysical Factors in Range-of-Motion Exercise," *The Physician and Sportsmedicine*, December 1981, pp. 57–65.

Scheuer, James, M.D., "Effects of Physical Training on Myocardial Vascularity and Perfusion," *Circulation*, September 1982, pp. 491–95.

Schnabel, A., et al., "Hormonal and Metabolic Consequences of Prolonged Running at the Individual Anaerobic Threshold," *International Journal of Sports Medicine*, 1982, pp. 163–68.

Seefeldt, V., "Critical Periods and Programs of Early Intervention," Paper presented at the National Meeting of the American Alliance for Health, Physical Education, and Recreation, Atlantic City, N.J., 1975.

Seefeldt, V., et al., "Skeletal Age and Body Size as Variables in Motor Performance," Paper presented at Third Symposium on Child Growth and Motor Development, University of Western Ontario, March 1976.

Shyne, Kevin, "Richard H. Dominguez, M.D.: To Stretch or Not to Stretch?," *The Physician and Sportsmedicine*, September 1982, pp. 137–39.

Singer, Robert N., "Sports Psychology: The Waves of the Future," *The Physician and Sports Science*, March 1981, pp. 153–56.

Slaughter, M. H., and T. G. Lohman, "An Objective Method for Measurement of Musculo-Skeletal Size to Characterize Body Physique with Application to the Athletic Population," *Medicine and Science in Sports and Exercise*, 1980, pp. 170–74.

Sperling, G., "The Information Available in Brief Visual Presentations," *Psychological Monographs*, 1960, pp. 69–81.

Stamford, Bryan A., et al., "Exercise Recovery Above and Below Anaerobic Threshold Following Maximal Work," *Journal of Applied Physiology*, 1981, pp. 840–44.

Surberg, Paul R., "Neuromuscular Facilitation in Sportsmedicine," *The Physician and Sportsmedicine*, September 1981, pp. 115–27.

Thompson, Walter, et al., "Physiological and Training Profiles of Ultramarathoners," *The Physician and Sportsmedicine*, May 1981, pp. 61–65.

Whipp, Brian J., et al., "A Test to Determine Parameters of Aerobic Function During Exercise," *Journal of Applied Physiology*, 1981, pp. 217–71.

Wilkerson, Gary B., "Developing Flexibility by Overcoming the Stretch Reflex," *The Physician and Sportsmedicine*, September 1981, pp. 189–90.

Wolfe, L. A., et al., "The Value of Combining Noninvasive Techniques in Exercise Testing," *Medicine and Science in Sports and Exercise*, 1980, pp. 200–204.

RECOMMENDED BOOKS AND PERIODICALS

ALPINE SKIING

Books

How the Racers Ski by Warren Witherell
How to Ski the New French Way by Georges Joubert and Jean Vuarnet

Journals and Magazines

Ski Racing
Skiing Magazine
Ski Magazine

TENNIS

Books

Vic Braden's Tennis for the Future by Vic Braden and Bill Bruns

Journals and Magazines

World Tennis Magazine

WINDSURFING

Books

Windsurfing by Ken Winner
Wherever There Is Water and Wind by Glen Taylor

Journals and Magazines

Windsurf Magazine

RUNNING

Books

The Complete Book of Running by James F. Fixx
Improving Your Running by Bill Squires and Raymond Krise
A Scientific Approach to Distance Running by David Costill
Stretching by Bob Anderson
Middle Distances and *Long Distances* by Jess Jarver (ed.)

Journals and Magazines

The Runner
Track and Field News
Runners' World

SWIMMING

Books

Competitive Swimming Manual by James E. Counsilman
Swimming Faster by Ernest Maglischo
Swimming for Total Fitness by Jane Katz

Journals and Magazines

Swim
Swim Magazine

CYCLING

Books

Inside the Cyclist by Ed Burke et al.
Beginning Bicycle Racing by Fred Matheny

Journals and Magazines

Velo News
Bicycling

CROSS-COUNTRY SKIING

Books

Citizen Racing by John Caldwell and Michael Brady
The Cross-Country Ski Book by John Caldwell

Journals and Magazines

Ski—XC
X-C Skier